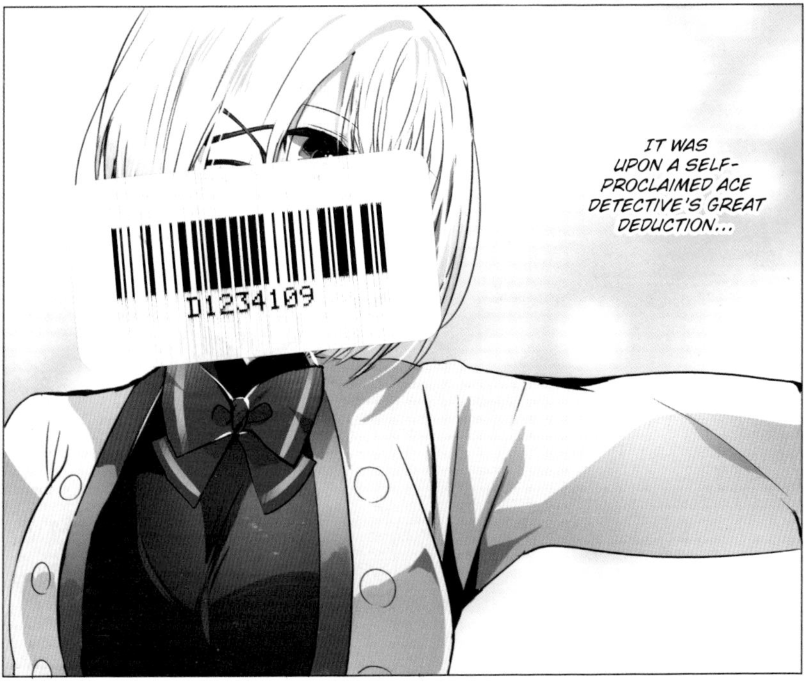
IT WAS UPON A SELF-PROCLAIMED ACE DETECTIVE'S GREAT DEDUCTION...

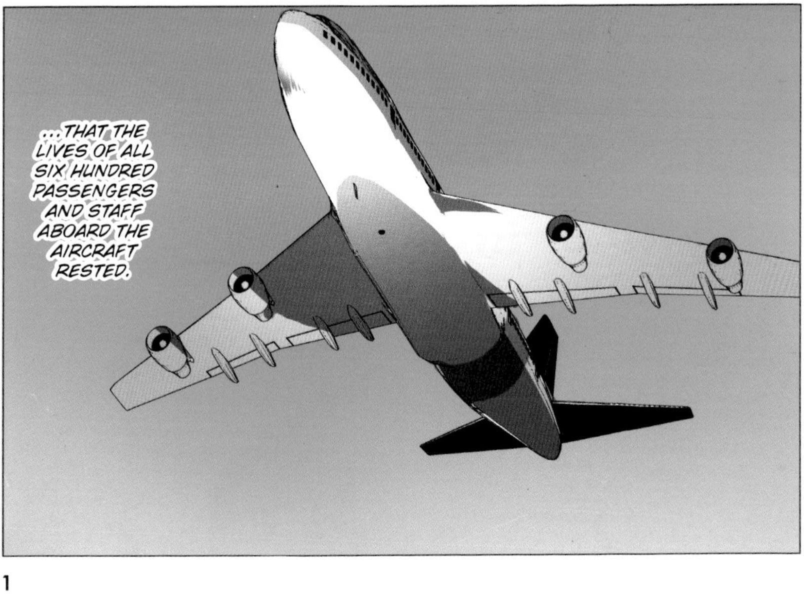
...THAT THE LIVES OF ALL SIX HUNDRED PASSENGERS AND STAFF ABOARD THE AIRCRAFT RESTED.

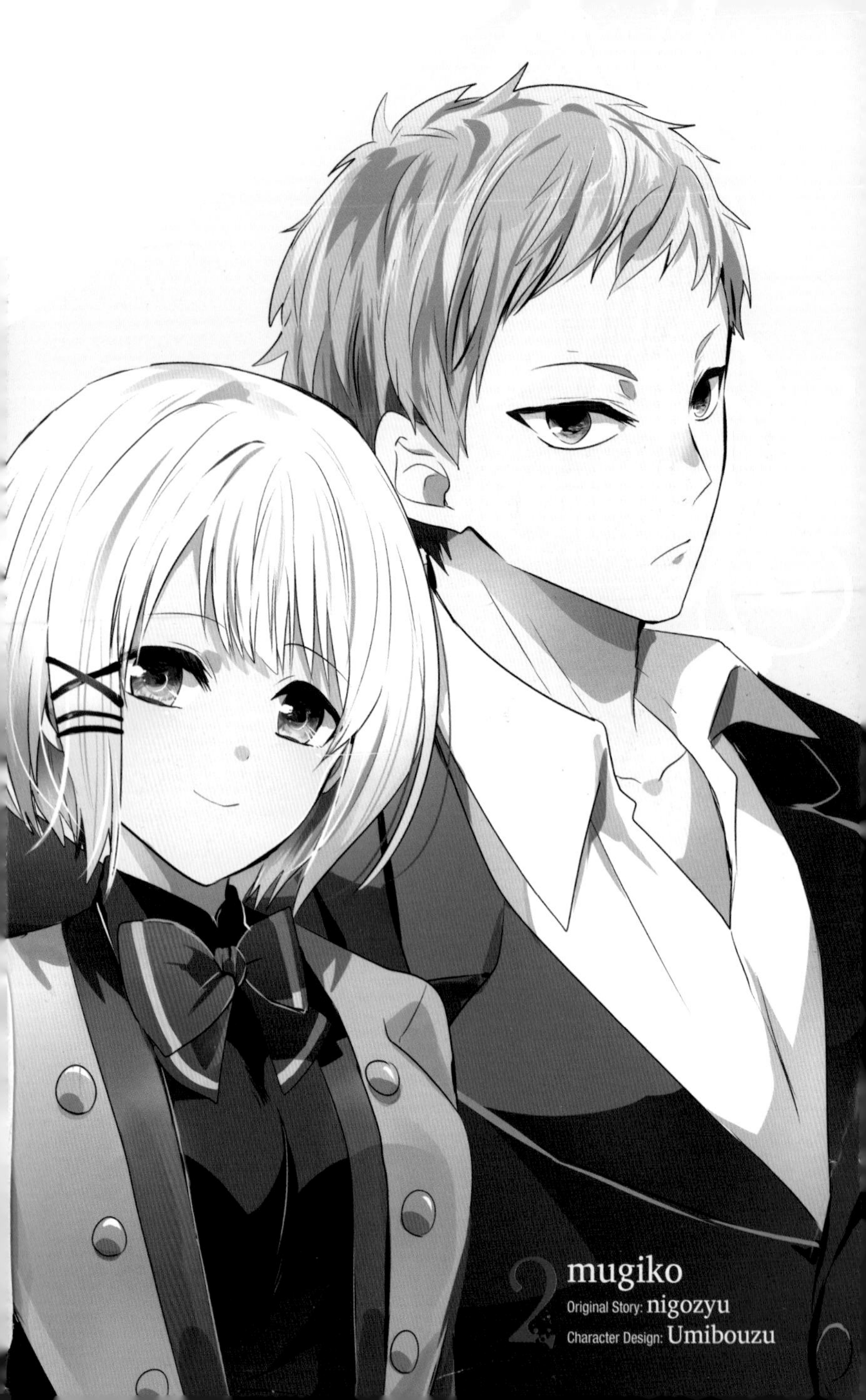
2
mugiko
Original Story: nigozyu
Character Design: Umibouzu

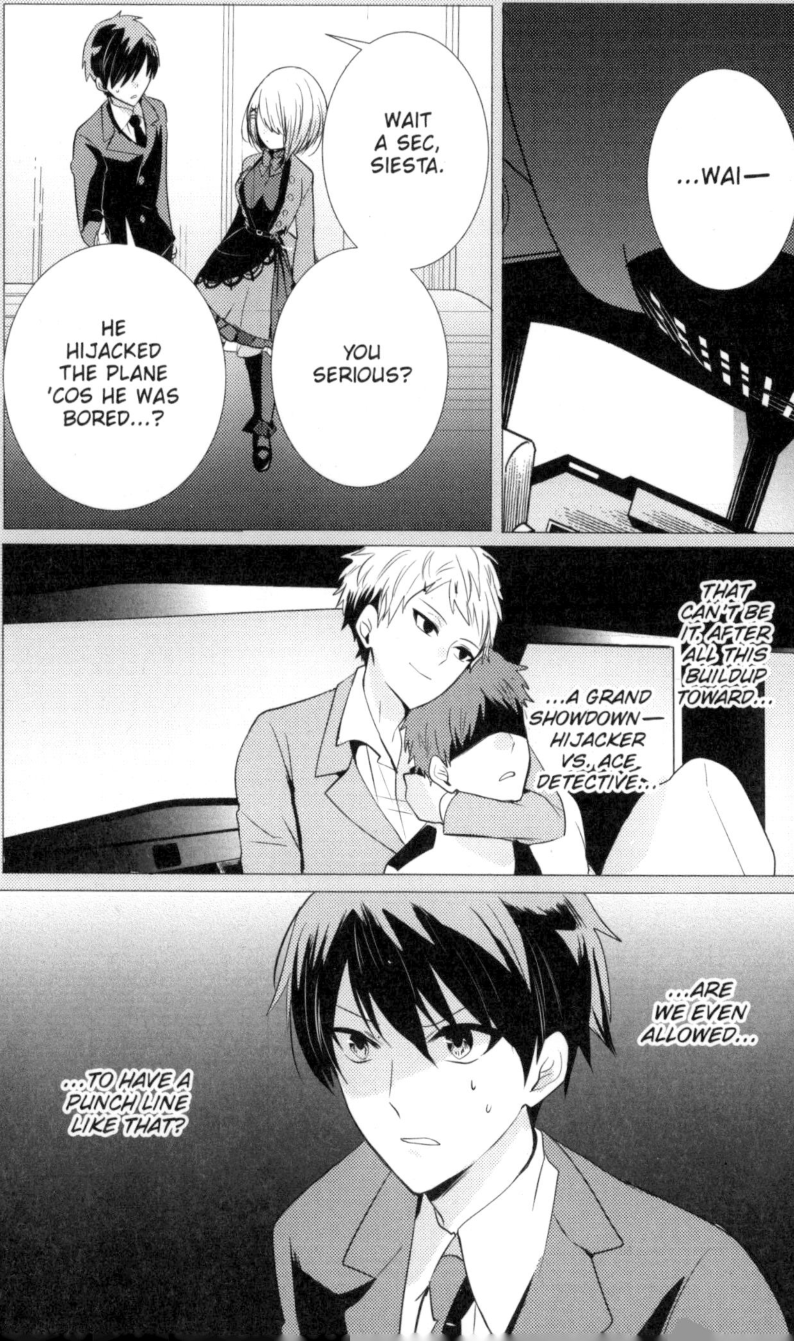
...WAI—
WAIT A SEC, SIESTA.
YOU SERIOUS?
HE HIJACKED THE PLANE 'COS HE WAS BORED...?
THAT CAN'T BE IT. AFTER ALL THIS BUILDUP TOWARD...
...A GRAND SHOWDOWN—HIJACKER VS. ACE DETECTIVE...
...ARE WE EVEN ALLOWED...
...TO HAVE A PUNCH LINE LIKE THAT?

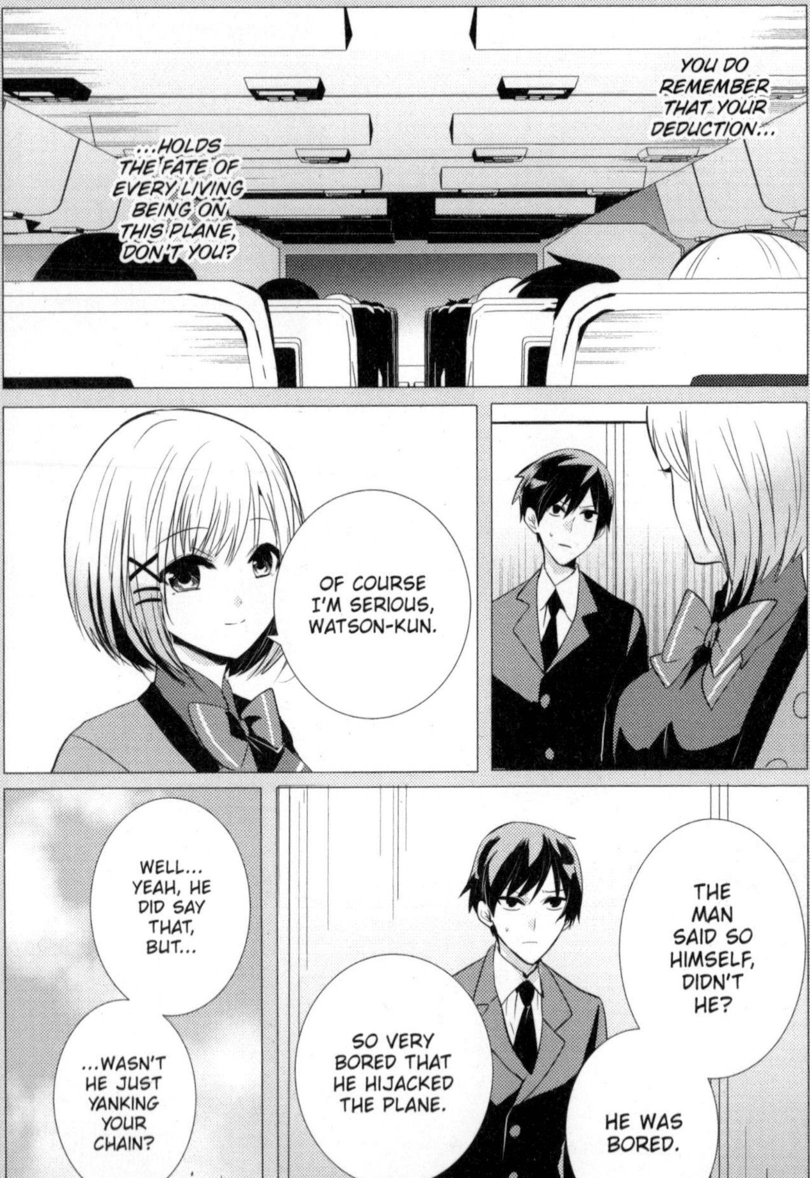
YOU DO REMEMBER THAT YOUR DEDUCTION...
...HOLDS THE FATE OF EVERY LIVING BEING ON THIS PLANE, DON'T YOU?
OF COURSE I'M SERIOUS, WATSON-KUN.
THE MAN SAID SO HIMSELF, DIDN'T HE?
HE WAS BORED.
SO VERY BORED THAT HE HIJACKED THE PLANE.
WELL... YEAH, HE DID SAY THAT, BUT...
...WASN'T HE JUST YANKING YOUR CHAIN?

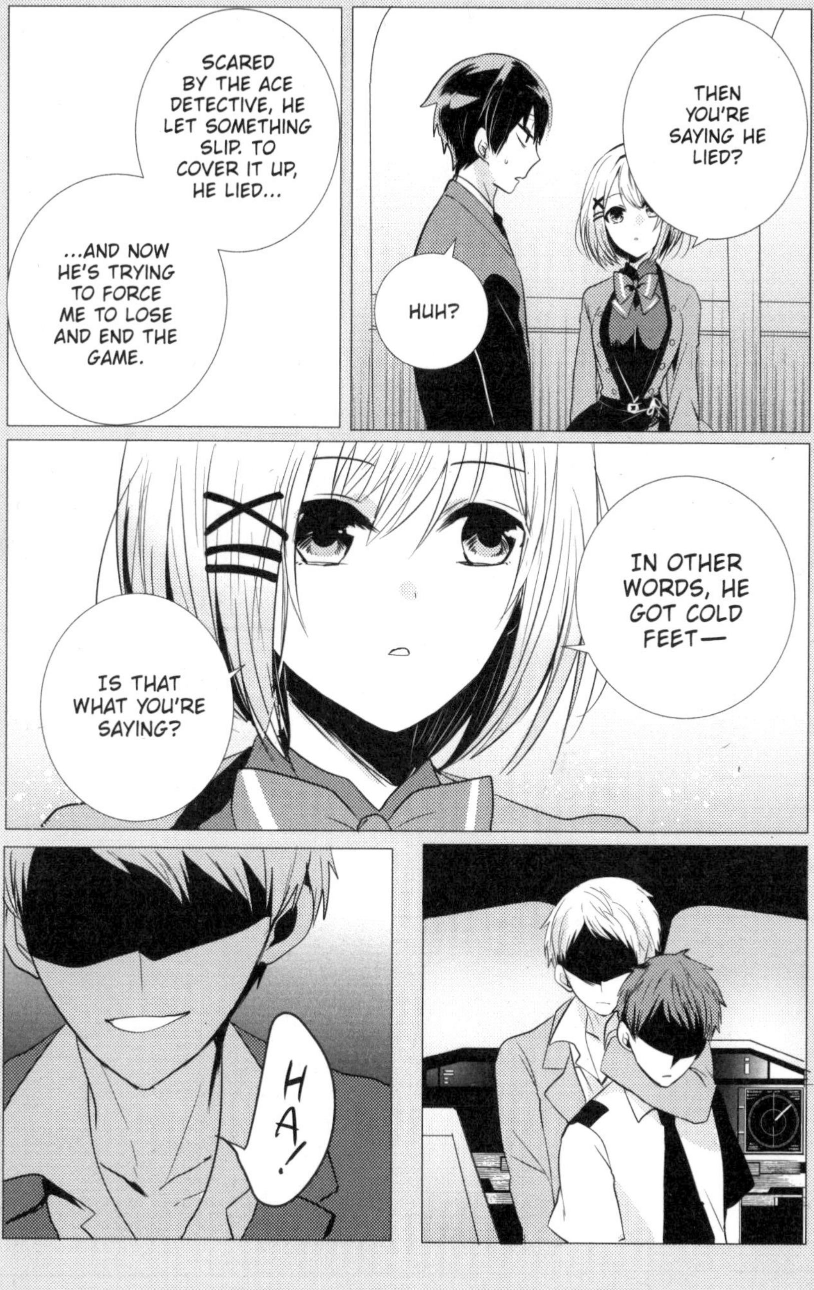
THEN YOU'RE SAYING HE LIED?
HUH?
SCARED BY THE ACE DETECTIVE, HE LET SOMETHING SLIP. TO COVER IT UP, HE LIED...
...AND NOW HE'S TRYING TO FORCE ME TO LOSE AND END THE GAME.
IN OTHER WORDS, HE GOT COLD FEET—
IS THAT WHAT YOU'RE SAYING?
HA!

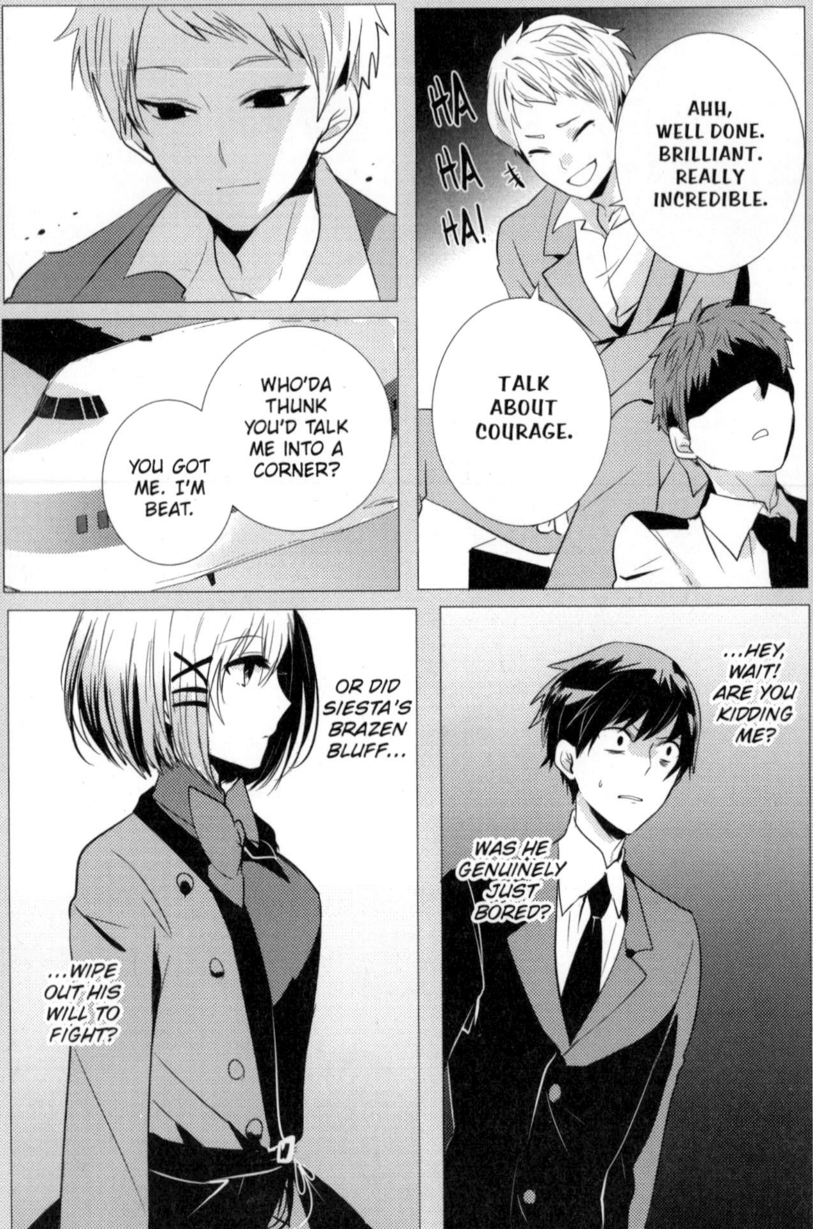
HA HA HA!
AHH, WELL DONE. BRILLIANT. REALLY INCREDIBLE.
TALK ABOUT COURAGE.
WHO'DA THUNK YOU'D TALK ME INTO A CORNER?
YOU GOT ME. I'M BEAT.
...HEY, WAIT! ARE YOU KIDDING ME?
WAS HE GENUINELY JUST BORED?
OR DID SIESTA'S BRAZEN BLUFF...
...WIPE OUT HIS WILL TO FIGHT?

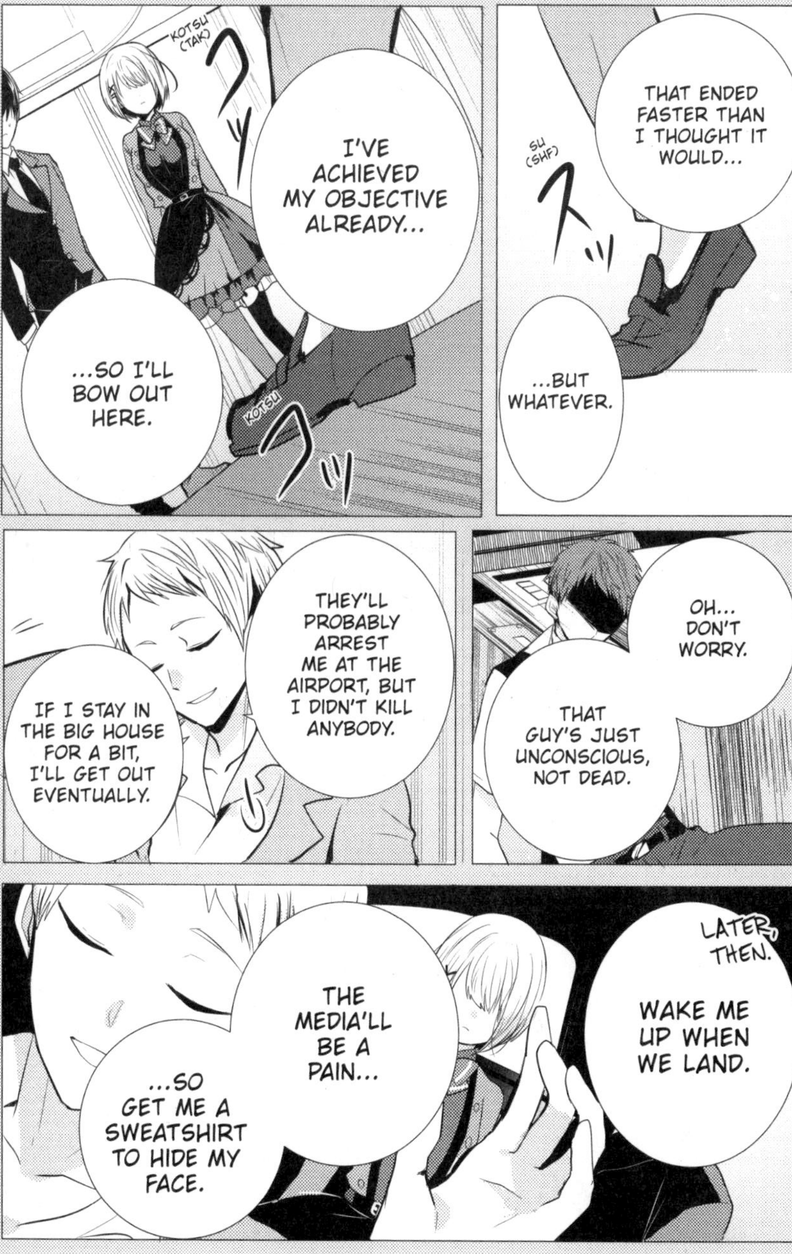
SU (SHF)
THAT ENDED FASTER THAN I THOUGHT IT WOULD...
...BUT WHATEVER.
KOTSU (TAK)
I'VE ACHIEVED MY OBJECTIVE ALREADY...
...SO I'LL BOW OUT HERE.
KOTSU
OH... DON'T WORRY.
THAT GUY'S JUST UNCONSCIOUS, NOT DEAD.
THEY'LL PROBABLY ARREST ME AT THE AIRPORT, BUT I DIDN'T KILL ANYBODY.
IF I STAY IN THE BIG HOUSE FOR A BIT, I'LL GET OUT EVENTUALLY.
LATER, THEN.
WAKE ME UP WHEN WE LAND.
THE MEDIA'LL BE A PAIN...
...SO GET ME A SWEATSHIRT TO HIDE MY FACE.

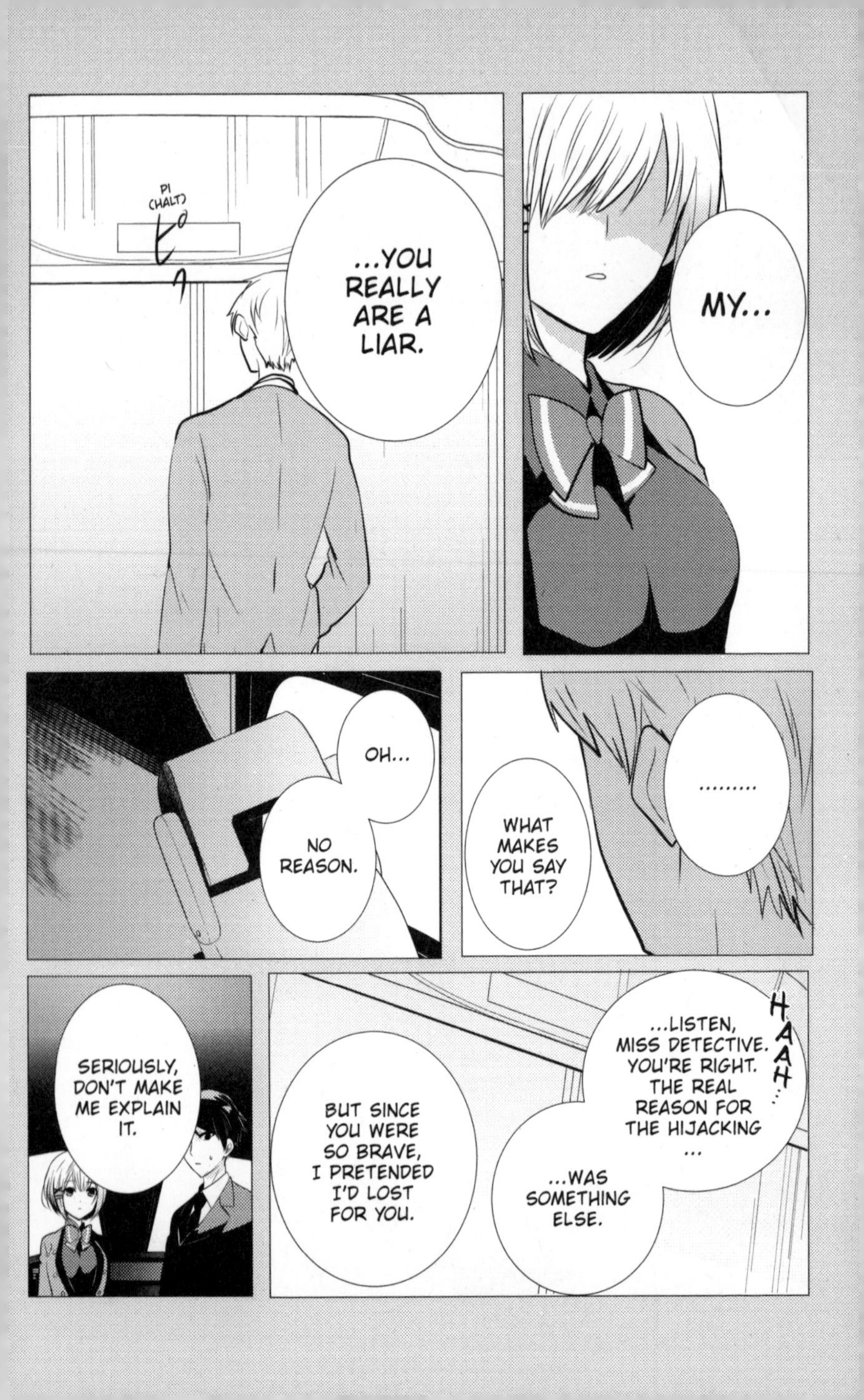
MY...
PI (HALT)
...YOU REALLY ARE A LIAR.
....
WHAT MAKES YOU SAY THAT?
OH...
NO REASON.
HAAH...
...LISTEN, MISS DETECTIVE. YOU'RE RIGHT. THE REAL REASON FOR THE HIJACKING...
...WAS SOMETHING ELSE.
BUT SINCE YOU WERE SO BRAVE, I PRETENDED I'D LOST FOR YOU.
SERIOUSLY, DON'T MAKE ME EXPLAIN IT.

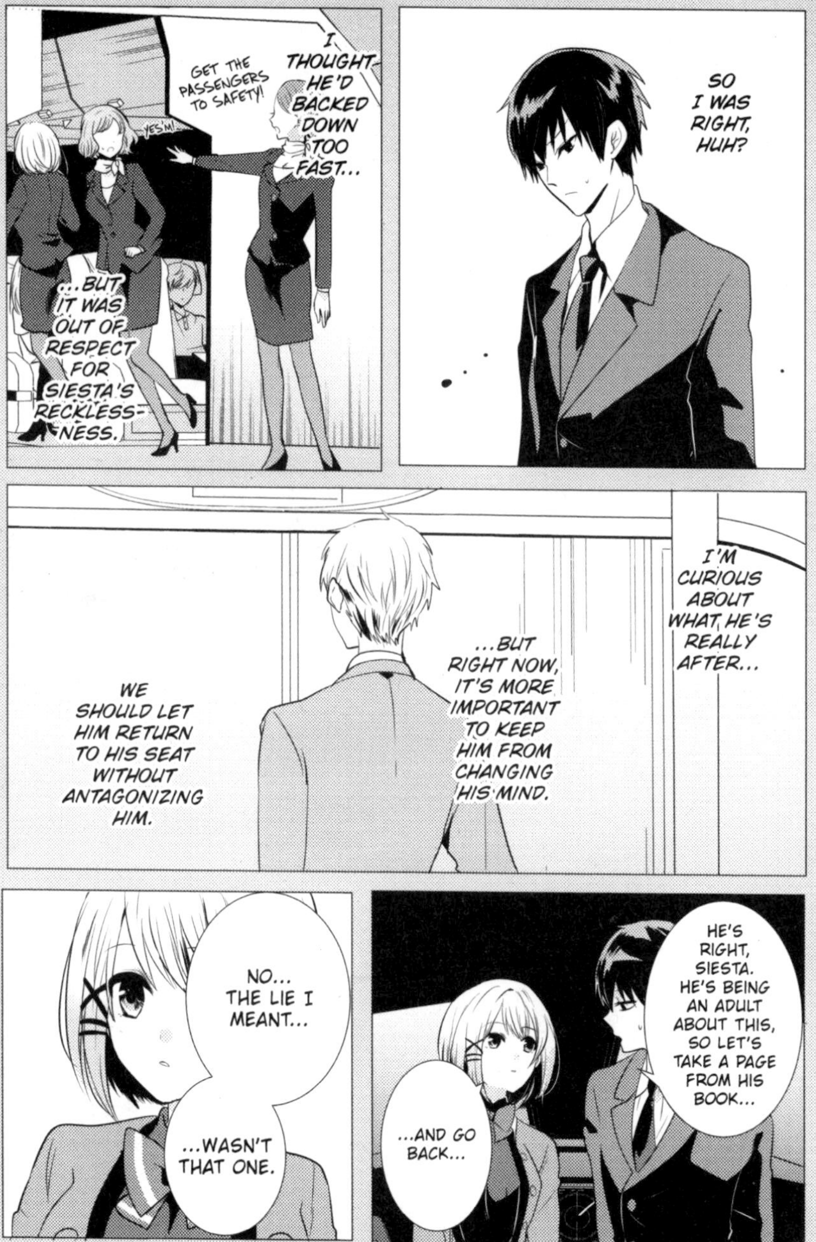
SO I WAS RIGHT, HUH?
I THOUGHT HE'D BACKED DOWN TOO FAST...
GET THE PASSENGERS TO SAFETY!
YES'M!
...BUT IT WAS OUT OF RESPECT FOR SIESTA'S RECKLESS-NESS.
I'M CURIOUS ABOUT WHAT HE'S REALLY AFTER...
...BUT RIGHT NOW, IT'S MORE IMPORTANT TO KEEP HIM FROM CHANGING HIS MIND.
WE SHOULD LET HIM RETURN TO HIS SEAT WITHOUT ANTAGONIZING HIM.
HE'S RIGHT, SIESTA. HE'S BEING AN ADULT ABOUT THIS, SO LET'S TAKE A PAGE FROM HIS BOOK...
...AND GO BACK...
NO... THE LIE I MEANT...
...WASN'T THAT ONE.

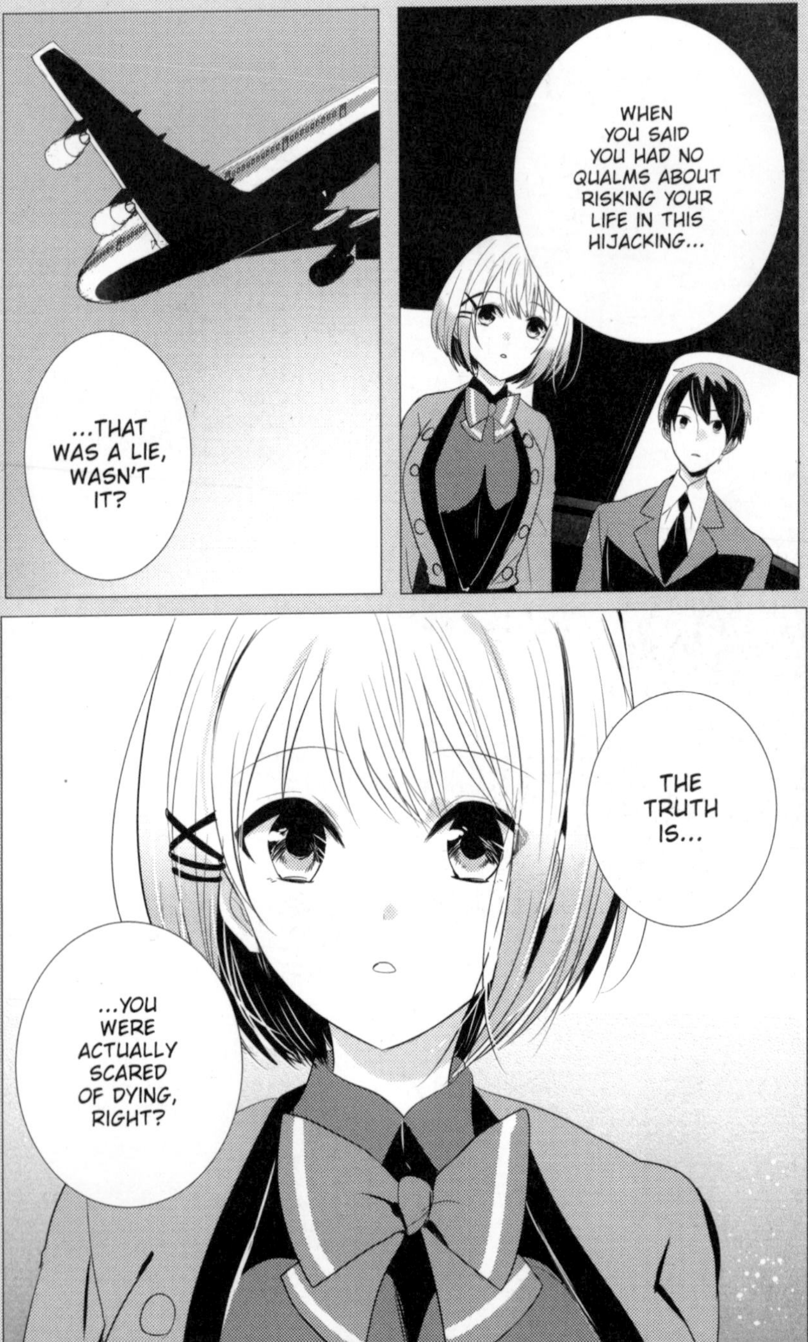
WHEN YOU SAID YOU HAD NO QUALMS ABOUT RISKING YOUR LIFE IN THIS HIJACKING...
...THAT WAS A LIE, WASN'T IT?
THE TRUTH IS...
...YOU WERE ACTUALLY SCARED OF DYING, RIGHT?

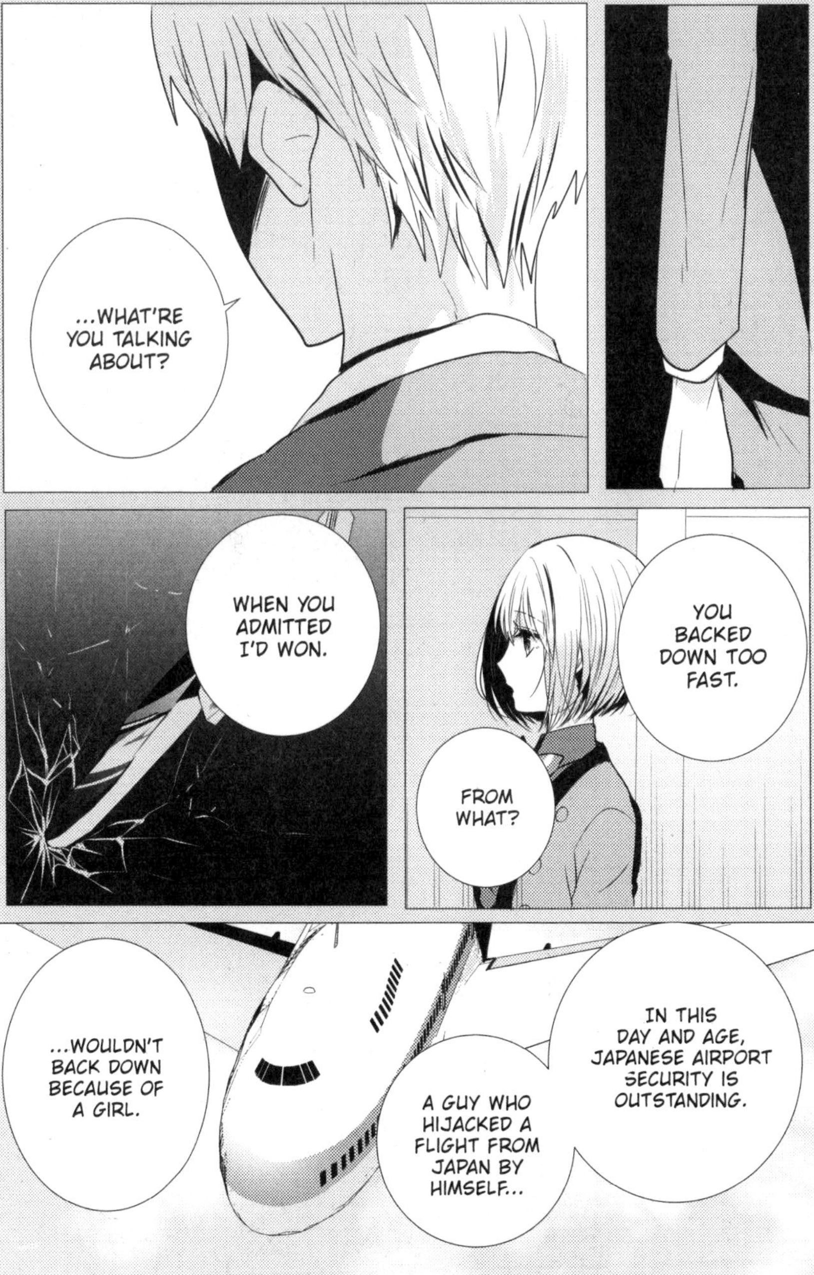
...WHAT'RE YOU TALKING ABOUT?
YOU BACKED DOWN TOO FAST.
FROM WHAT?
WHEN YOU ADMITTED I'D WON.
IN THIS DAY AND AGE, JAPANESE AIRPORT SECURITY IS OUTSTANDING.
A GUY WHO HIJACKED A FLIGHT FROM JAPAN BY HIMSELF...
...WOULDN'T BACK DOWN BECAUSE OF A GIRL.

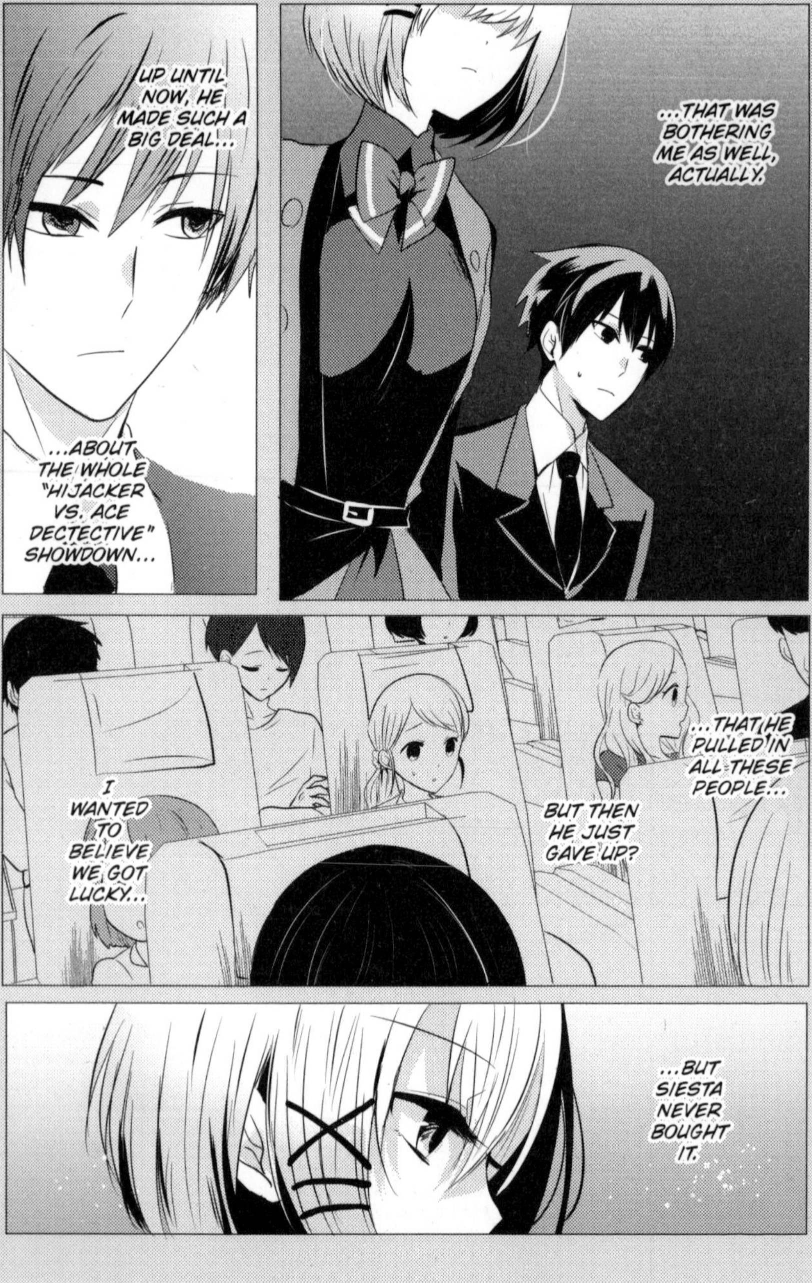
...THAT WAS BOTHERING ME AS WELL, ACTUALLY.
UP UNTIL NOW, HE MADE SUCH A BIG DEAL...
...ABOUT THE WHOLE "HIJACKER VS. ACE DECTECTIVE" SHOWDOWN...
...THAT HE PULLED IN ALL THESE PEOPLE...
BUT THEN HE JUST GAVE UP?
I WANTED TO BELIEVE WE GOT LUCKY...
...BUT SIESTA NEVER BOUGHT IT.

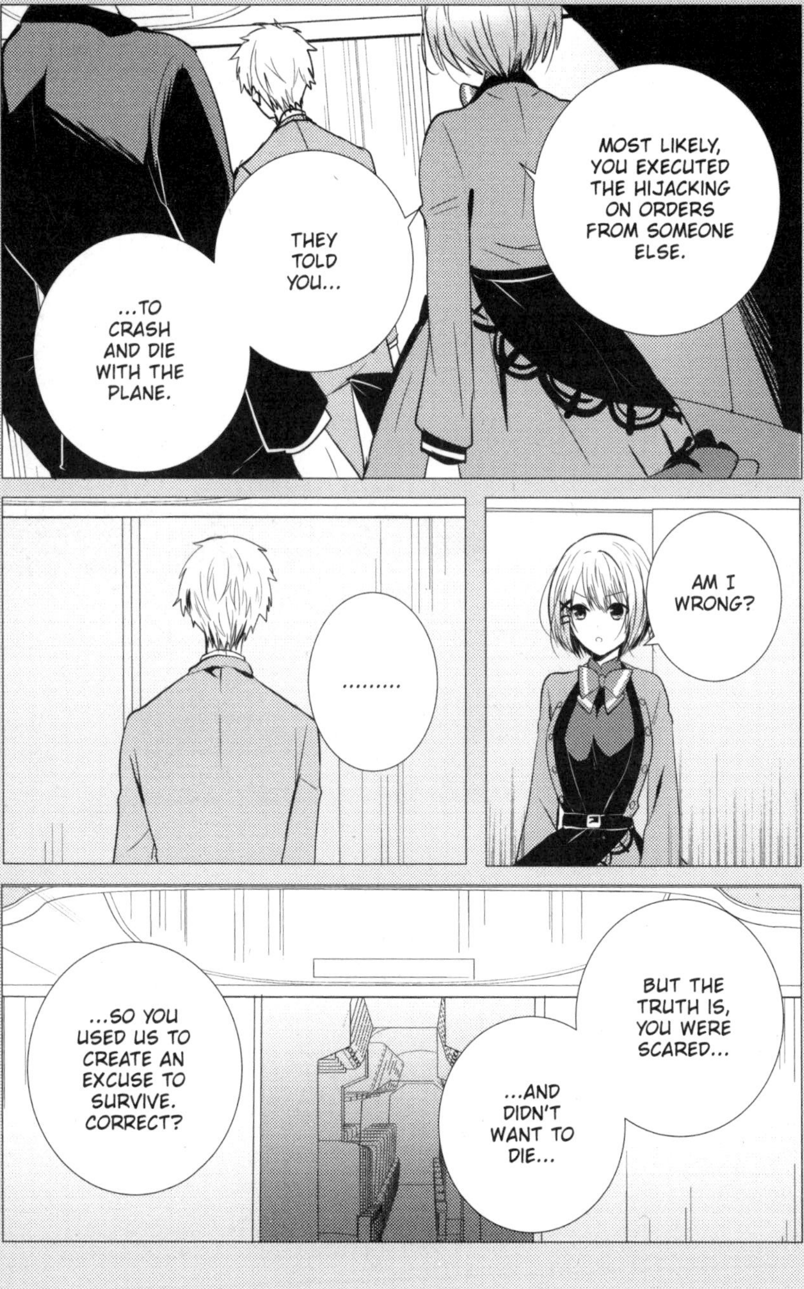
MOST LIKELY, YOU EXECUTED THE HIJACKING ON ORDERS FROM SOMEONE ELSE.
THEY TOLD YOU...
...TO CRASH AND DIE WITH THE PLANE.
AM I WRONG?
....
BUT THE TRUTH IS, YOU WERE SCARED...
...AND DIDN'T WANT TO DIE...
...SO YOU USED US TO CREATE AN EXCUSE TO SURVIVE. CORRECT?

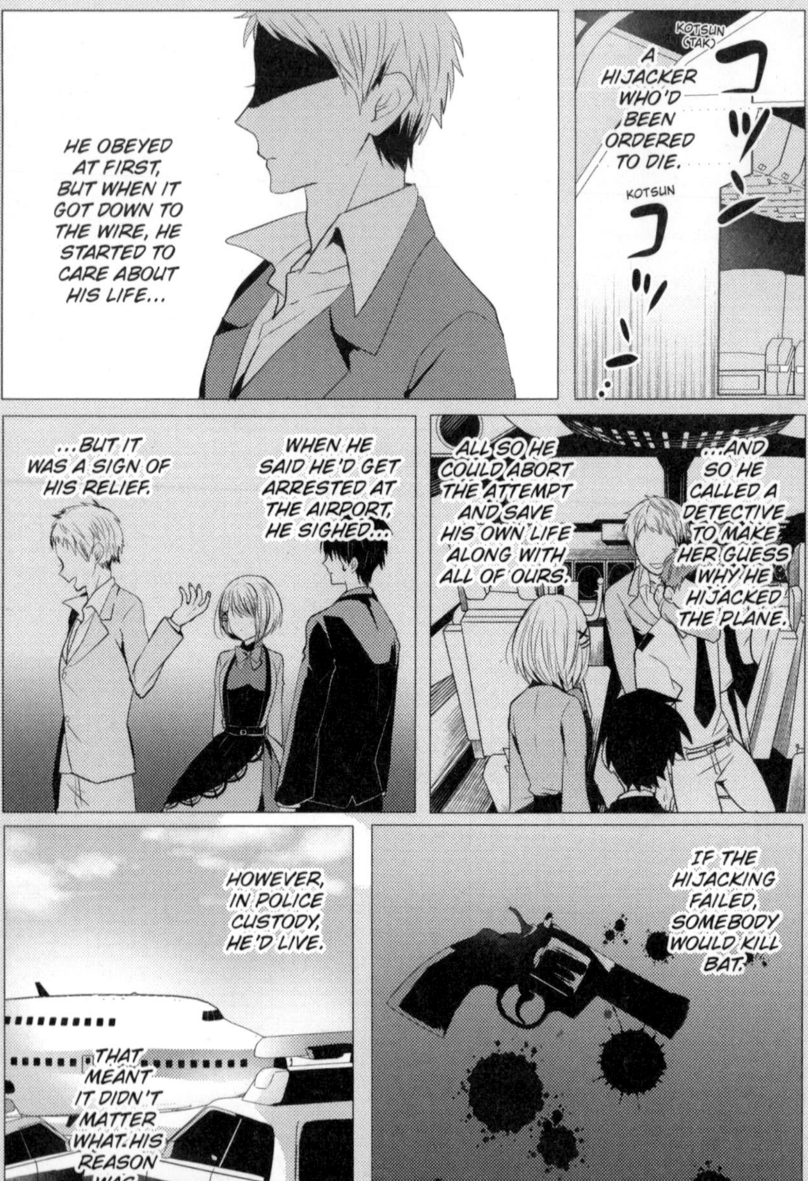
KOTSUN (TAK)
A HIJACKER WHO'D BEEN ORDERED TO DIE.
KOTSUN
HE OBEYED AT FIRST, BUT WHEN IT GOT DOWN TO THE WIRE, HE STARTED TO CARE ABOUT HIS LIFE...
...AND SO HE CALLED A DETECTIVE TO MAKE HER GUESS WHY HE HIJACKED THE PLANE.
ALL SO HE COULD ABORT THE ATTEMPT AND SAVE HIS OWN LIFE ALONG WITH ALL OF OURS.
WHEN HE SAID HE'D GET ARRESTED AT THE AIRPORT, HE SIGHED...
...BUT IT WAS A SIGN OF HIS RELIEF.
IF THE HIJACKING FAILED, SOMEBODY WOULD KILL BAT.
HOWEVER, IN POLICE CUSTODY, HE'D LIVE.
THAT MEANT IT DIDN'T MATTER WHAT HIS REASON WAS.

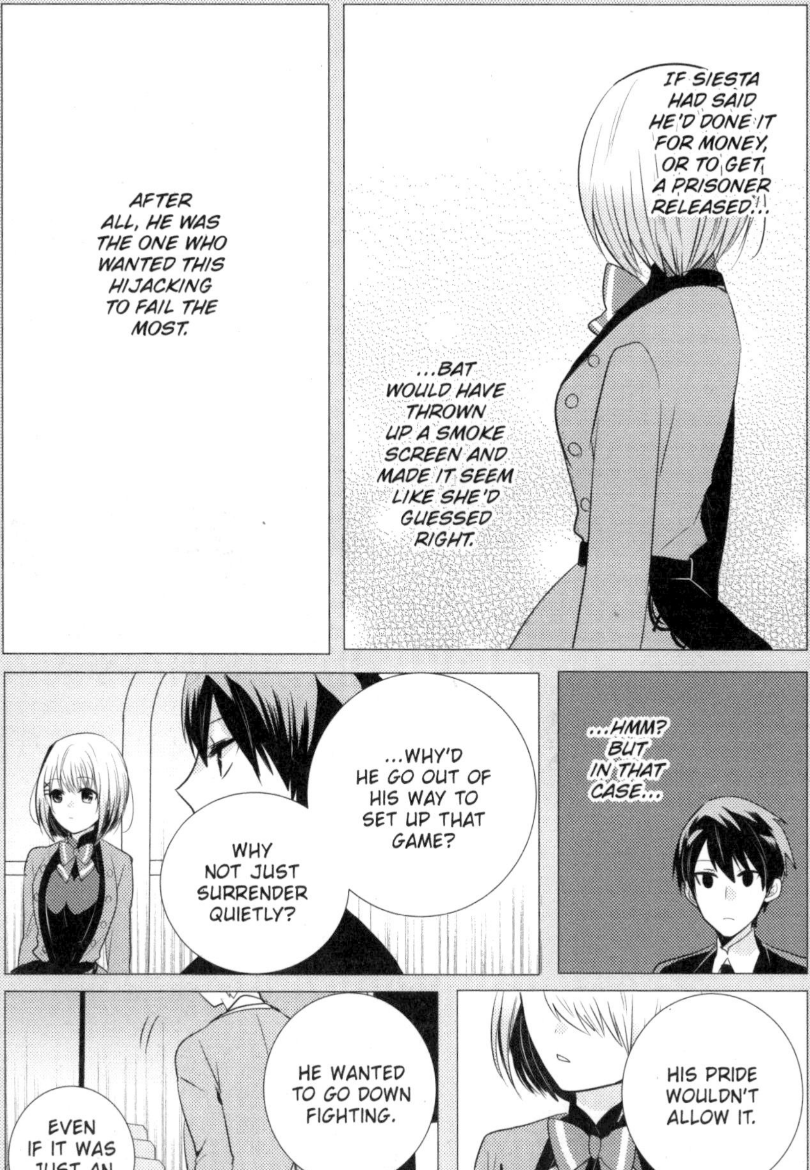
IF SIESTA HAD SAID HE'D DONE IT FOR MONEY, OR TO GET A PRISONER RELEASED...
...BAT WOULD HAVE THROWN UP A SMOKE SCREEN AND MADE IT SEEM LIKE SHE'D GUESSED RIGHT.
AFTER ALL, HE WAS THE ONE WHO WANTED THIS HIJACKING TO FAIL THE MOST.
...HMM? BUT IN THAT CASE...
...WHY'D HE GO OUT OF HIS WAY TO SET UP THAT GAME?
WHY NOT JUST SURRENDER QUIETLY?
HIS PRIDE WOULDN'T ALLOW IT.
HE WANTED TO GO DOWN FIGHTING.
EVEN IF IT WAS JUST AN ACT.

PON
(SMACK)

OKAY.

...WAS THAT HOW IT WAS?

LET'S GO BACK TO OUR SEATS.

CASE CLOSED.

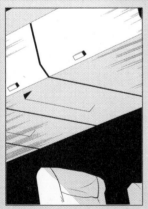

HEY. TELL ME ONE THING BEFORE *THE END.*

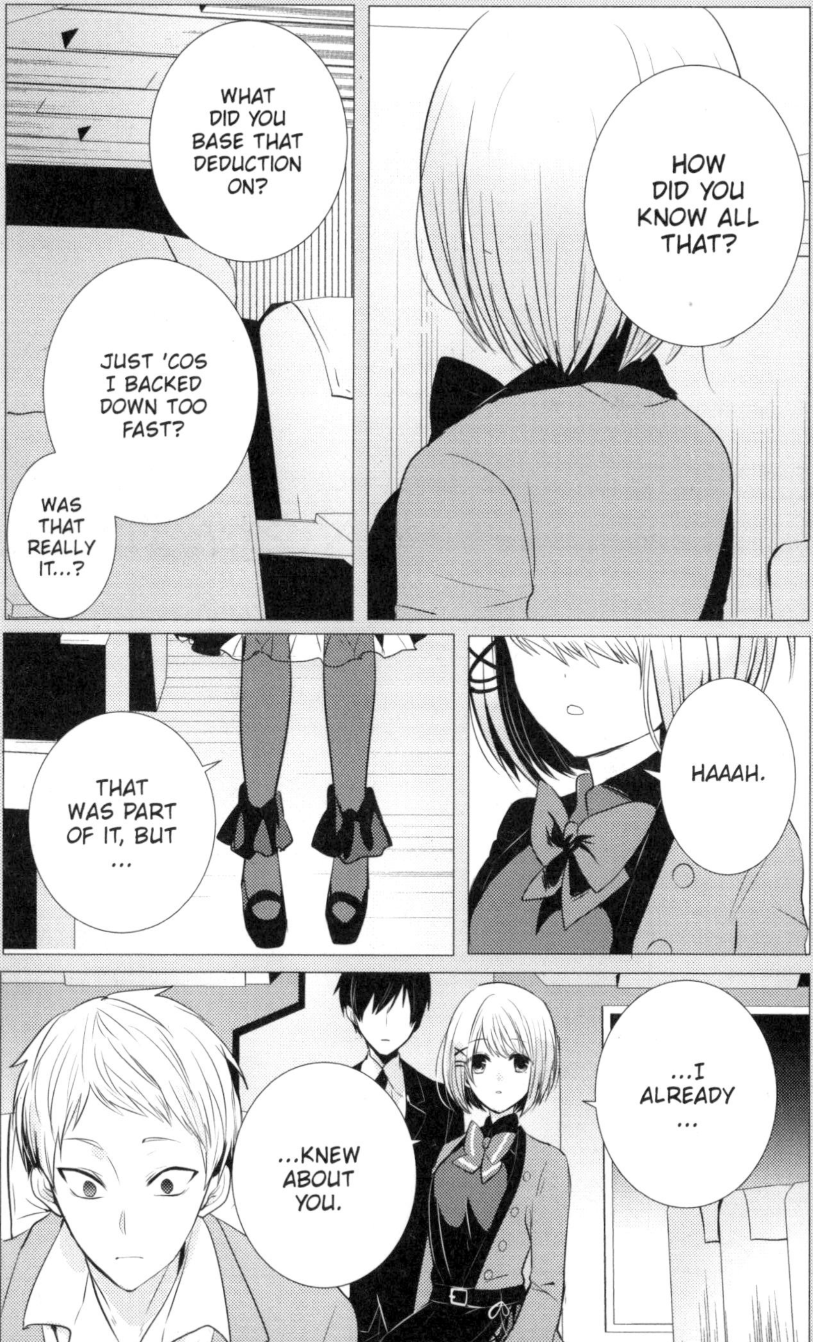
HOW DID YOU KNOW ALL THAT?
WHAT DID YOU BASE THAT DEDUCTION ON?
JUST 'COS I BACKED DOWN TOO FAST?
WAS THAT REALLY IT...?
HAAAH.
THAT WAS PART OF IT, BUT ...
...I ALREADY ...
...KNEW ABOUT YOU.

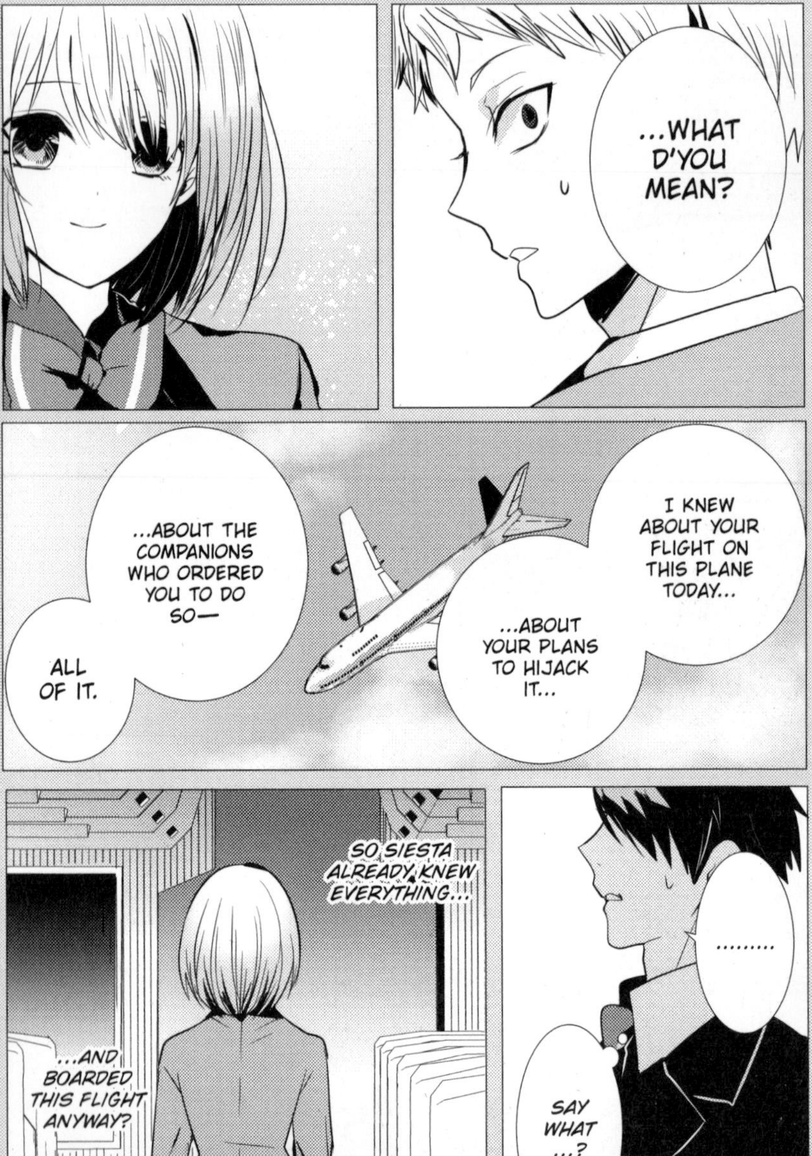
...WHAT D'YOU MEAN?
I KNEW ABOUT YOUR FLIGHT ON THIS PLANE TODAY...
...ABOUT YOUR PLANS TO HIJACK IT...
...ABOUT THE COMPANIONS WHO ORDERED YOU TO DO SO—
ALL OF IT.
....
SAY WHAT ...?
SO SIESTA ALREADY KNEW EVERYTHING...
...AND BOARDED THIS FLIGHT ANYWAY?

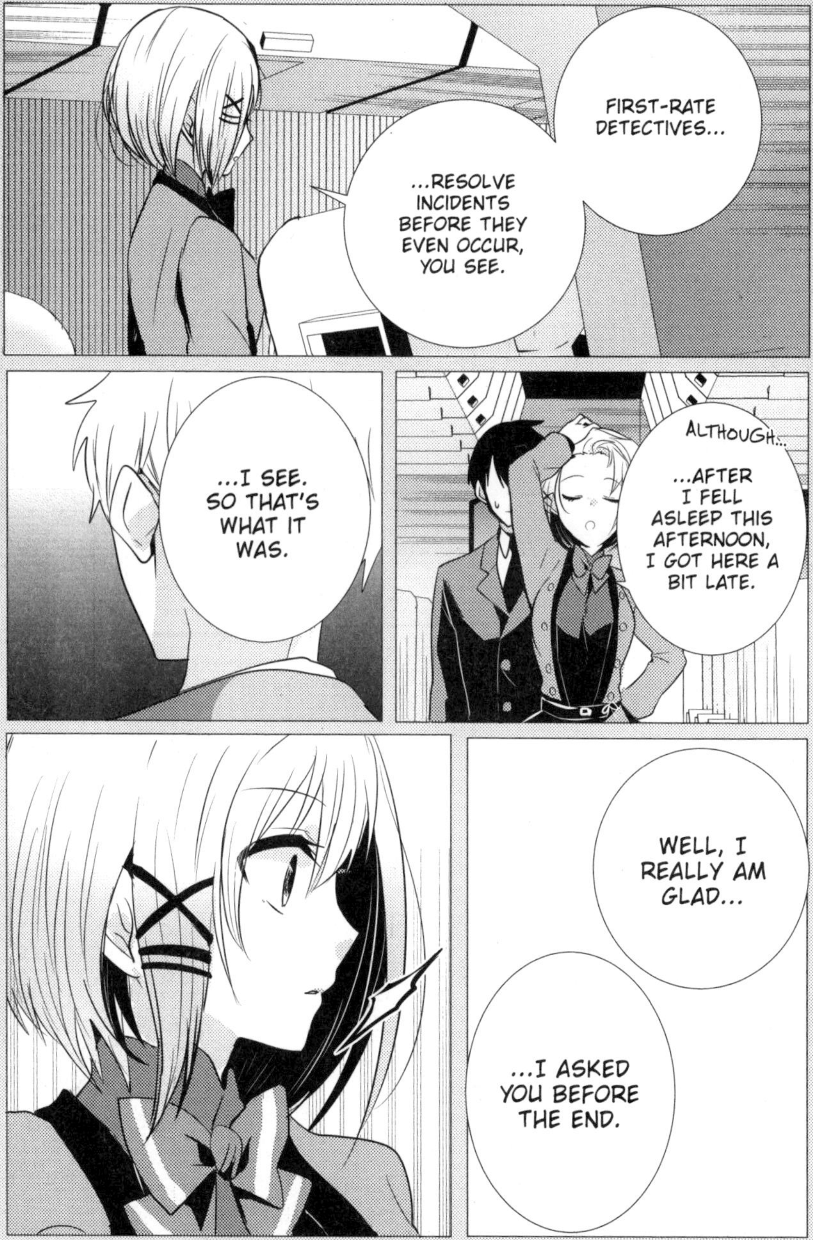
FIRST-RATE DETECTIVES...
...RESOLVE INCIDENTS BEFORE THEY EVEN OCCUR, YOU SEE.
ALTHOUGH...
...AFTER I FELL ASLEEP THIS AFTERNOON, I GOT HERE A BIT LATE.
...I SEE. SO THAT'S WHAT IT WAS.
WELL, I REALLY AM GLAD...
...I ASKED YOU BEFORE THE END.

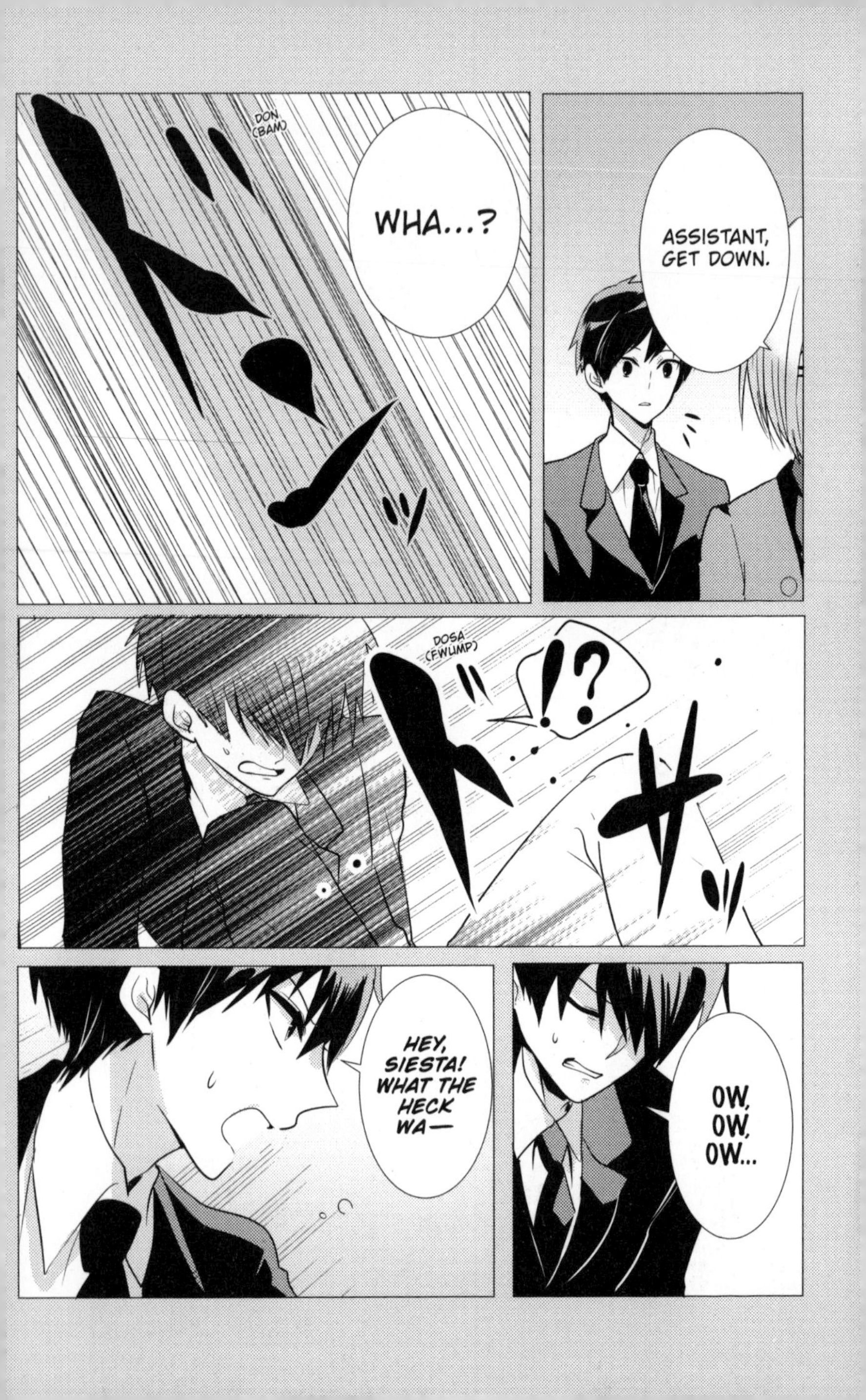
ASSISTANT, GET DOWN.
DON (BAM)
WHA...?
DOSA (FWUMP)
!?
OW, OW, OW...
HEY, SIESTA! WHAT THE HECK WA—

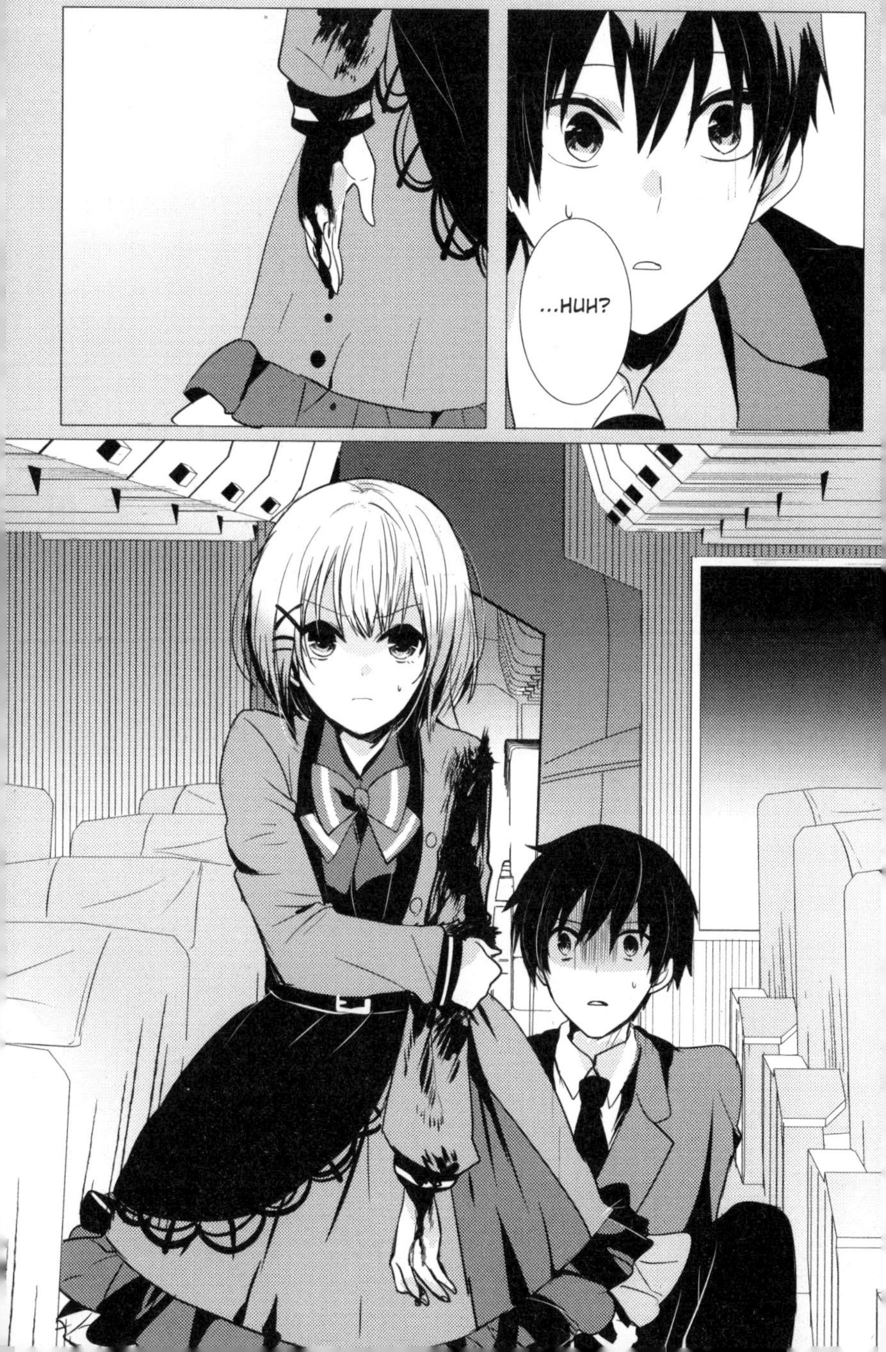
...HUH?

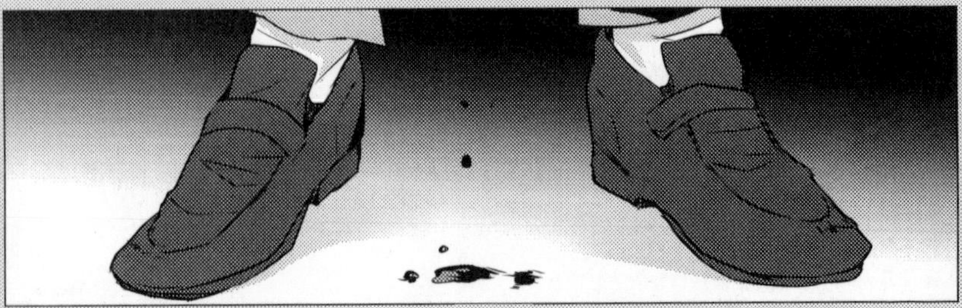

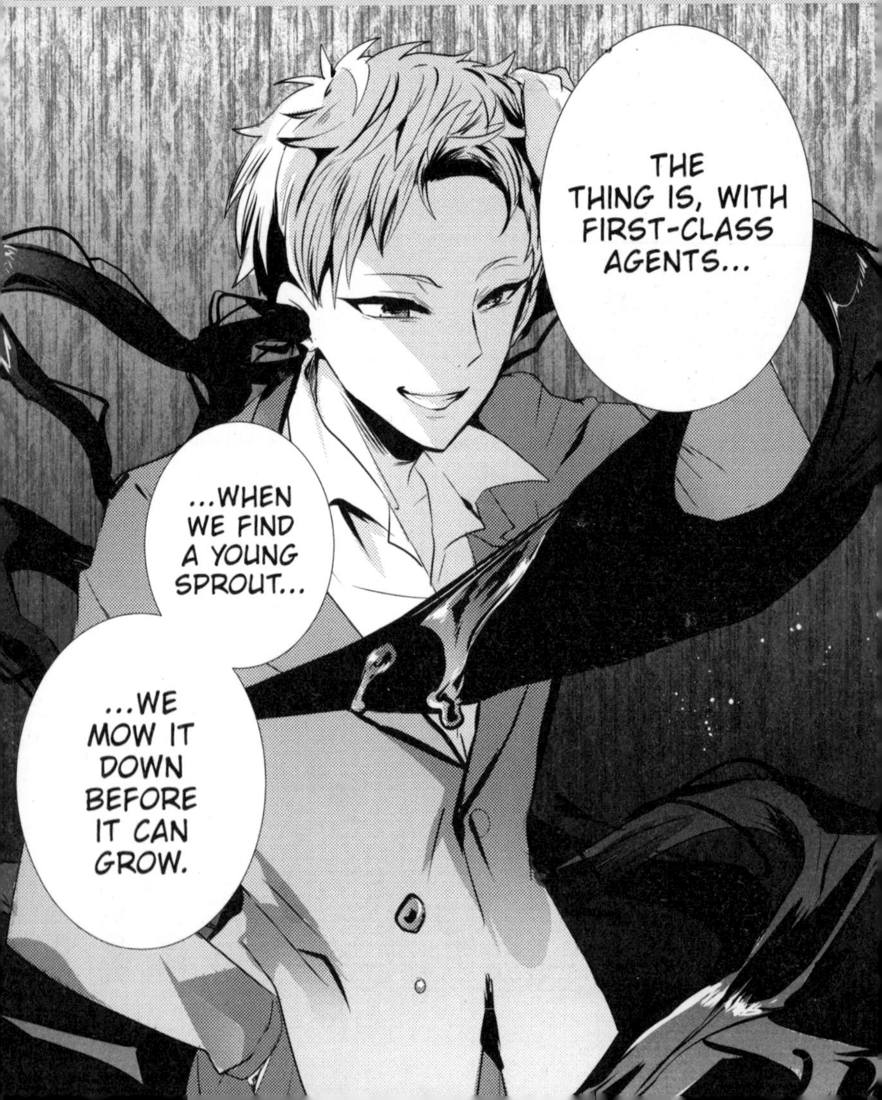
THE THING IS, WITH FIRST-CLASS AGENTS...
...WHEN WE FIND A YOUNG SPROUT...
...WE MOW IT DOWN BEFORE IT CAN GROW.

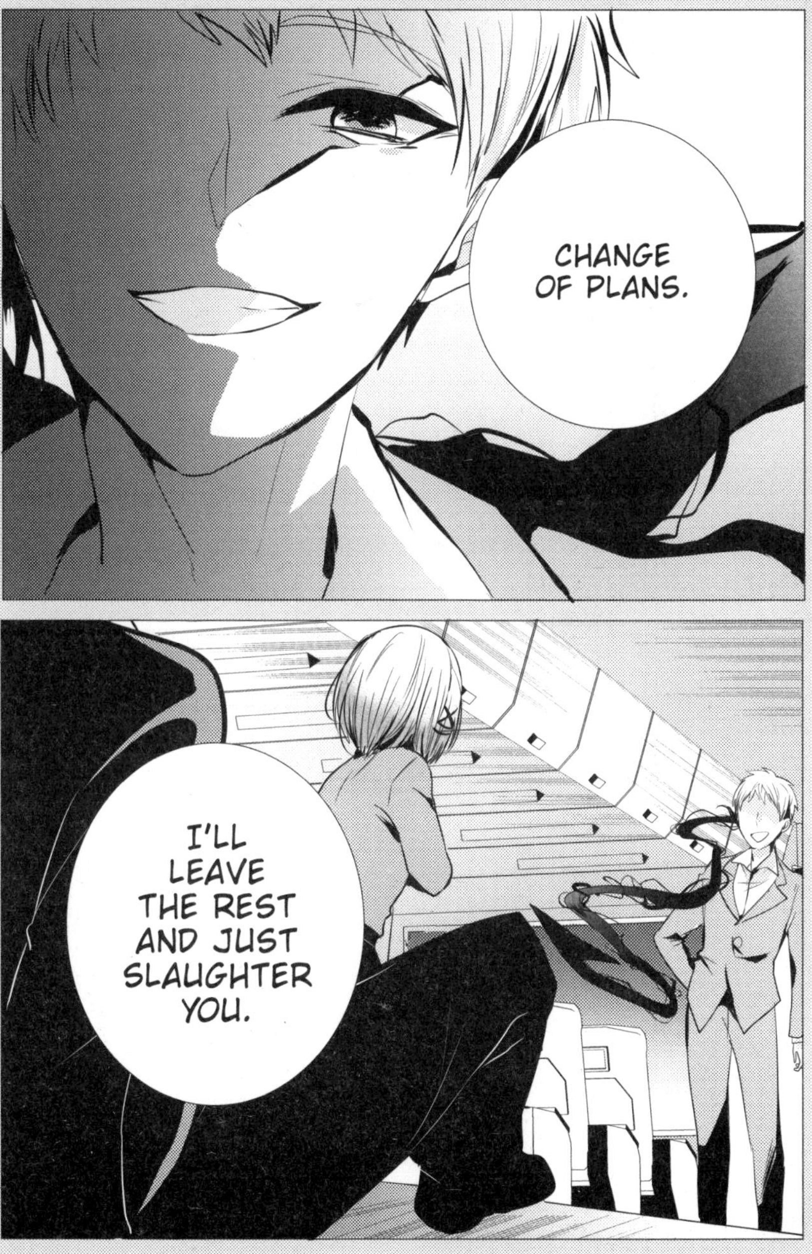
CHANGE OF PLANS.
I'LL LEAVE THE REST AND JUST SLAUGHTER YOU.

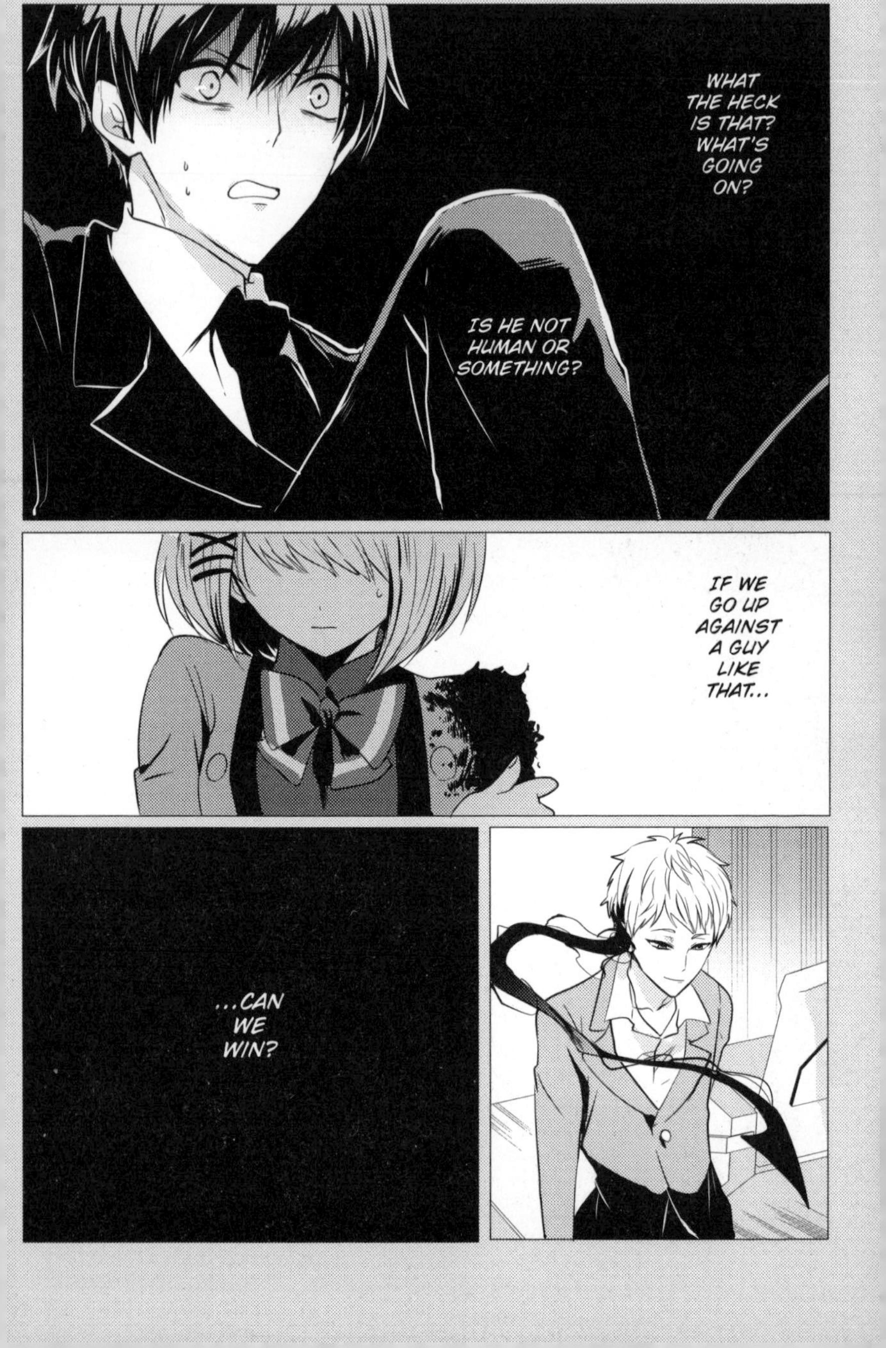
WHAT THE HECK IS THAT? WHAT'S GOING ON?
IS HE NOT HUMAN OR SOMETHING?
IF WE GO UP AGAINST A GUY LIKE THAT...
...CAN WE WIN?

The Detective Is Already Dead

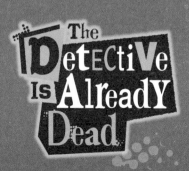

The Detective Is Already Dead

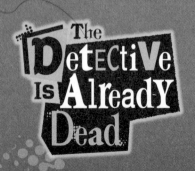

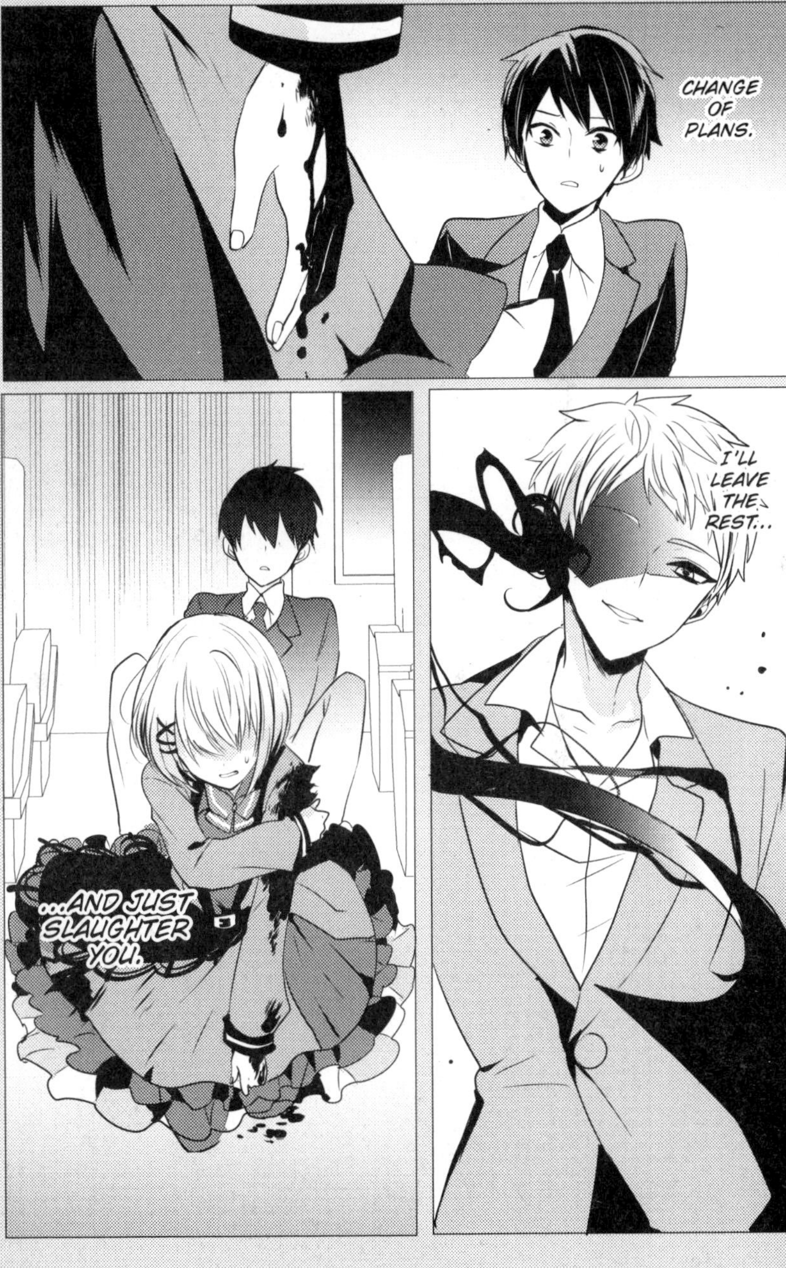
CHANGE OF PLANS.
I'LL LEAVE THE REST...
...AND JUST SLAUGHTER YOU.

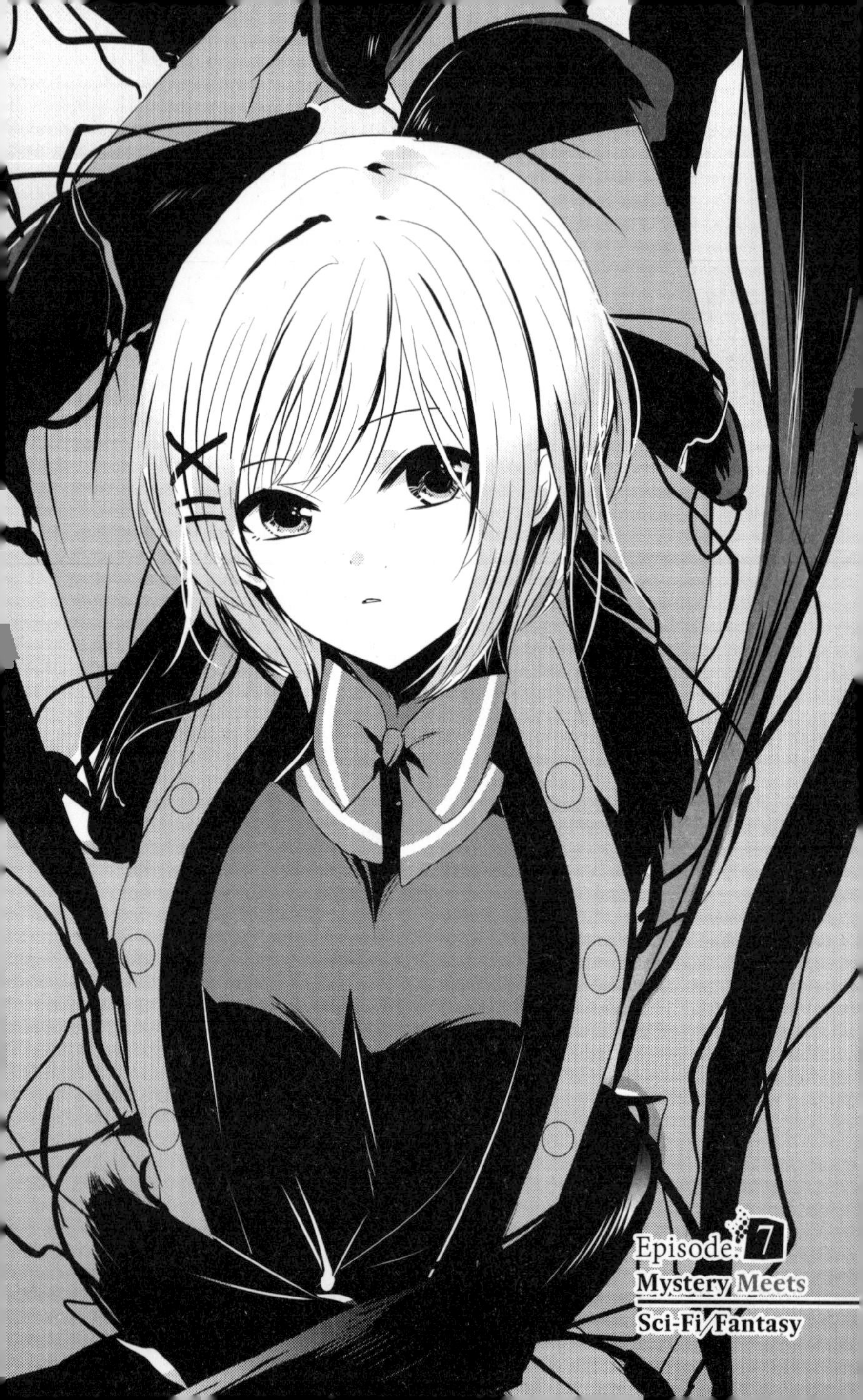

Episode 7 Mystery Meets Sci-Fi/Fantasy

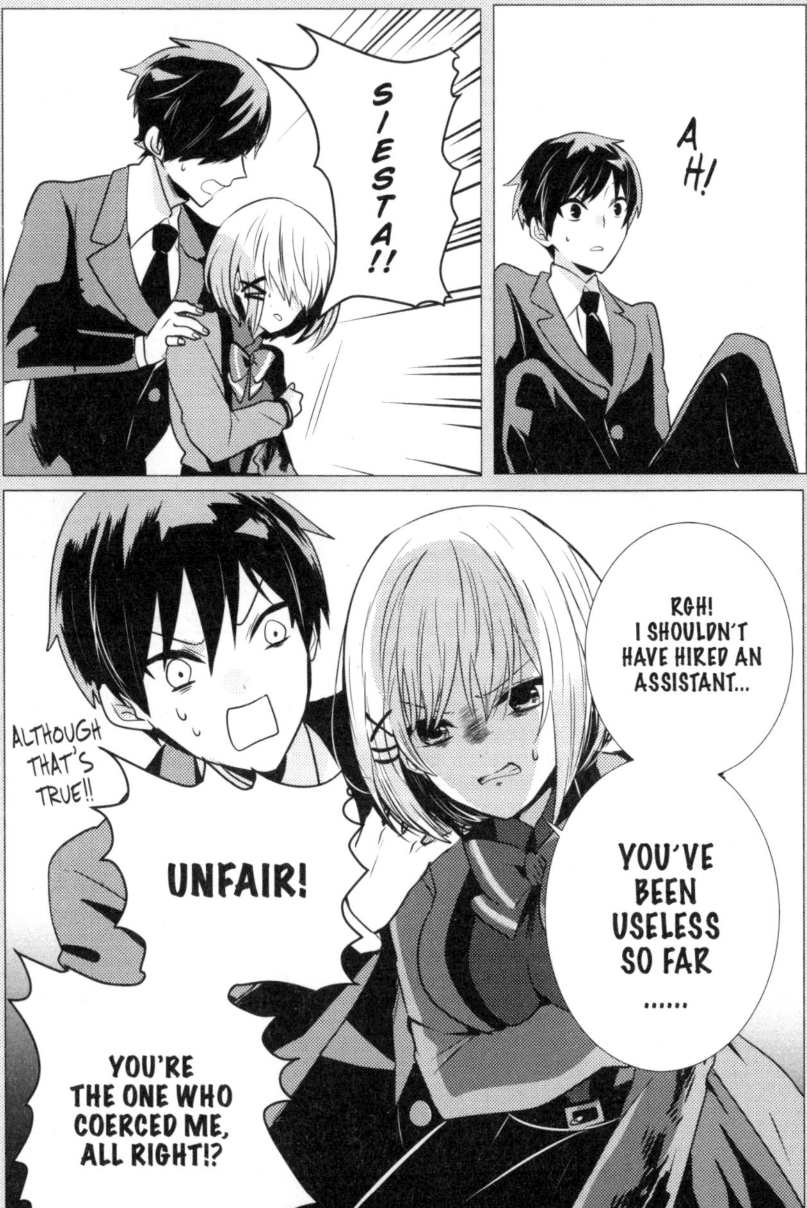
AH!
SIESTA!!
RGH! I SHOULDN'T HAVE HIRED AN ASSISTANT...
YOU'VE BEEN USELESS SO FAR ......
ALTHOUGH THAT'S TRUE!!
UNFAIR!
YOU'RE THE ONE WHO COERCED ME, ALL RIGHT!?

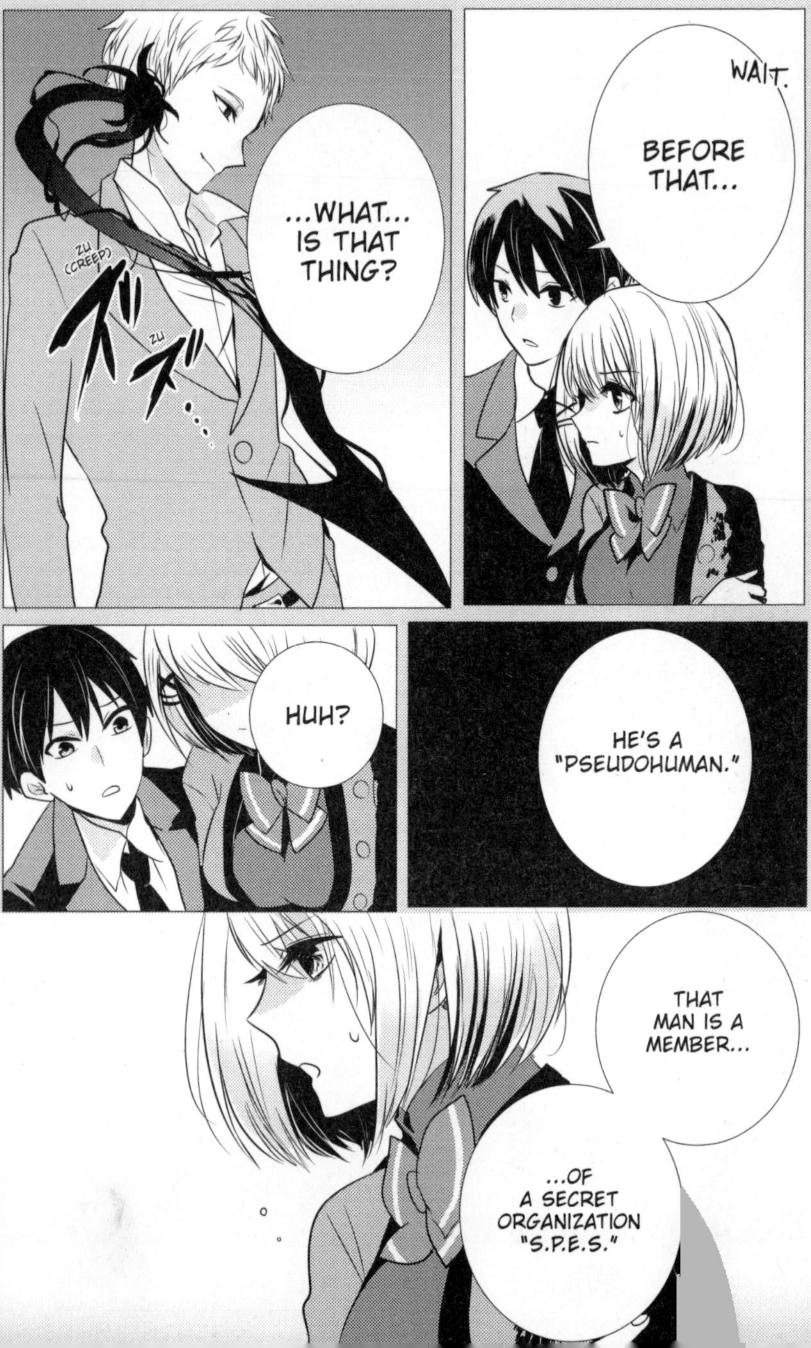
WAIT.
BEFORE THAT...
...WHAT... IS THAT THING?
ZU (CREEP)
ZU
HE'S A "PSEUDOHUMAN."
HUH?
THAT MAN IS A MEMBER...
...OF A SECRET ORGANIZATION "S.P.E.S."

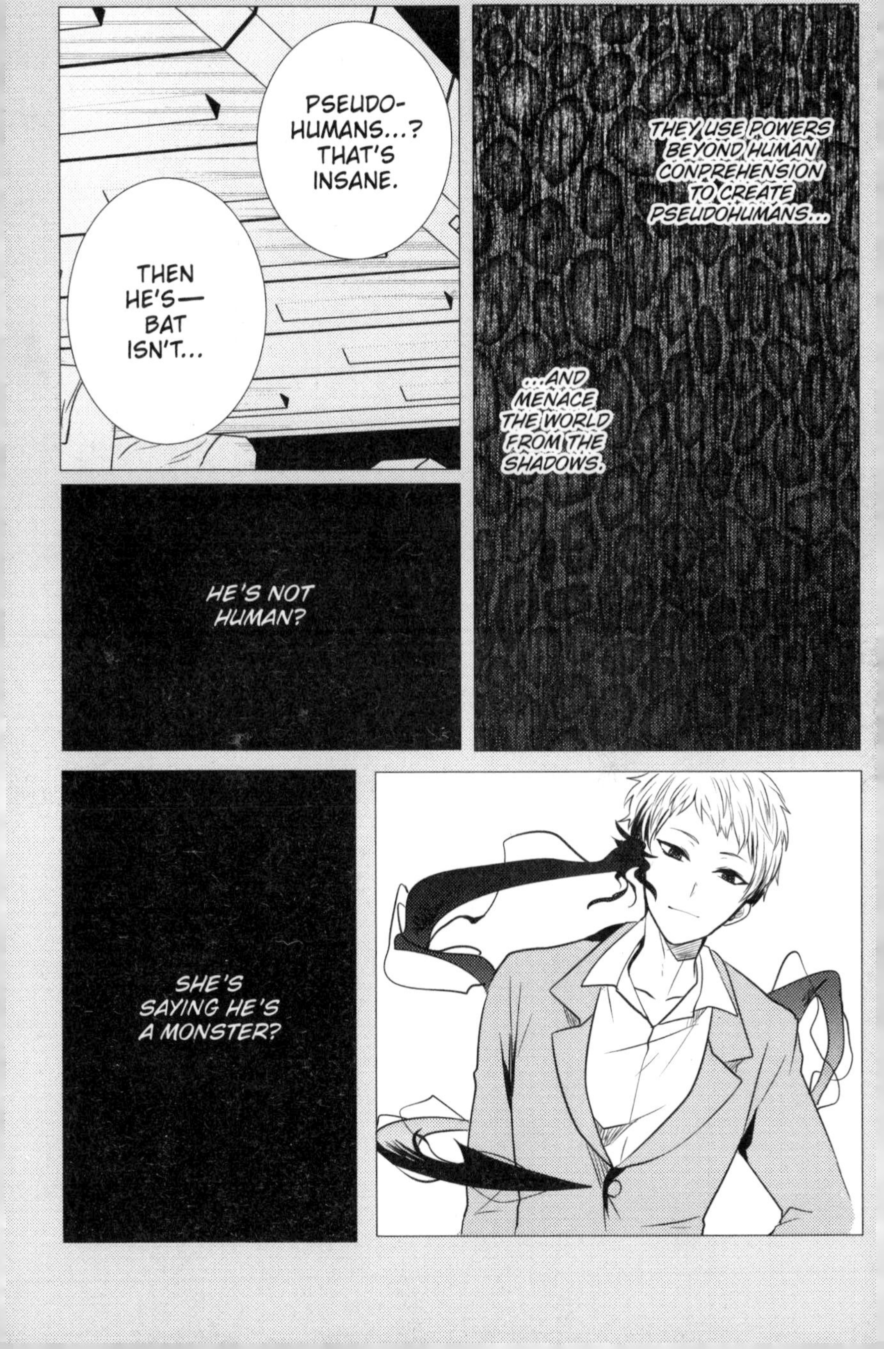
THEY USE POWERS BEYOND HUMAN CONPREHENSION TO CREATE PSEUDOHUMANS...
...AND MENACE THE WORLD FROM THE SHADOWS.
PSEUDO-HUMANS...? THAT'S INSANE.
THEN HE'S— BAT ISN'T...
HE'S NOT HUMAN?
SHE'S SAYING HE'S A MONSTER?

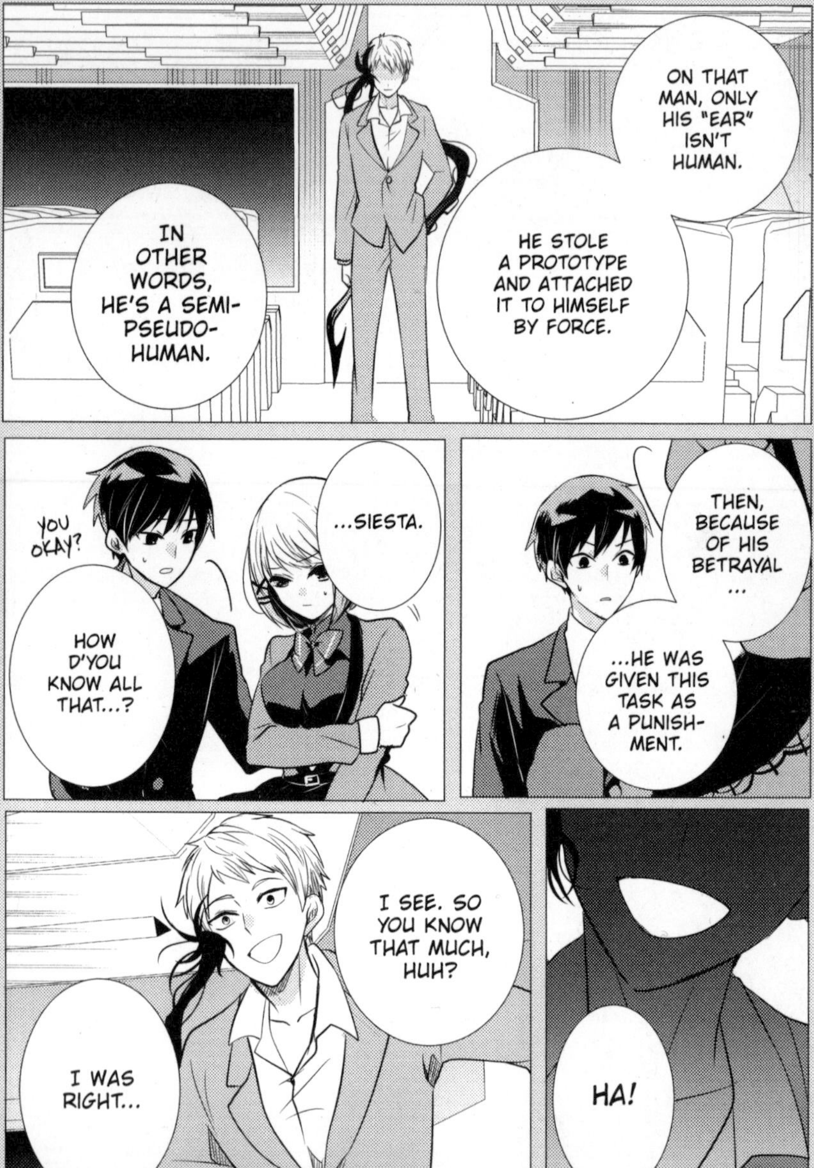
ON THAT MAN, ONLY HIS "EAR" ISN'T HUMAN.
HE STOLE A PROTOTYPE AND ATTACHED IT TO HIMSELF BY FORCE.
IN OTHER WORDS, HE'S A SEMI-PSEUDO-HUMAN.
THEN, BECAUSE OF HIS BETRAYAL...
...HE WAS GIVEN THIS TASK AS A PUNISHMENT.
...SIESTA.
YOU OKAY?
HOW D'YOU KNOW ALL THAT...?
HA!
I SEE. SO YOU KNOW THAT MUCH, HUH?
I WAS RIGHT...

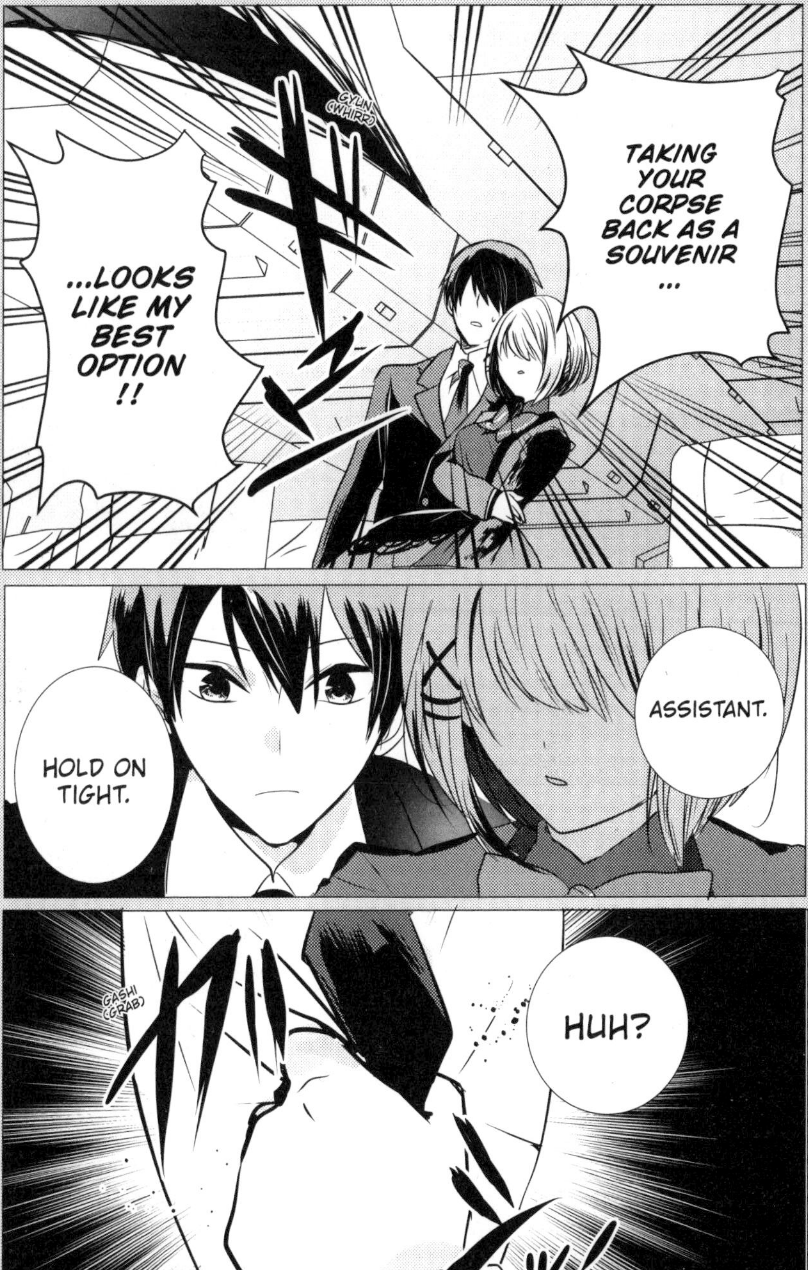
TAKING YOUR CORPSE BACK AS A SOUVENIR...
GYUN (WHIRR)
...LOOKS LIKE MY BEST OPTION!!
ASSISTANT.
HOLD ON TIGHT.
HUH?
GASHI (GRAB)

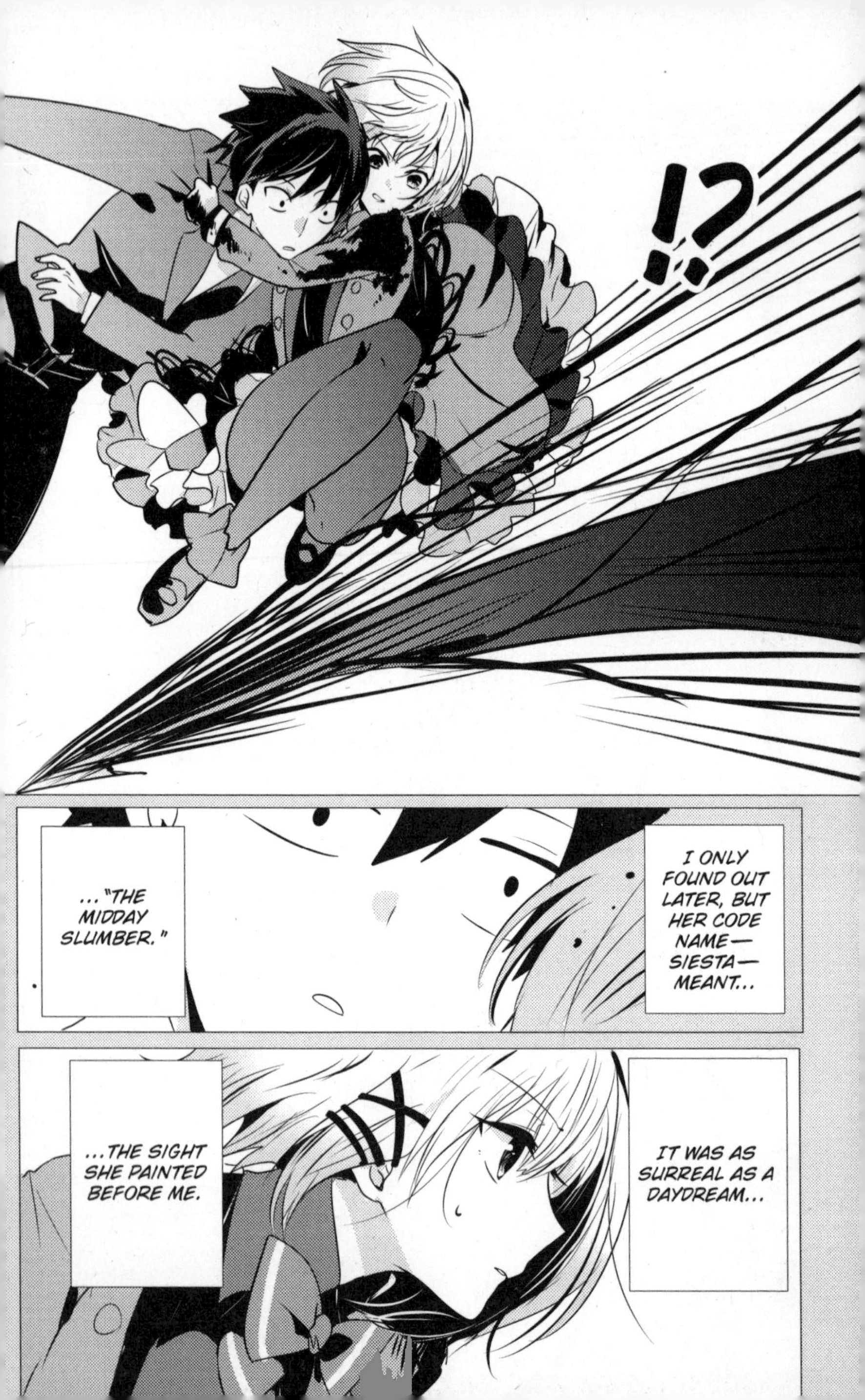
!?
I ONLY FOUND OUT LATER, BUT HER CODE NAME—SIESTA—MEANT...
..."THE MIDDAY SLUMBER."
IT WAS AS SURREAL AS A DAYDREAM...
...THE SIGHT SHE PAINTED BEFORE ME.

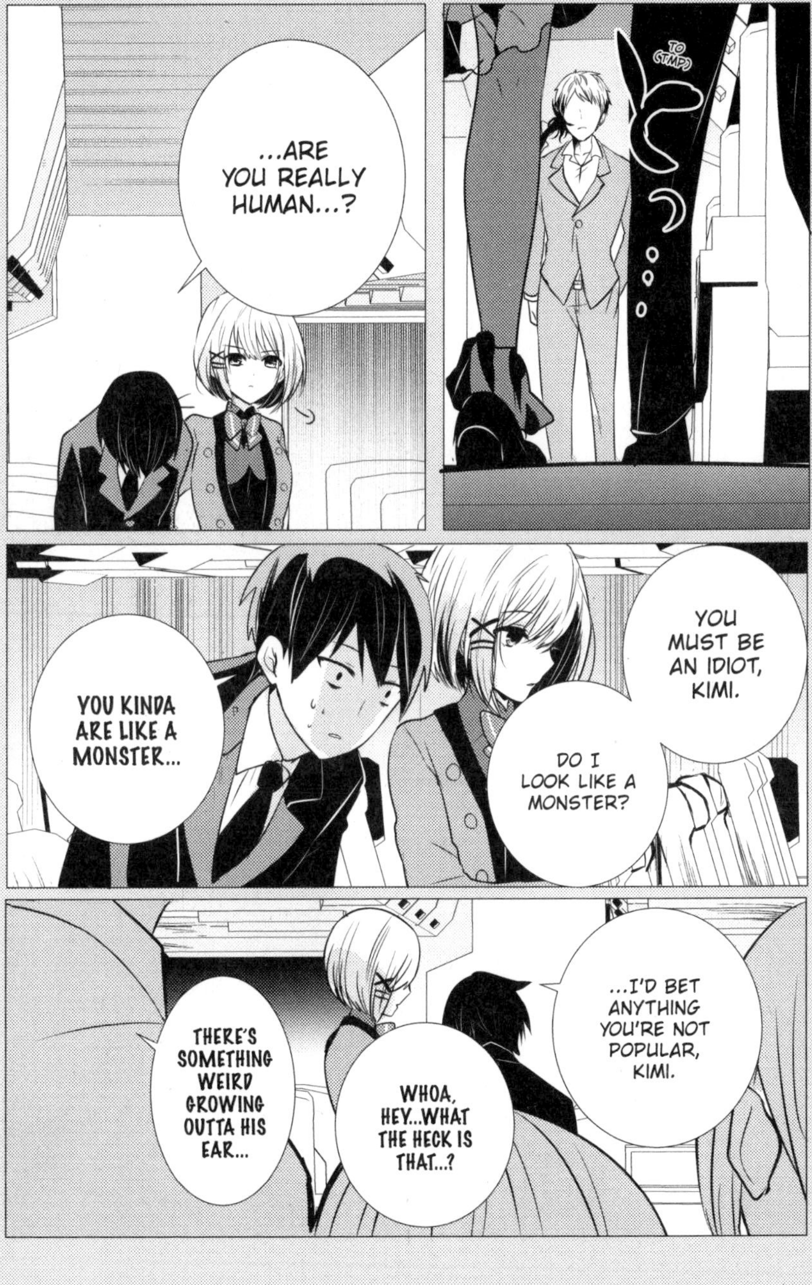
TO (TMP)
...ARE YOU REALLY HUMAN...?
YOU MUST BE AN IDIOT, KIMI.
DO I LOOK LIKE A MONSTER?
YOU KINDA ARE LIKE A MONSTER...
...I'D BET ANYTHING YOU'RE NOT POPULAR, KIMI.
WHOA, HEY...WHAT THE HECK IS THAT...?
THERE'S SOMETHING WEIRD GROWING OUTTA HIS EAR...

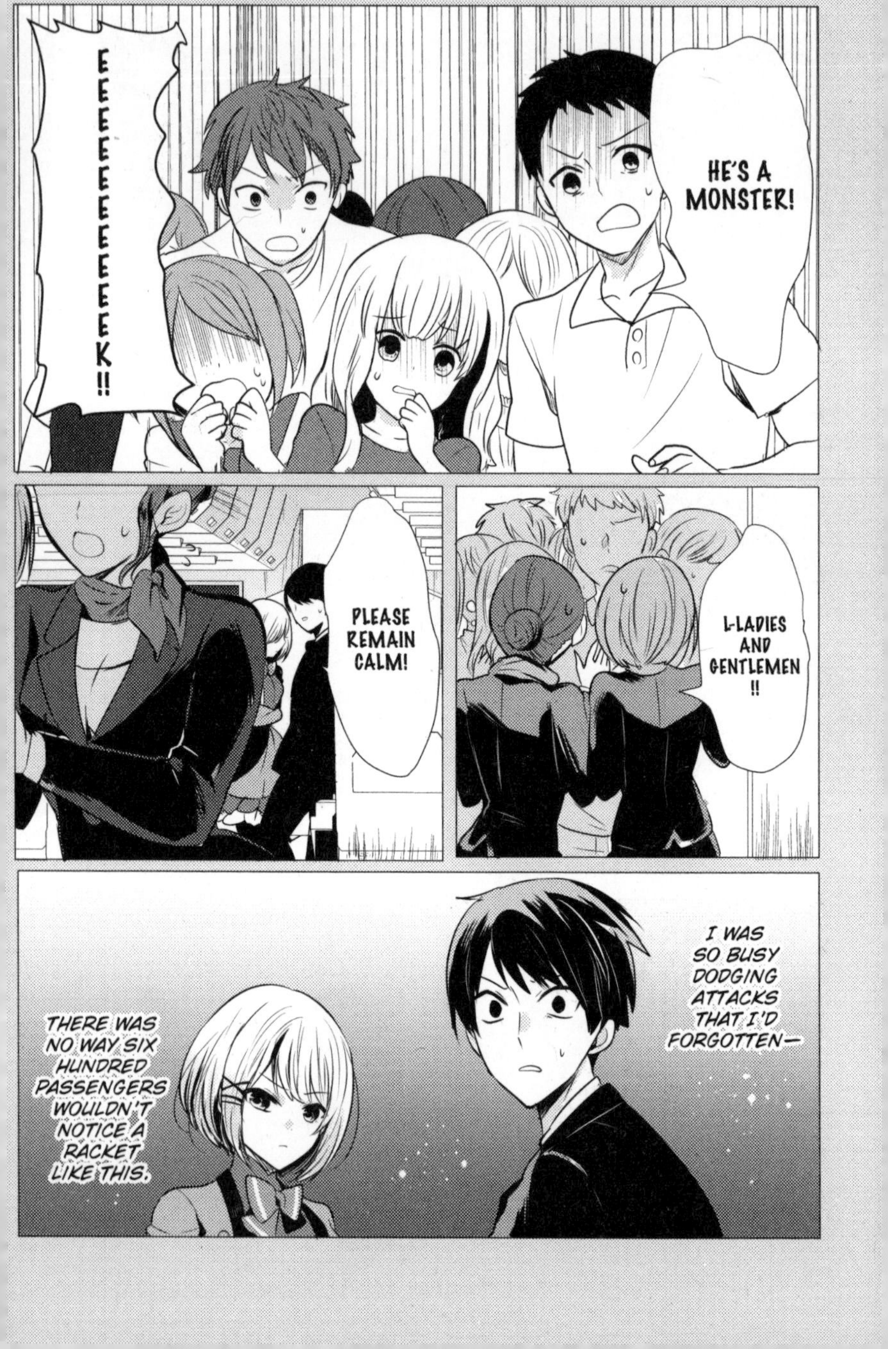
HE'S A MONSTER!
EEEEEEEEEEEEK!!
L-LADIES AND GENTLEMEN!!
PLEASE REMAIN CALM!
I WAS SO BUSY DODGING ATTACKS THAT I'D FORGOTTEN—
THERE WAS NO WAY SIX HUNDRED PASSENGERS WOULDN'T NOTICE A RACKET LIKE THIS.

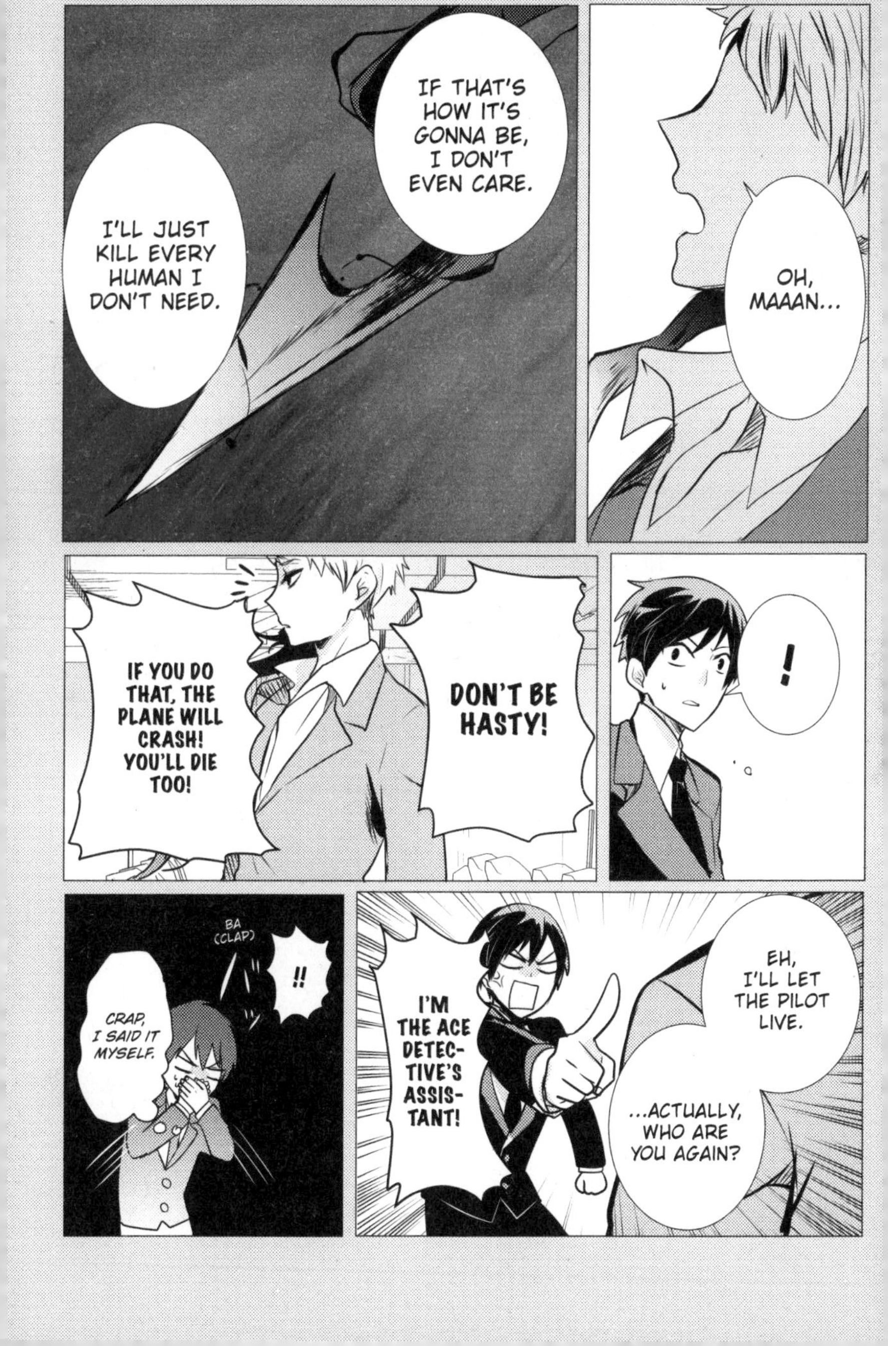
OH, MAAAN…
IF THAT'S HOW IT'S GONNA BE, I DON'T EVEN CARE.
I'LL JUST KILL EVERY HUMAN I DON'T NEED.
!
DON'T BE HASTY!
IF YOU DO THAT, THE PLANE WILL CRASH! YOU'LL DIE TOO!
EH, I'LL LET THE PILOT LIVE.
…ACTUALLY, WHO ARE YOU AGAIN?
I'M THE ACE DETECTIVE'S ASSISTANT!
BA (CLAP)
!!
CRAP, I SAID IT MYSELF.

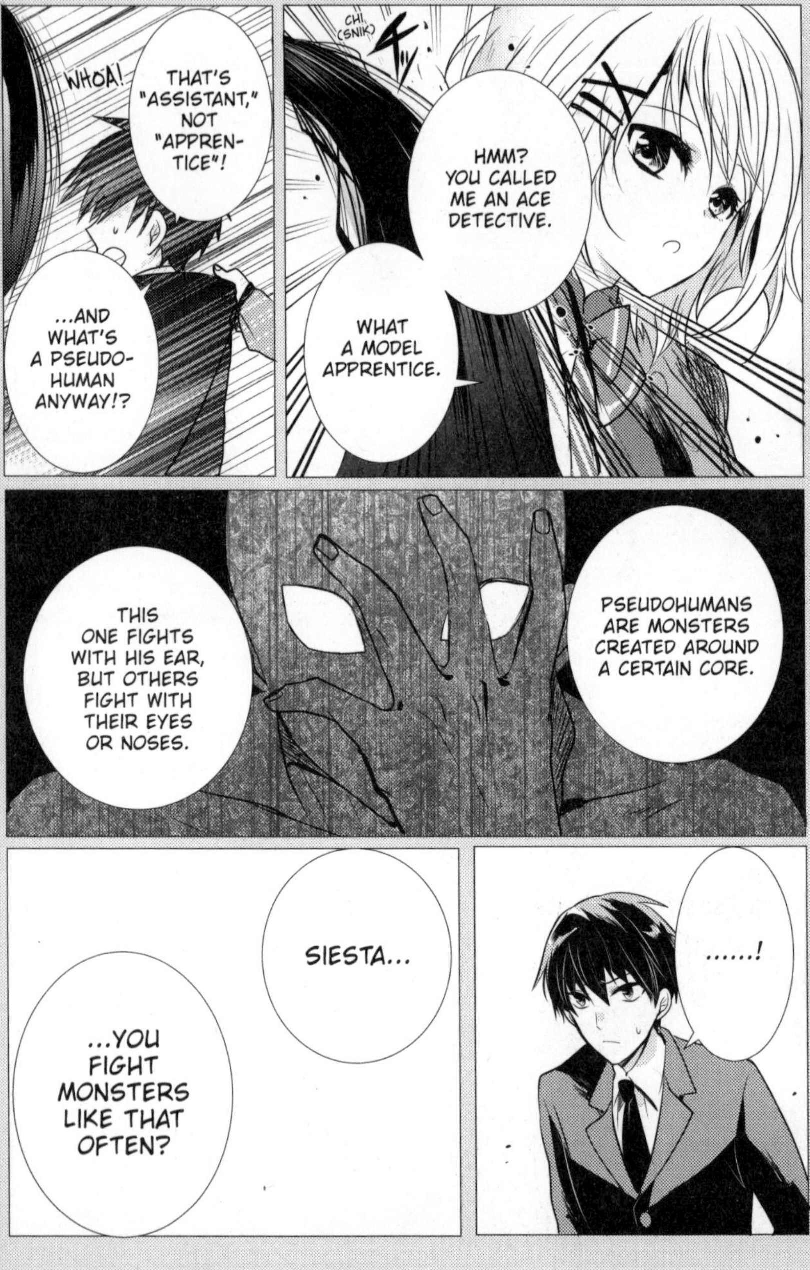
CHI (SNIK)
HMM? YOU CALLED ME AN ACE DETECTIVE.
WHAT A MODEL APPRENTICE.
THAT'S "ASSISTANT," NOT "APPRENTICE"!
WHOA!
...AND WHAT'S A PSEUDOHUMAN ANYWAY!?
PSEUDOHUMANS ARE MONSTERS CREATED AROUND A CERTAIN CORE.
THIS ONE FIGHTS WITH HIS EAR, BUT OTHERS FIGHT WITH THEIR EYES OR NOSES.
......!
SIESTA...
...YOU FIGHT MONSTERS LIKE THAT OFTEN?

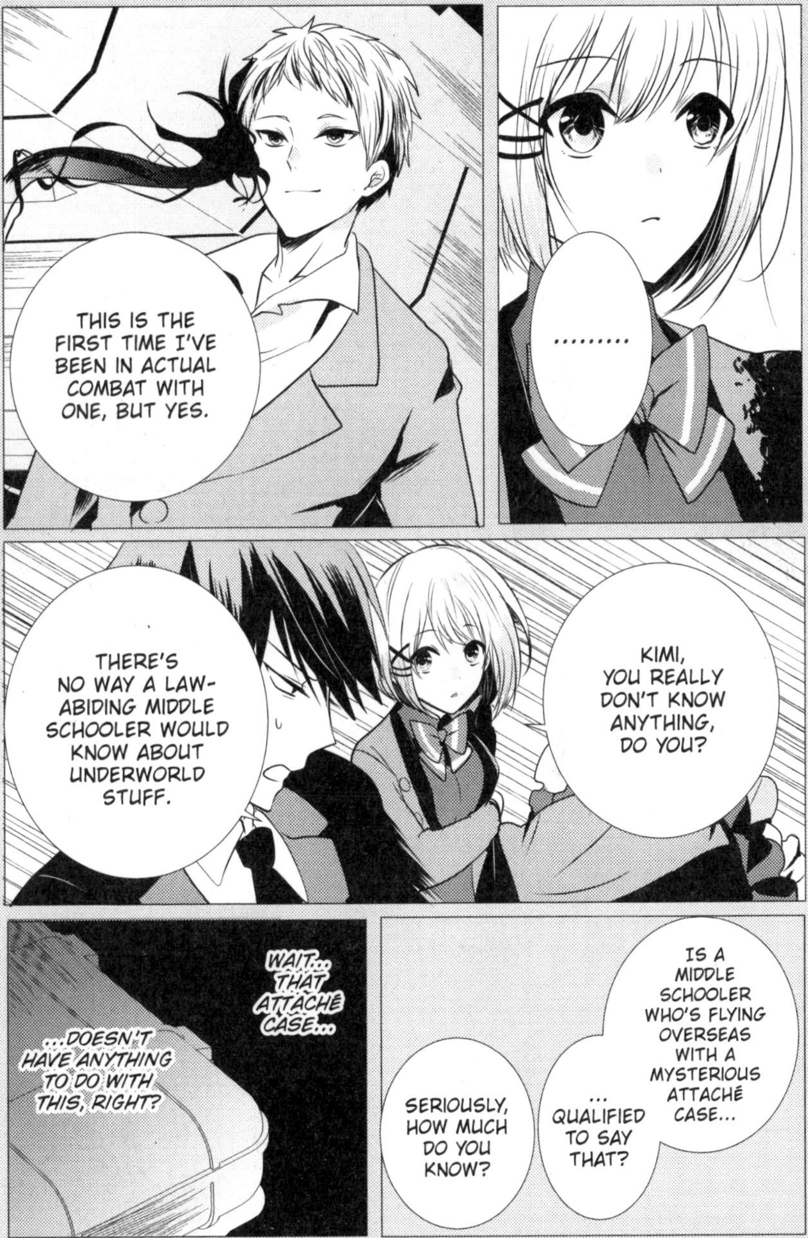
....
THIS IS THE FIRST TIME I'VE BEEN IN ACTUAL COMBAT WITH ONE, BUT YES.
KIMI, YOU REALLY DON'T KNOW ANYTHING, DO YOU?
THERE'S NO WAY A LAW-ABIDING MIDDLE SCHOOLER WOULD KNOW ABOUT UNDERWORLD STUFF.
IS A MIDDLE SCHOOLER WHO'S FLYING OVERSEAS WITH A MYSTERIOUS ATTACHÉ CASE...
... QUALIFIED TO SAY THAT?
SERIOUSLY, HOW MUCH DO YOU KNOW?
WAIT... THAT ATTACHÉ CASE...
...DOESN'T HAVE ANYTHING TO DO WITH THIS, RIGHT?

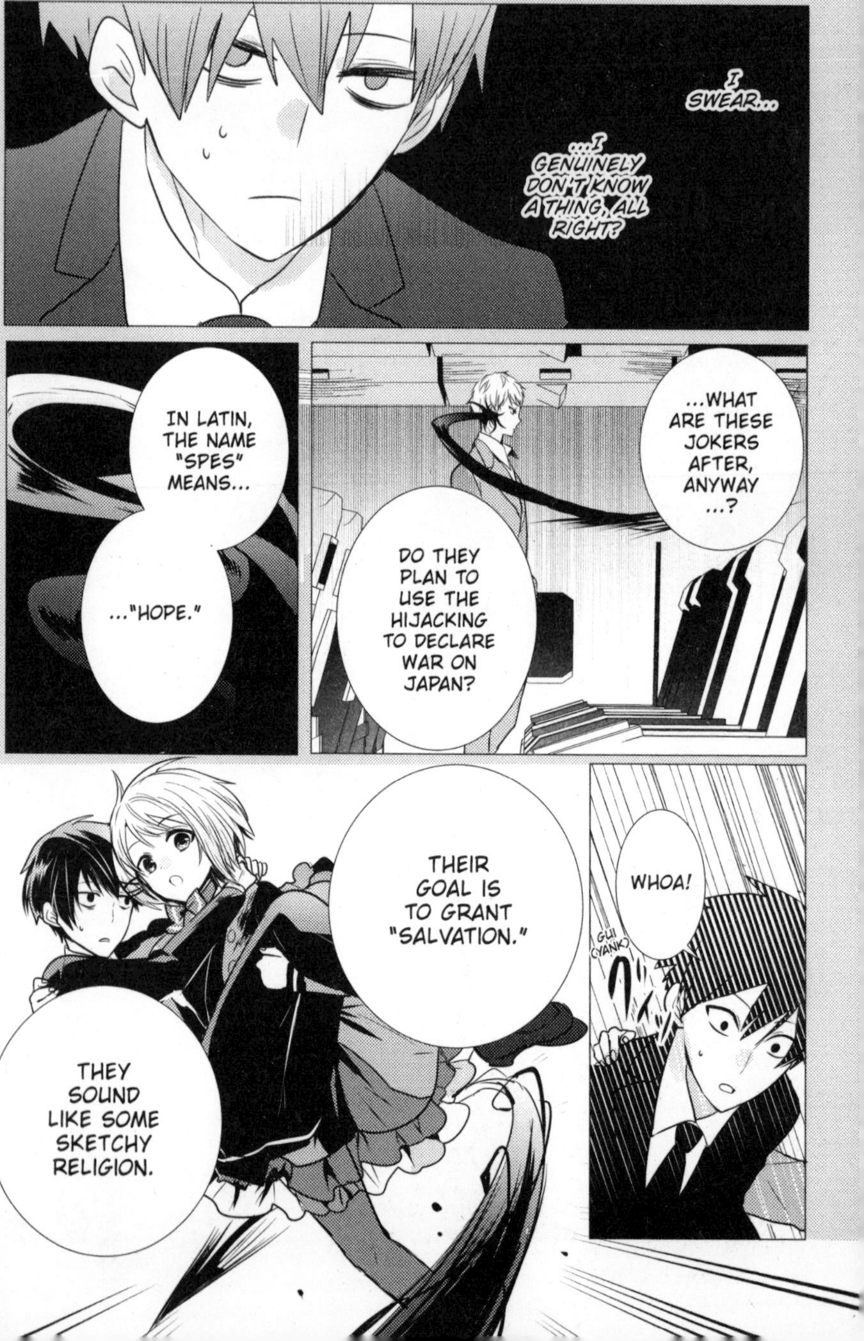
I SWEAR...
...I GENUINELY DON'T KNOW A THING, ALL RIGHT?
...WHAT ARE THESE JOKERS AFTER, ANYWAY...?
DO THEY PLAN TO USE THE HIJACKING TO DECLARE WAR ON JAPAN?
IN LATIN, THE NAME "SPES" MEANS...
..."HOPE."
WHOA!
GUI (YANK)
THEIR GOAL IS TO GRANT "SALVATION."
THEY SOUND LIKE SOME SKETCHY RELIGION.

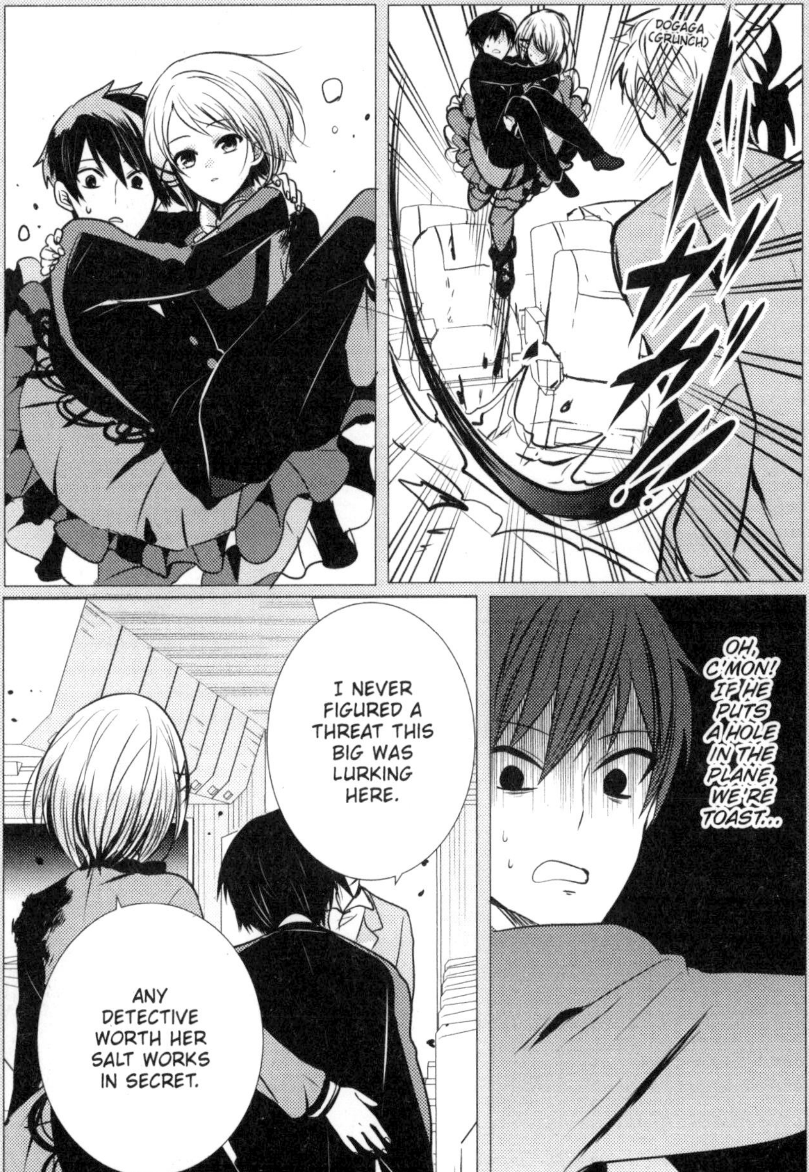
DOGAGA (CRUNCH)
OH, C'MON! IF HE PUTS A HOLE IN THE PLANE, WE'RE TOAST...
I NEVER FIGURED A THREAT THIS BIG WAS LURKING HERE.
ANY DETECTIVE WORTH HER SALT WORKS IN SECRET.

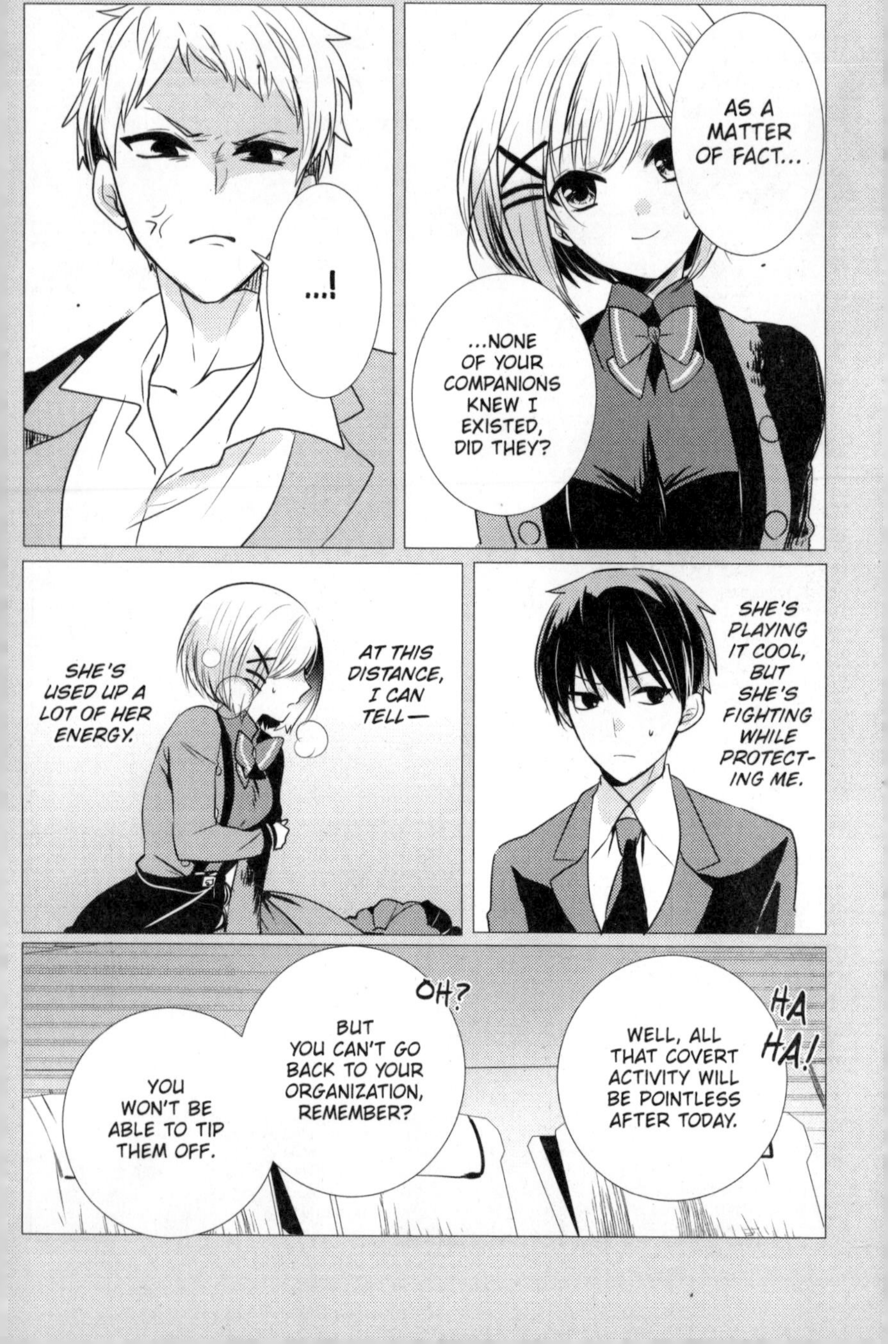
AS A MATTER OF FACT...
...NONE OF YOUR COMPANIONS KNEW I EXISTED, DID THEY?
...!
SHE'S PLAYING IT COOL, BUT SHE'S FIGHTING WHILE PROTECT-ING ME.
AT THIS DISTANCE, I CAN TELL—
SHE'S USED UP A LOT OF HER ENERGY.
HA HA!
WELL, ALL THAT COVERT ACTIVITY WILL BE POINTLESS AFTER TODAY.
OH?
BUT YOU CAN'T GO BACK TO YOUR ORGANIZATION, REMEMBER?
YOU WON'T BE ABLE TO TIP THEM OFF.

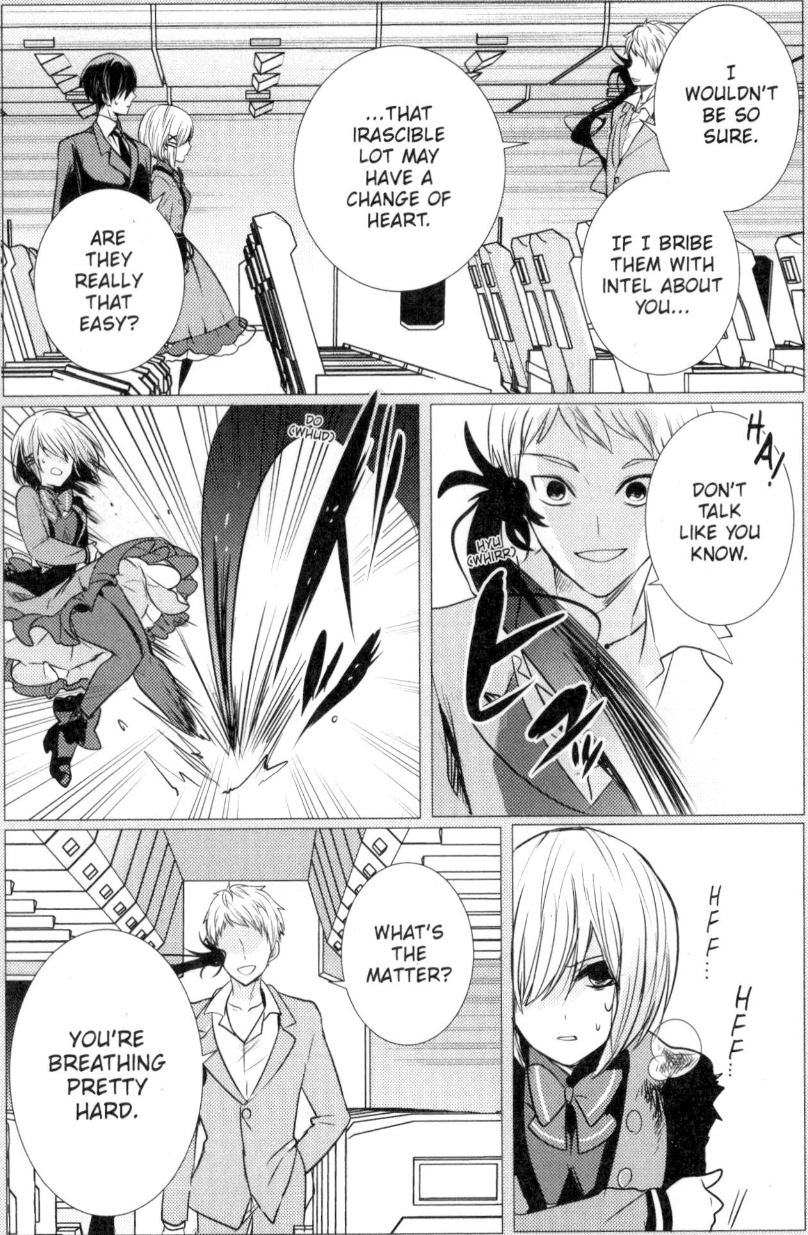
I WOULDN'T BE SO SURE.
IF I BRIBE THEM WITH INTEL ABOUT YOU...
...THAT IRASCIBLE LOT MAY HAVE A CHANGE OF HEART.
ARE THEY REALLY THAT EASY?
HA!
DON'T TALK LIKE YOU KNOW.
HYU (WHIRR)
DO (WHUD)
HFF...
HFF...
WHAT'S THE MATTER?
YOU'RE BREATHING PRETTY HARD.

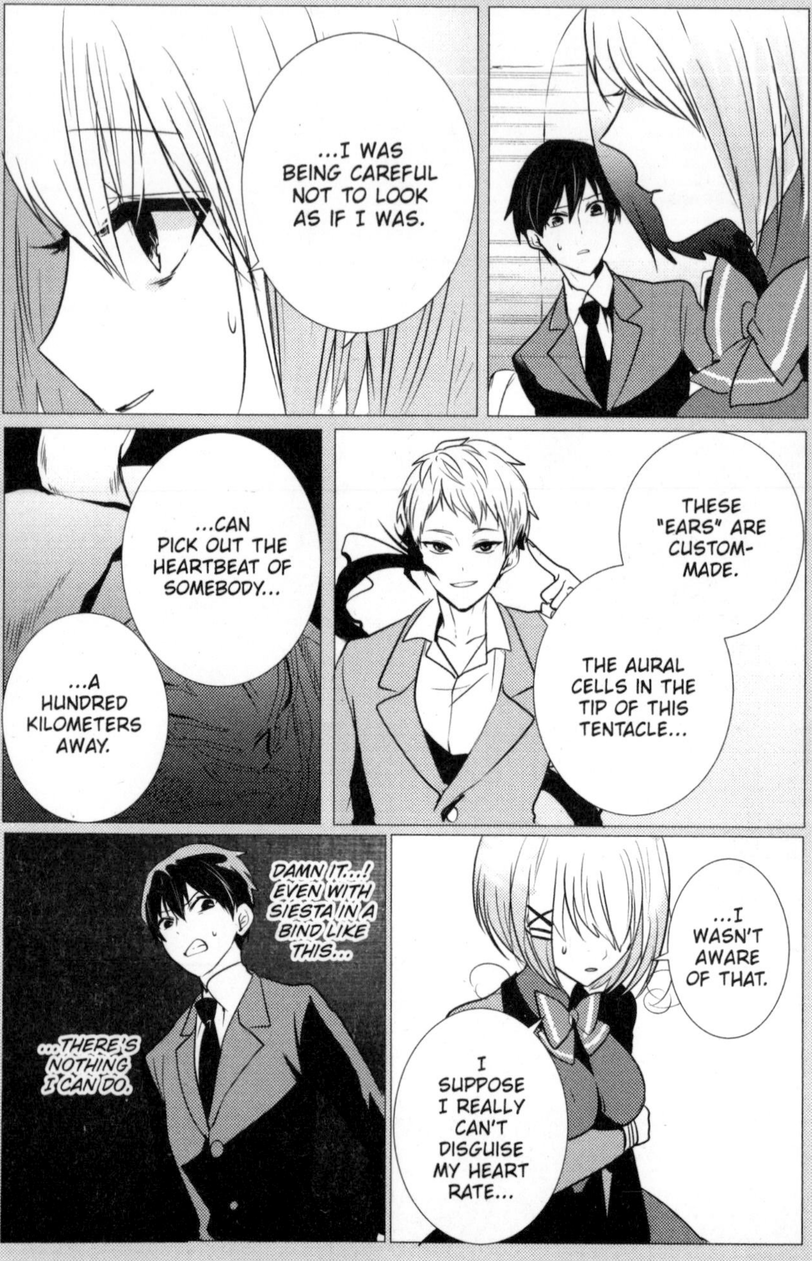
...I WAS BEING CAREFUL NOT TO LOOK AS IF I WAS.
THESE "EARS" ARE CUSTOM-MADE.
THE AURAL CELLS IN THE TIP OF THIS TENTACLE...
...CAN PICK OUT THE HEARTBEAT OF SOMEBODY...
...A HUNDRED KILOMETERS AWAY.
...I WASN'T AWARE OF THAT.
I SUPPOSE I REALLY CAN'T DISGUISE MY HEART RATE...
DAMN IT...! EVEN WITH SIESTA IN A BIND LIKE THIS...
...THERE'S NOTHING I CAN DO.

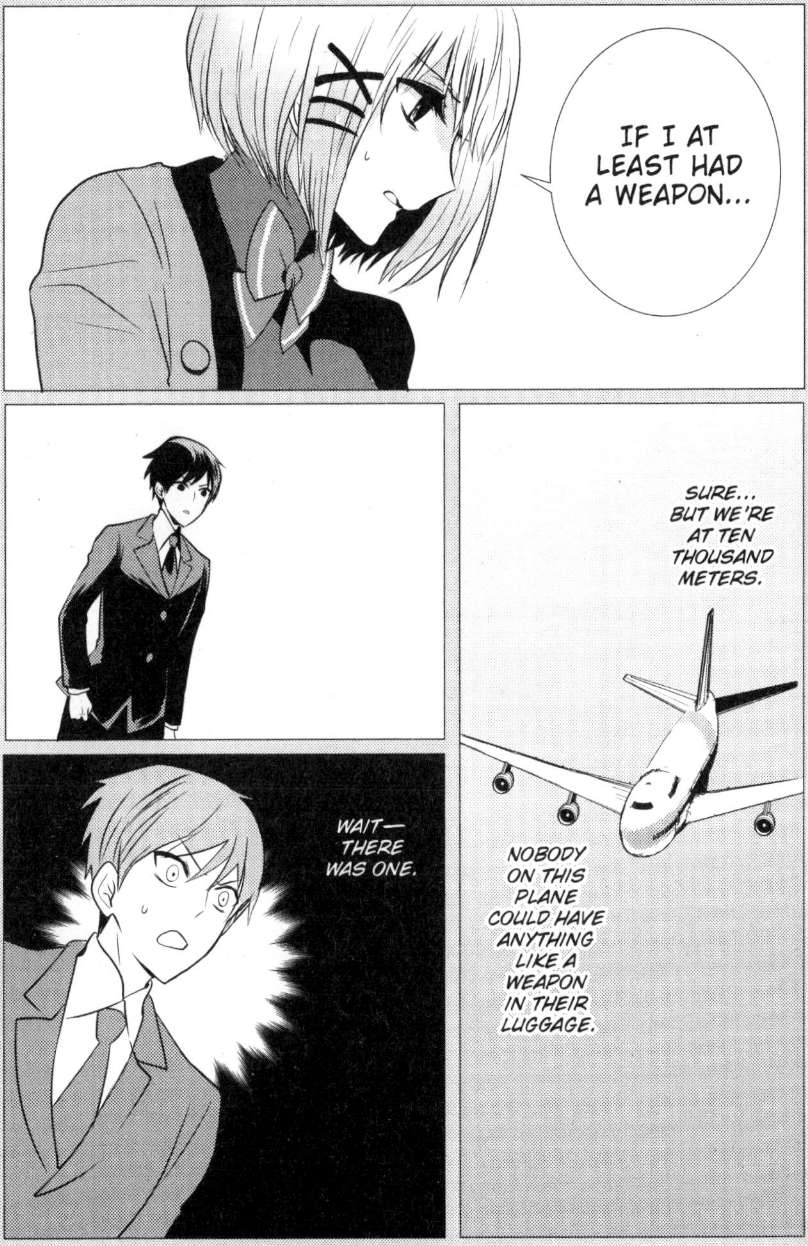
IF I AT LEAST HAD A WEAPON...
SURE... BUT WE'RE AT TEN THOUSAND METERS.
NOBODY ON THIS PLANE COULD HAVE ANYTHING LIKE A WEAPON IN THEIR LUGGAGE.
WAIT—THERE WAS ONE.

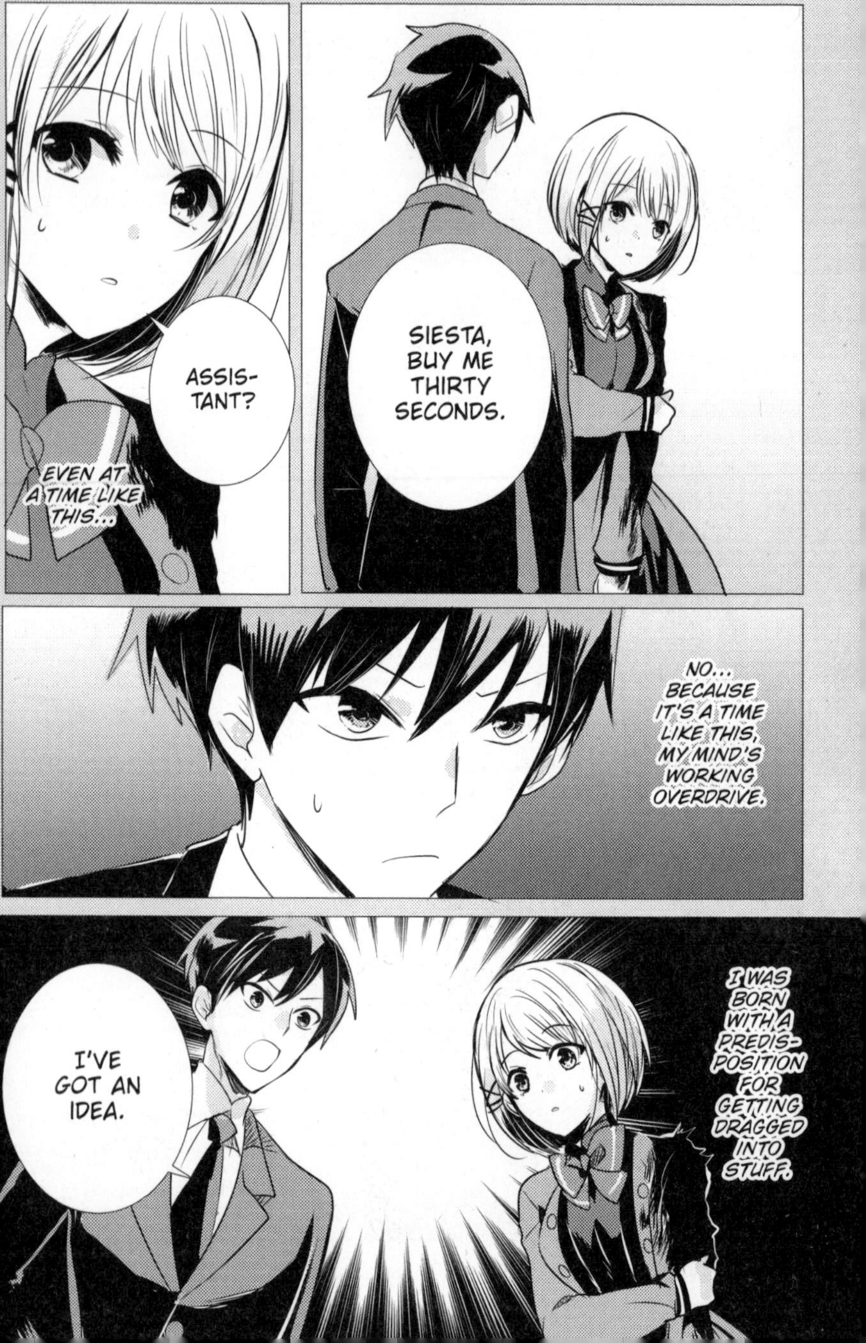
SIESTA, BUY ME THIRTY SECONDS.
ASSIS-TANT?
EVEN AT A TIME LIKE THIS...
NO... BECAUSE IT'S A TIME LIKE THIS, MY MIND'S WORKING OVERDRIVE.
I WAS BORN WITH A PREDIS-POSITION FOR GETTING DRAGGED INTO STUFF.
I'VE GOT AN IDEA.

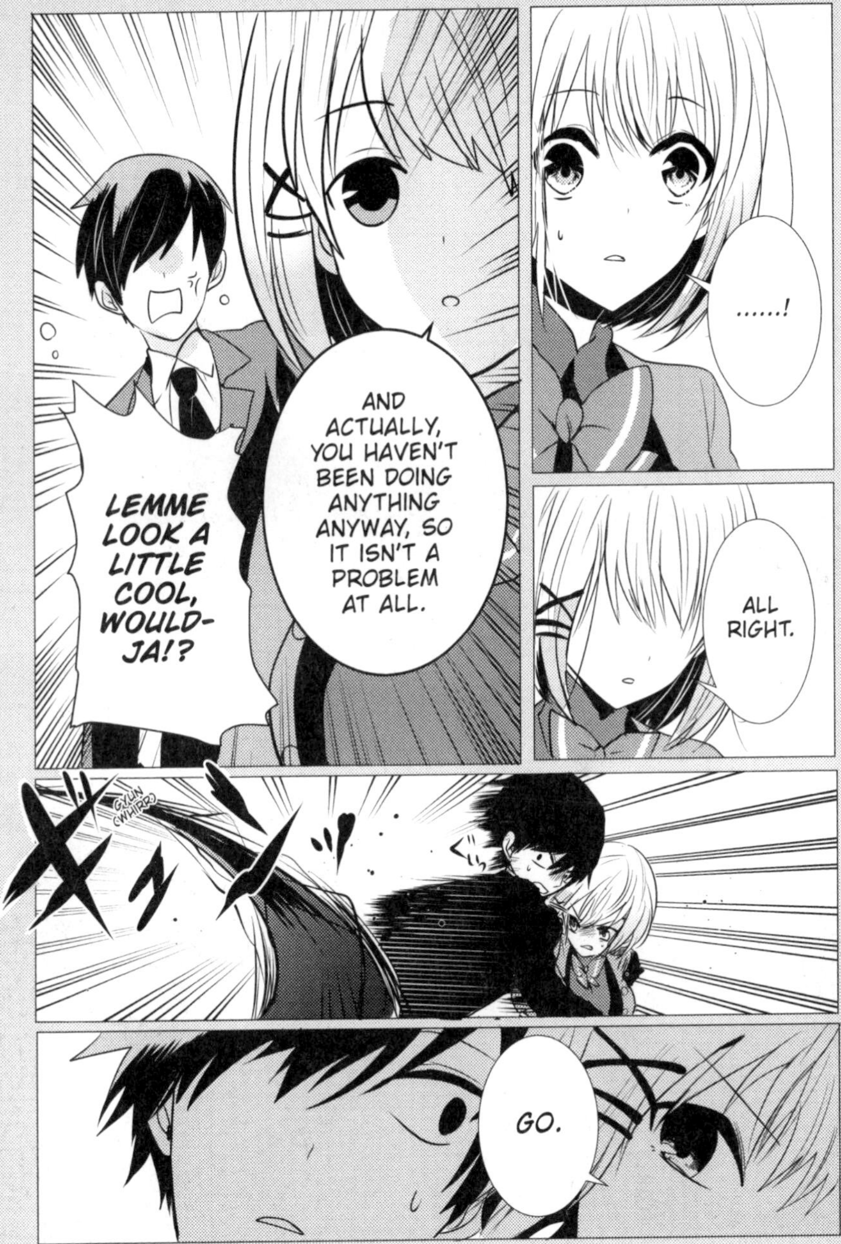
......!
ALL RIGHT.
AND ACTUALLY, YOU HAVEN'T BEEN DOING ANYTHING ANYWAY, SO IT ISN'T A PROBLEM AT ALL.
LEMME LOOK A LITTLE COOL, WOULD-JA!?
GYUN (WHIRR)
GO.

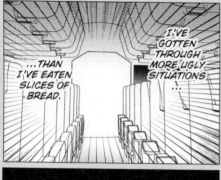

DA (DASH)
I'VE GOTTEN THROUGH MORE UGLY SITUATIONS...
...THAN I'VE EATEN SLICES OF BREAD.
THIS HUNCH HAS TO BE...
...THE BEST SOLUTION—BACKED UP BY PAST EXPERIENCE.
THAT ATTACHÉ CASE UNDER MY SEAT.
GA (GRAB)
OF COURSE... I DON'T KNOW WHAT'S IN THIS THING.

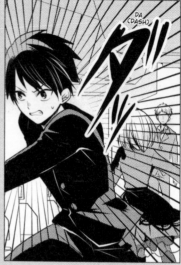

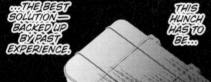

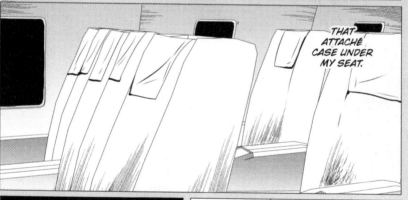

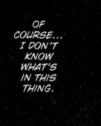

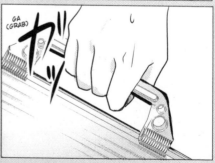

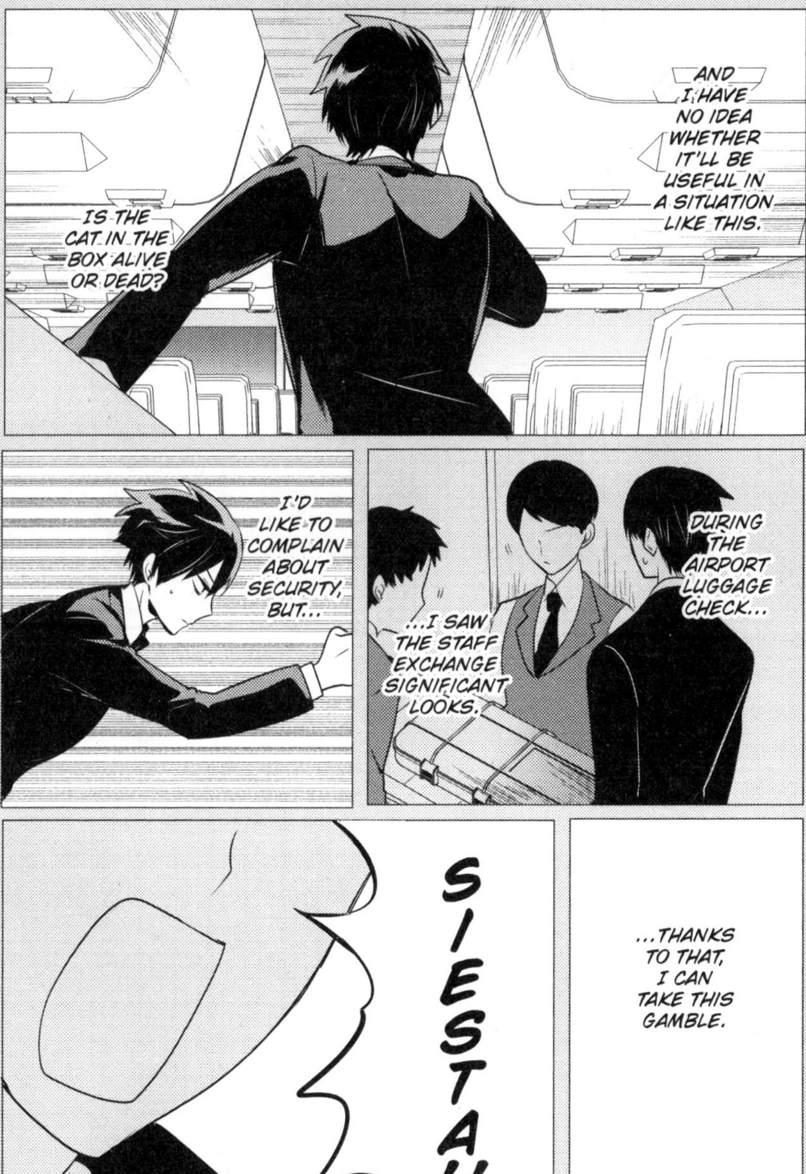
AND I HAVE NO IDEA WHETHER IT'LL BE USEFUL IN A SITUATION LIKE THIS.
IS THE CAT IN THE BOX ALIVE OR DEAD?
DURING THE AIRPORT LUGGAGE CHECK...
...I SAW THE STAFF EXCHANGE SIGNIFICANT LOOKS.
I'D LIKE TO COMPLAIN ABOUT SECURITY, BUT...
...THANKS TO THAT, I CAN TAKE THIS GAMBLE.
SIESTA!!

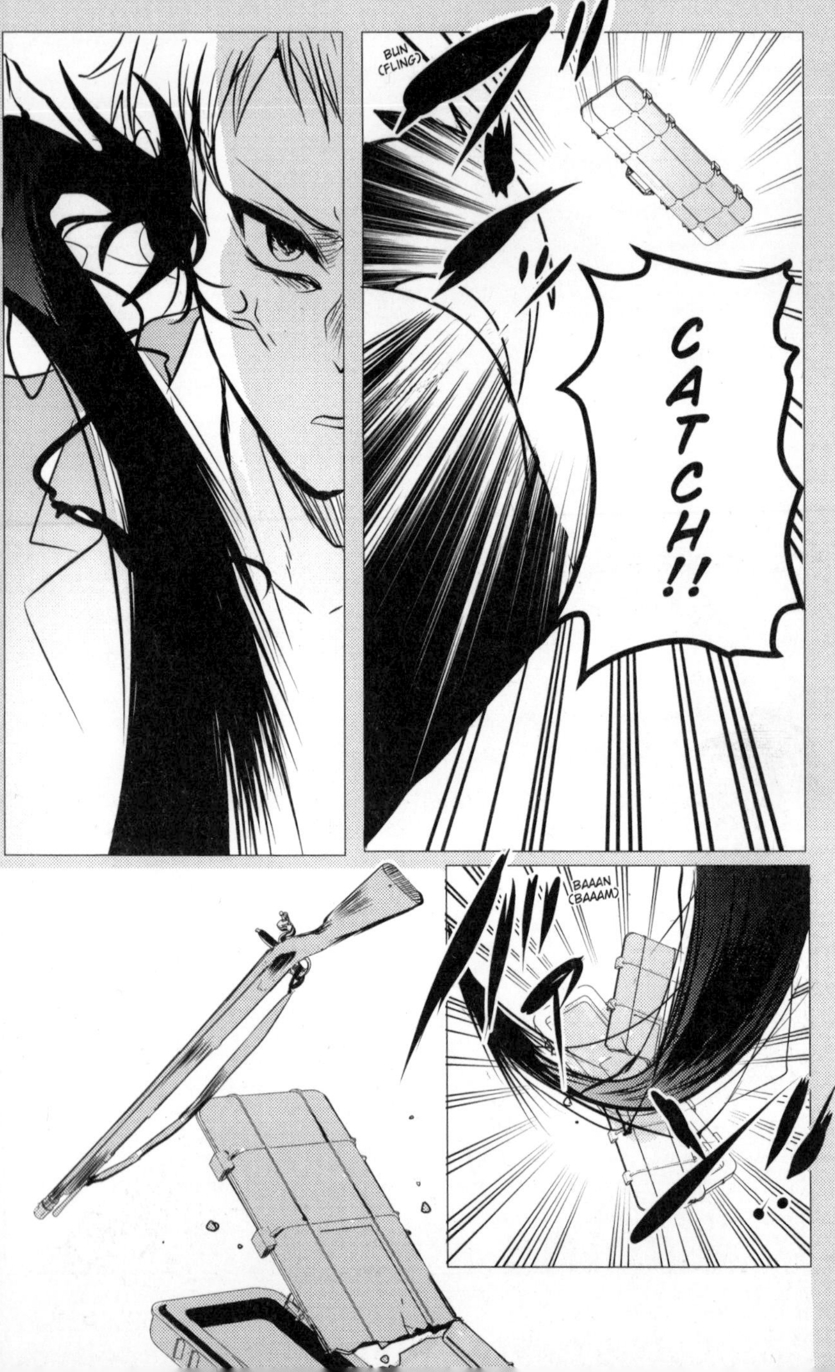
BUN
(FLING)
CATCH!!
BAAAN
(BAAAM)

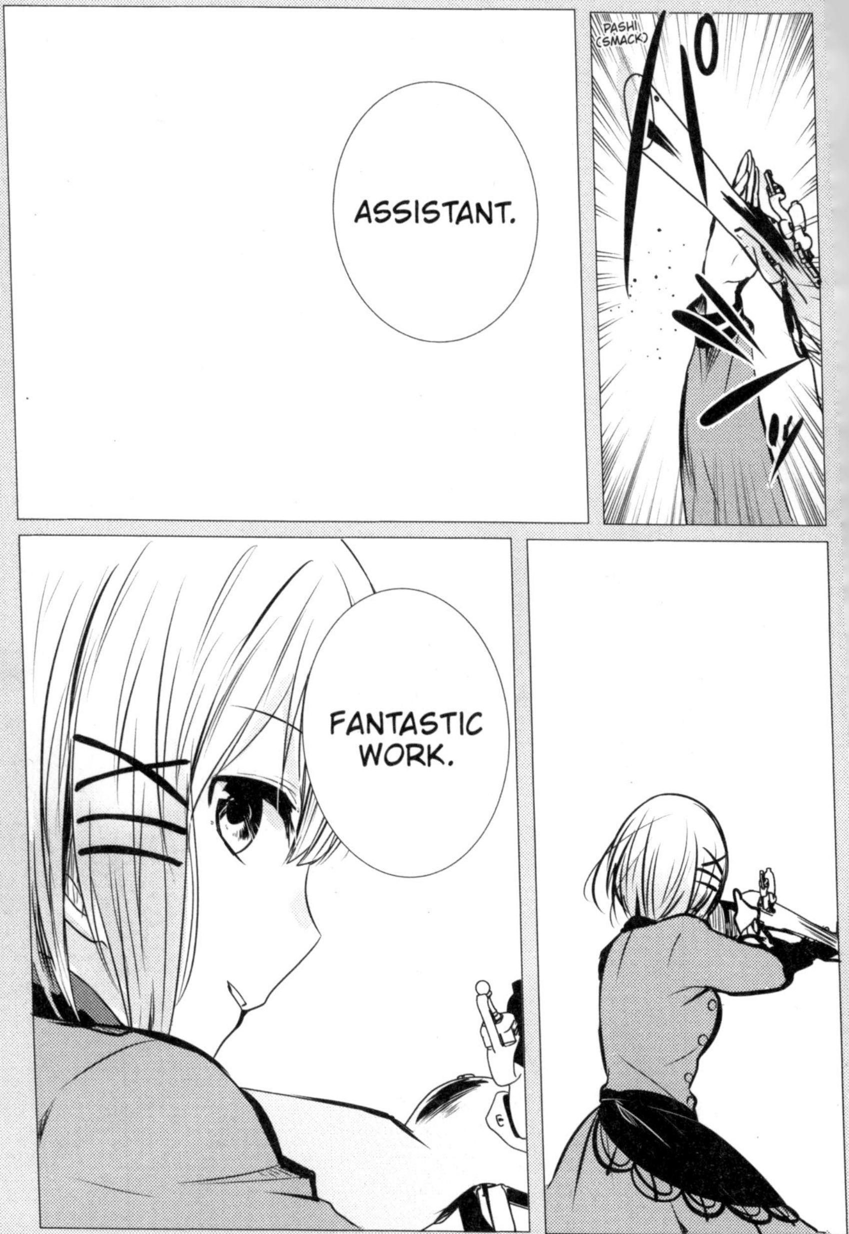
PASHI (SMACK)
ASSISTANT.
FANTASTIC WORK.

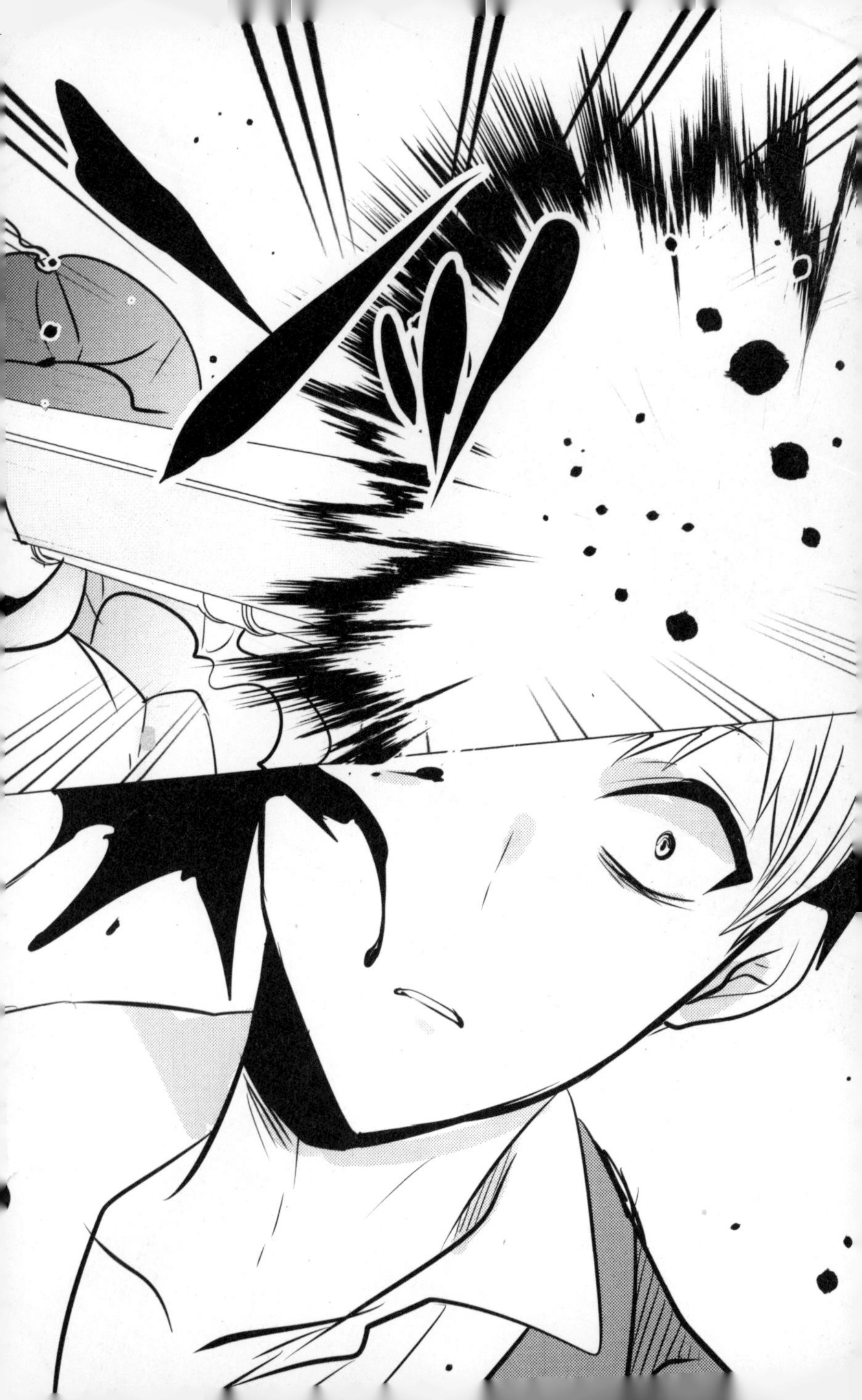

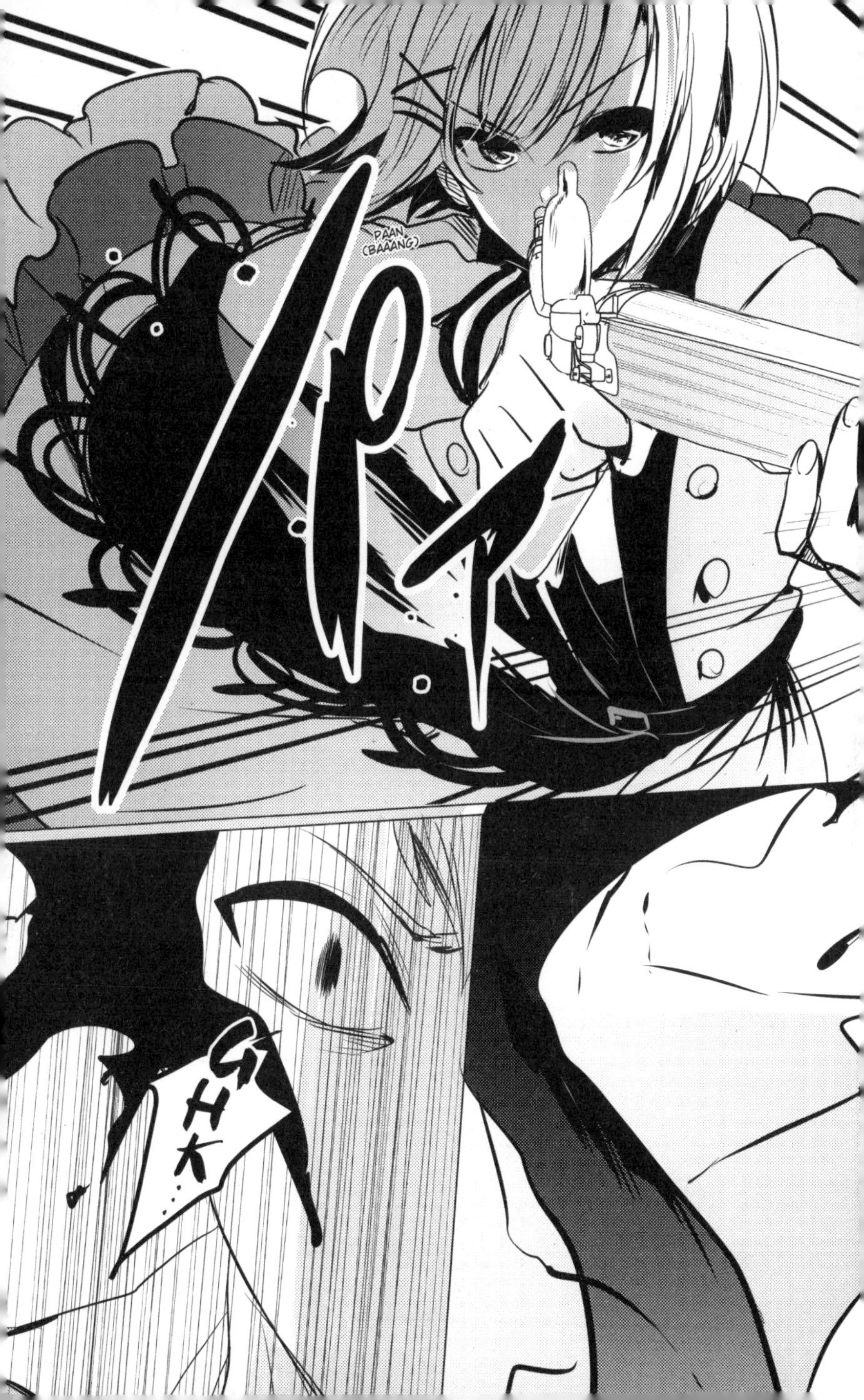
PAAN
(BAAANG)
GHK...

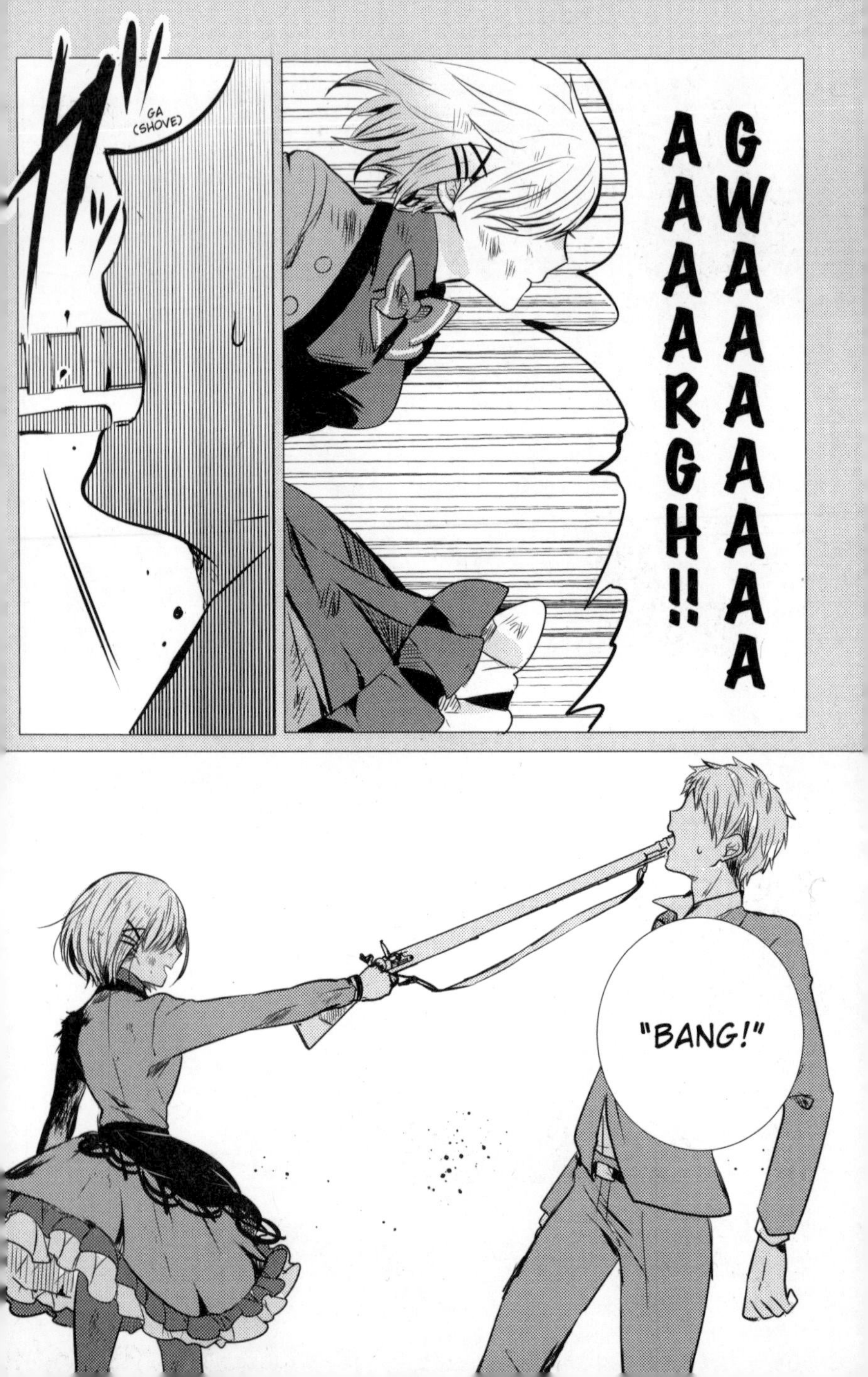
GWAAAAAAA
AAAARGH!!
GA (SHOVE)
"BANG!"

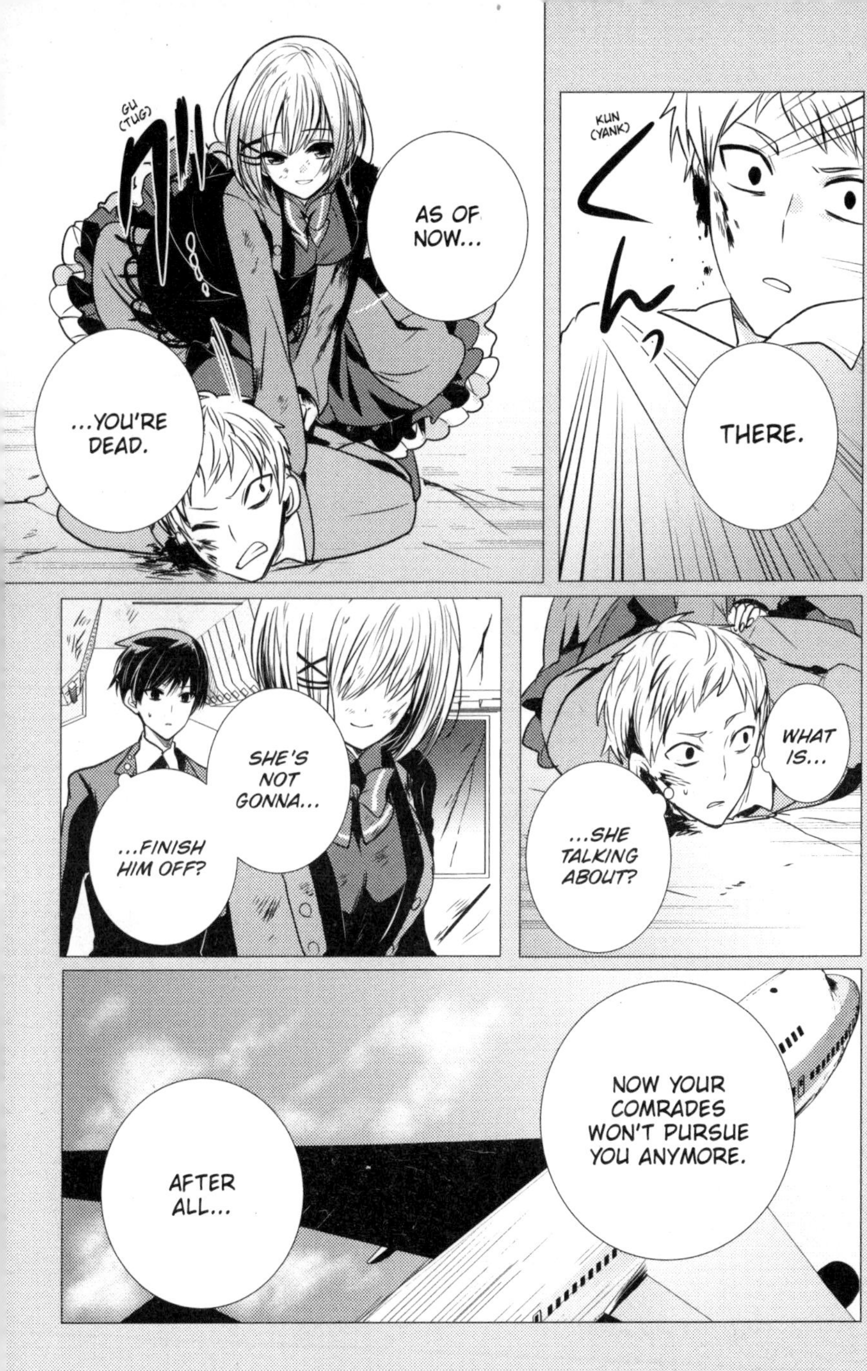
KUN (YANK)
THERE.
GU (TUG)
AS OF NOW...
...YOU'RE DEAD.
WHAT IS...
...SHE TALKING ABOUT?
SHE'S NOT GONNA...
...FINISH HIM OFF?
NOW YOUR COMRADES WON'T PURSUE YOU ANYMORE.
AFTER ALL...

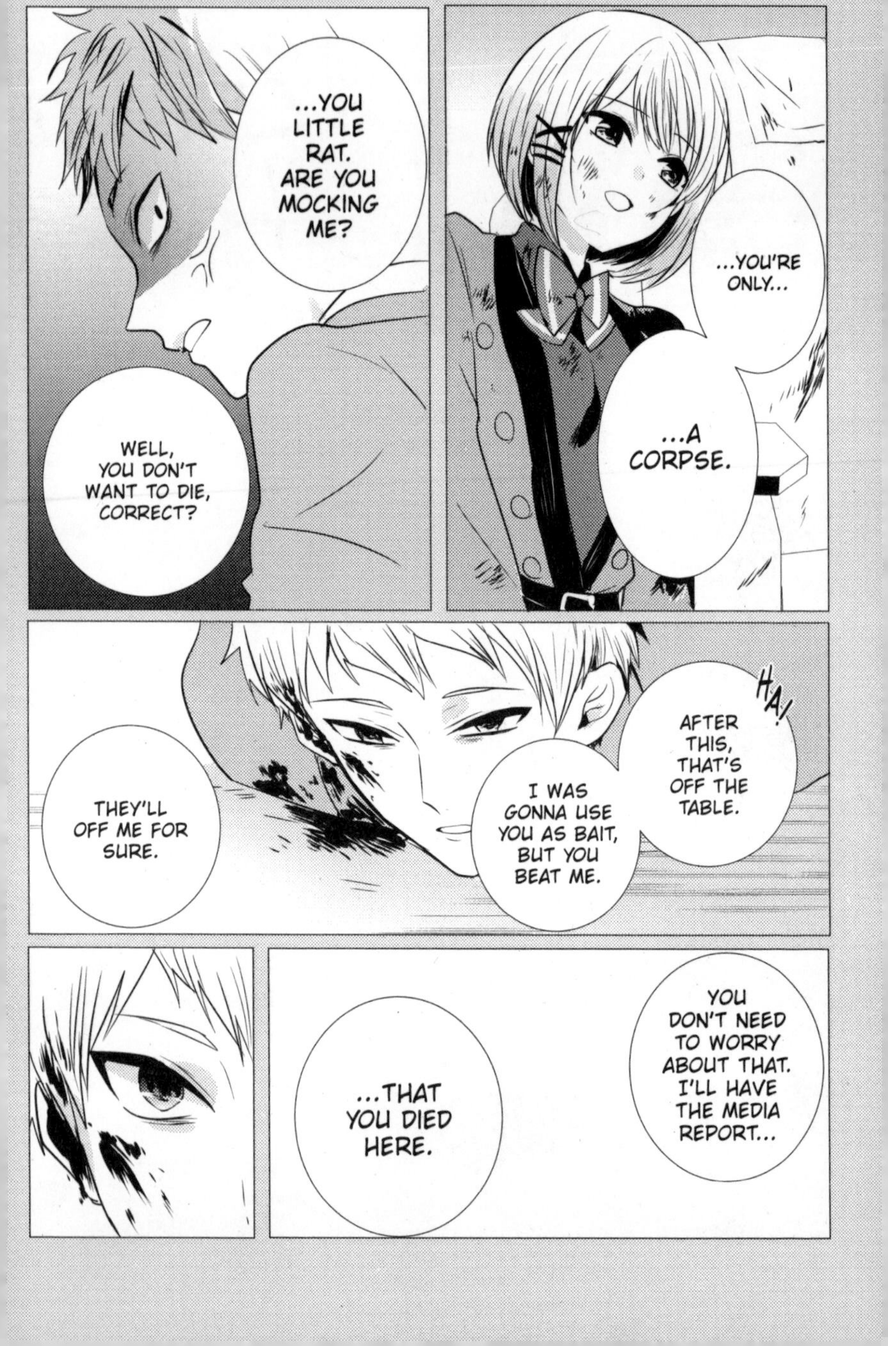
...YOU'RE ONLY...
...A CORPSE.
...YOU LITTLE RAT. ARE YOU MOCKING ME?
WELL, YOU DON'T WANT TO DIE, CORRECT?
HA!
AFTER THIS, THAT'S OFF THE TABLE.
I WAS GONNA USE YOU AS BAIT, BUT YOU BEAT ME.
THEY'LL OFF ME FOR SURE.
YOU DON'T NEED TO WORRY ABOUT THAT. I'LL HAVE THE MEDIA REPORT...
...THAT YOU DIED HERE.

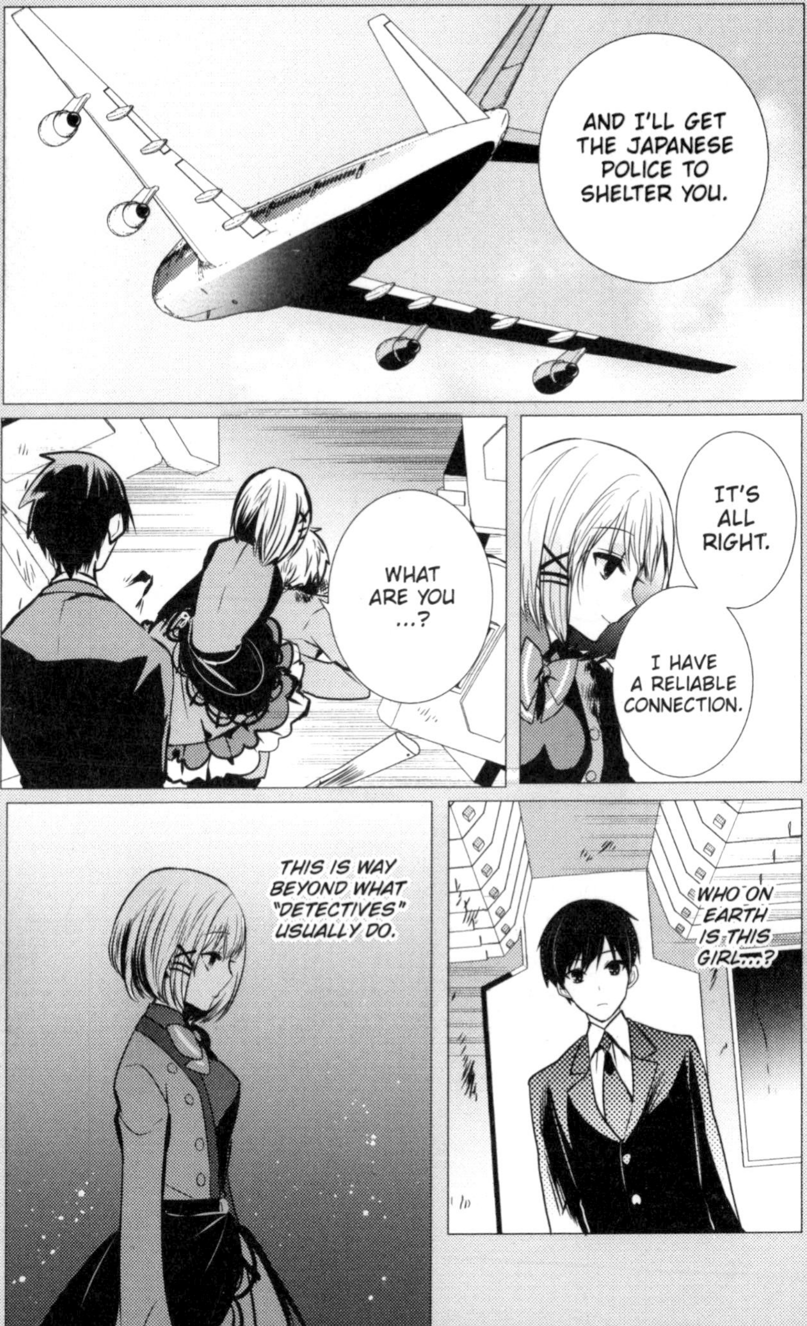
AND I'LL GET THE JAPANESE POLICE TO SHELTER YOU.
IT'S ALL RIGHT.
I HAVE A RELIABLE CONNECTION.
WHAT ARE YOU ...?
WHO ON EARTH IS THIS GIRL...?
THIS IS WAY BEYOND WHAT "DETECTIVES" USUALLY DO.

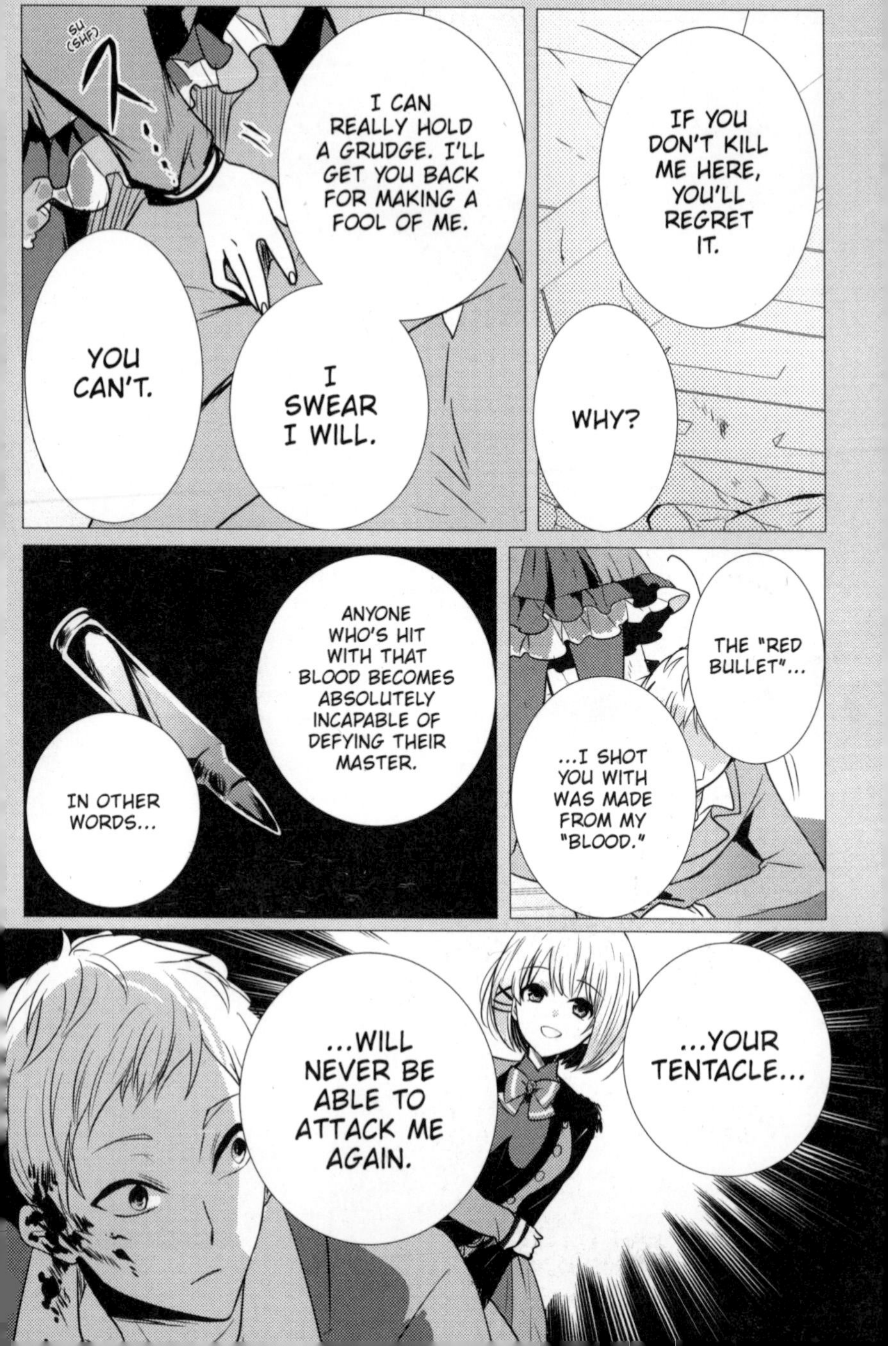
IF YOU DON'T KILL ME HERE, YOU'LL REGRET IT.
WHY?
I CAN REALLY HOLD A GRUDGE. I'LL GET YOU BACK FOR MAKING A FOOL OF ME.
SU (SHF)
I SWEAR I WILL.
YOU CAN'T.
THE "RED BULLET"...
...I SHOT YOU WITH WAS MADE FROM MY "BLOOD."
ANYONE WHO'S HIT WITH THAT BLOOD BECOMES ABSOLUTELY INCAPABLE OF DEFYING THEIR MASTER.
IN OTHER WORDS...
...YOUR TENTACLE...
...WILL NEVER BE ABLE TO ATTACK ME AGAIN.

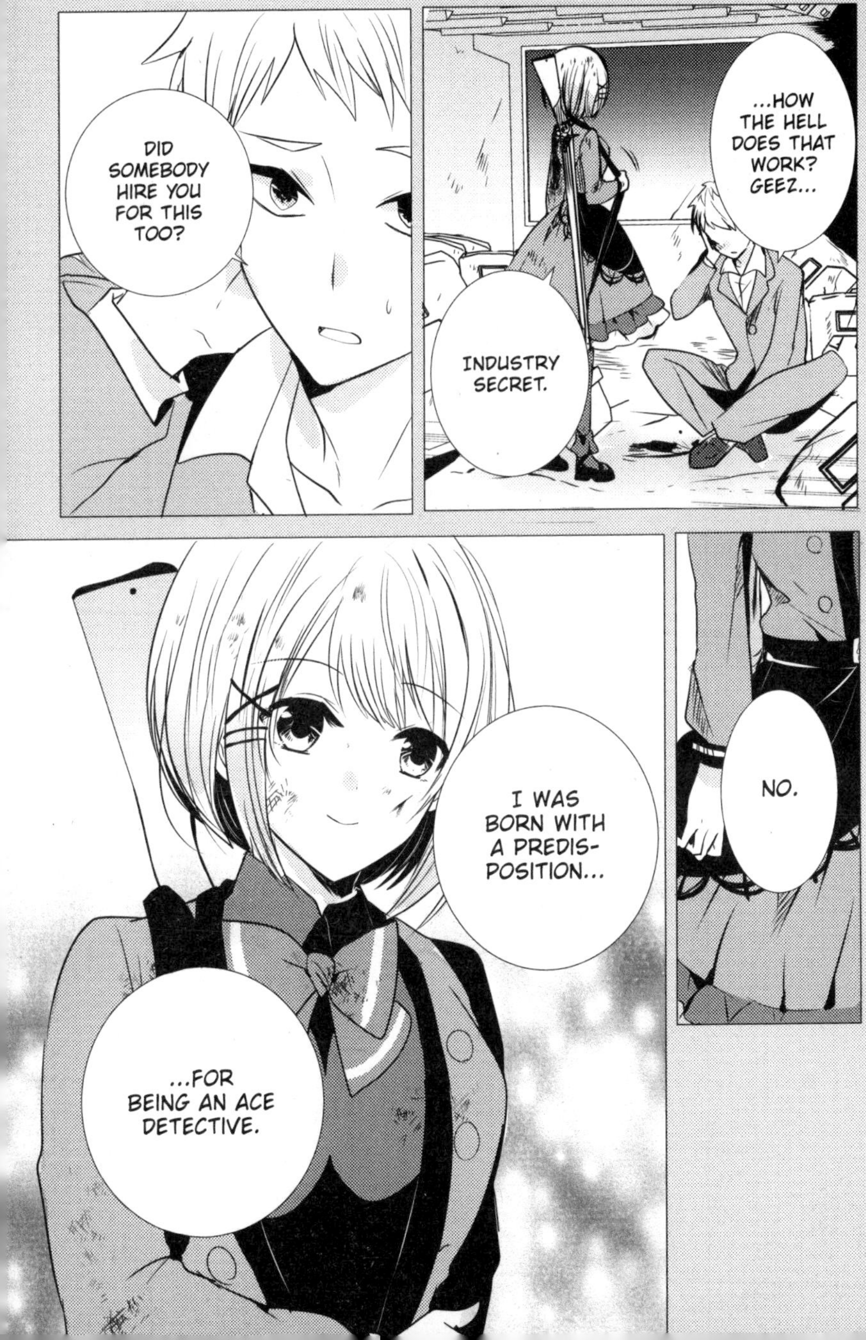
...HOW THE HELL DOES THAT WORK? GEEZ...
INDUSTRY SECRET.
DID SOMEBODY HIRE YOU FOR THIS TOO?
NO.
I WAS BORN WITH A PREDIS-POSITION...
...FOR BEING AN ACE DETECTIVE.

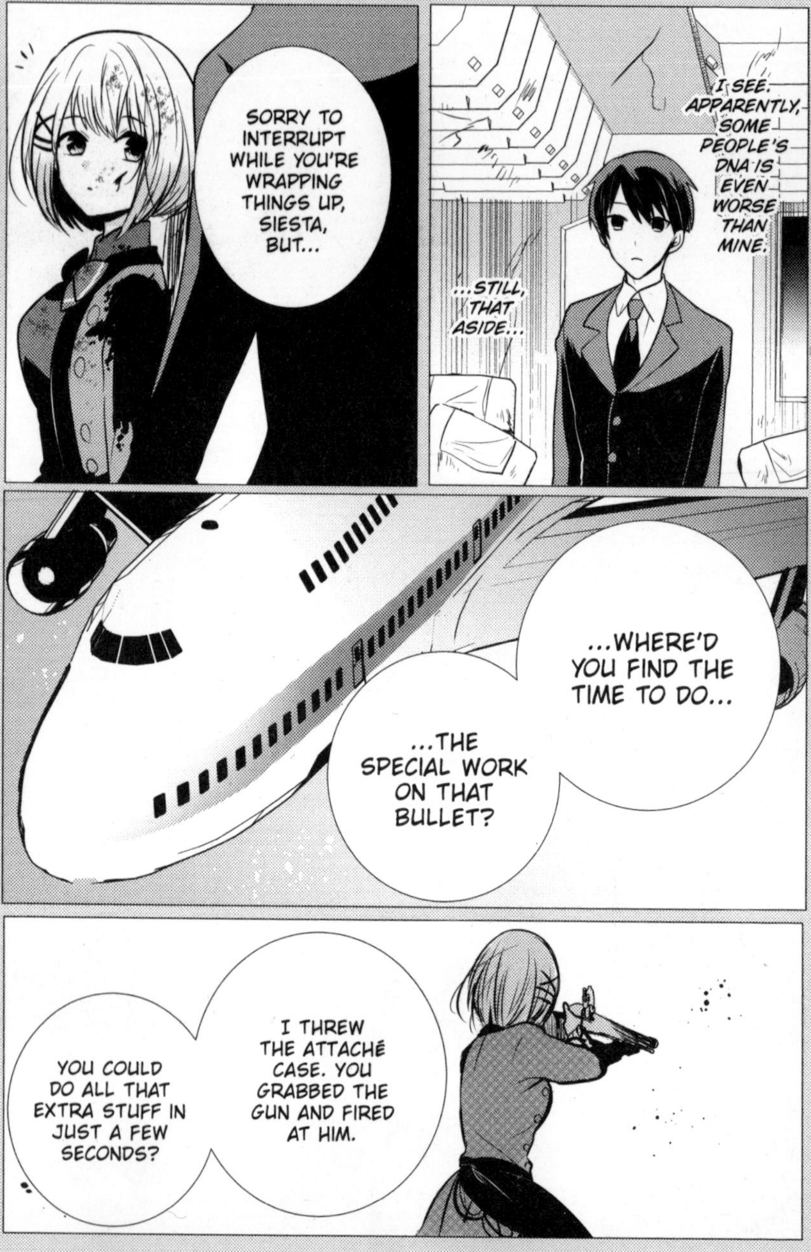
I SEE. APPARENTLY, SOME PEOPLE'S DNA IS EVEN WORSE THAN MINE.
...STILL, THAT ASIDE...
SORRY TO INTERRUPT WHILE YOU'RE WRAPPING THINGS UP, SIESTA, BUT...
...WHERE'D YOU FIND THE TIME TO DO...
...THE SPECIAL WORK ON THAT BULLET?
I THREW THE ATTACHÉ CASE. YOU GRABBED THE GUN AND FIRED AT HIM.
YOU COULD DO ALL THAT EXTRA STUFF IN JUST A FEW SECONDS?

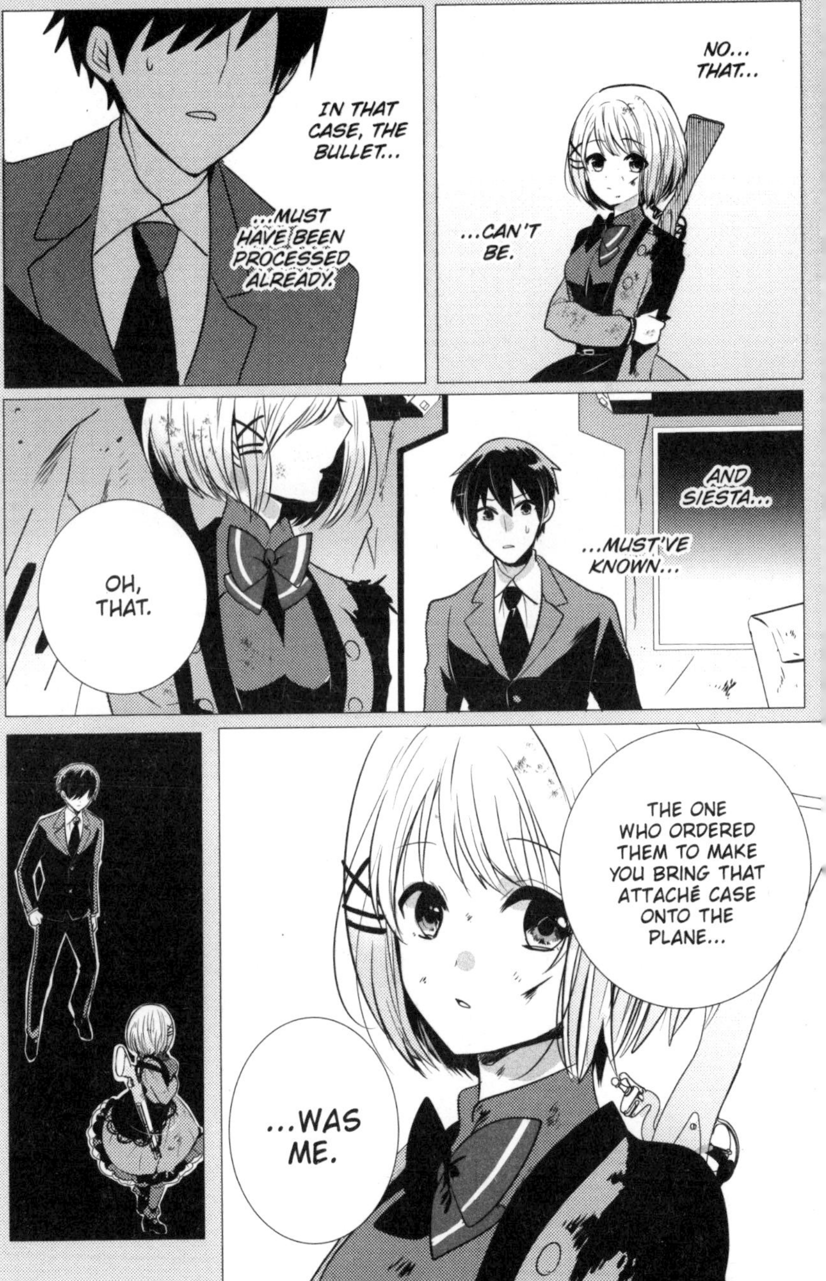
NO... THAT...
...CAN'T BE.
IN THAT CASE, THE BULLET...
...MUST HAVE BEEN PROCESSED ALREADY.
AND SIESTA...
...MUST'VE KNOWN...
OH, THAT.
THE ONE WHO ORDERED THEM TO MAKE YOU BRING THAT ATTACHÉ CASE ONTO THE PLANE...
...WAS ME.

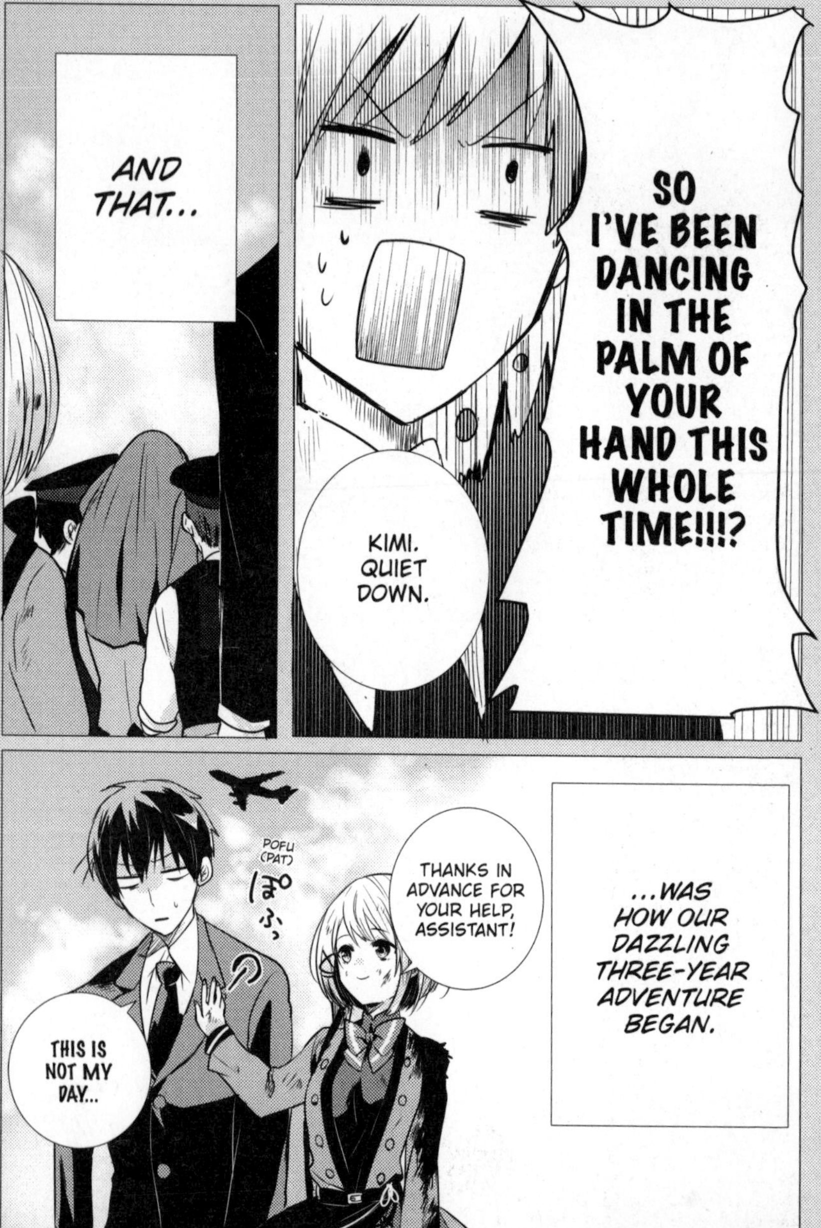
SO I'VE BEEN DANCING IN THE PALM OF YOUR HAND THIS WHOLE TIME!!!?
KIMI. QUIET DOWN.
AND THAT...
...WAS HOW OUR DAZZLING THREE-YEAR ADVENTURE BEGAN.
THANKS IN ADVANCE FOR YOUR HELP, ASSISTANT!
POFU (PAT)
ぽふっ
THIS IS NOT MY DAY...

The Detective Is Already Dead

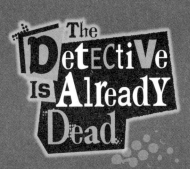

The Detective Is Already Dead

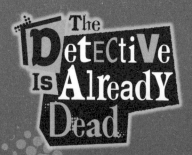

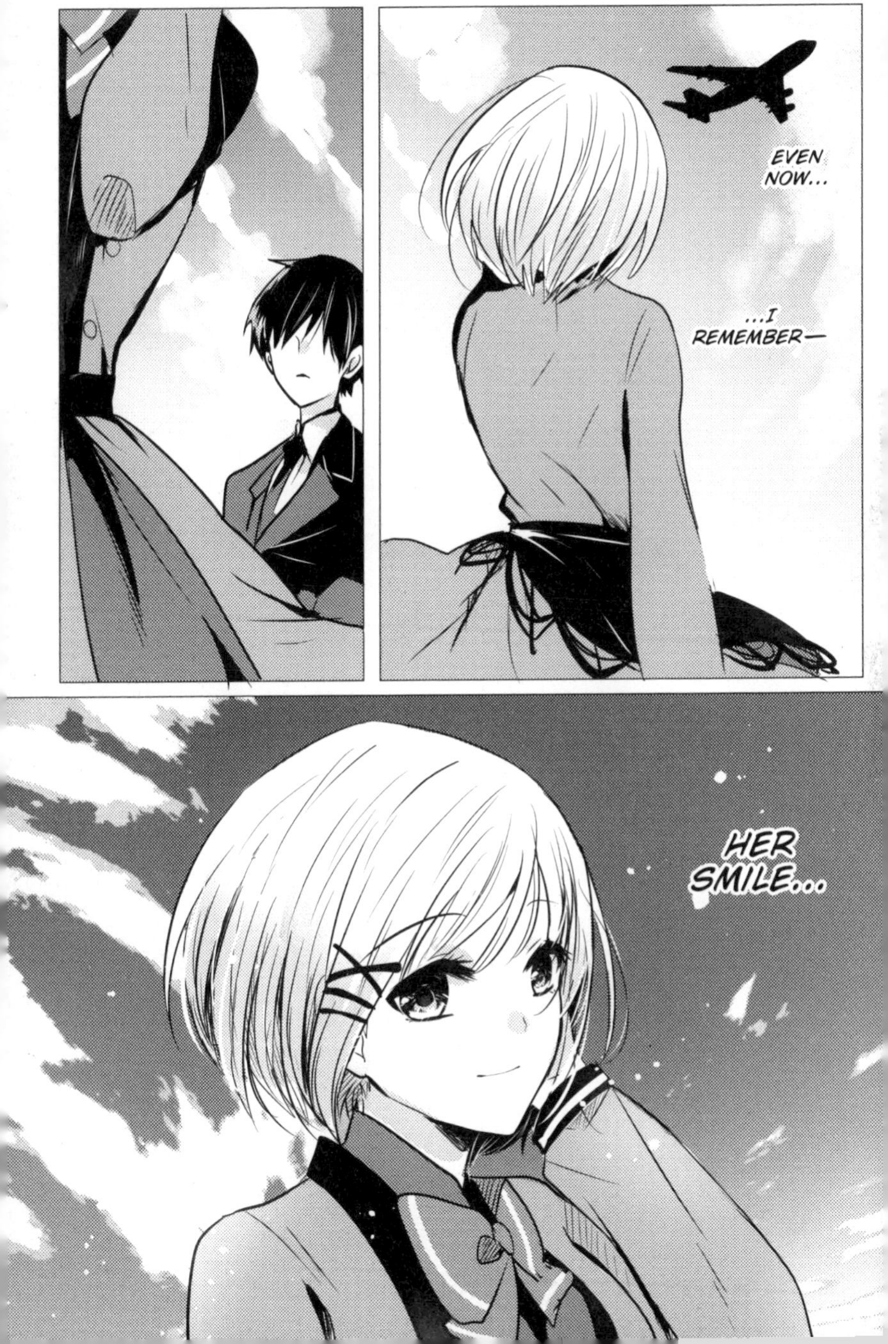
EVEN NOW...
...I REMEMBER—
HER SMILE...

Episode. 8
Even Now, I Remember

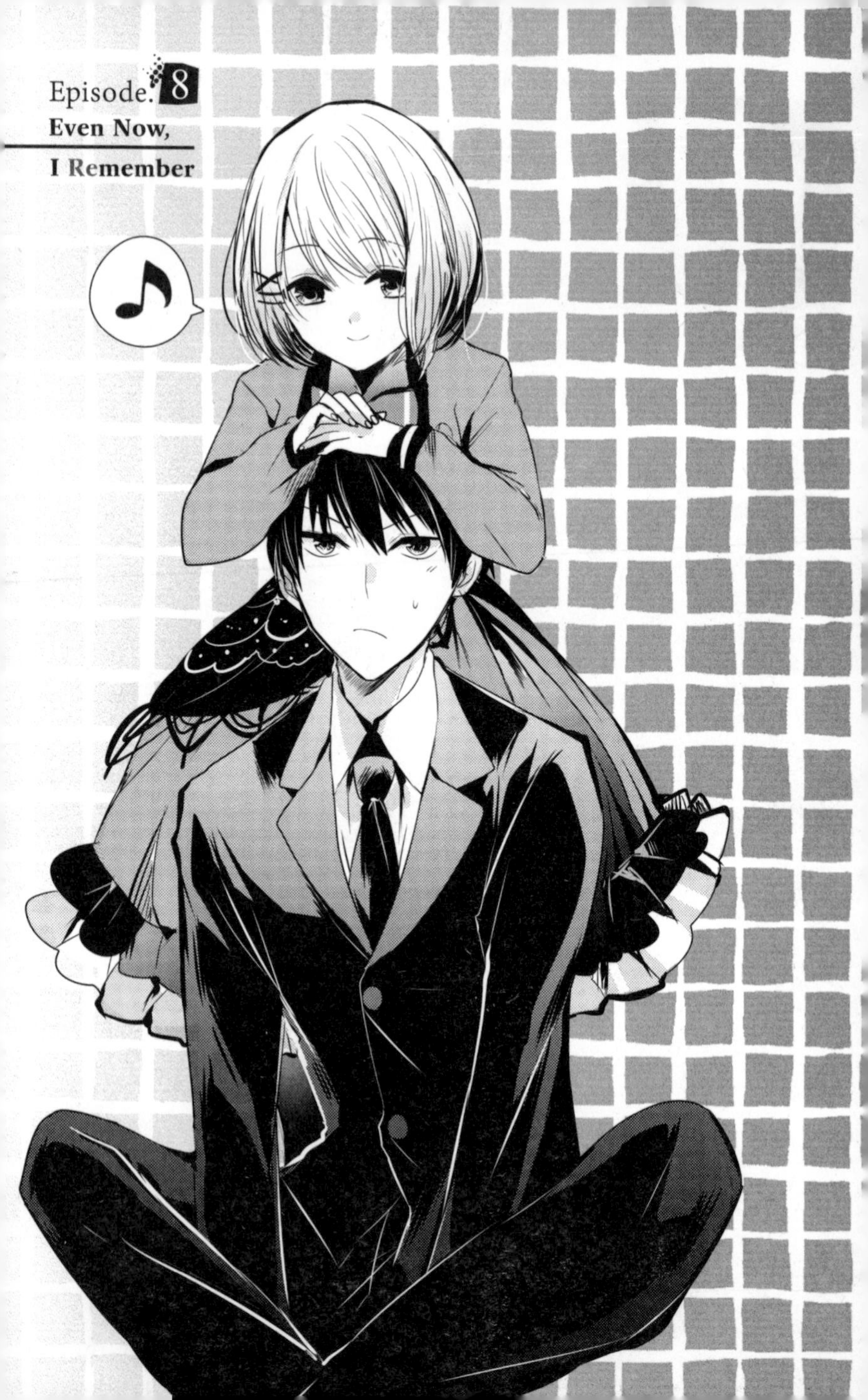

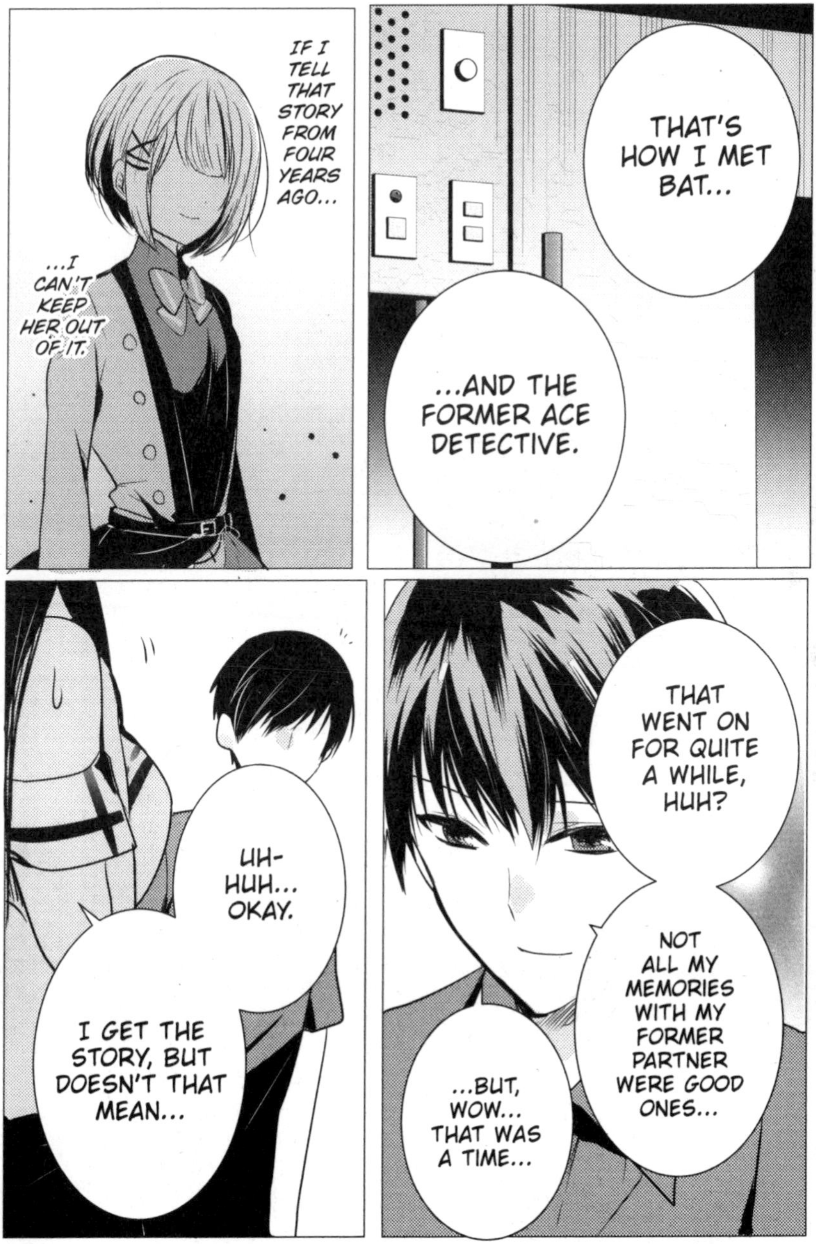
THAT'S HOW I MET BAT...
...AND THE FORMER ACE DETECTIVE.
IF I TELL THAT STORY FROM FOUR YEARS AGO...
...I CAN'T KEEP HER OUT OF IT.
THAT WENT ON FOR QUITE A WHILE, HUH?
NOT ALL MY MEMORIES WITH MY FORMER PARTNER WERE GOOD ONES...
...BUT, WOW... THAT WAS A TIME...
UH-HUH... OKAY.
I GET THE STORY, BUT DOESN'T THAT MEAN...

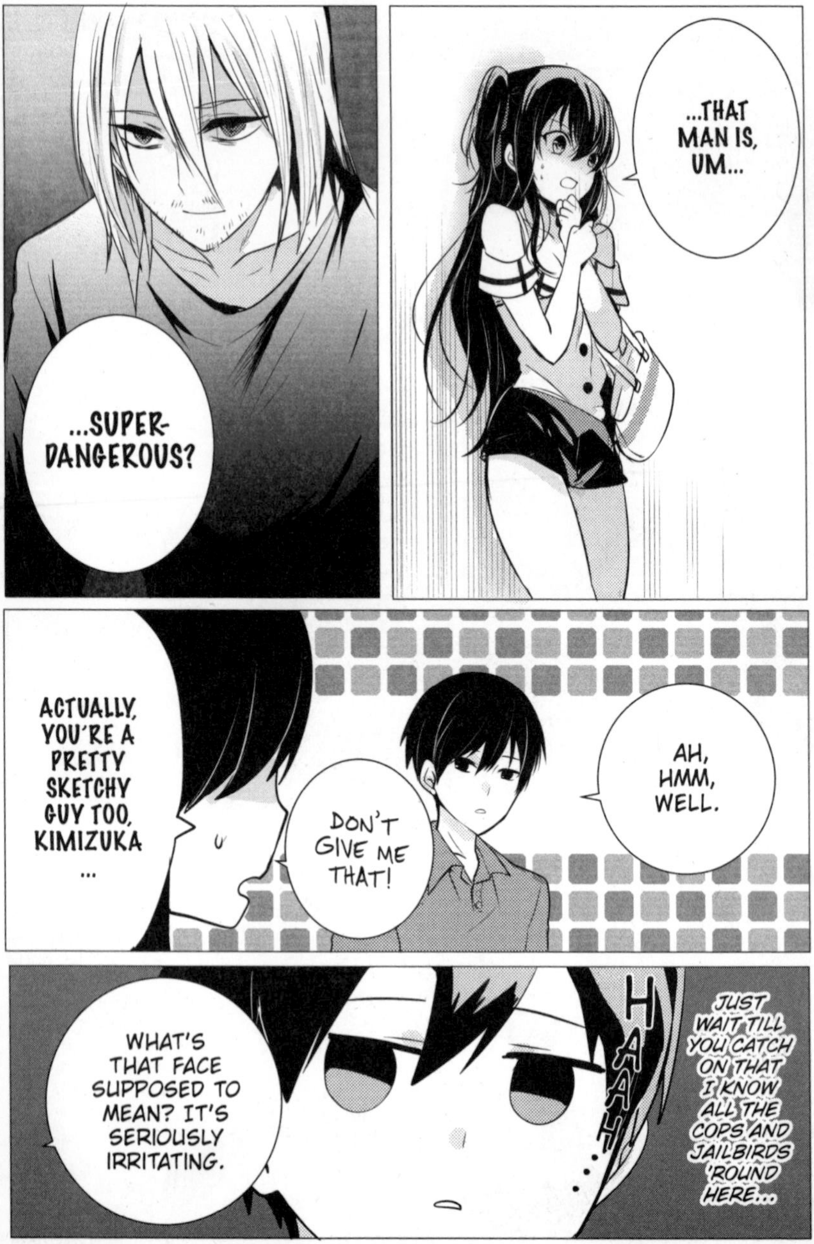
...THAT MAN IS, UM...
...SUPER-DANGEROUS?
AH, HMM, WELL.
DON'T GIVE ME THAT!
ACTUALLY, YOU'RE A PRETTY SKETCHY GUY TOO, KIMIZUKA...
JUST WAIT TILL YOU CATCH ON THAT I KNOW ALL THE COPS AND JAILBIRDS 'ROUND HERE...
HAAAH...
WHAT'S THAT FACE SUPPOSED TO MEAN? IT'S SERIOUSLY IRRITATING.

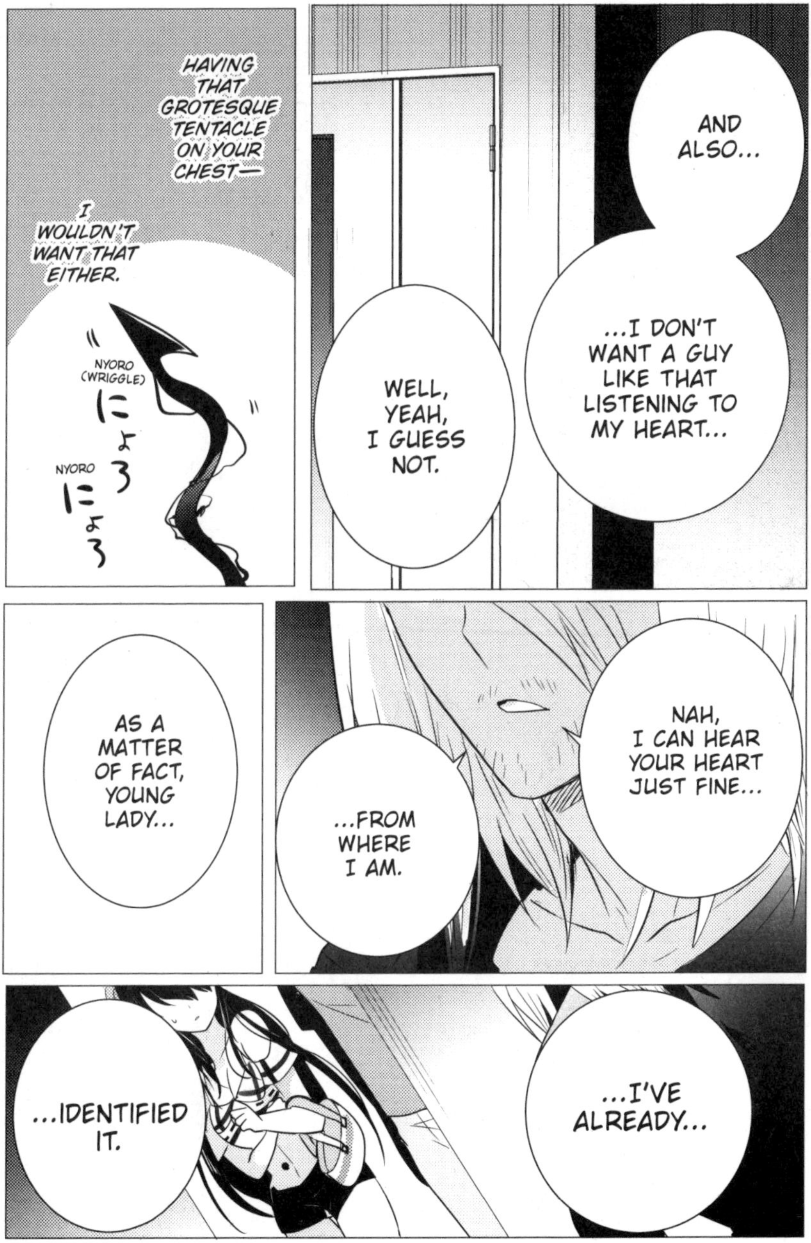
AND ALSO...
...I DON'T WANT A GUY LIKE THAT LISTENING TO MY HEART...
WELL, YEAH, I GUESS NOT.
HAVING THAT GROTESQUE TENTACLE ON YOUR CHEST—
I WOULDN'T WANT THAT EITHER.
NYORO (WRIGGLE)
にょろ
NYORO
にょろ
NAH, I CAN HEAR YOUR HEART JUST FINE...
...FROM WHERE I AM.
AS A MATTER OF FACT, YOUNG LADY...
...I'VE ALREADY...
...IDENTIFIED IT.

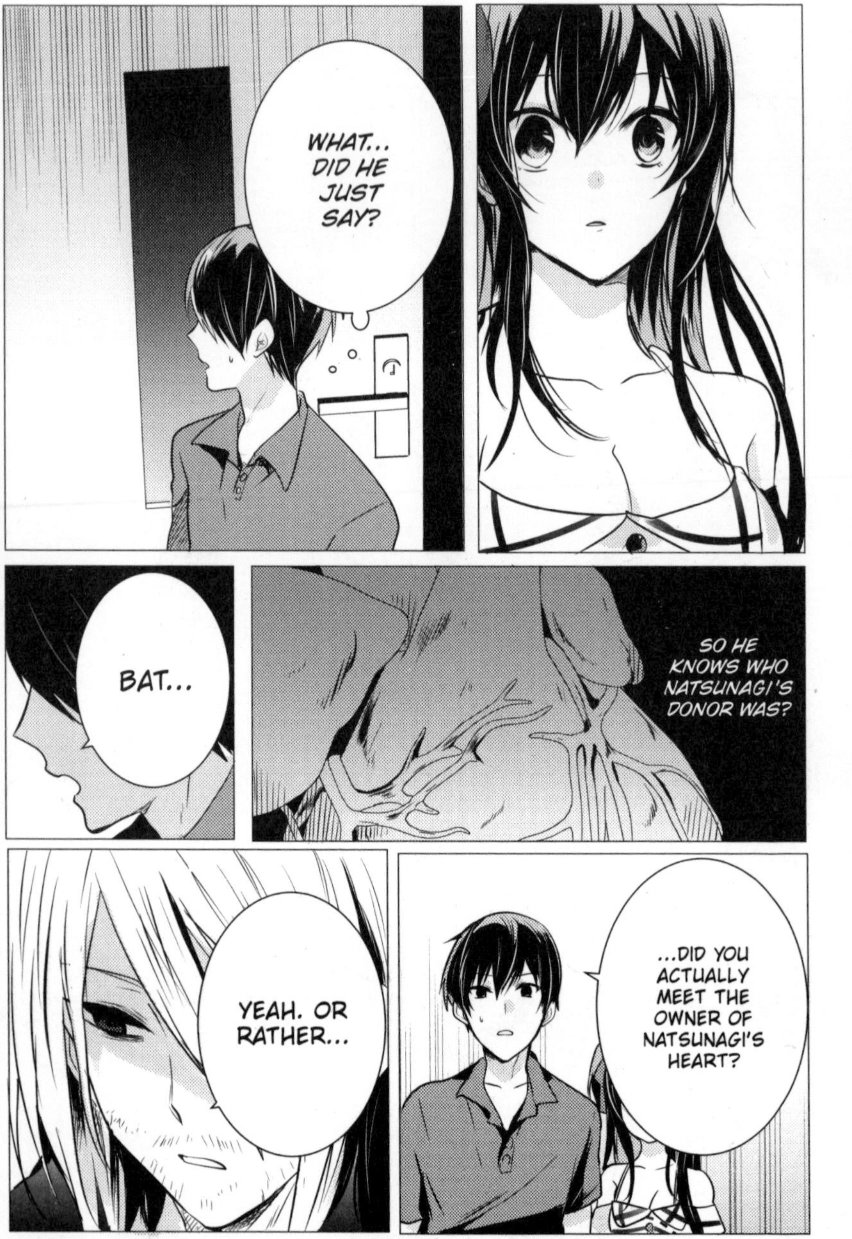
WHAT... DID HE JUST SAY?
SO HE KNOWS WHO NATSUNAGI'S DONOR WAS?
BAT...
...DID YOU ACTUALLY MEET THE OWNER OF NATSUNAGI'S HEART?
YEAH. OR RATHER...

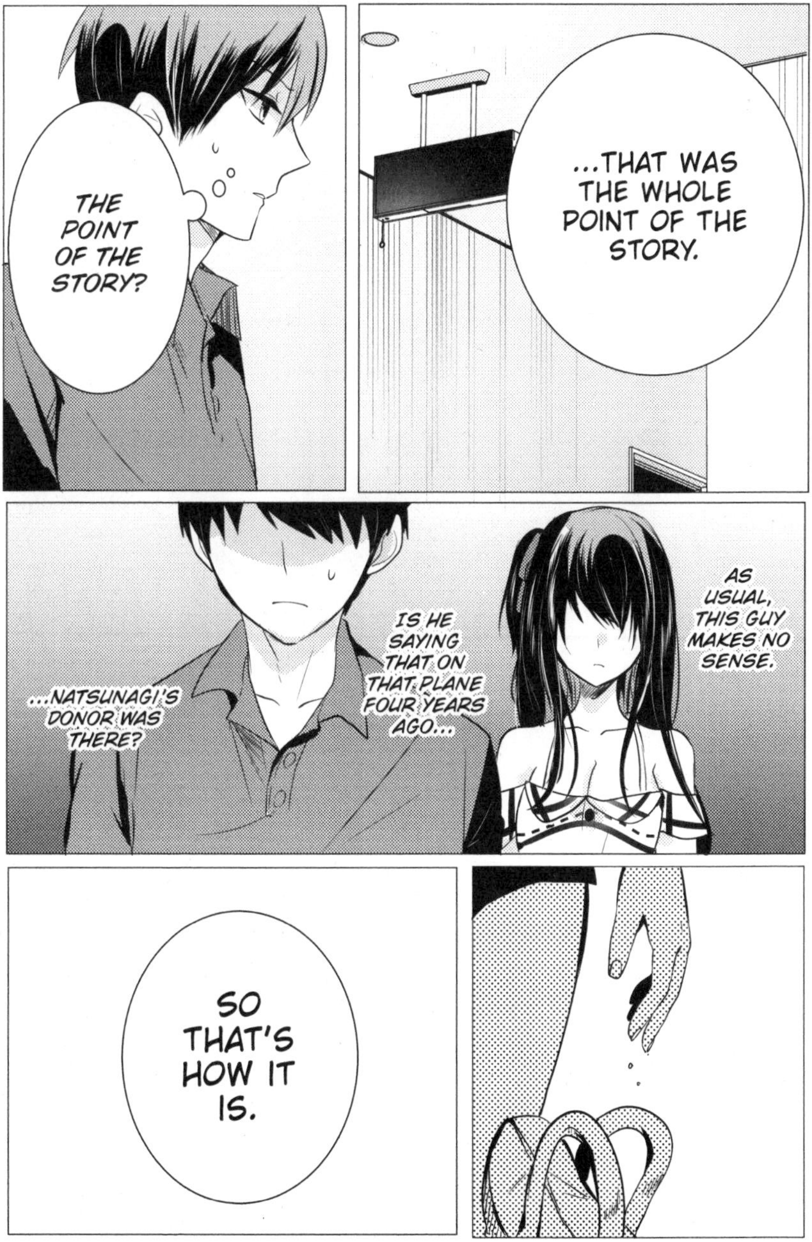
...THAT WAS THE WHOLE POINT OF THE STORY.
THE POINT OF THE STORY?
AS USUAL, THIS GUY MAKES NO SENSE.
IS HE SAYING THAT ON THAT PLANE FOUR YEARS AGO...
...NATSUNAGI'S DONOR WAS THERE?
SO THAT'S HOW IT IS.

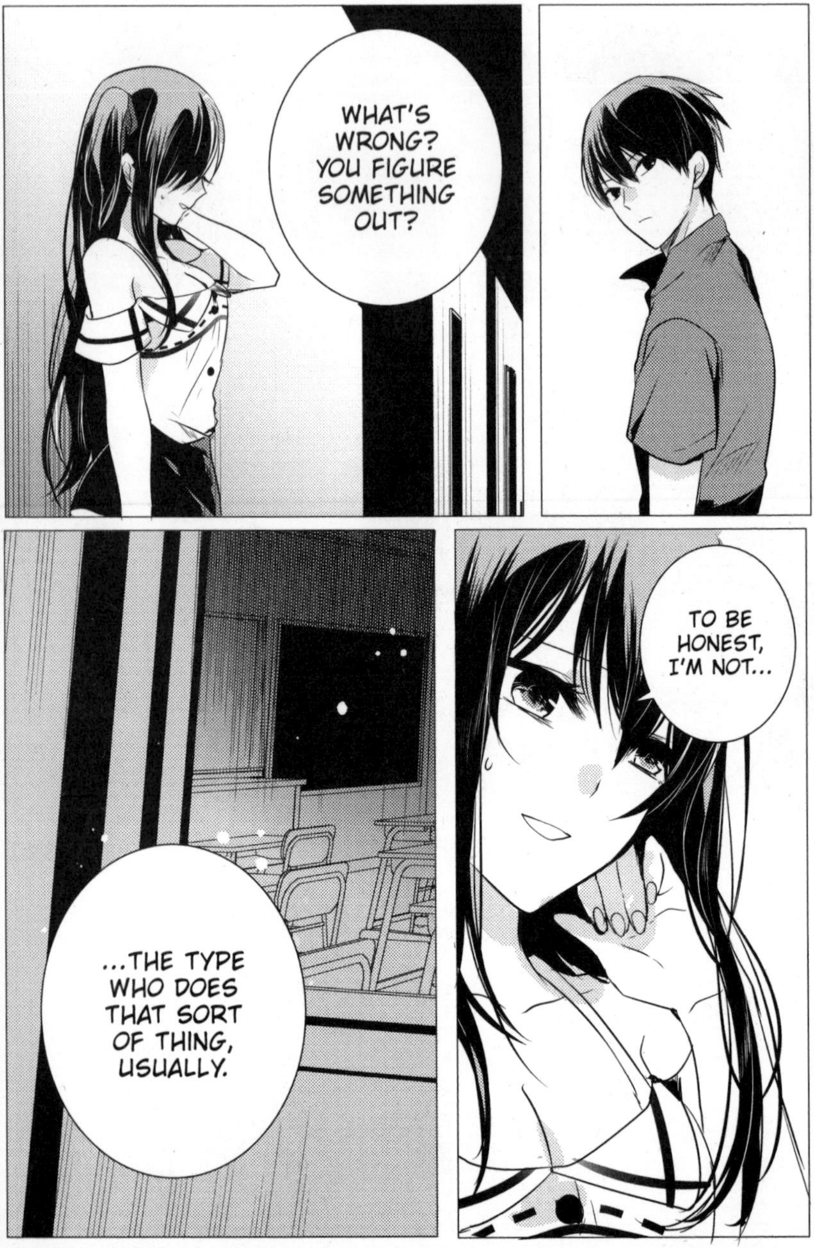
WHAT'S WRONG? YOU FIGURE SOMETHING OUT?
TO BE HONEST, I'M NOT...
...THE TYPE WHO DOES THAT SORT OF THING, USUALLY.

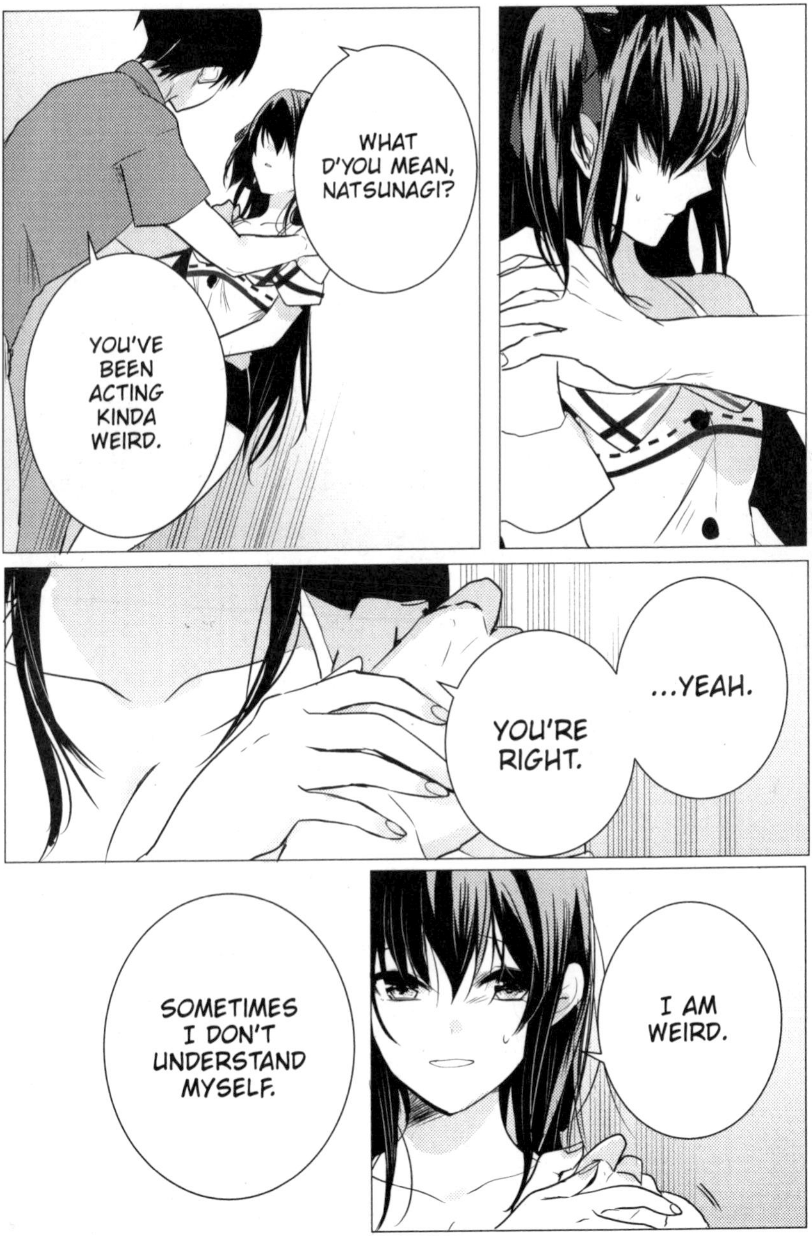
WHAT D'YOU MEAN, NATSUNAGI?
YOU'VE BEEN ACTING KINDA WEIRD.
...YEAH.
YOU'RE RIGHT.
I AM WEIRD.
SOMETIMES I DON'T UNDERSTAND MYSELF.

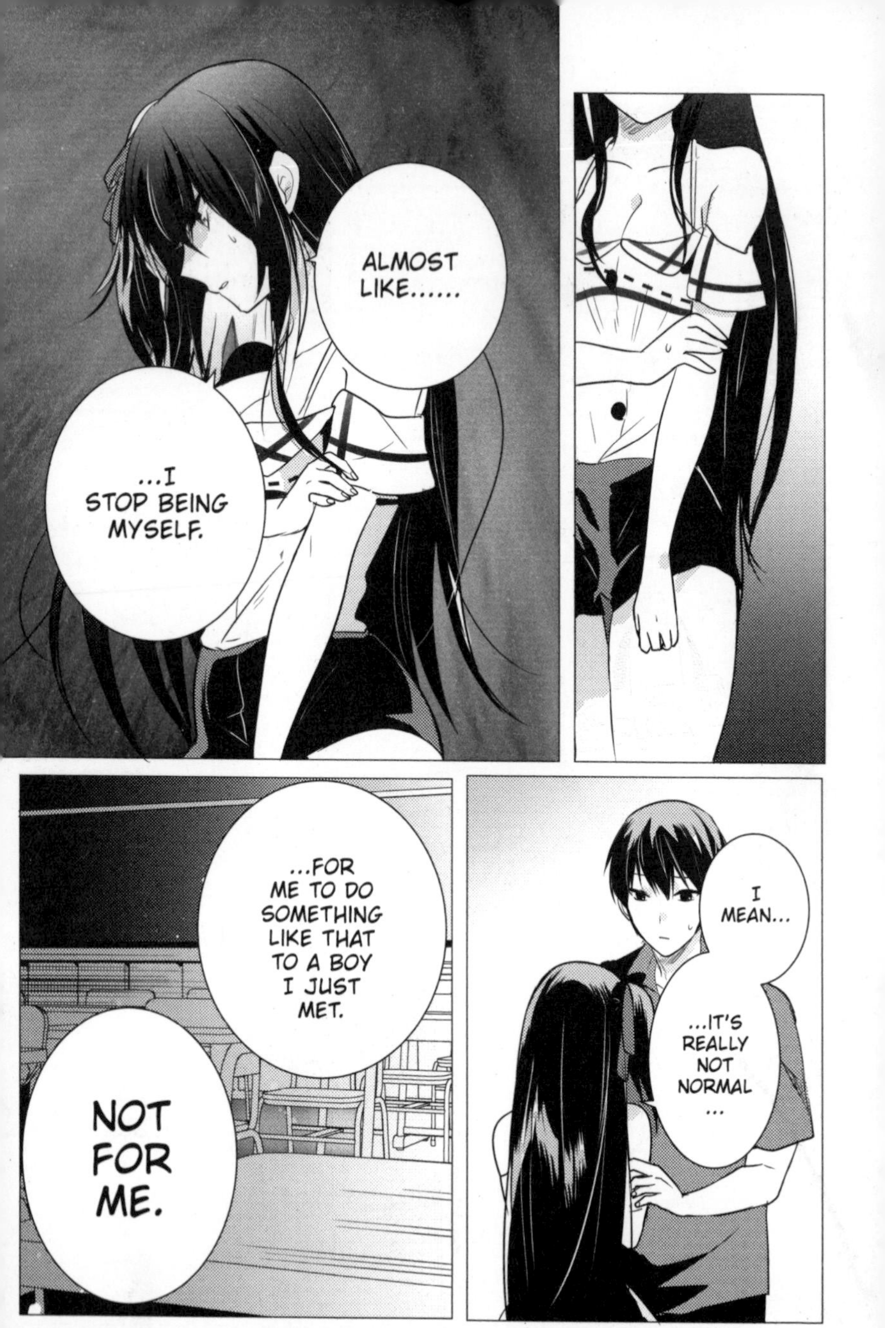
ALMOST LIKE......
...I STOP BEING MYSELF.
I MEAN...
...IT'S REALLY NOT NORMAL ...
...FOR ME TO DO SOMETHING LIKE THAT TO A BOY I JUST MET.
NOT FOR ME.

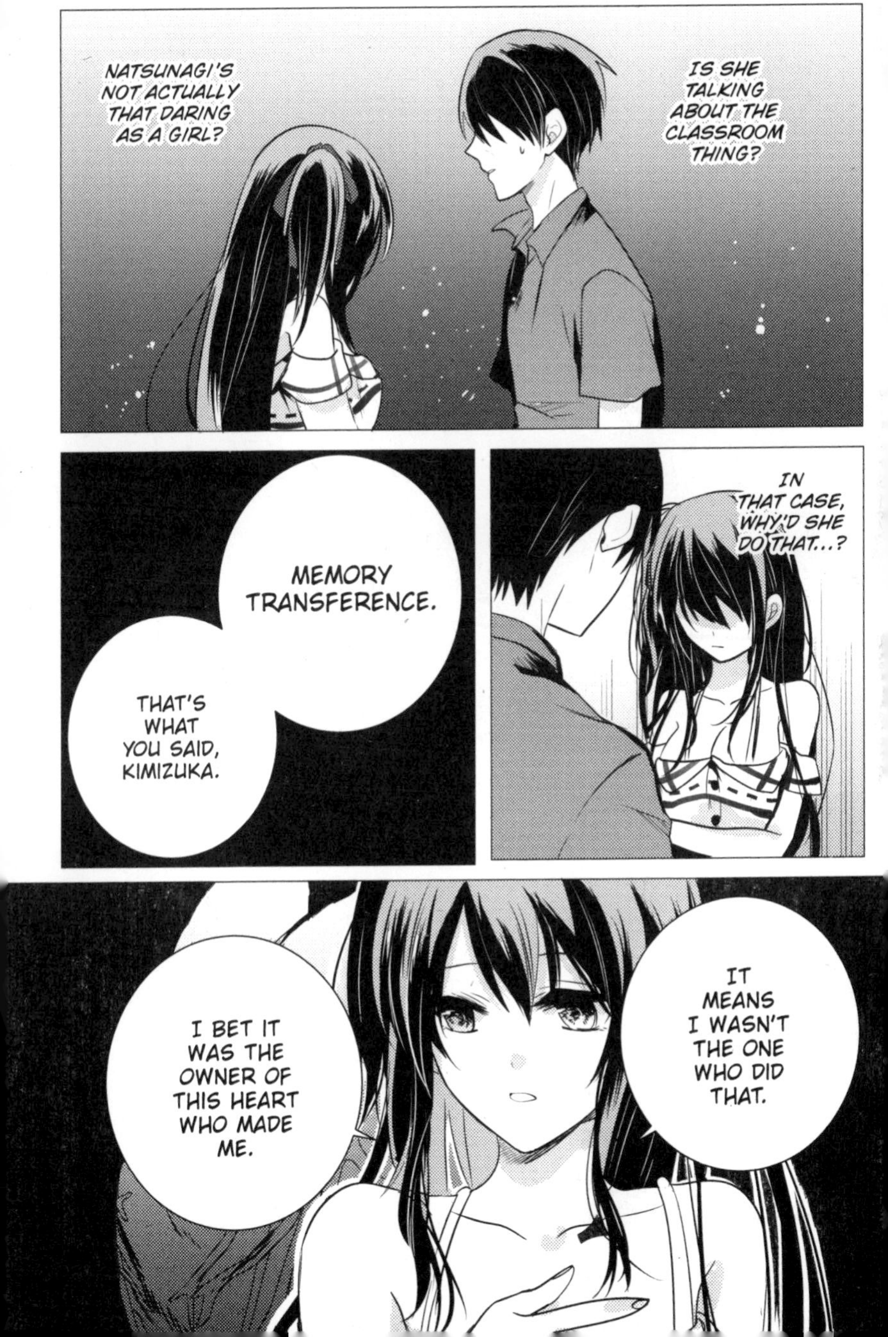
IS SHE TALKING ABOUT THE CLASSROOM THING?
NATSUNAGI'S NOT ACTUALLY THAT DARING AS A GIRL?
IN THAT CASE, WHY'D SHE DO THAT...?
MEMORY TRANSFERENCE.
THAT'S WHAT YOU SAID, KIMIZUKA.
IT MEANS I WASN'T THE ONE WHO DID THAT.
I BET IT WAS THE OWNER OF THIS HEART WHO MADE ME.

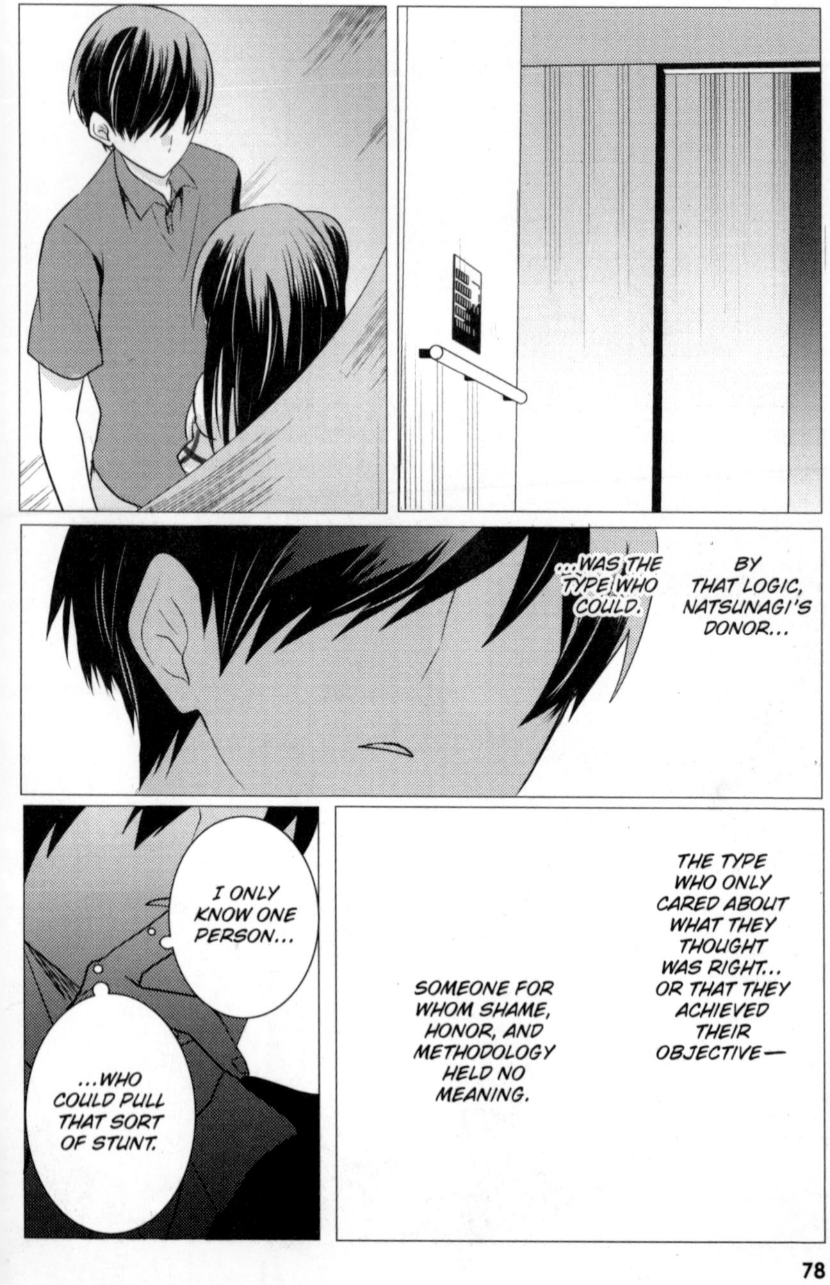
BY THAT LOGIC, NATSUNAGI'S DONOR...
...WAS THE TYPE WHO COULD.
THE TYPE WHO ONLY CARED ABOUT WHAT THEY THOUGHT WAS RIGHT... OR THAT THEY ACHIEVED THEIR OBJECTIVE—
SOMEONE FOR WHOM SHAME, HONOR, AND METHODOLOGY HELD NO MEANING.
I ONLY KNOW ONE PERSON...
...WHO COULD PULL THAT SORT OF STUNT.

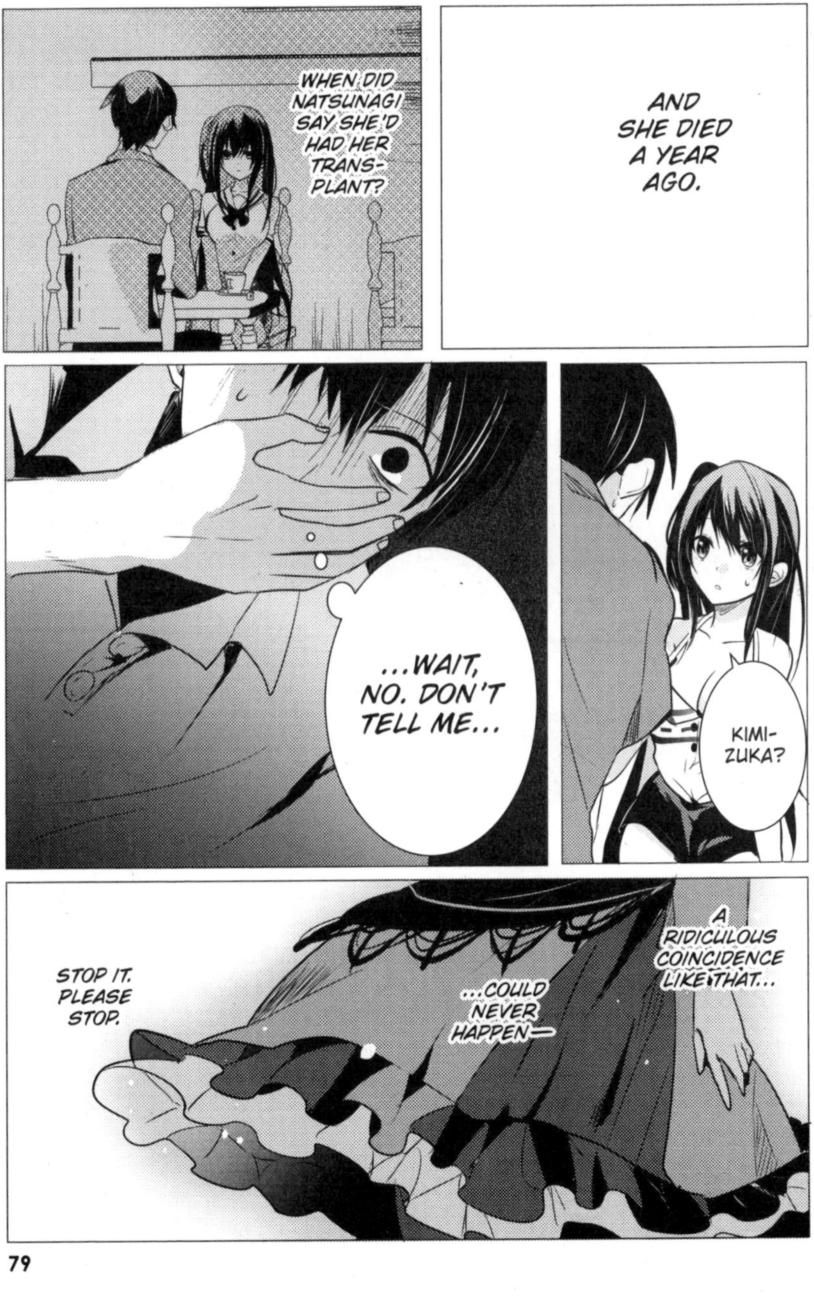
AND SHE DIED A YEAR AGO.
WHEN DID NATSUNAGI SAY SHE'D HAD HER TRANS-PLANT?
KIMI-ZUKA?
...WAIT, NO. DON'T TELL ME...
A RIDICULOUS COINCIDENCE LIKE THAT...
...COULD NEVER HAPPEN—
STOP IT. PLEASE STOP.

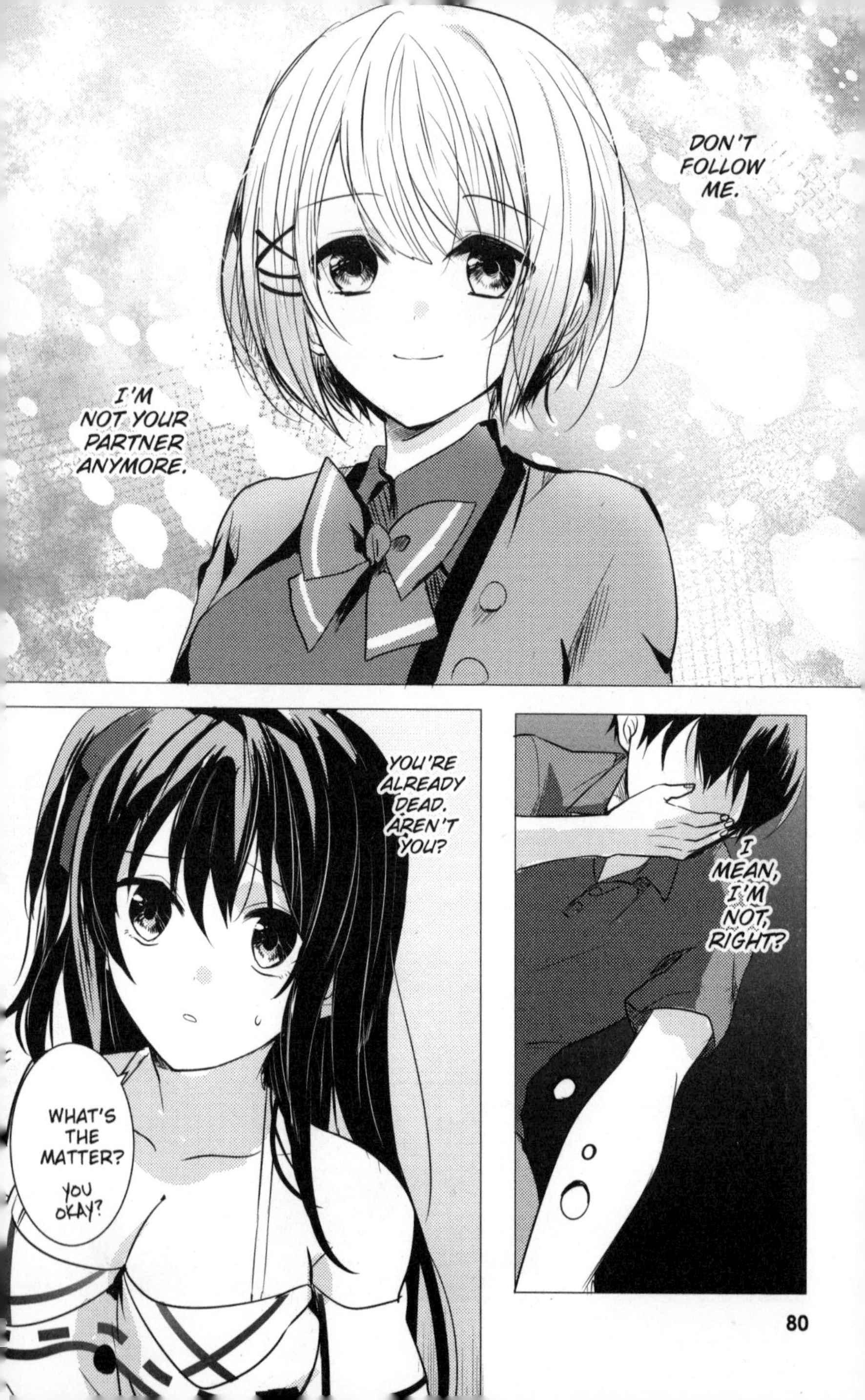
DON'T FOLLOW ME.
I'M NOT YOUR PARTNER ANYMORE.
I MEAN, I'M NOT, RIGHT?
YOU'RE ALREADY DEAD. AREN'T YOU?
WHAT'S THE MATTER?
YOU OKAY?

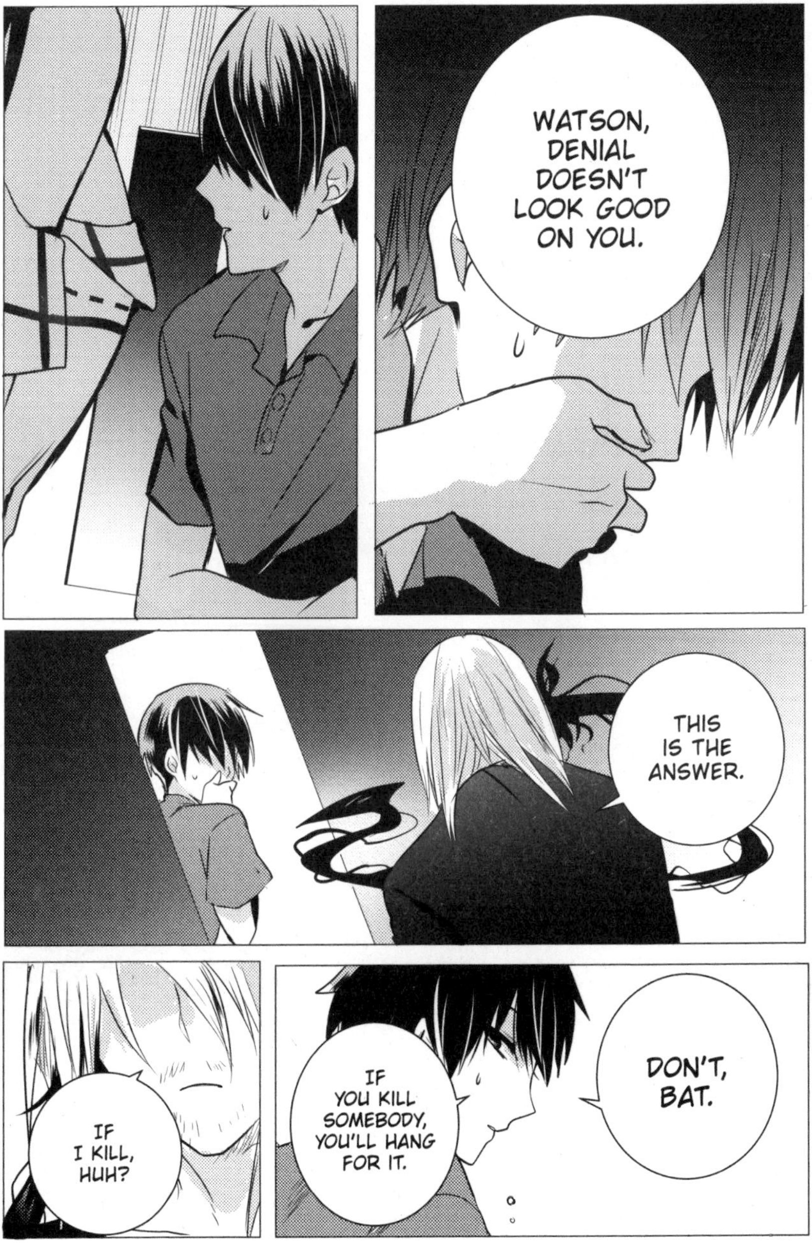
WATSON, DENIAL DOESN'T LOOK GOOD ON YOU.
THIS IS THE ANSWER.
DON'T, BAT.
IF YOU KILL SOMEBODY, YOU'LL HANG FOR IT.
IF I KILL, HUH?

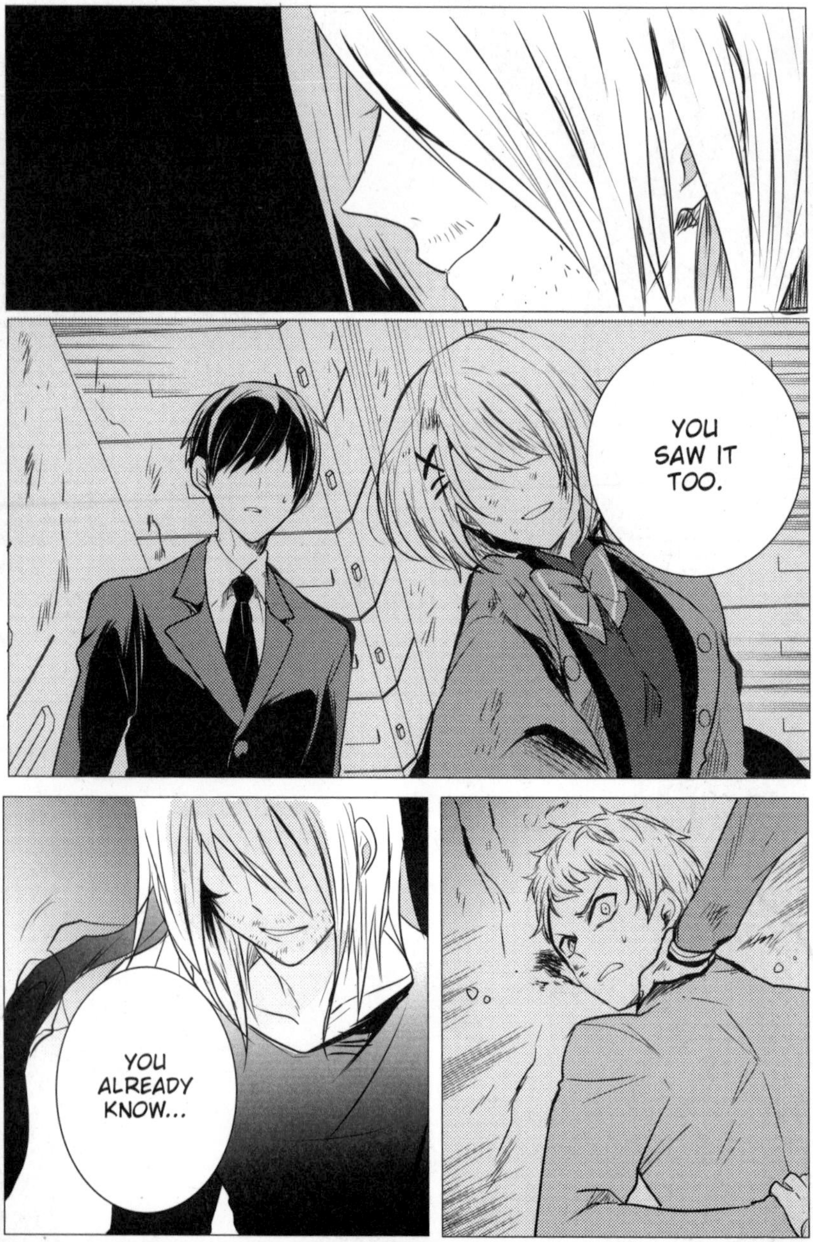
YOU SAW IT TOO.
YOU ALREADY KNOW...

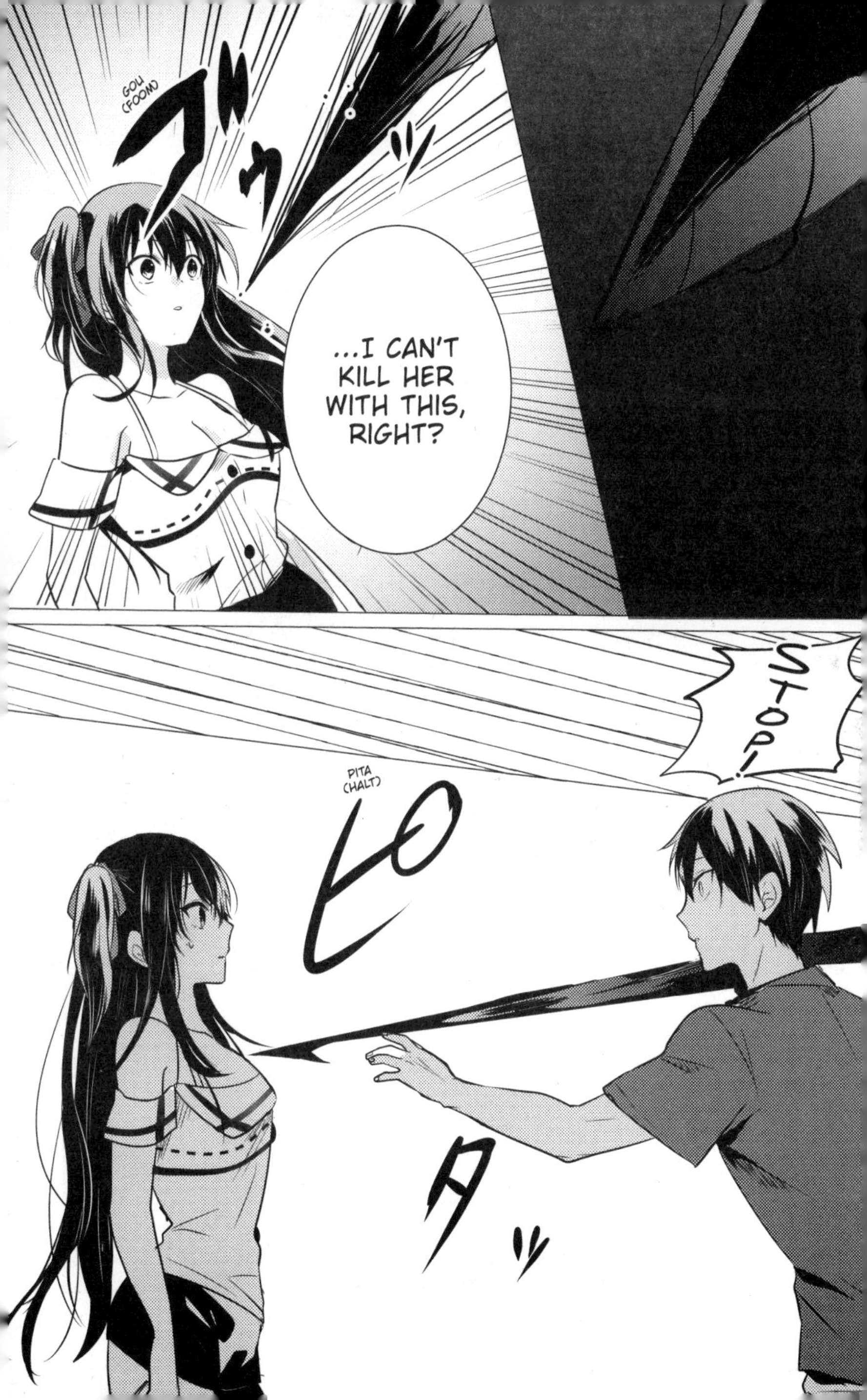
GOU (FOOM)
...I CAN'T KILL HER WITH THIS, RIGHT?
STOP!!
PITA (HALT)

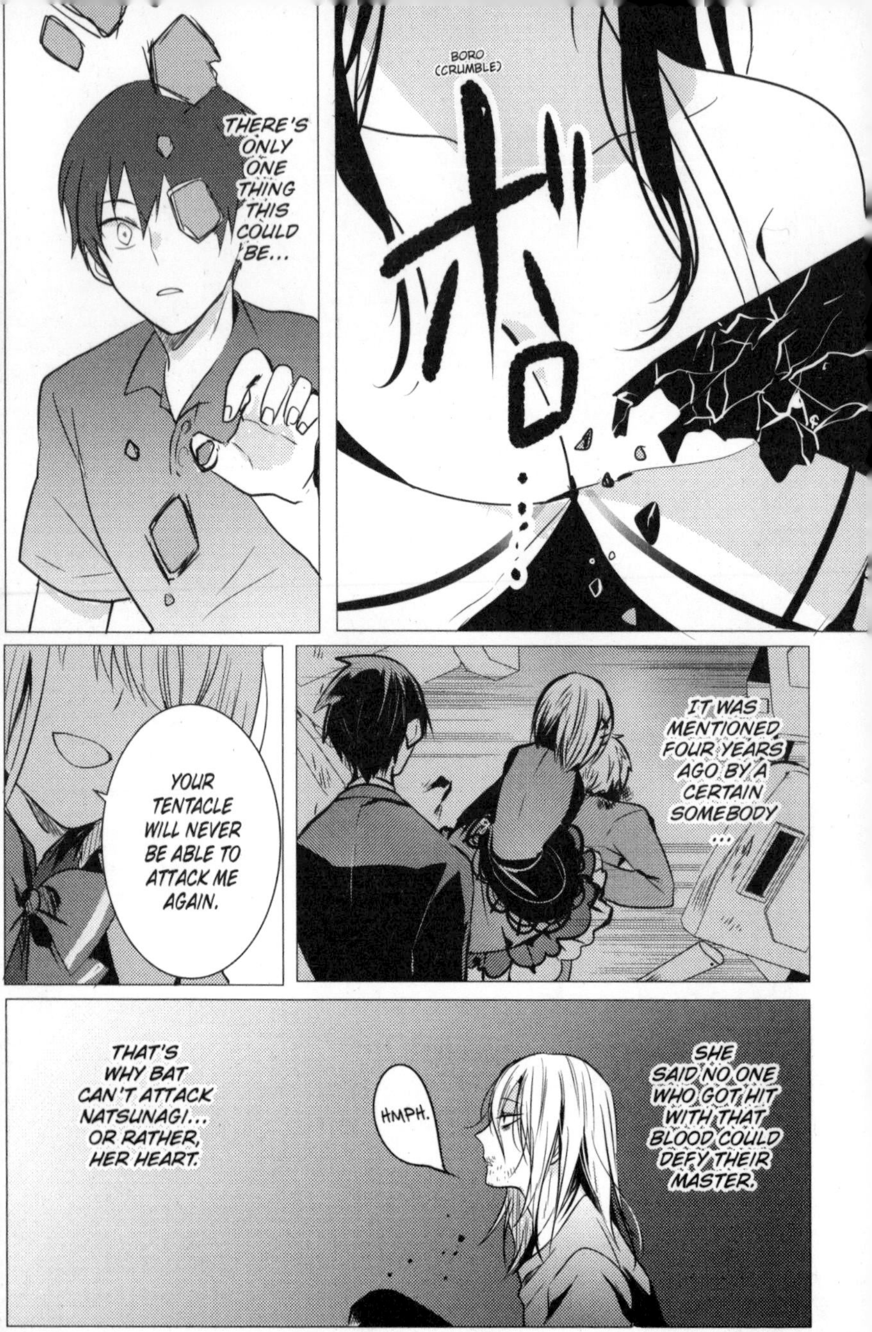
BORO (CRUMBLE)
THERE'S ONLY ONE THING THIS COULD BE...
IT WAS MENTIONED FOUR YEARS AGO BY A CERTAIN SOMEBODY...
YOUR TENTACLE WILL NEVER BE ABLE TO ATTACK ME AGAIN.
SHE SAID NO ONE WHO GOT HIT WITH THAT BLOOD COULD DEFY THEIR MASTER.
HMPH.
THAT'S WHY BAT CAN'T ATTACK NATSUNAGI... OR RATHER, HER HEART.

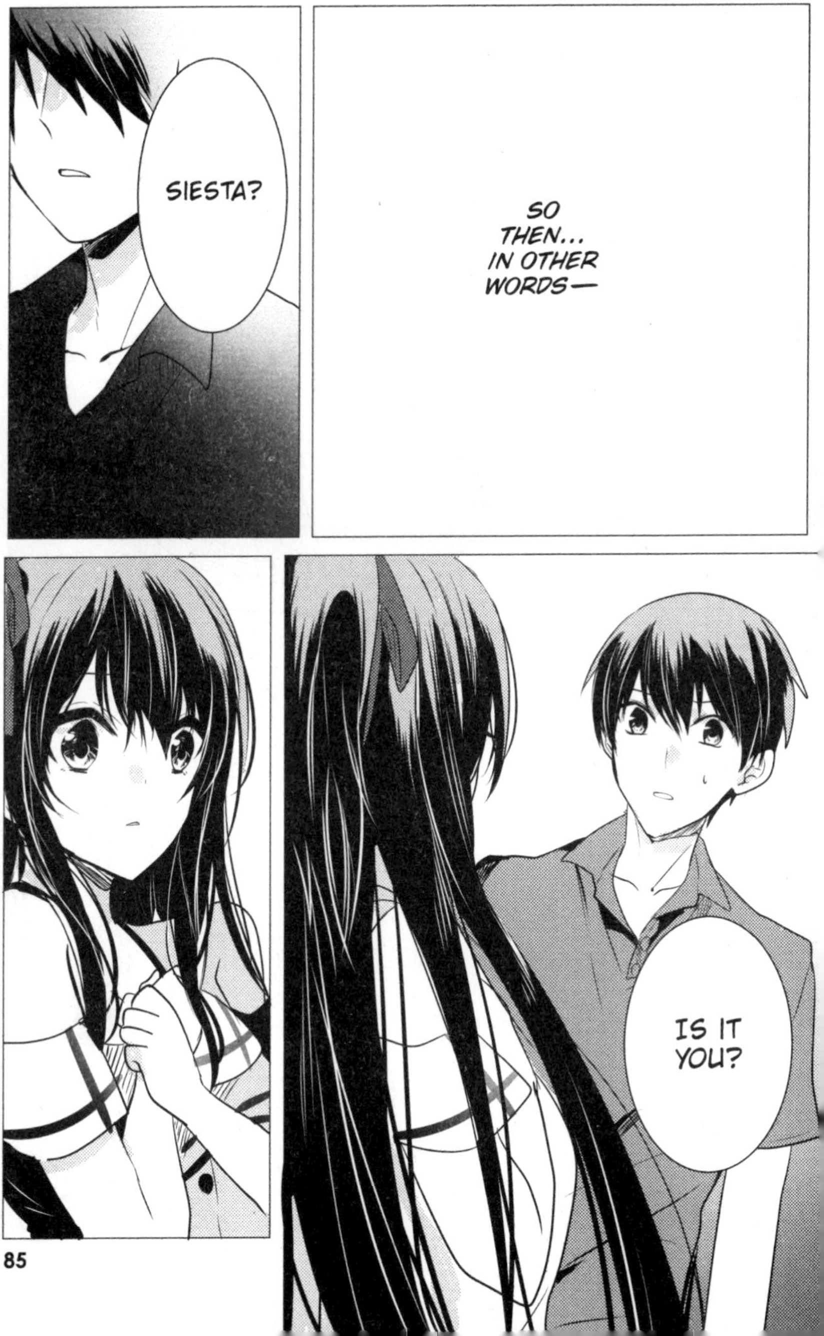
SO THEN... IN OTHER WORDS—
SIESTA?
IS IT YOU?

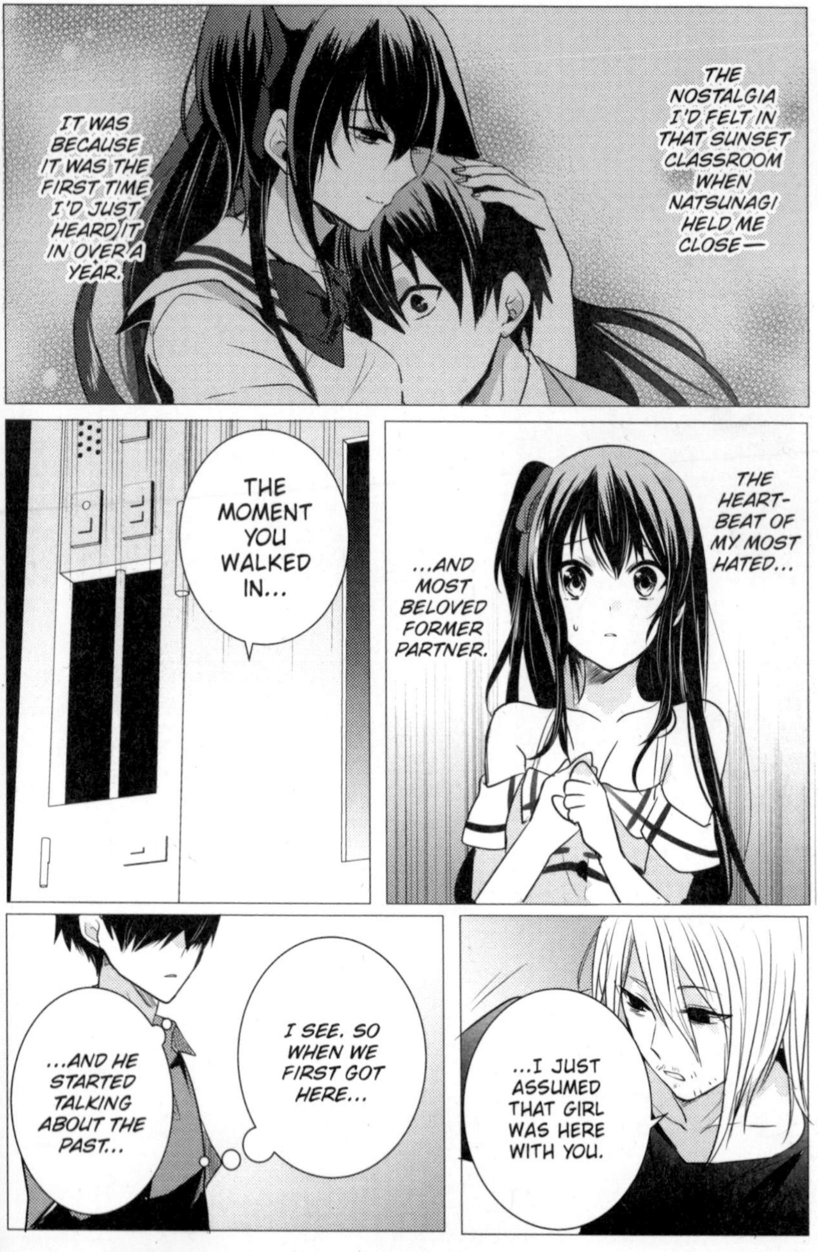
THE NOSTALGIA I'D FELT IN THAT SUNSET CLASSROOM WHEN NATSUNAGI HELD ME CLOSE—
IT WAS BECAUSE IT WAS THE FIRST TIME I'D JUST HEARD IT IN OVER A YEAR.
THE HEART-BEAT OF MY MOST HATED...
...AND MOST BELOVED FORMER PARTNER.
THE MOMENT YOU WALKED IN...
...I JUST ASSUMED THAT GIRL WAS HERE WITH YOU.
I SEE. SO WHEN WE FIRST GOT HERE...
...AND HE STARTED TALKING ABOUT THE PAST...

IT WAS BECAUSE HE'D HEARD HIS MORTAL ENEMY'S HEART?
BAT CAN'T SEE, SO HE MISTOOK NATSUNAGI FOR SIESTA.
NO WONDER OUR CONVERSATION DIDN'T MESH.
WHEN DID THE ACE DETECTIVE DIE?
......
...A YEAR AGO. ON A FARAWAY ISLAND IN A DISTANT OCEAN.

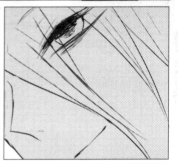

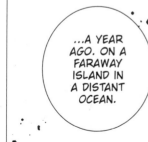

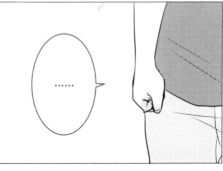

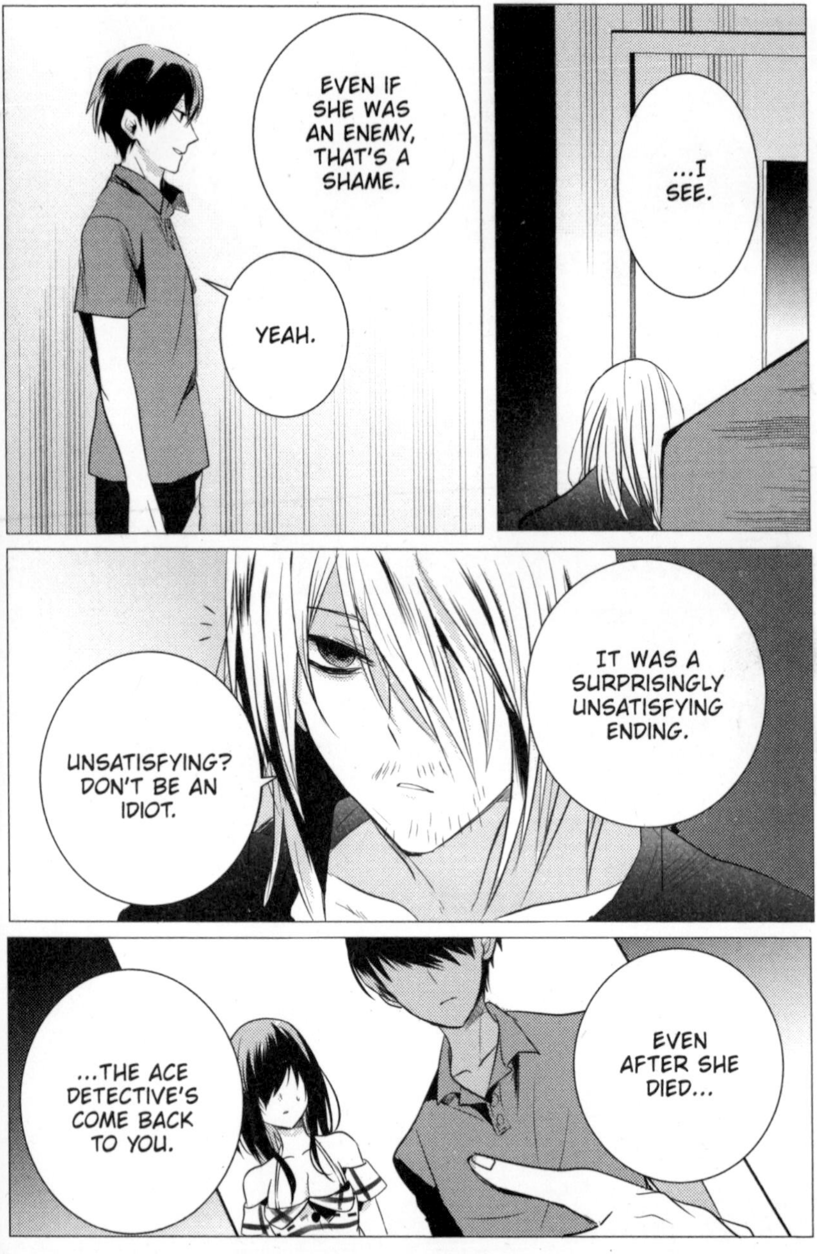
...I SEE.
EVEN IF SHE WAS AN ENEMY, THAT'S A SHAME.
YEAH.
IT WAS A SURPRISINGLY UNSATISFYING ENDING.
UNSATISFYING? DON'T BE AN IDIOT.
EVEN AFTER SHE DIED...
...THE ACE DETECTIVE'S COME BACK TO YOU.

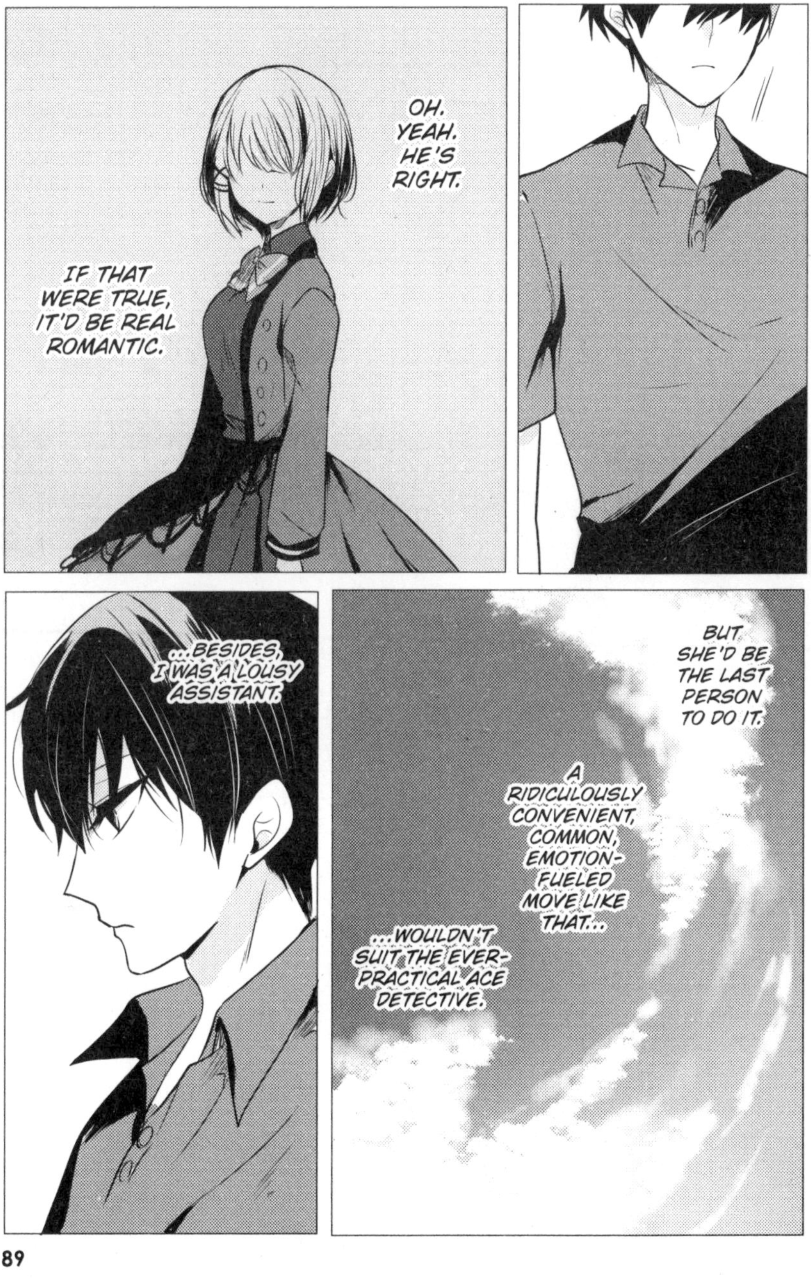
OH. YEAH. HE'S RIGHT.
IF THAT WERE TRUE, IT'D BE REAL ROMANTIC.
BUT SHE'D BE THE LAST PERSON TO DO IT.
A RIDICULOUSLY CONVENIENT, COMMON, EMOTION-FUELED MOVE LIKE THAT...
...WOULDN'T SUIT THE EVER-PRACTICAL ACE DETECTIVE.
...BESIDES, I WAS A LOUSY ASSISTANT.

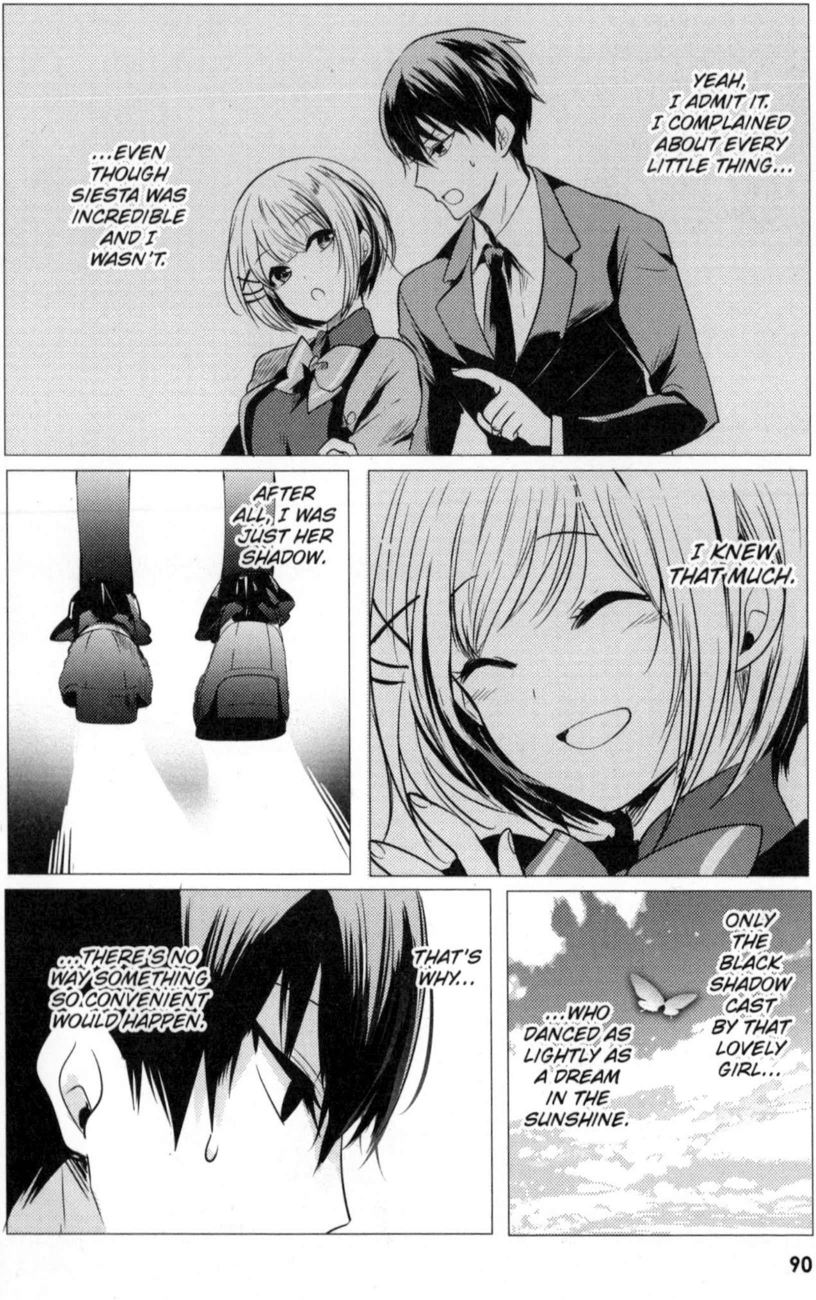

YEAH, I ADMIT IT. I COMPLAINED ABOUT EVERY LITTLE THING...
...EVEN THOUGH SIESTA WAS INCREDIBLE AND I WASN'T.
I KNEW THAT MUCH.
AFTER ALL, I WAS JUST HER SHADOW.
ONLY THE BLACK SHADOW CAST BY THAT LOVELY GIRL...
...WHO DANCED AS LIGHTLY AS A DREAM IN THE SUNSHINE.
THAT'S WHY...
...THERE'S NO WAY SOMETHING SO CONVENIENT WOULD HAPPEN.

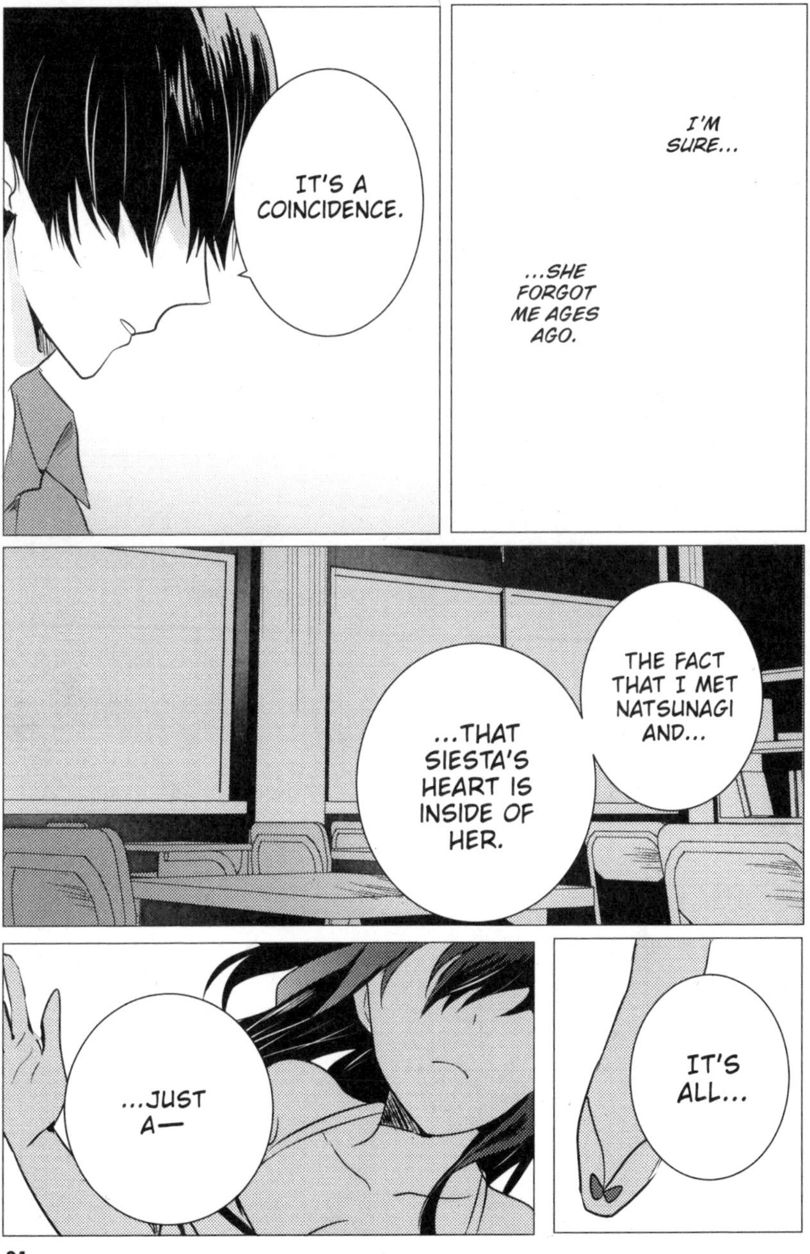
I'M SURE...
...SHE FORGOT ME AGES AGO.
IT'S A COINCIDENCE.
THE FACT THAT I MET NATSUNAGI AND...
...THAT SIESTA'S HEART IS INSIDE OF HER.
IT'S ALL...
...JUST A—

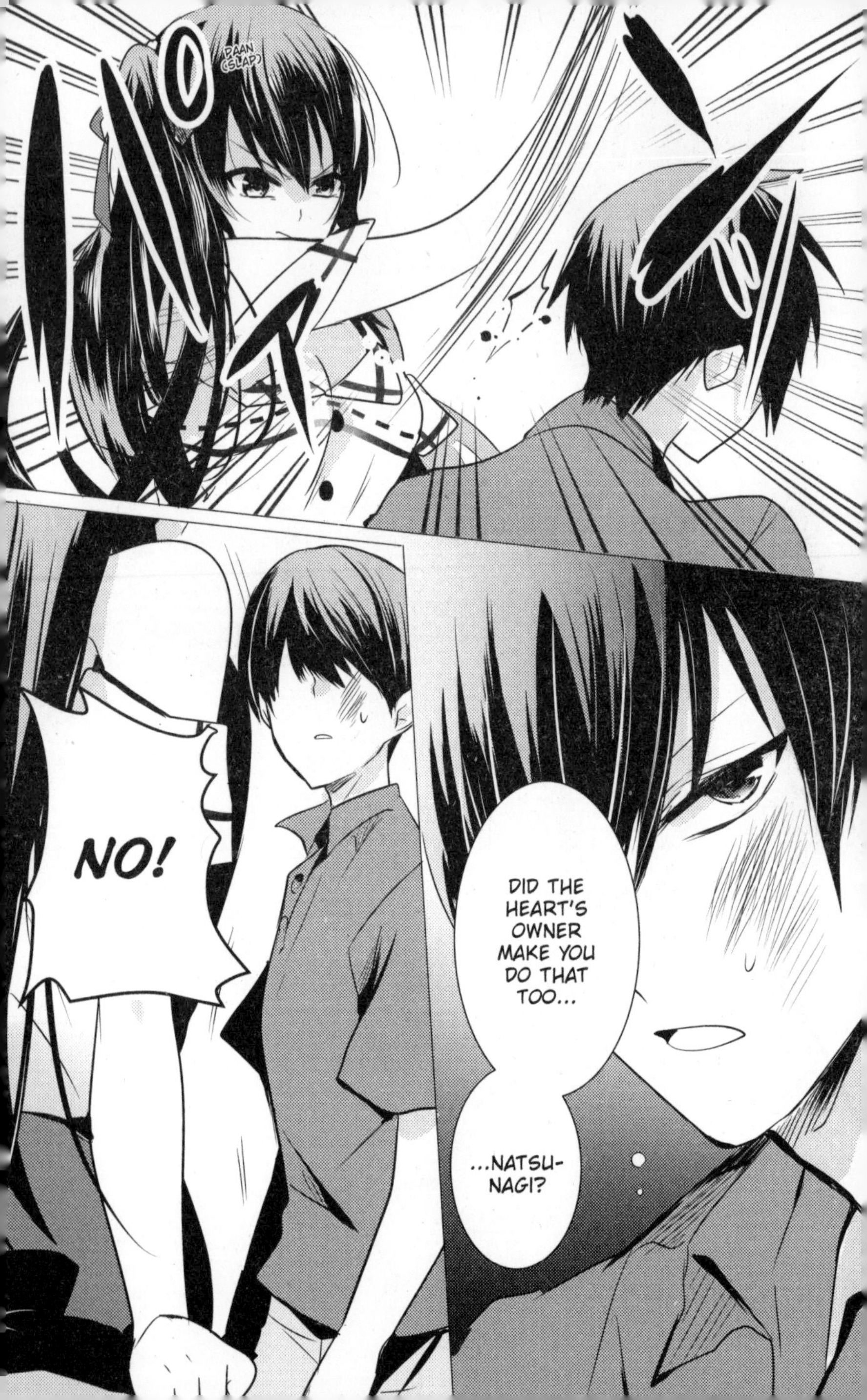
PAAN (SLAP)
DID THE HEART'S OWNER MAKE YOU DO THAT TOO...
...NATSU-NAGI?
NO!

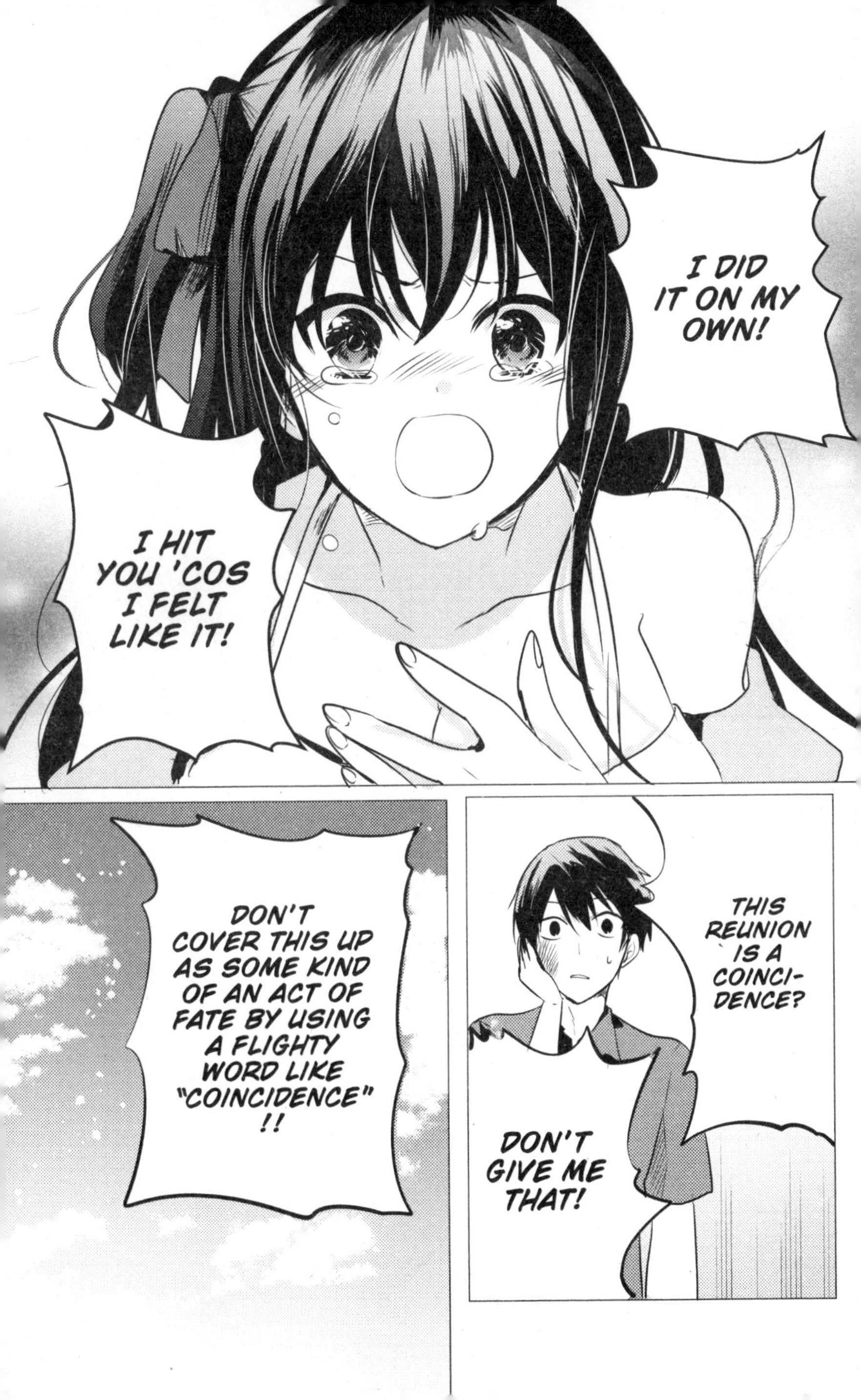
I DID IT ON MY OWN!
I HIT YOU 'COS I FELT LIKE IT!
THIS REUNION IS A COINCI-DENCE?
DON'T GIVE ME THAT!
DON'T COVER THIS UP AS SOME KIND OF AN ACT OF FATE BY USING A FLIGHTY WORD LIKE "COINCIDENCE" !!

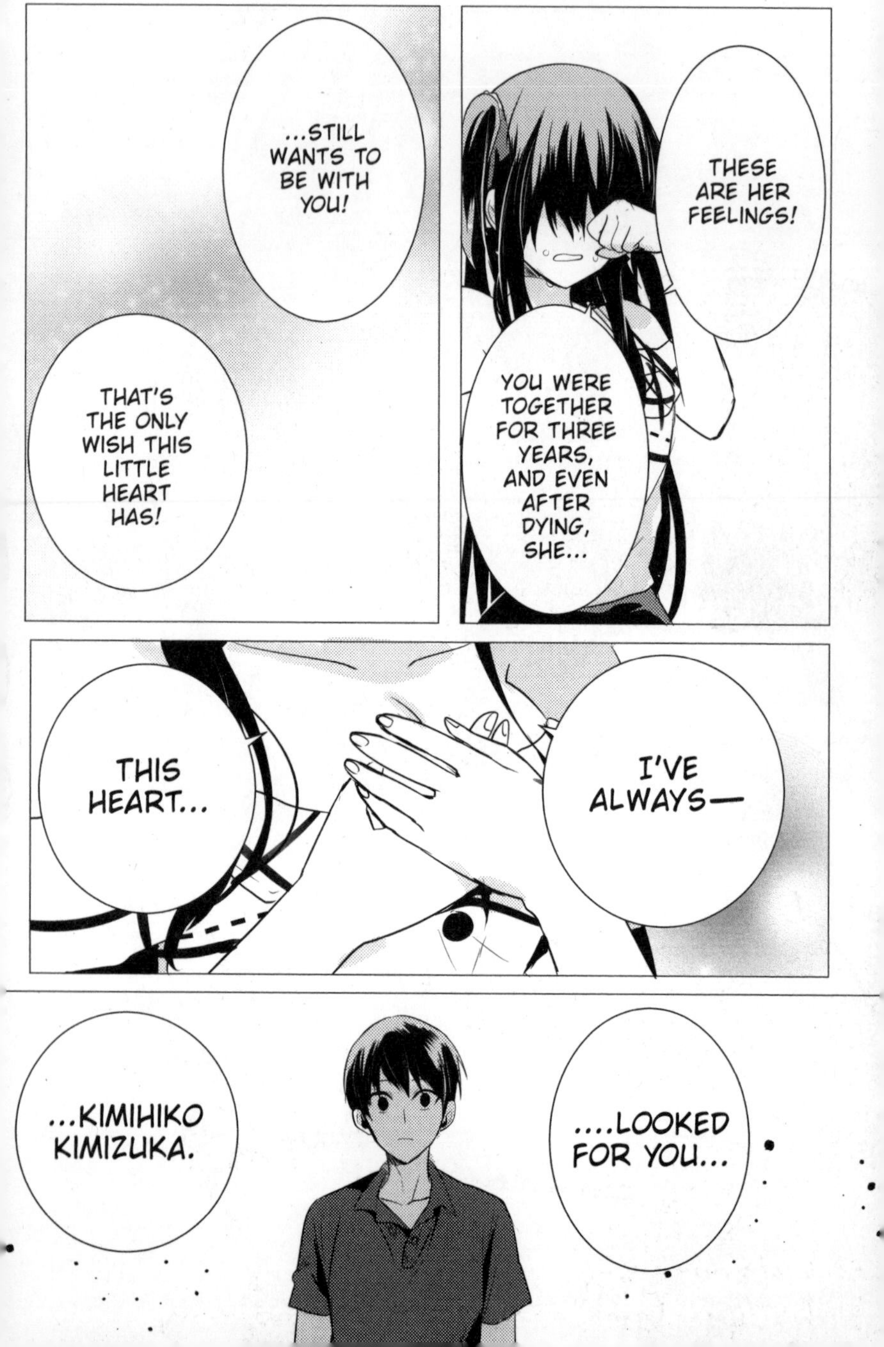
THESE ARE HER FEELINGS!
YOU WERE TOGETHER FOR THREE YEARS, AND EVEN AFTER DYING, SHE...
...STILL WANTS TO BE WITH YOU!
THAT'S THE ONLY WISH THIS LITTLE HEART HAS!
I'VE ALWAYS—
THIS HEART...
....LOOKED FOR YOU...
...KIMIHIKO KIMIZUKA.

SO IT... COULD SEE YOU AGAIN...
AND YOU JUST—
DON'T YOU DARE WRITE THAT OFF AS "COINCIDENCE"!
DON'T MAKE FUN OF PEOPLE'S FEELINGS—!!

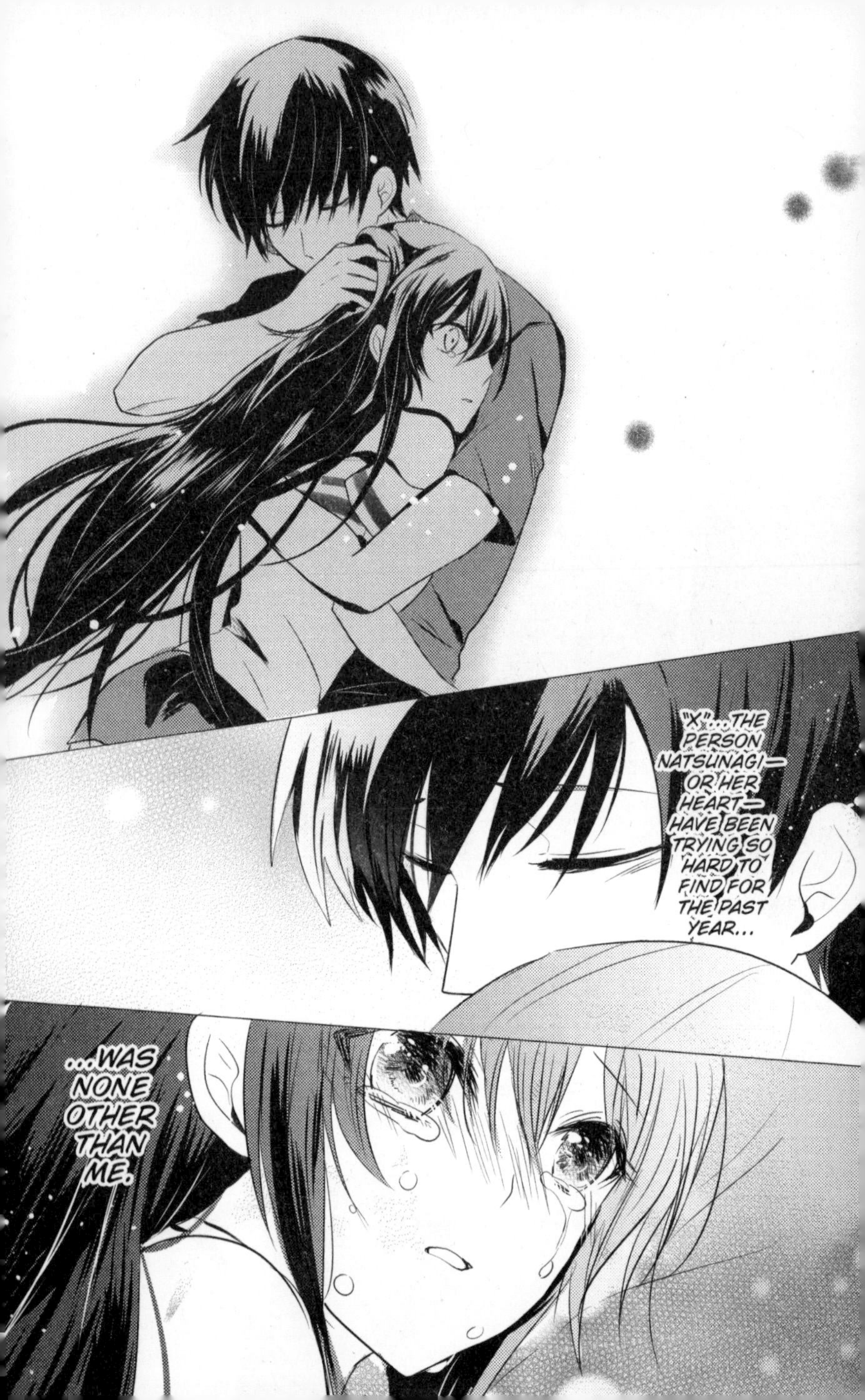
"X"... THE PERSON NATSUNAGI—OR HER HEART—HAVE BEEN TRYING SO HARD TO FIND FOR THE PAST YEAR...
...WAS NONE OTHER THAN ME.

...WANTED TO SEE ME?

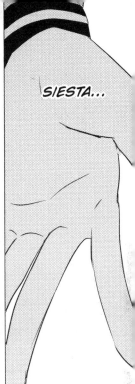

SIESTA...

ARE YOU THERE?

NO ANSWER. WELL, DUH... 'COURSE NOT.

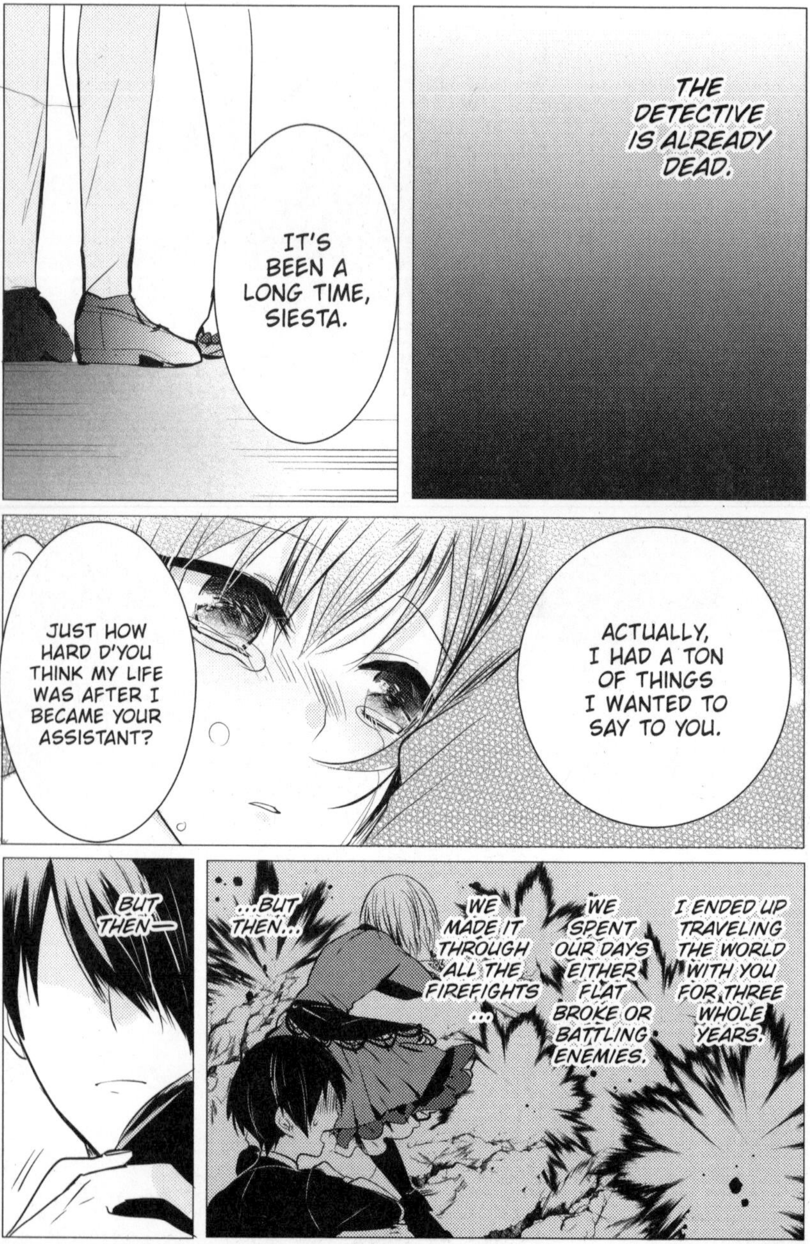
THE DETECTIVE IS ALREADY DEAD.
IT'S BEEN A LONG TIME, SIESTA.
ACTUALLY, I HAD A TON OF THINGS I WANTED TO SAY TO YOU.
JUST HOW HARD D'YOU THINK MY LIFE WAS AFTER I BECAME YOUR ASSISTANT?
I ENDED UP TRAVELING THE WORLD WITH YOU FOR THREE WHOLE YEARS.
WE SPENT OUR DAYS EITHER FLAT BROKE OR BATTLING ENEMIES.
WE MADE IT THROUGH ALL THE FIREFIGHTS...
...BUT THEN...
BUT THEN—

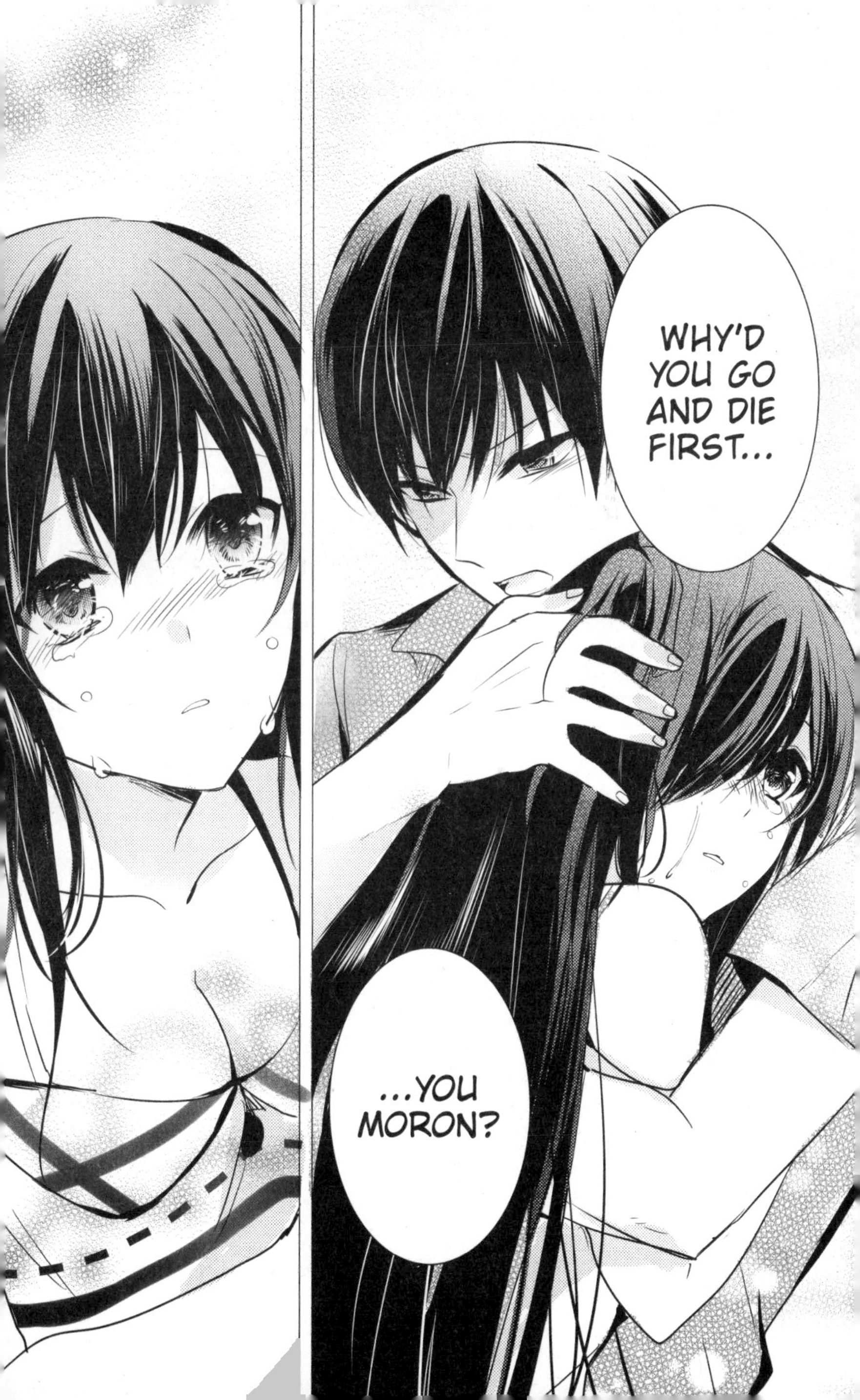
WHY'D YOU GO AND DIE FIRST...
...YOU MORON?

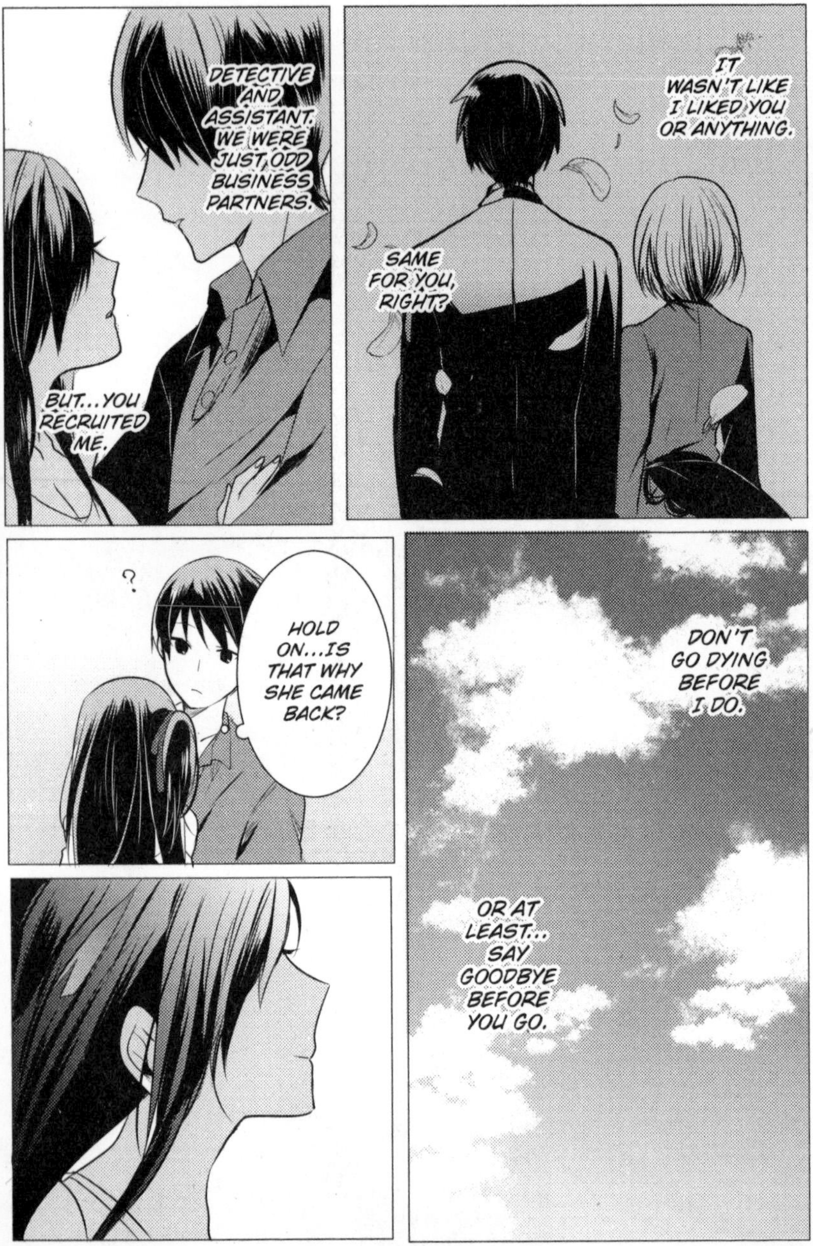
IT WASN'T LIKE I LIKED YOU OR ANYTHING.
SAME FOR YOU, RIGHT?
DETECTIVE AND ASSISTANT. WE WERE JUST ODD BUSINESS PARTNERS.
BUT...YOU RECRUITED ME.
DON'T GO DYING BEFORE I DO.
OR AT LEAST... SAY GOODBYE BEFORE YOU GO.
?
HOLD ON...IS THAT WHY SHE CAME BACK?

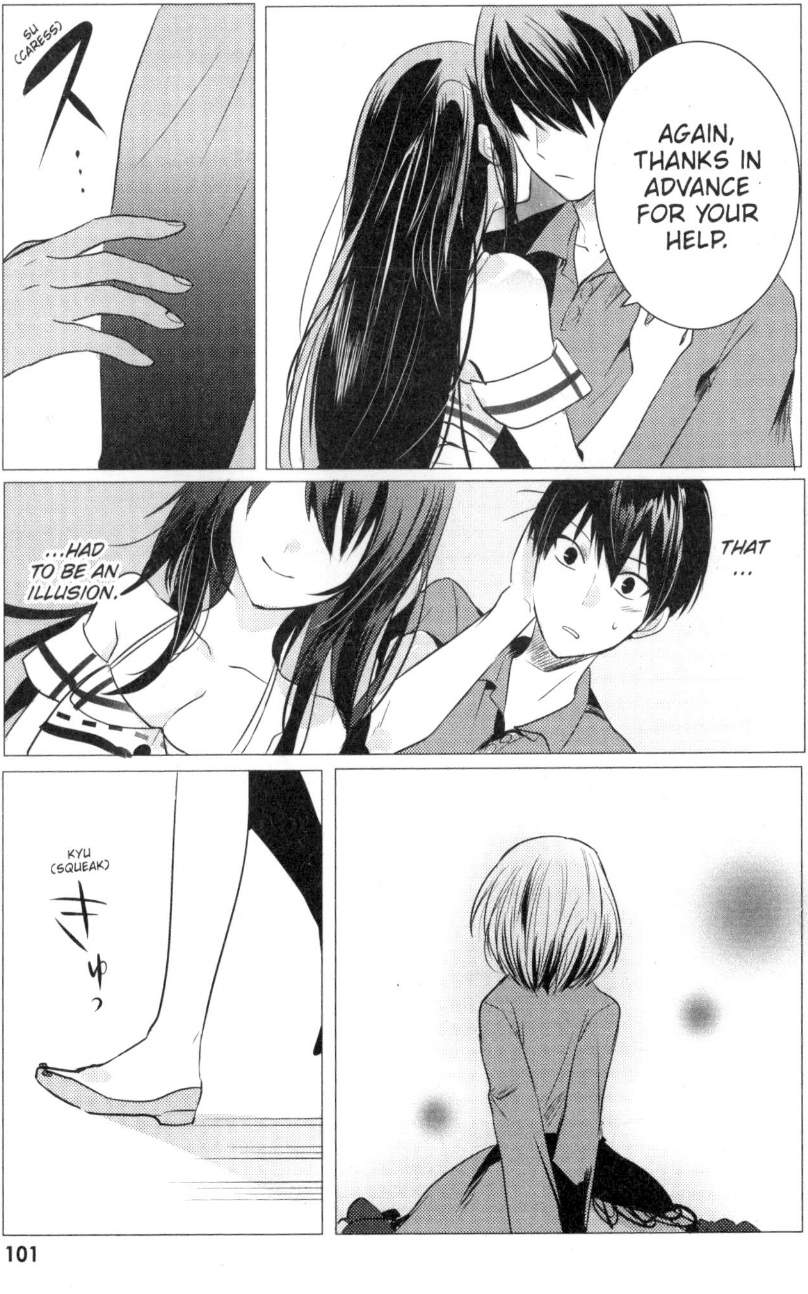
AGAIN, THANKS IN ADVANCE FOR YOUR HELP.
SU (CARESS)
ス…
THAT ...
...HAD TO BE AN ILLUSION.
KYU (SQUEAK)
きゅっ

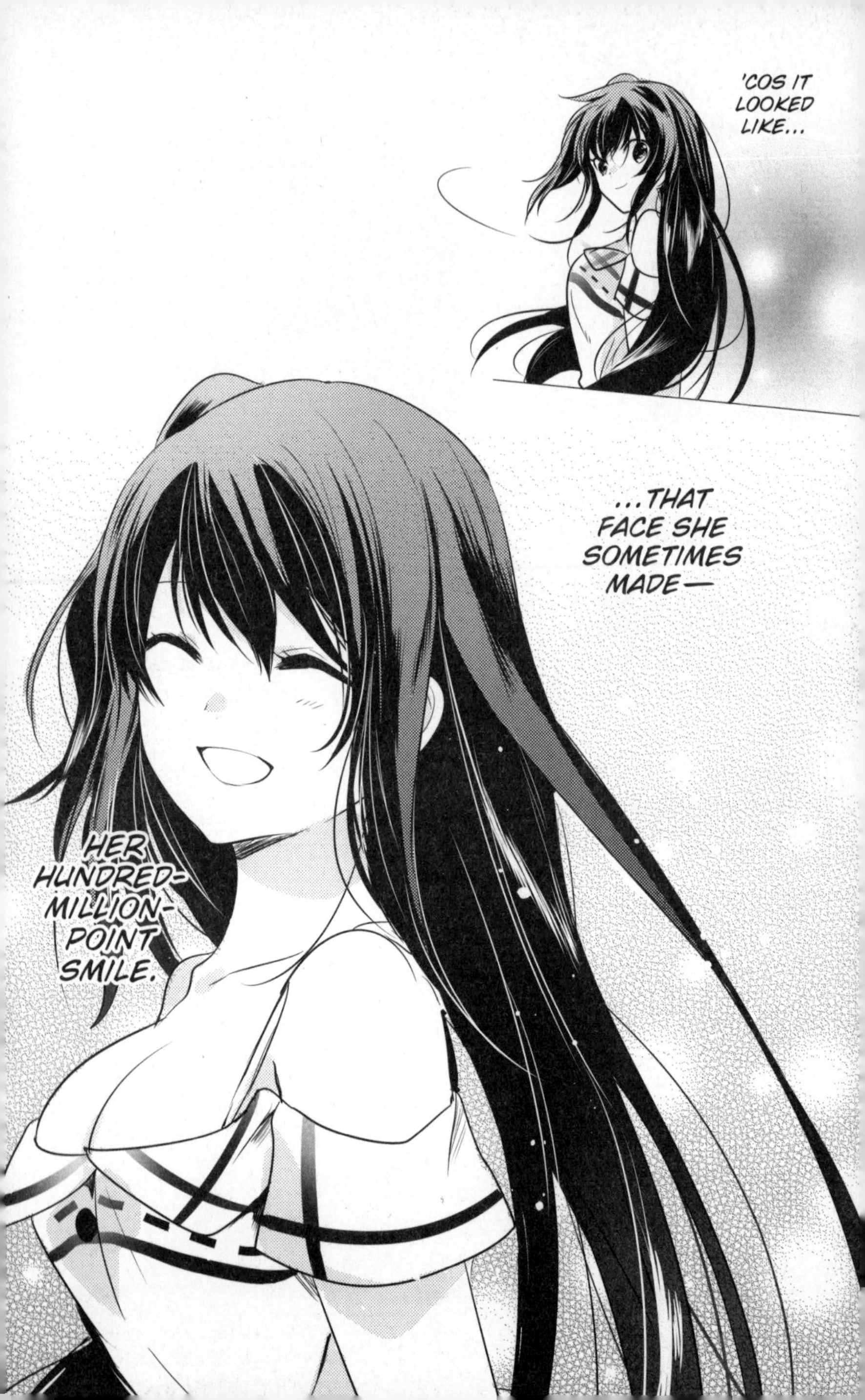
'COS IT LOOKED LIKE...
...THAT FACE SHE SOMETIMES MADE—
HER HUNDRED-MILLION-POINT SMILE.

The Detective Is Already Dead

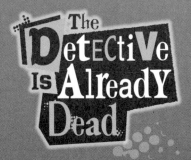

The Detective Is Already Dead

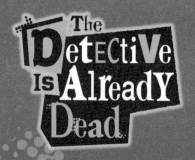

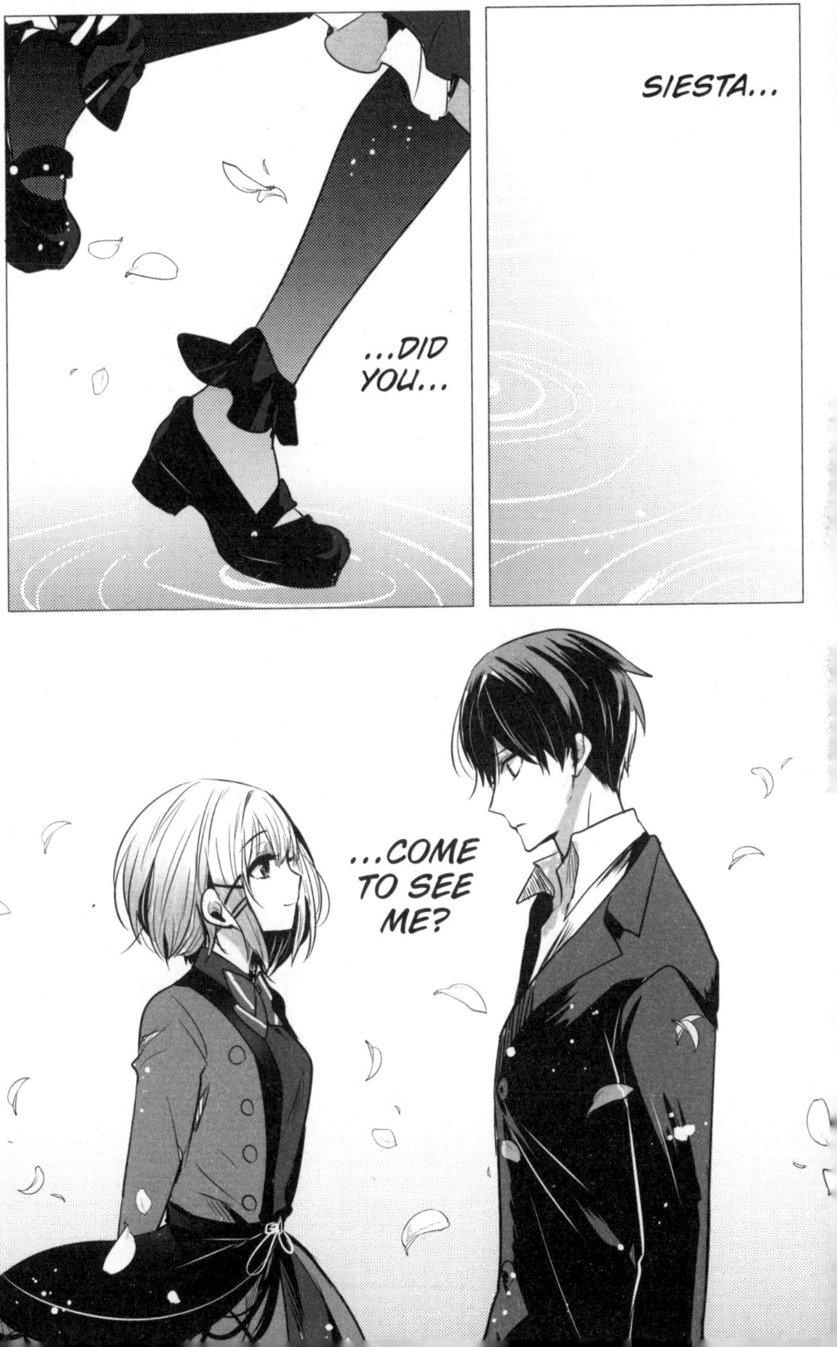
SIESTA...
...DID YOU...
...COME TO SEE ME?

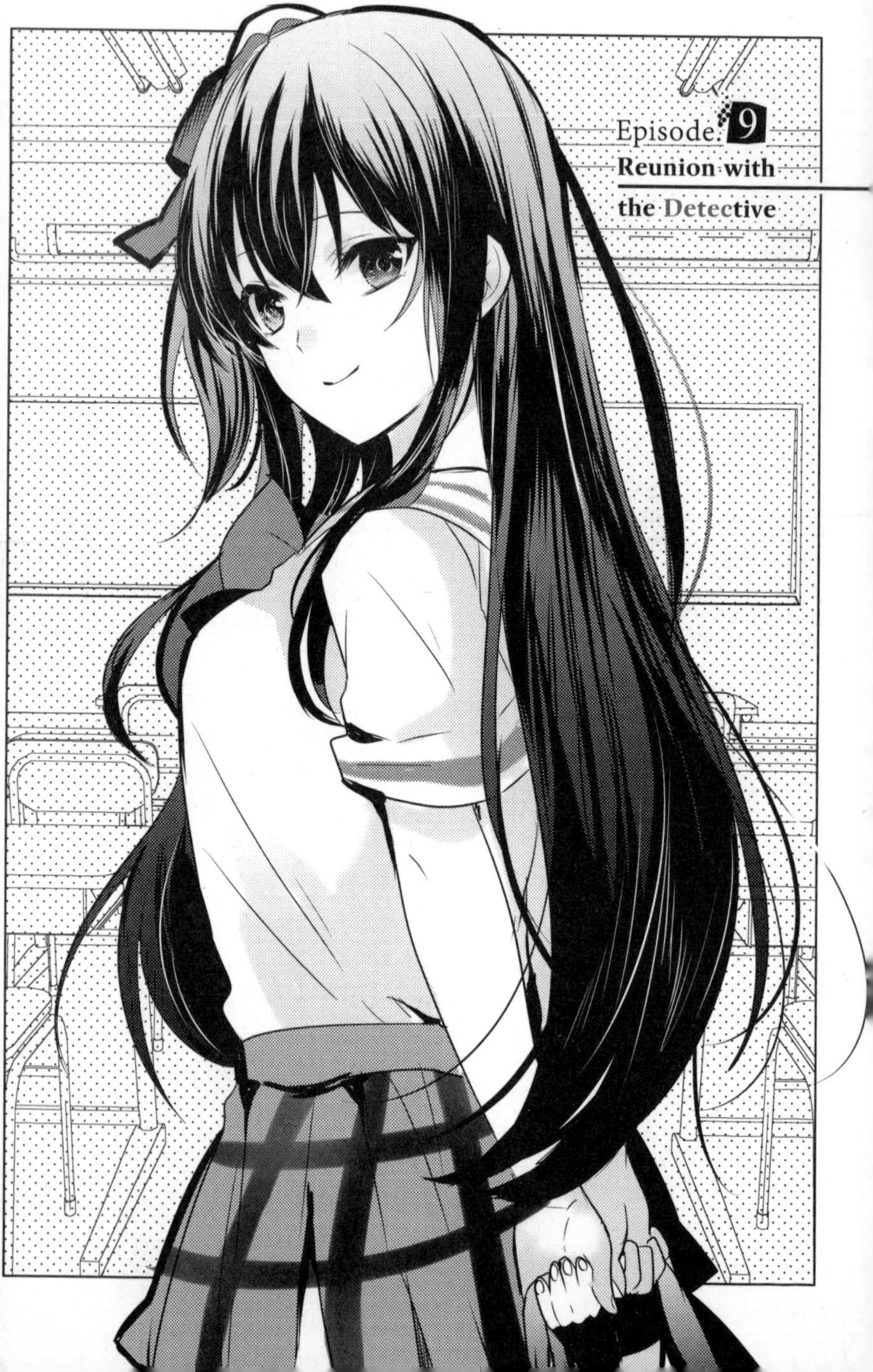
Episode. 9
Reunion with the Detective

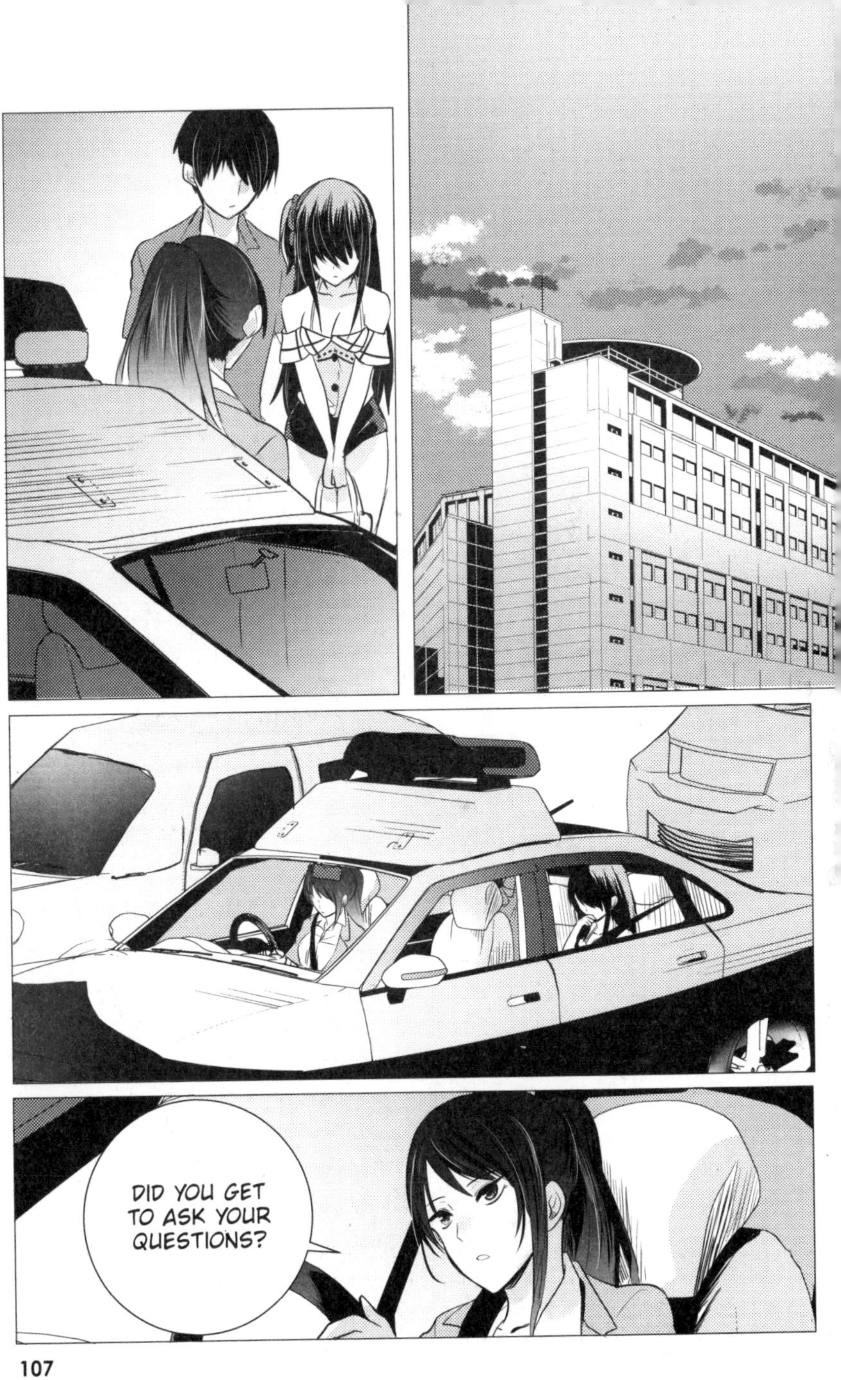
DID YOU GET TO ASK YOUR QUESTIONS?

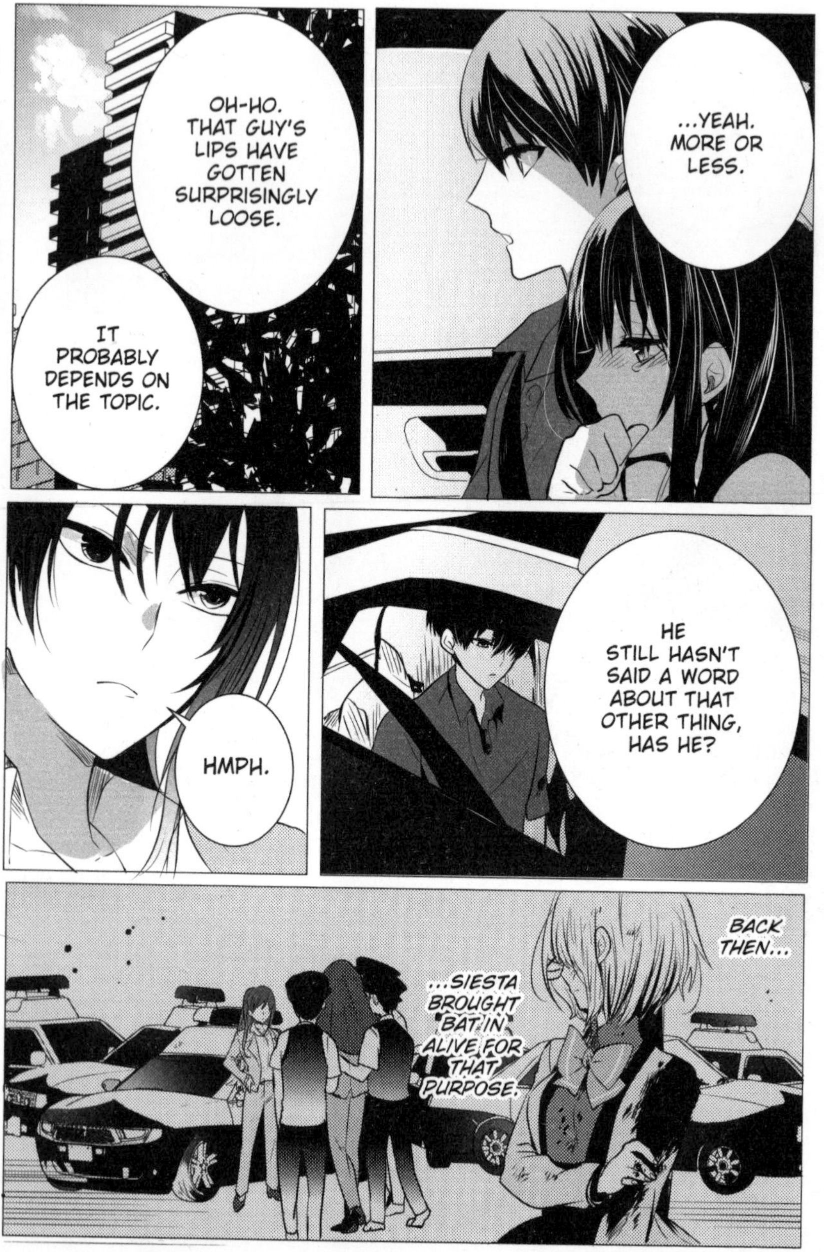
...YEAH. MORE OR LESS.
OH-HO. THAT GUY'S LIPS HAVE GOTTEN SURPRISINGLY LOOSE.
IT PROBABLY DEPENDS ON THE TOPIC.
HE STILL HASN'T SAID A WORD ABOUT THAT OTHER THING, HAS HE?
HMPH.
BACK THEN...
...SIESTA BROUGHT BAT IN ALIVE FOR THAT PURPOSE.

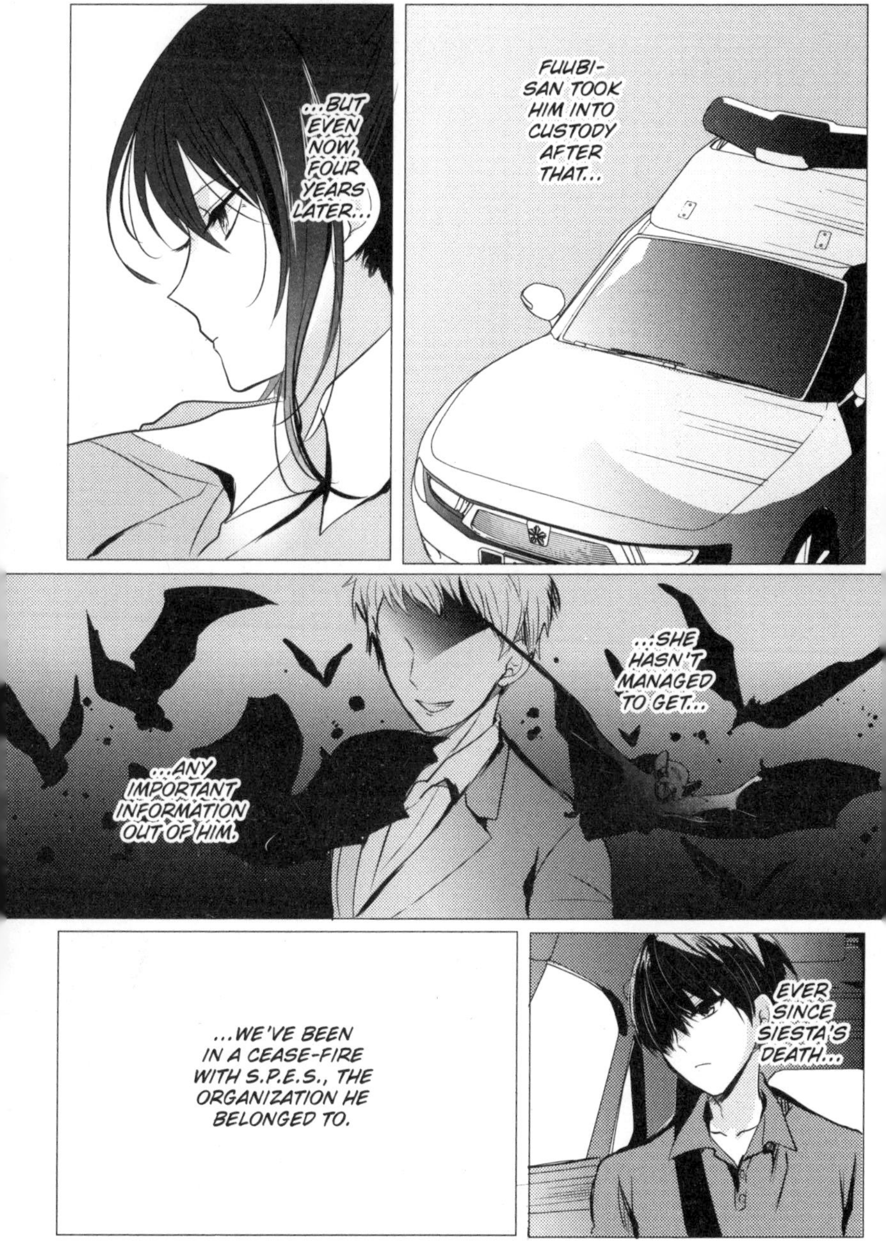
FUUBI-SAN TOOK HIM INTO CUSTODY AFTER THAT...
...BUT EVEN NOW, FOUR YEARS LATER...
...SHE HASN'T MANAGED TO GET...
...ANY IMPORTANT INFORMATION OUT OF HIM.
EVER SINCE SIESTA'S DEATH...
...WE'VE BEEN IN A CEASE-FIRE WITH S.P.E.S., THE ORGANIZATION HE BELONGED TO.

OR, TO BE ACCURATE, THEY STOPPED GOING OUT OF THEIR WAY TO FIGHT ME.

IT'S SAD TO SAY, BUT I GUESS...

...TO THEM, I WAS ONLY EVER...

...THE ACE DETECTIVE'S FLUNKY.

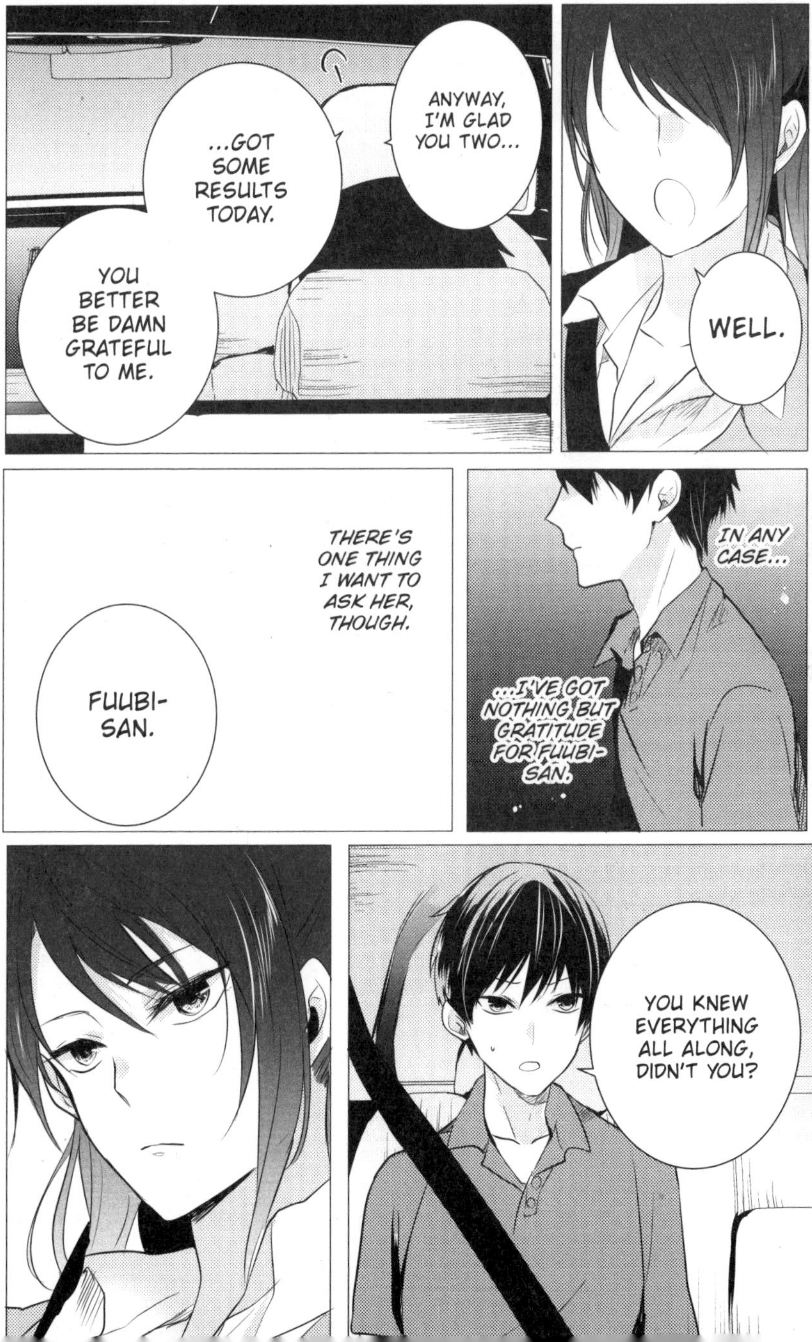
WELL.
ANYWAY, I'M GLAD YOU TWO...
...GOT SOME RESULTS TODAY.
YOU BETTER BE DAMN GRATEFUL TO ME.
IN ANY CASE...
...I'VE GOT NOTHING BUT GRATITUDE FOR FUUBI-SAN.
THERE'S ONE THING I WANT TO ASK HER, THOUGH.
FUUBI-SAN.
YOU KNEW EVERYTHING ALL ALONG, DIDN'T YOU?

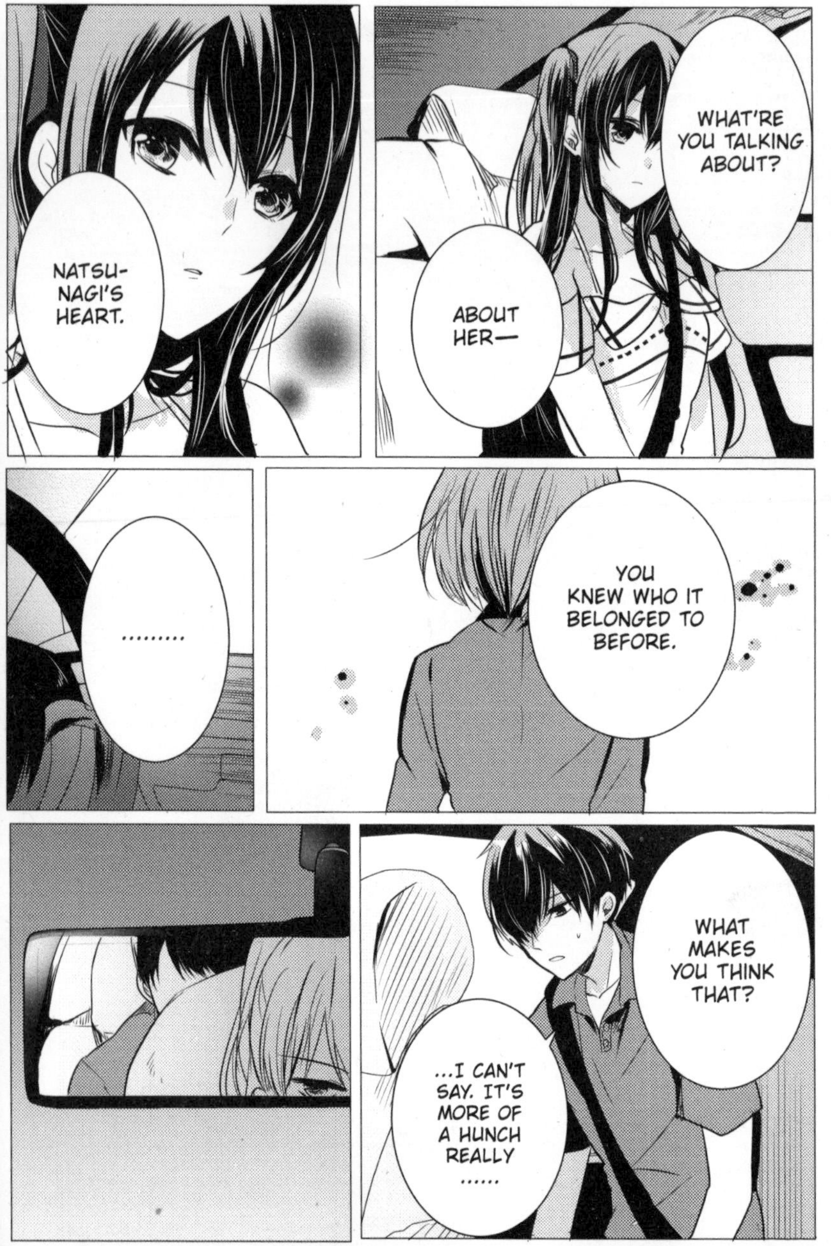
WHAT'RE YOU TALKING ABOUT?
ABOUT HER—
NATSU-NAGI'S HEART.
YOU KNEW WHO IT BELONGED TO BEFORE.
....
WHAT MAKES YOU THINK THAT?
...I CAN'T SAY. IT'S MORE OF A HUNCH REALLY ......

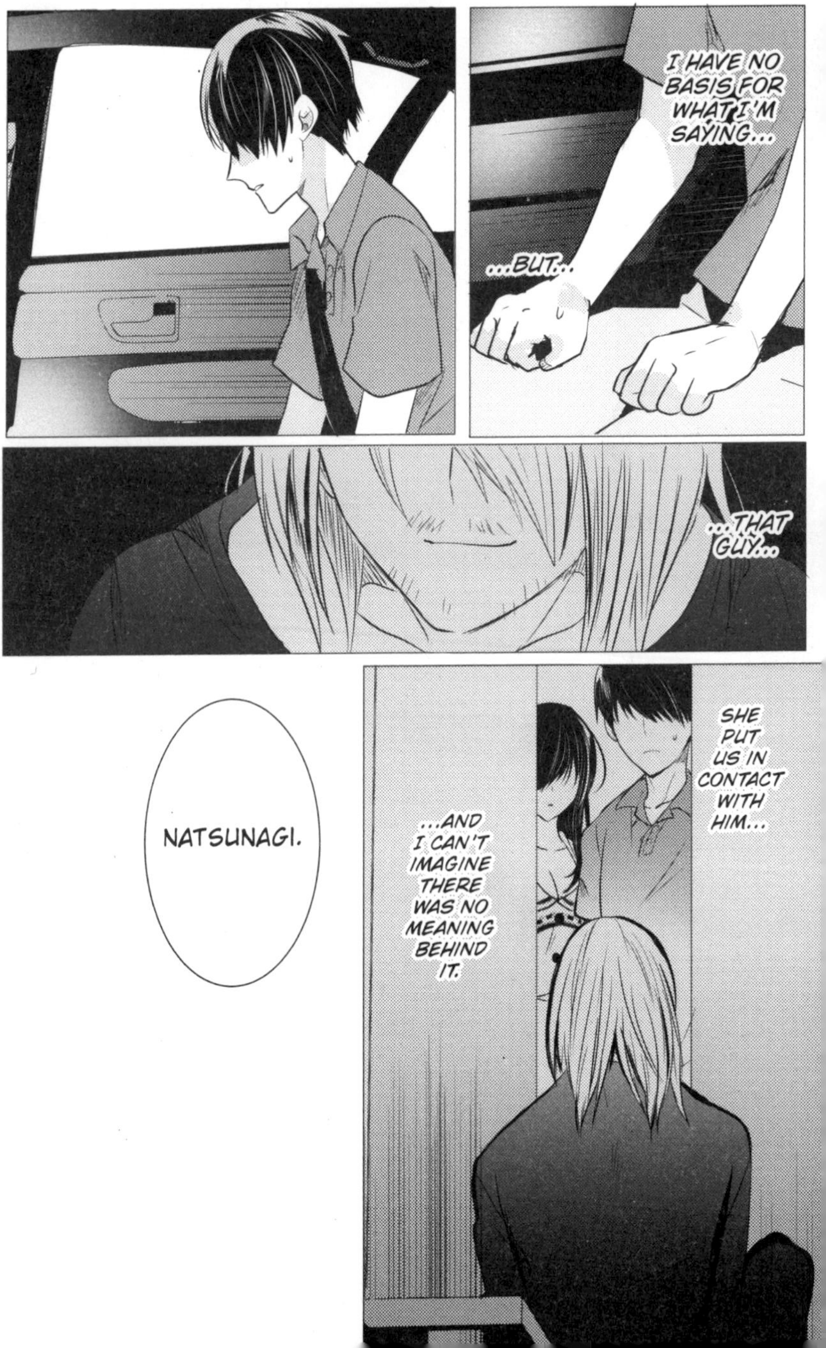
I HAVE NO BASIS FOR WHAT I'M SAYING...
...BUT...
...THAT GUY...
SHE PUT US IN CONTACT WITH HIM...
...AND I CAN'T IMAGINE THERE WAS NO MEANING BEHIND IT.
NATSUNAGI.

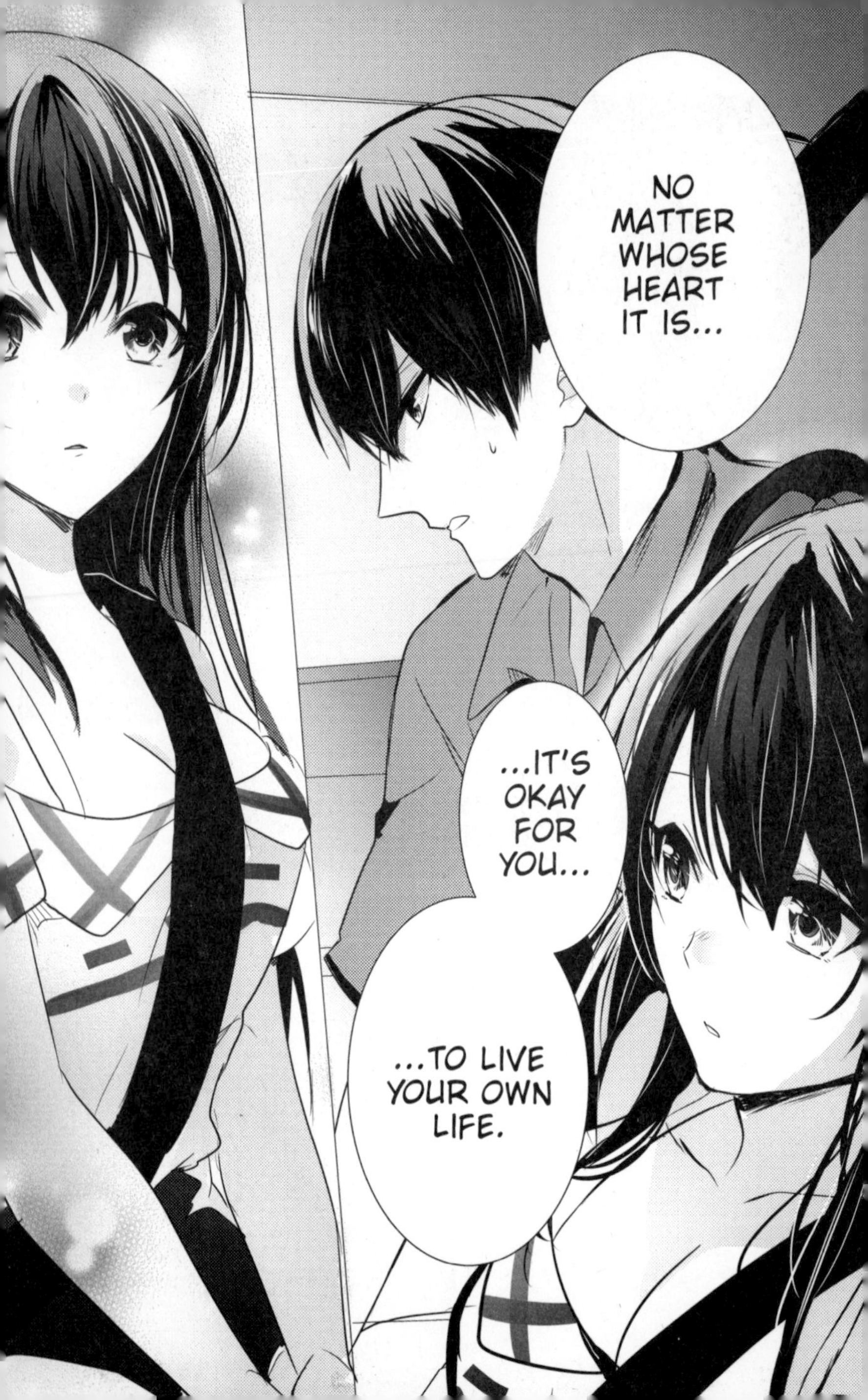
NO MATTER WHOSE HEART IT IS...
...IT'S OKAY FOR YOU...
...TO LIVE YOUR OWN LIFE.

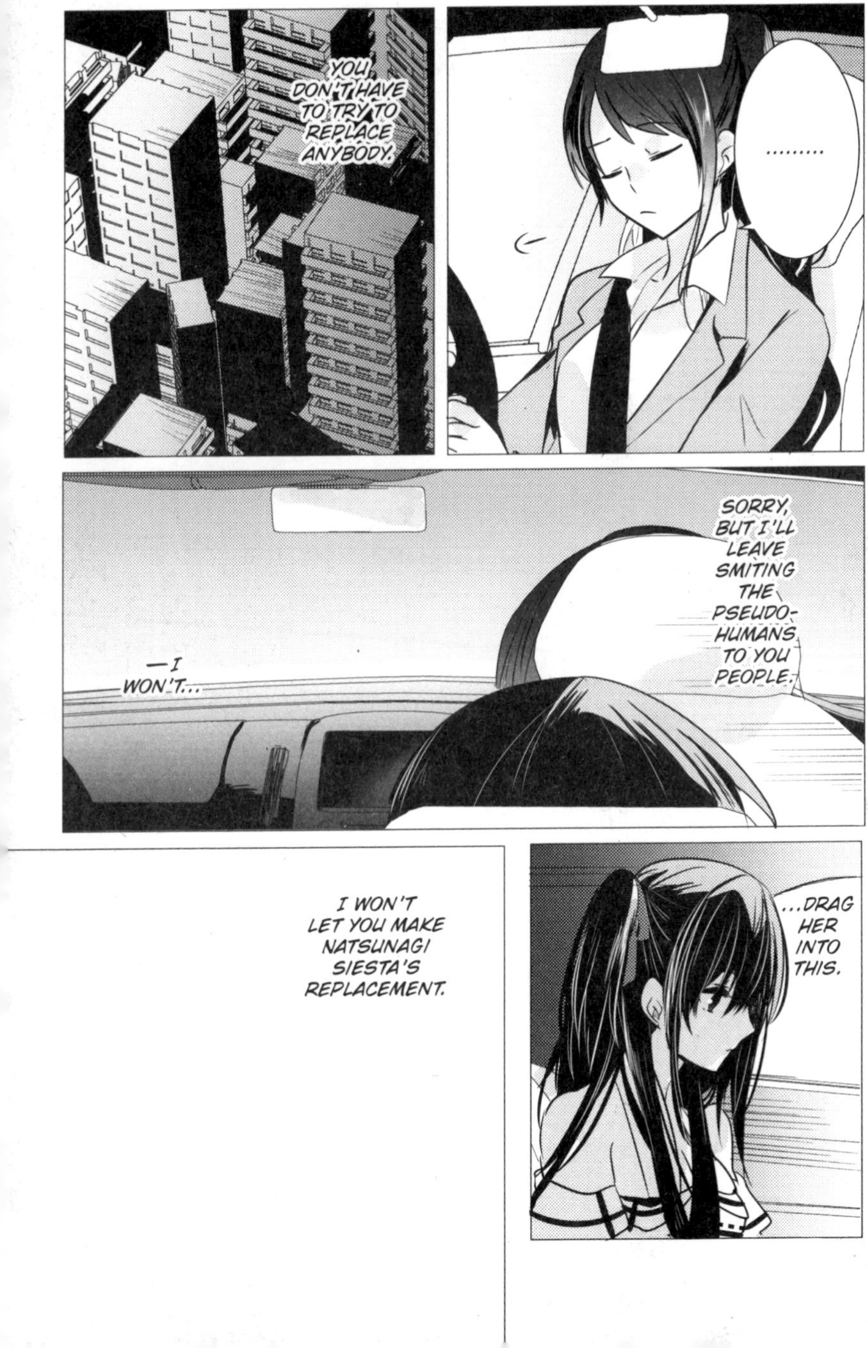
....
YOU DON'T HAVE TO TRY TO REPLACE ANYBODY.
SORRY, BUT I'LL LEAVE SMITING THE PSEUDO-HUMANS TO YOU PEOPLE.
—I WON'T...
...DRAG HER INTO THIS.
I WON'T LET YOU MAKE NATSUNAGI SIESTA'S REPLACEMENT.

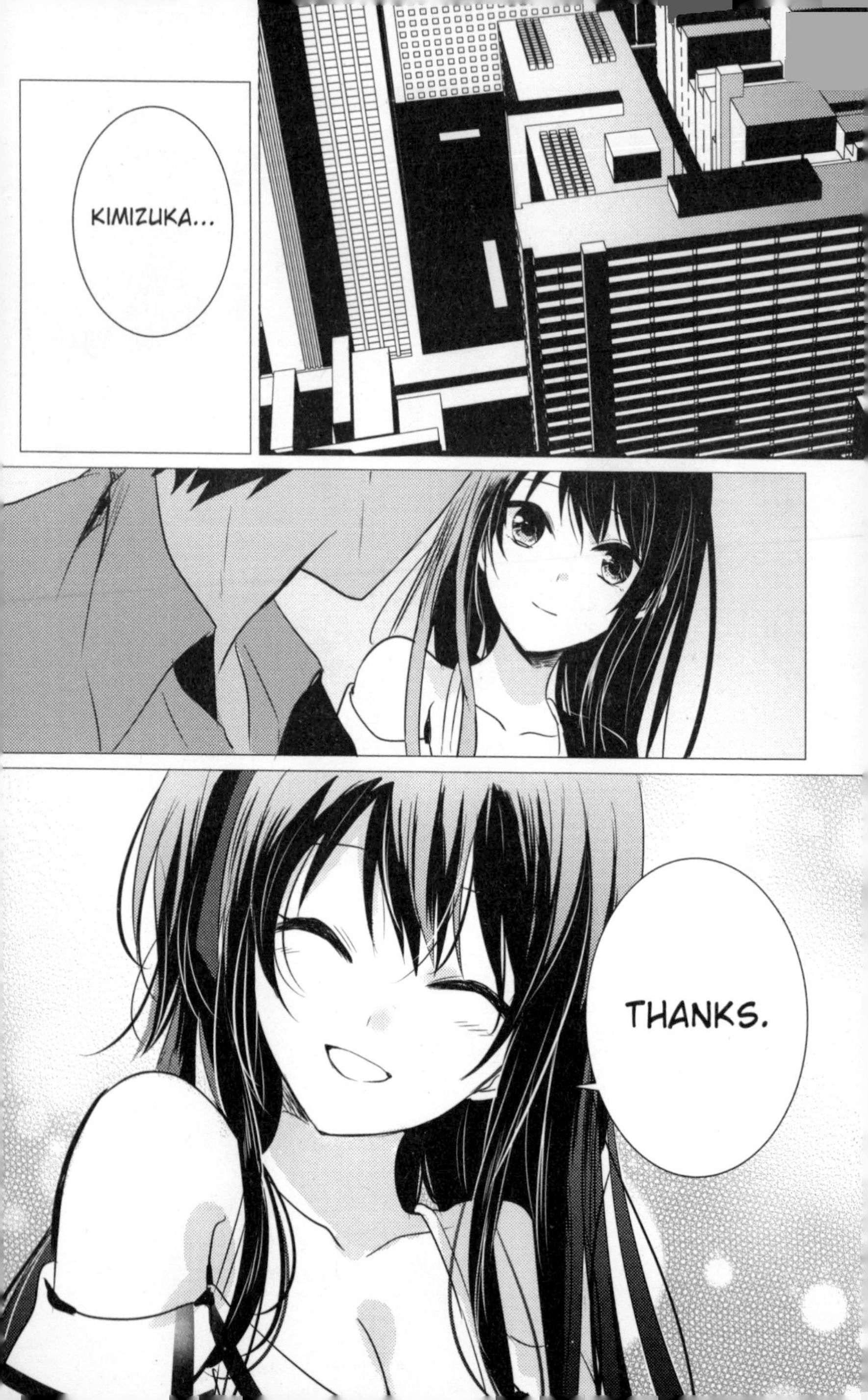
KIMIZUKA...
THANKS.

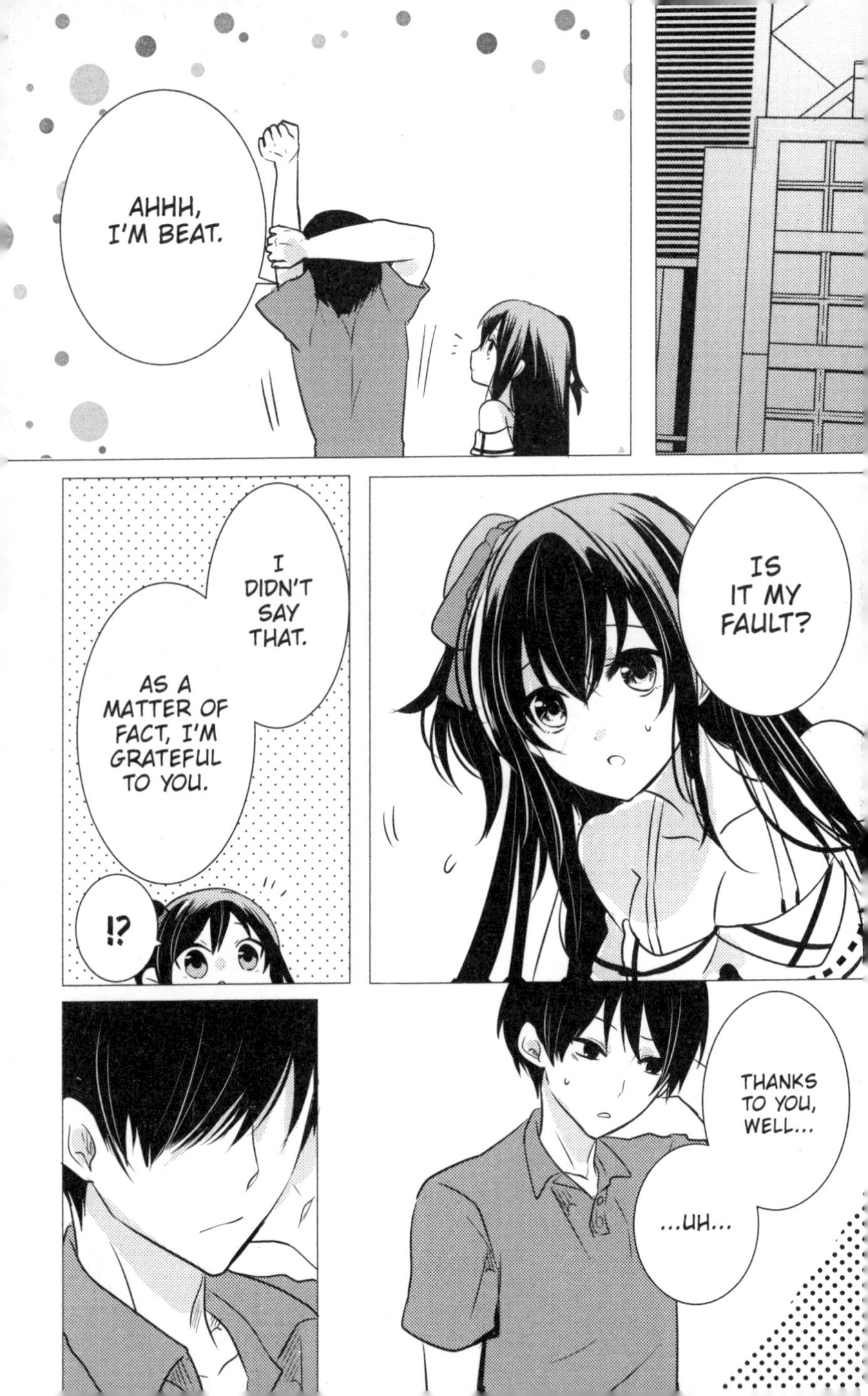
AHHH, I'M BEAT.
IS IT MY FAULT?
I DIDN'T SAY THAT.
AS A MATTER OF FACT, I'M GRATEFUL TO YOU.
!?
THANKS TO YOU, WELL...
...UH...

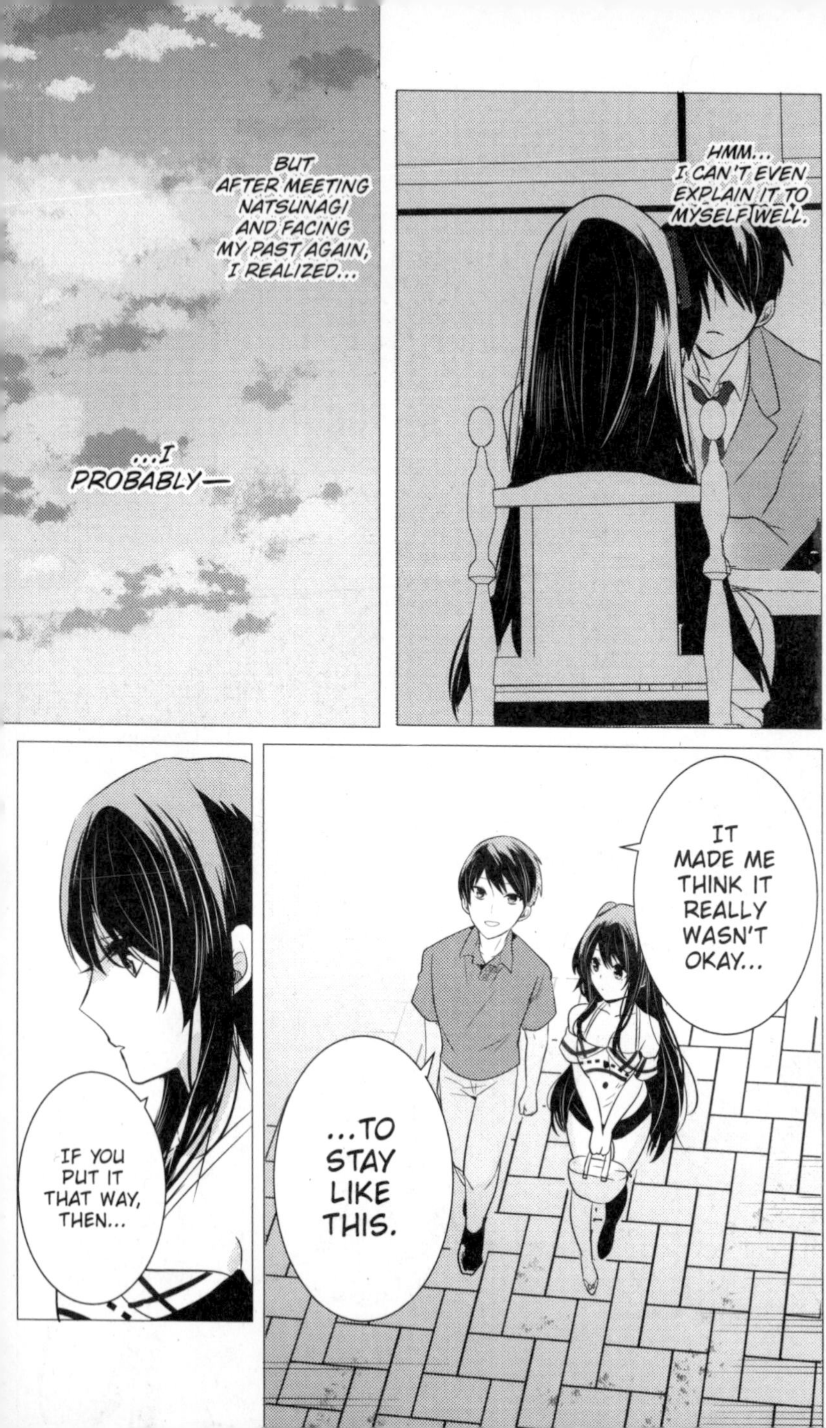
HMM... I CAN'T EVEN EXPLAIN IT TO MYSELF WELL.
BUT AFTER MEETING NATSUNAGI AND FACING MY PAST AGAIN, I REALIZED...
...I PROBABLY—
IT MADE ME THINK IT REALLY WASN'T OKAY...
...TO STAY LIKE THIS.
IF YOU PUT IT THAT WAY, THEN...

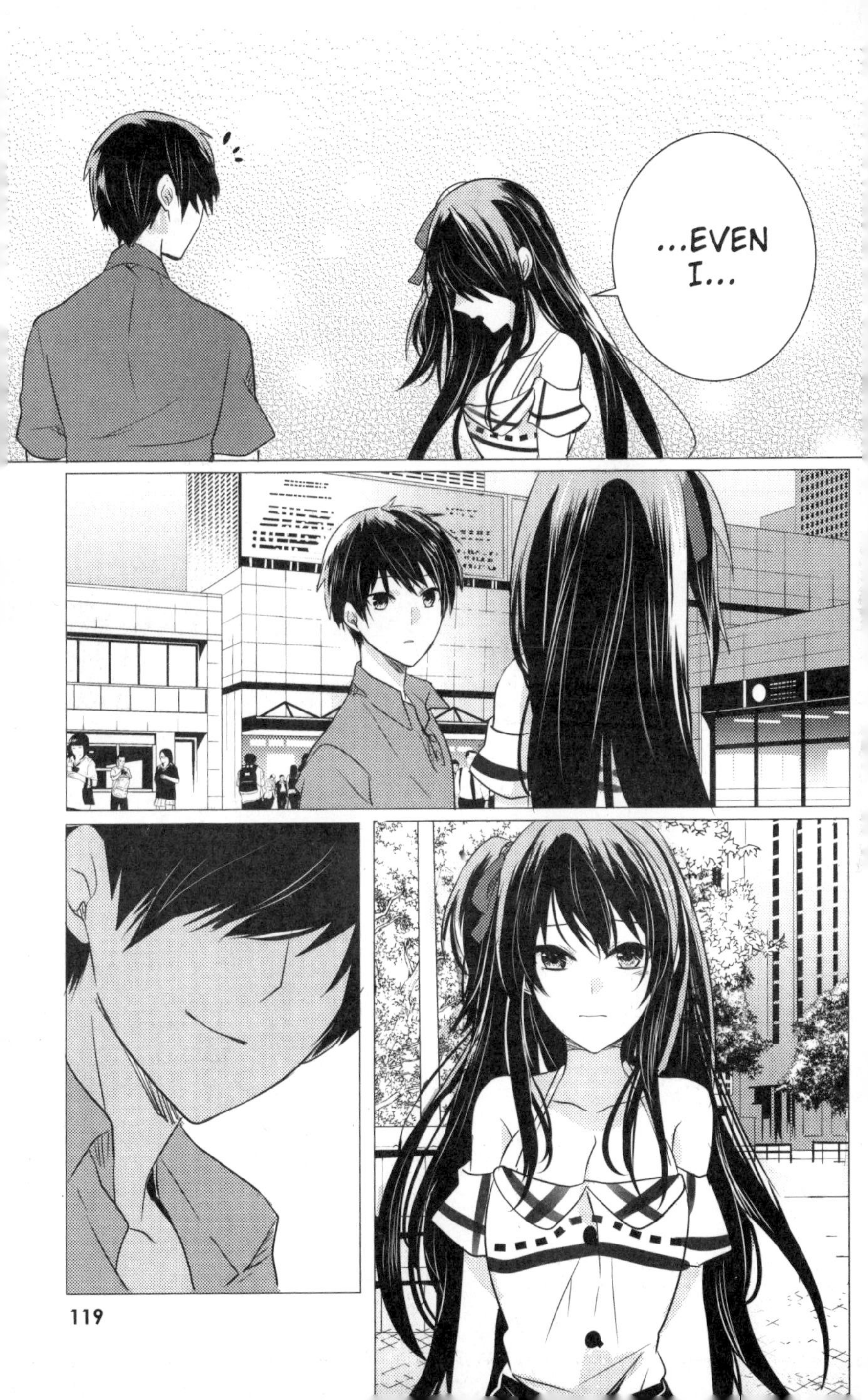
...EVEN I...

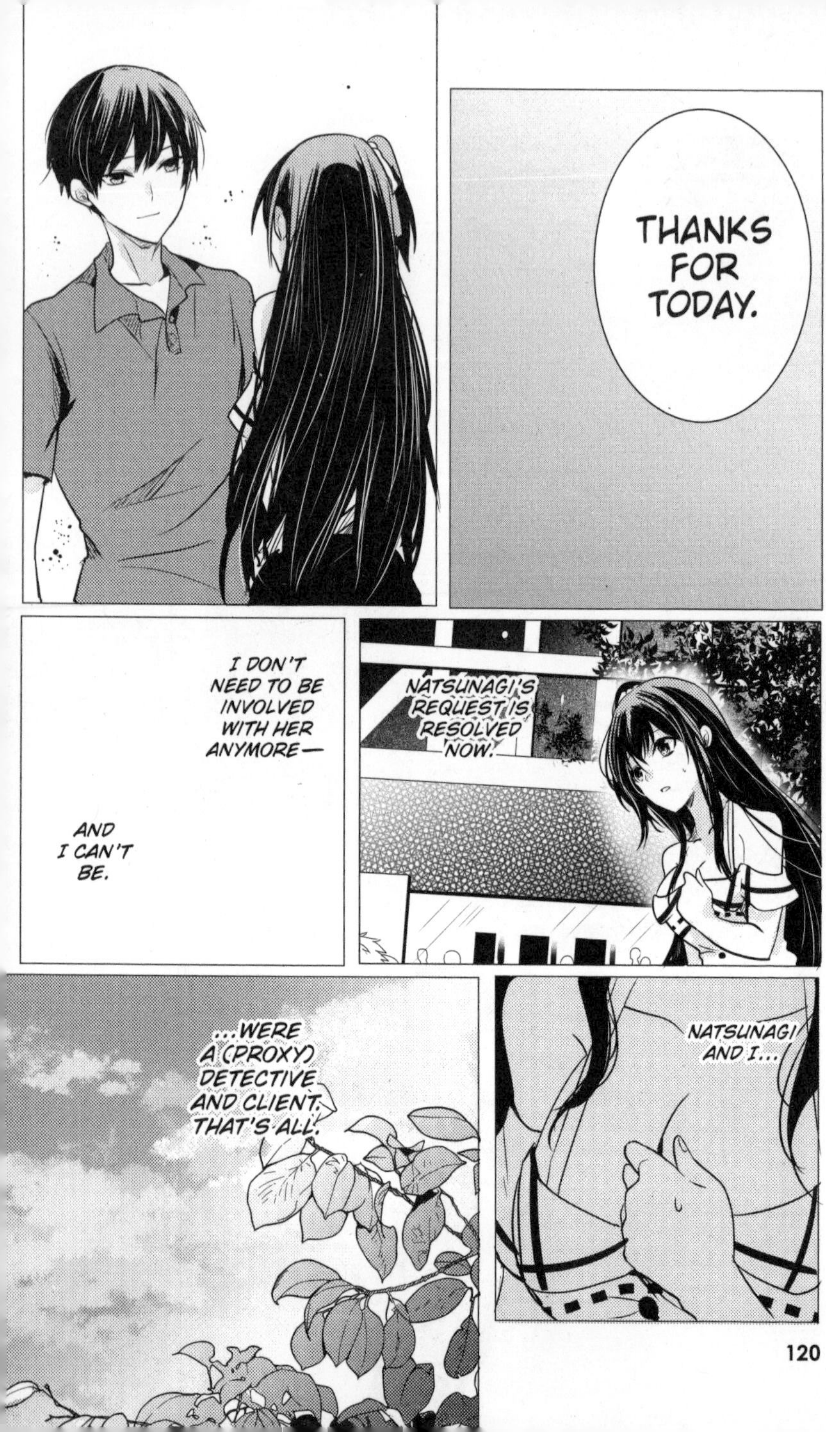
THANKS FOR TODAY.
NATSUNAGI'S REQUEST IS RESOLVED NOW.
I DON'T NEED TO BE INVOLVED WITH HER ANYMORE—
AND I CAN'T BE.
NATSUNAGI AND I...
...WERE A (PROXY) DETECTIVE AND CLIENT. THAT'S ALL.

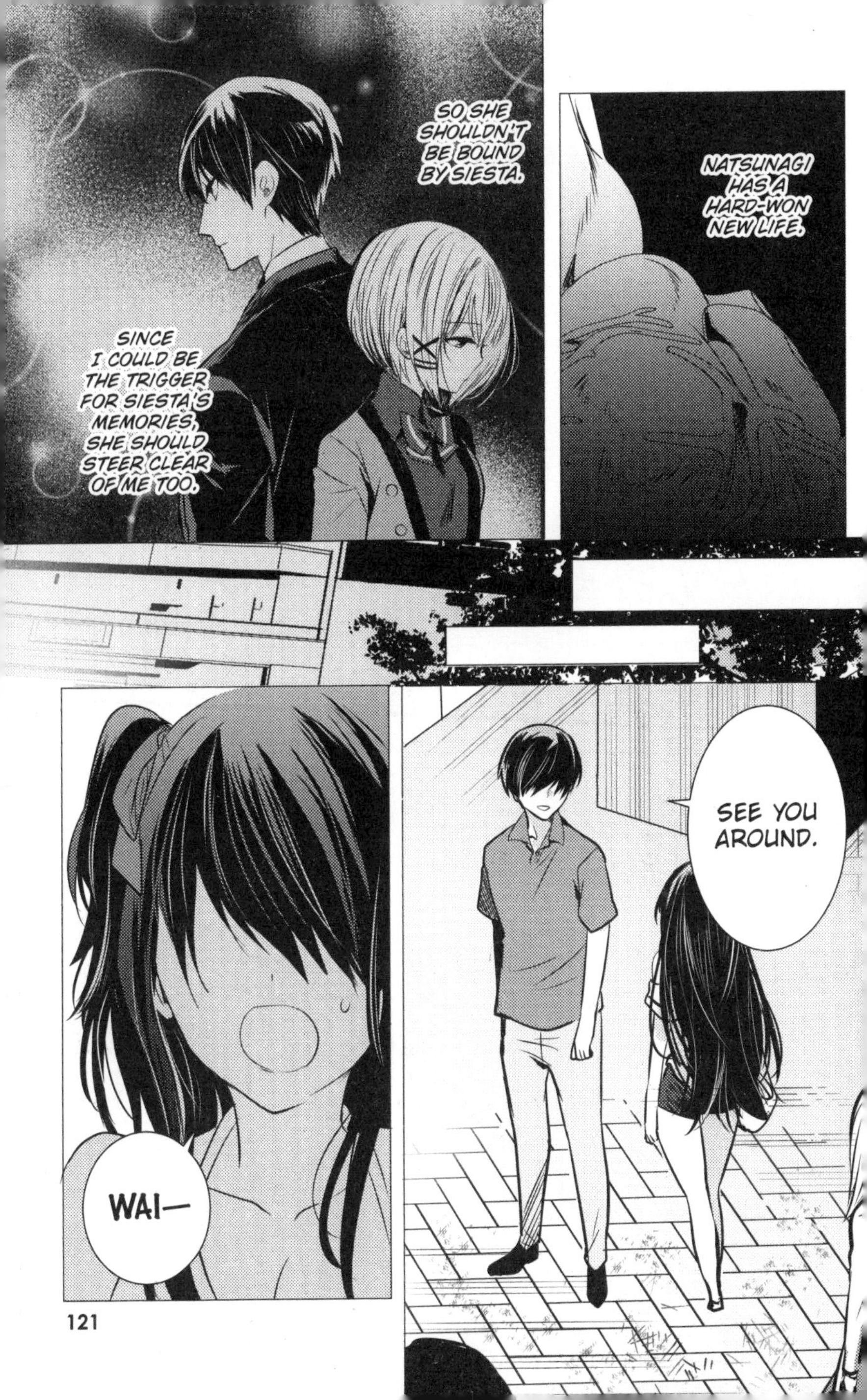
NATSUNAGI HAS A HARD-WON NEW LIFE.
SO SHE SHOULDN'T BE BOUND BY SIESTA.
SINCE I COULD BE THE TRIGGER FOR SIESTA'S MEMORIES, SHE SHOULD STEER CLEAR OF ME TOO.
SEE YOU AROUND.
WAI—

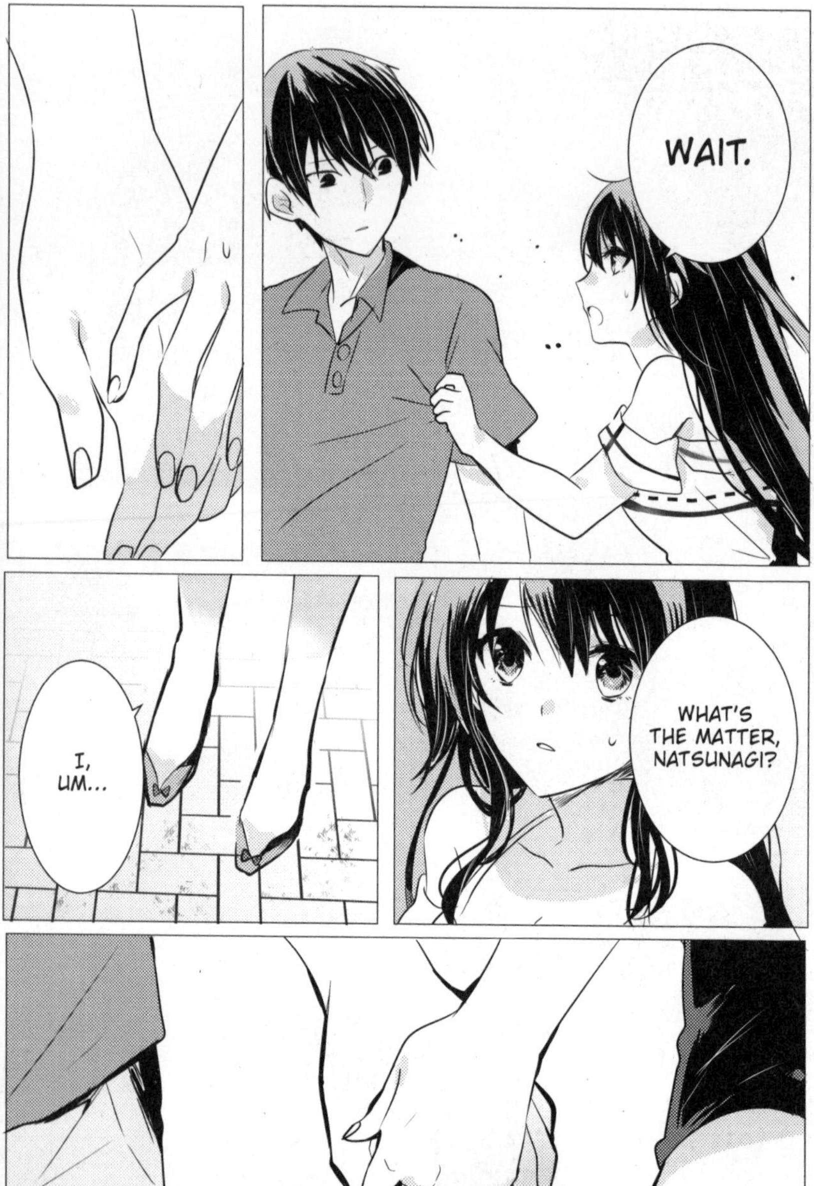
WAIT.
WHAT'S THE MATTER, NATSUNAGI?
I, UM...

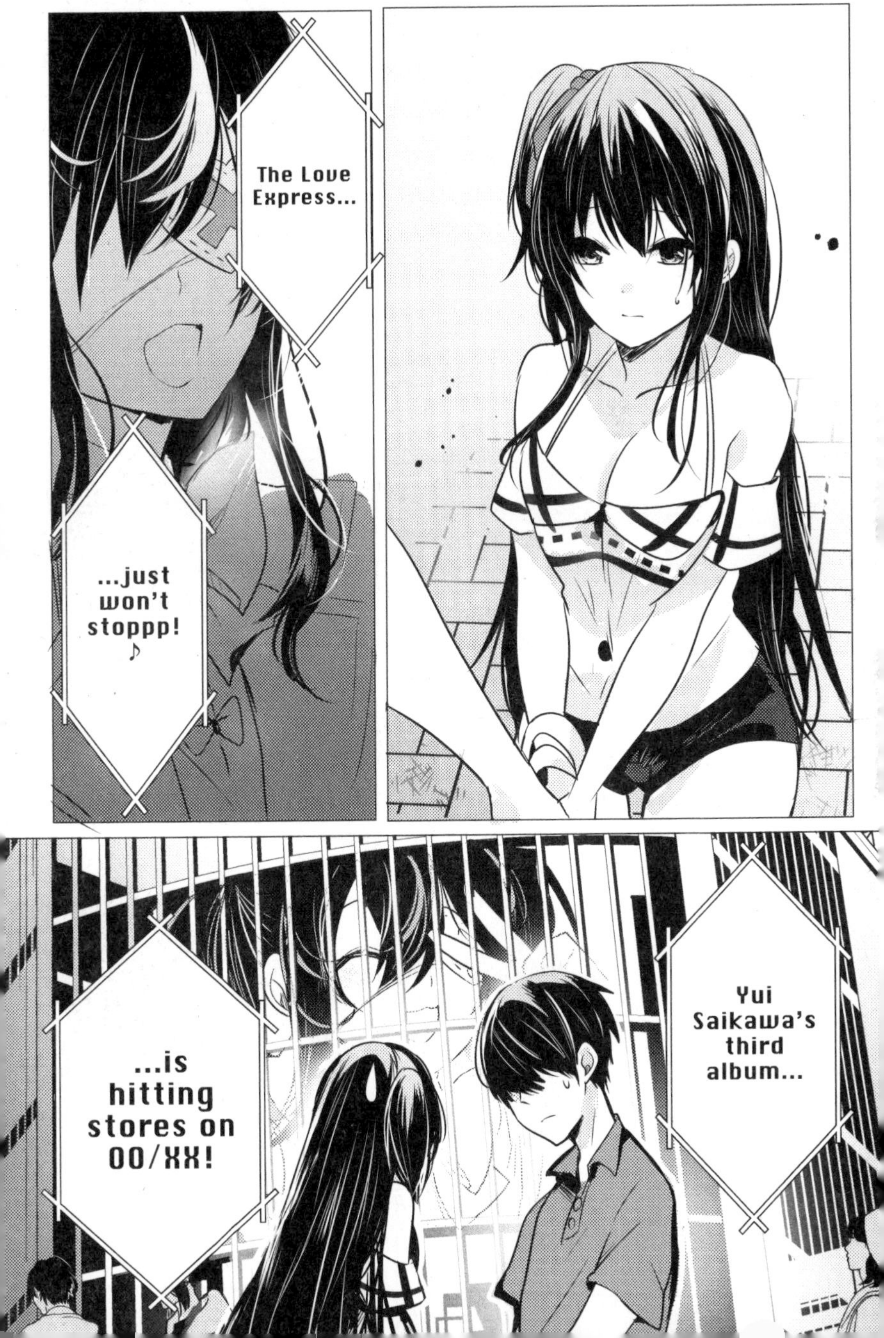
The Love Express...
...just won't stoppp! ♪
Yui Saikawa's third album...
...is hitting stores on OO/XX!

IF YOU DON'T HAVE ANYTHING TO SAY, I'M LEAVING.

...YOU'RE SUCH A JERK, KIMIZUKA.

I'M A FAILURE OF A HUMAN BEING.

SORRY ABOUT THAT.

YES, I AM.

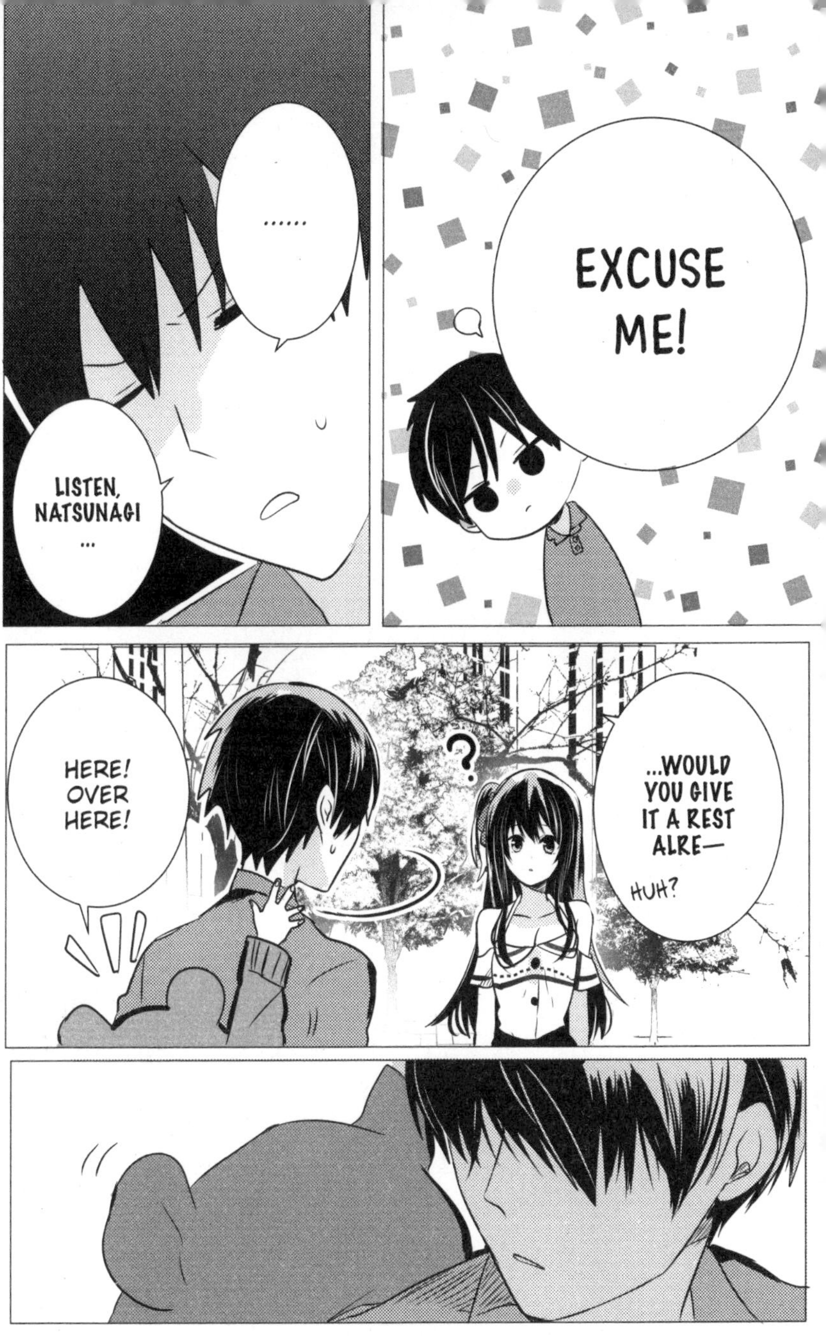
EXCUSE ME!
......
LISTEN, NATSUNAGI...
...WOULD YOU GIVE IT A REST ALRE—
HUH?
HERE! OVER HERE!

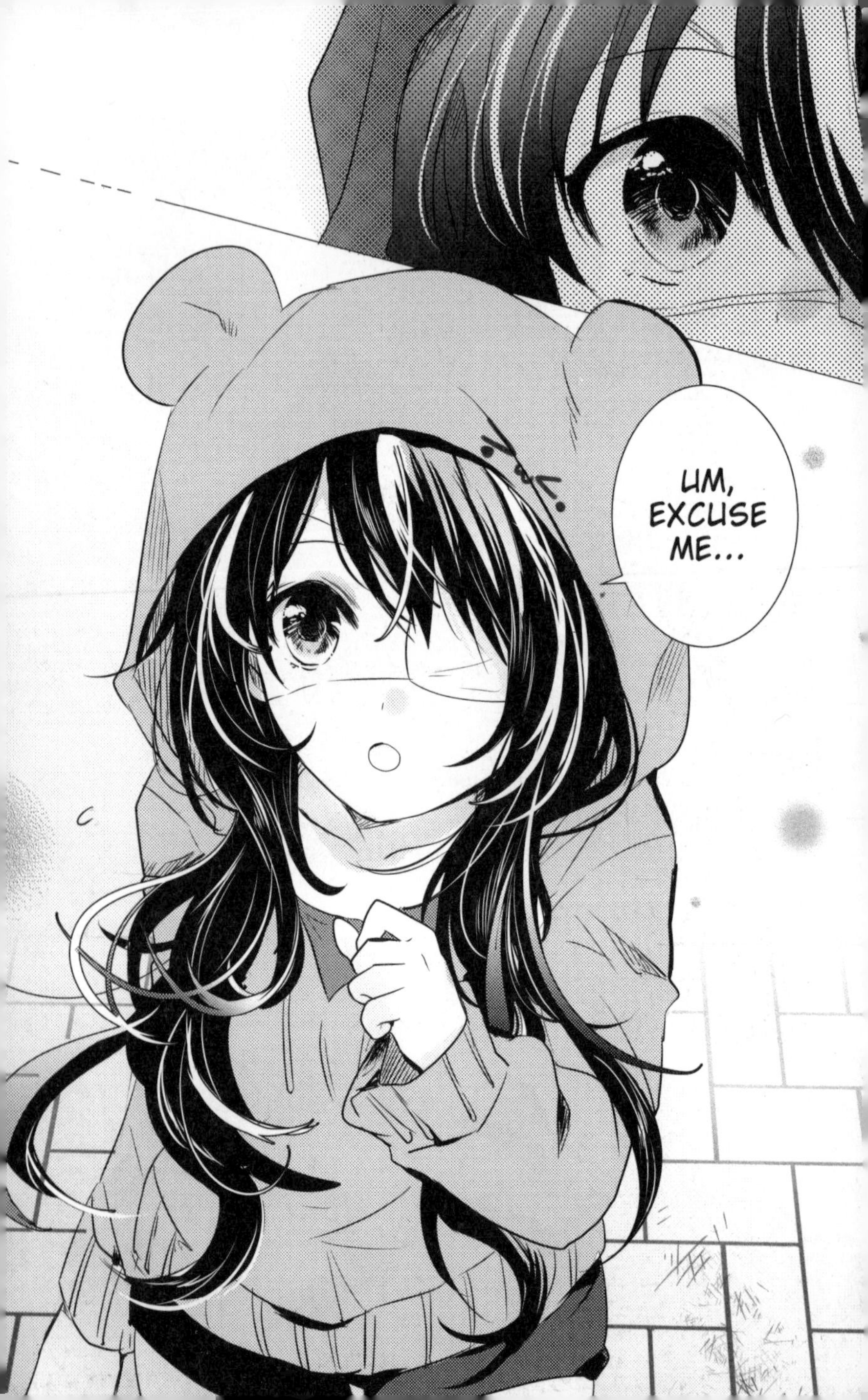
UM, EXCUSE ME...

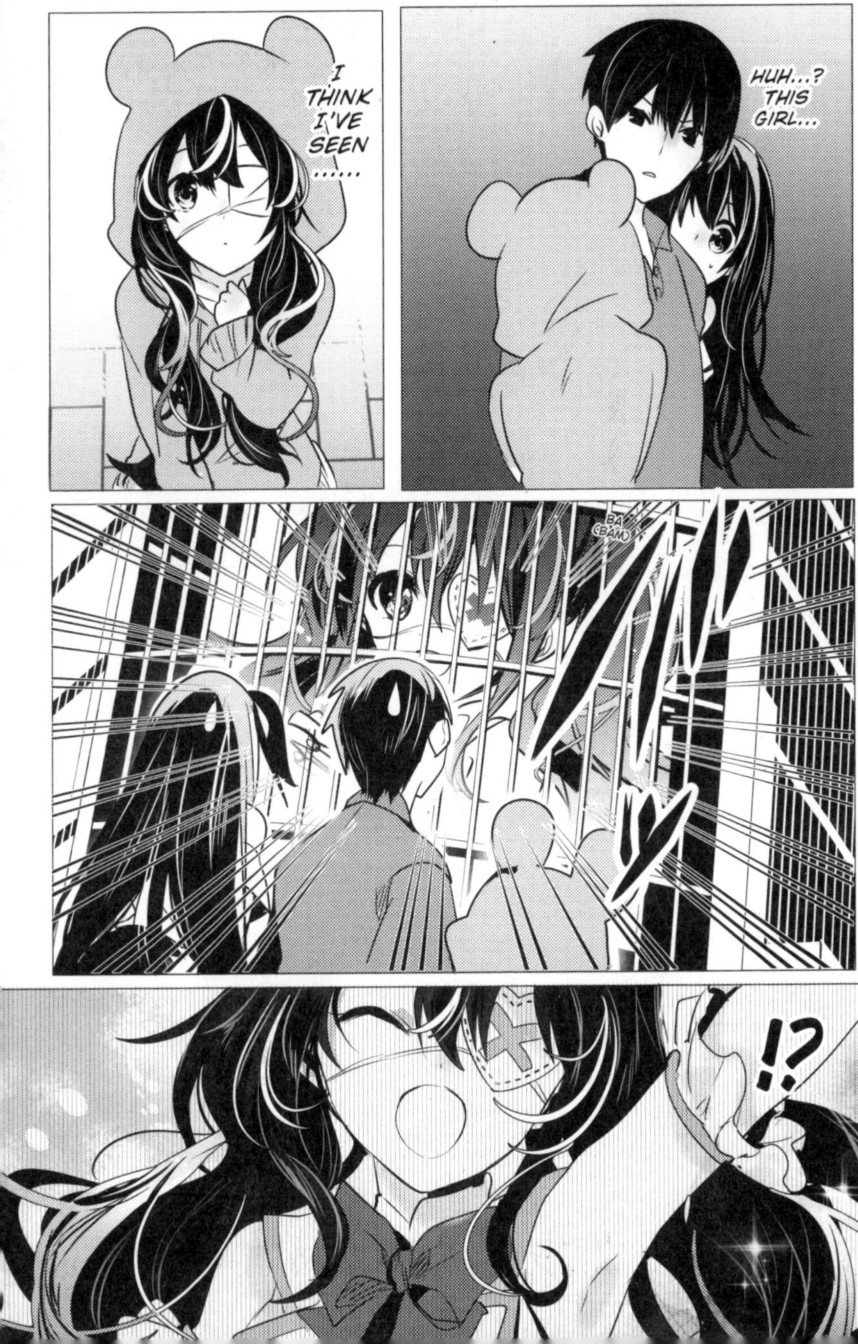
HUH...? THIS GIRL...
I THINK I'VE SEEN ......
BA (BAM)
!?

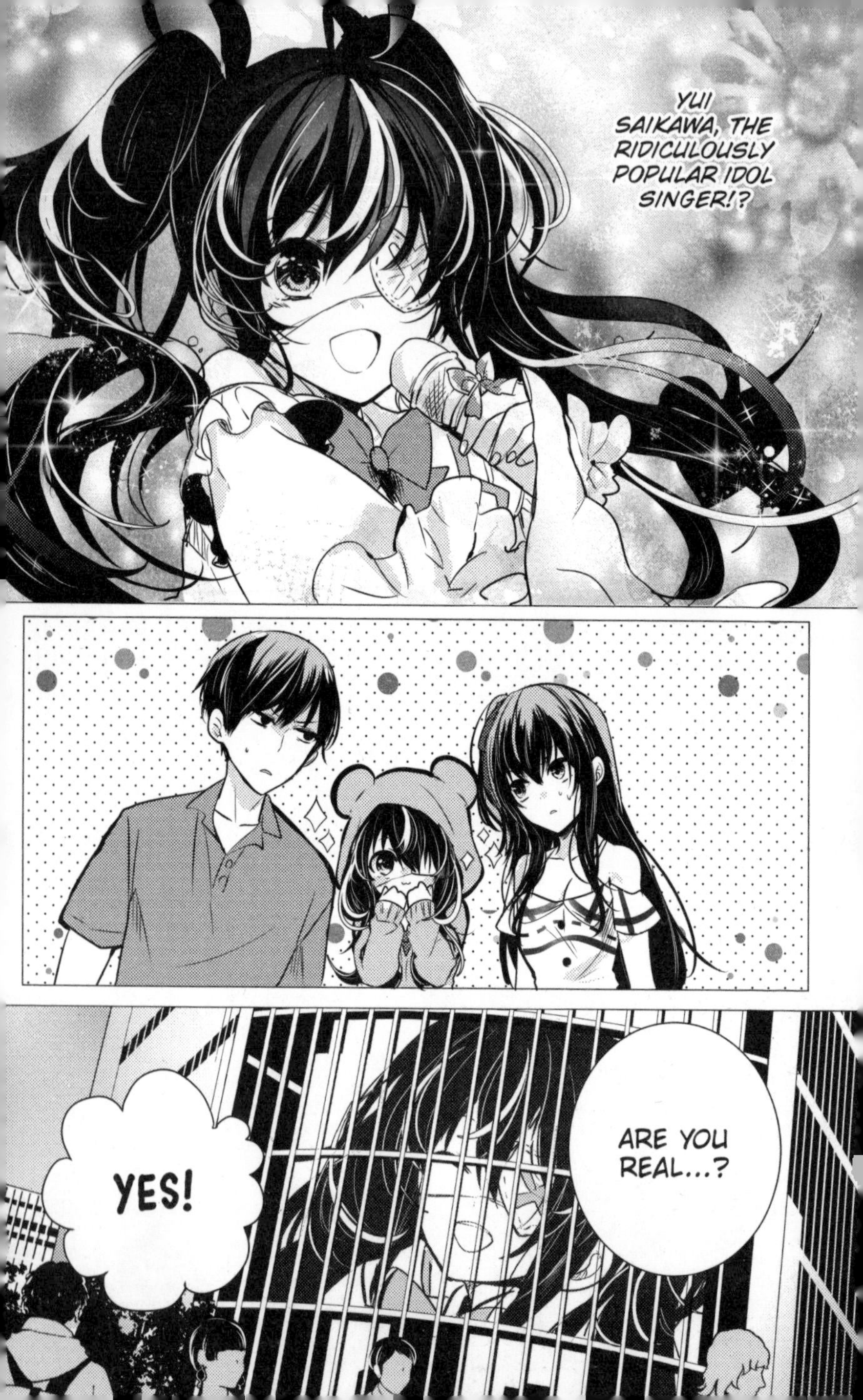
YUI SAIKAWA, THE RIDICULOUSLY POPULAR IDOL SINGER!?
ARE YOU REAL...?
YES!

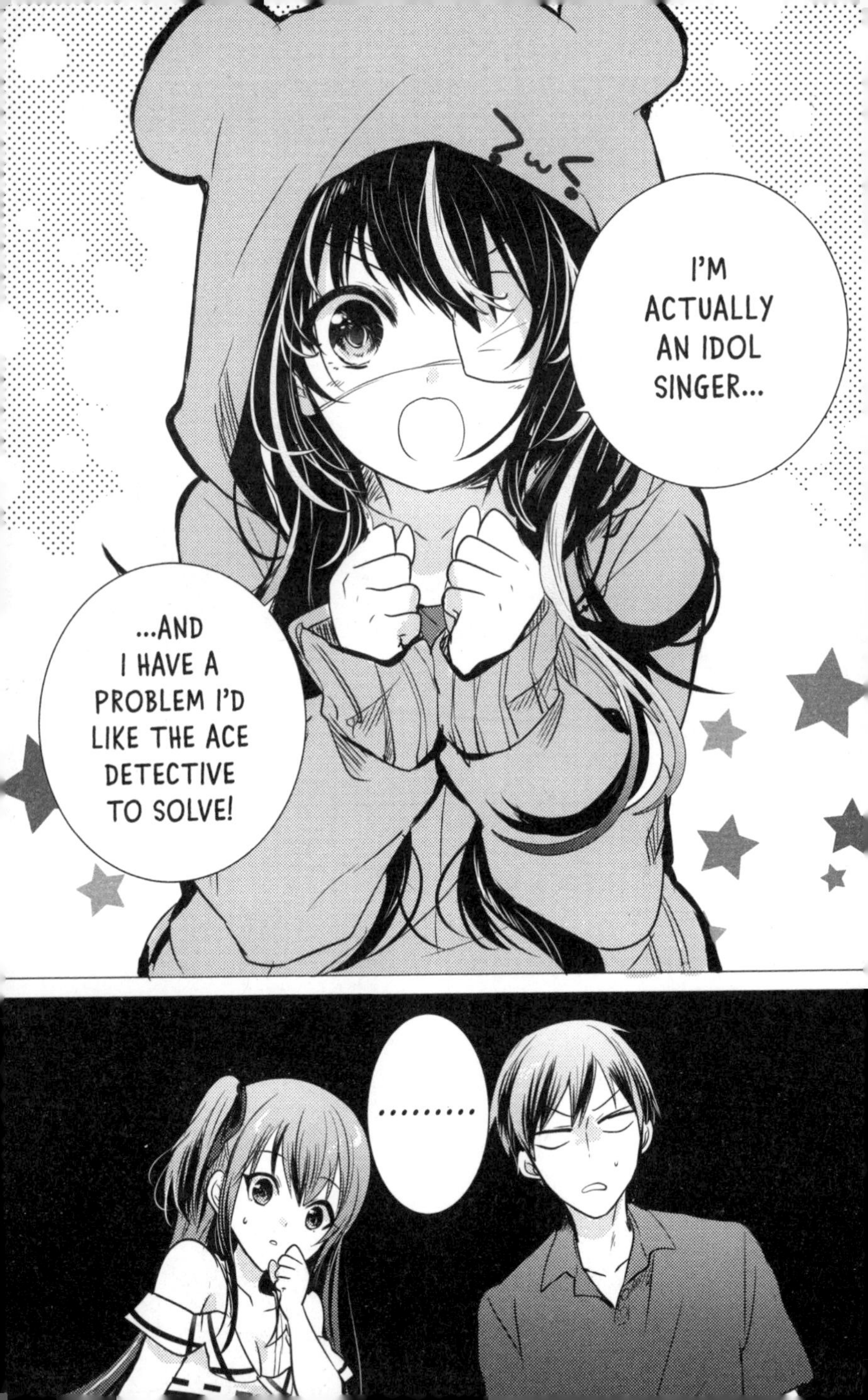
I'M ACTUALLY AN IDOL SINGER...
...AND I HAVE A PROBLEM I'D LIKE THE ACE DETECTIVE TO SOLVE!
....

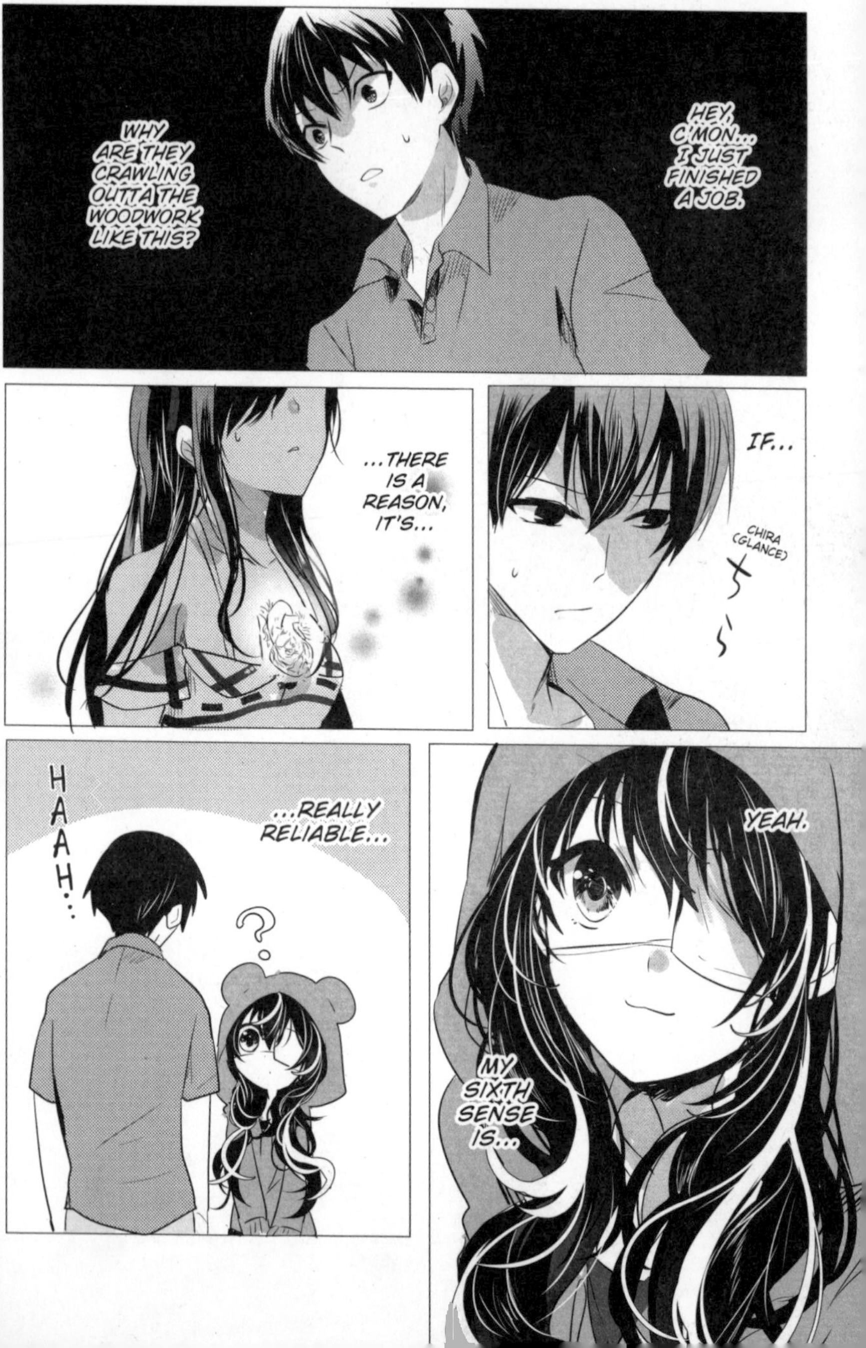
HEY, C'MON... I JUST FINISHED A JOB.
WHY ARE THEY CRAWLING OUTTA THE WOODWORK LIKE THIS?
IF...
CHIRA (GLANCE)
ちら
...THERE IS A REASON, IT'S...
YEAH.
MY SIXTH SENSE IS...
...REALLY RELIABLE...
HAAAH...

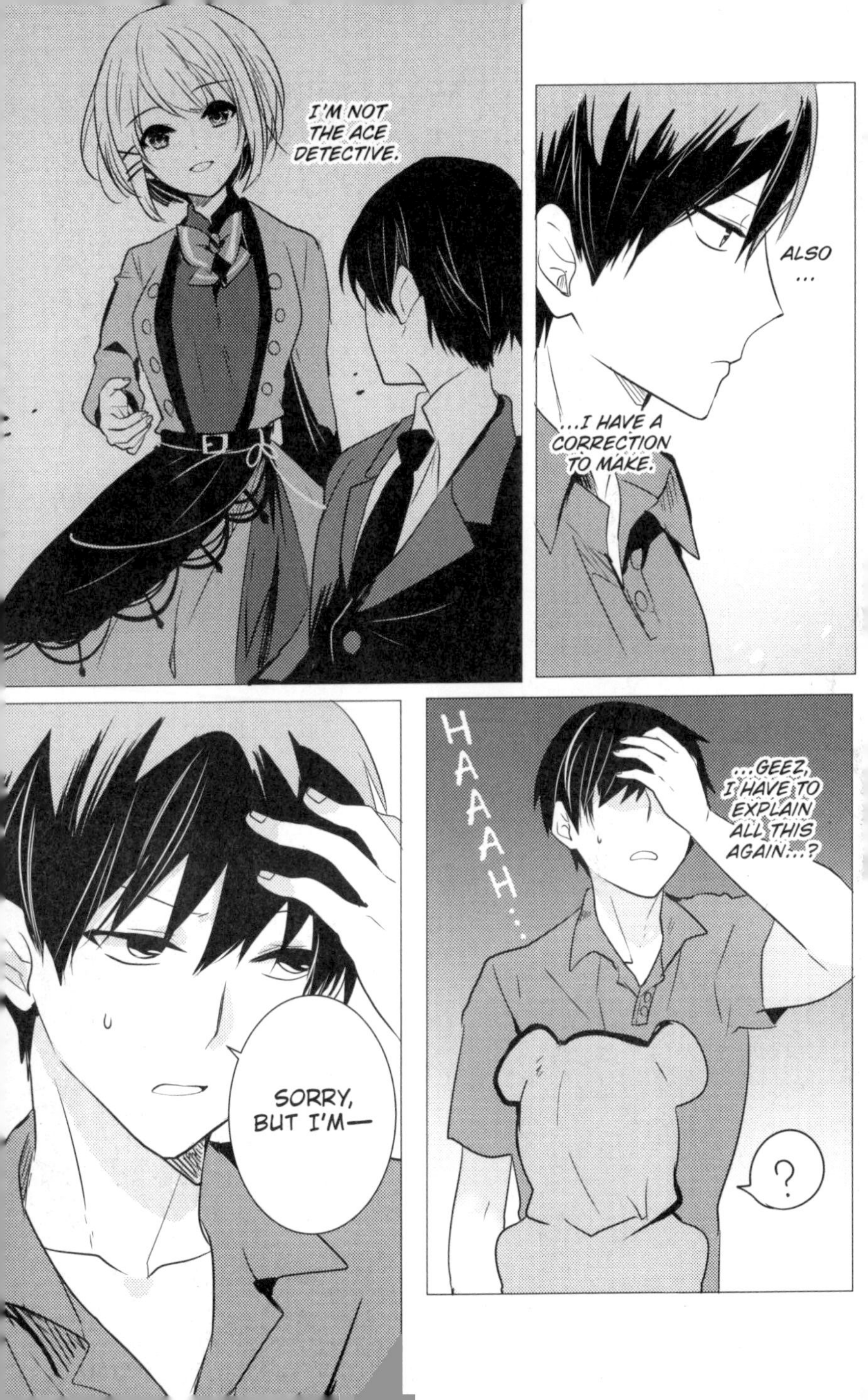
ALSO ...
...I HAVE A CORRECTION TO MAKE.
I'M NOT THE ACE DETECTIVE.
HAAAH...
...GEEZ, I HAVE TO EXPLAIN ALL THIS AGAIN...?
?
SORRY, BUT I'M—

YEAH, SORRY. THIS APATHETIC-LOOKING GUY...

...IS ONLY AN ASSISTANT.

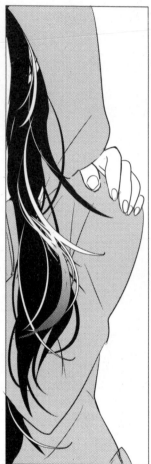

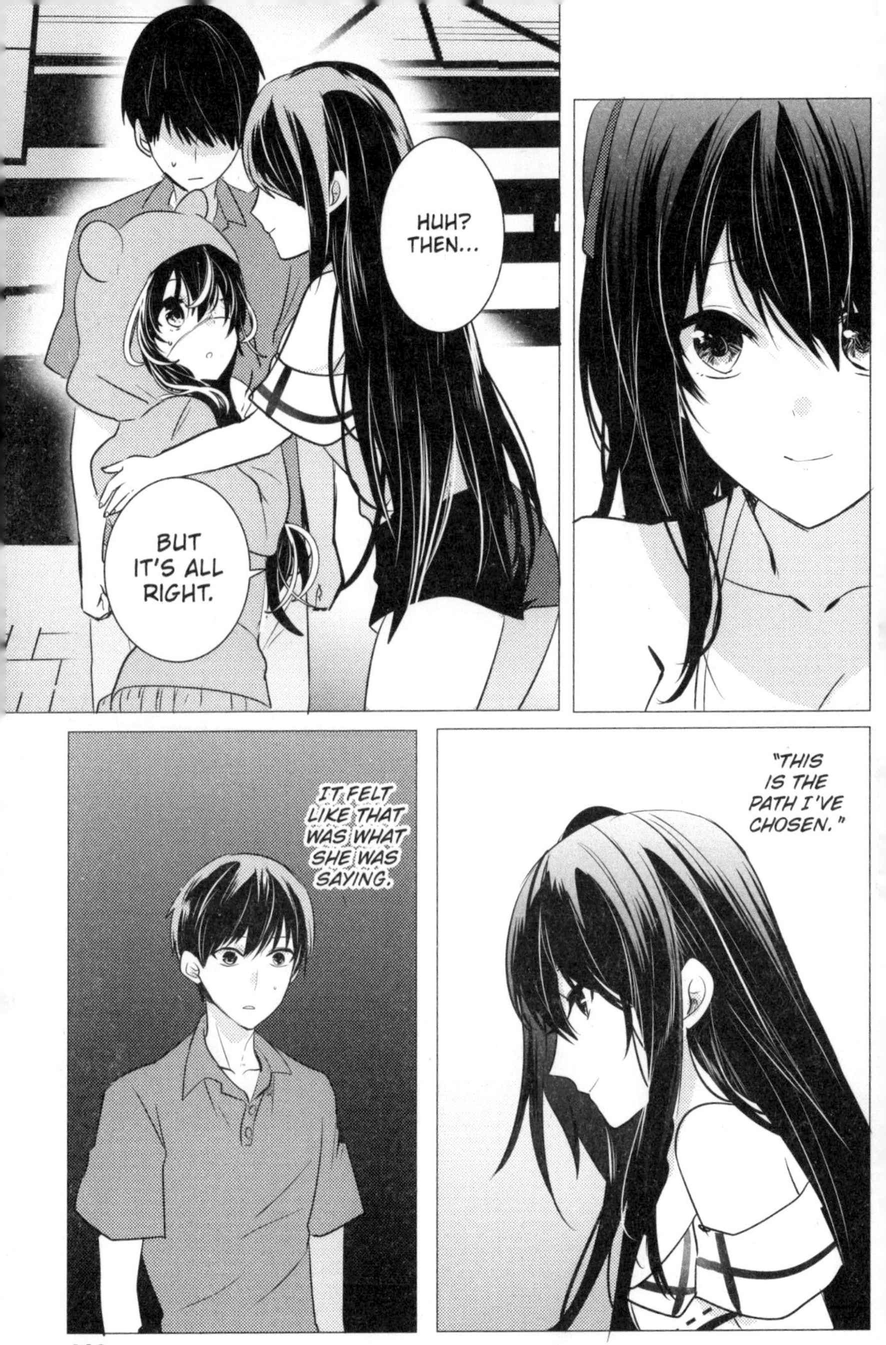
HUH? THEN...
BUT IT'S ALL RIGHT.
"THIS IS THE PATH I'VE CHOSEN."
IT FELT LIKE THAT WAS WHAT SHE WAS SAYING.

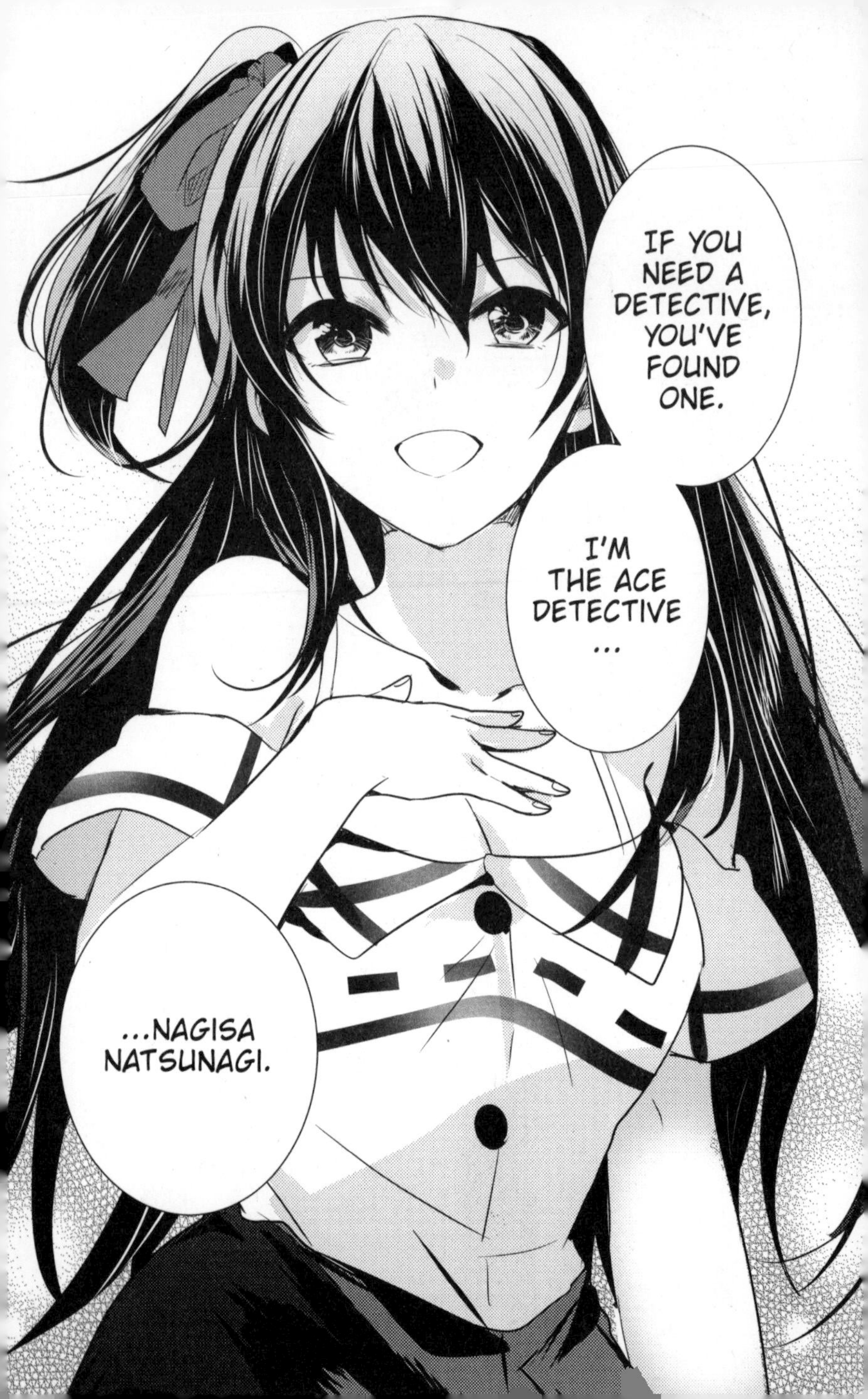
IF YOU NEED A DETECTIVE, YOU'VE FOUND ONE.
I'M THE ACE DETECTIVE ...
...NAGISA NATSUNAGI.

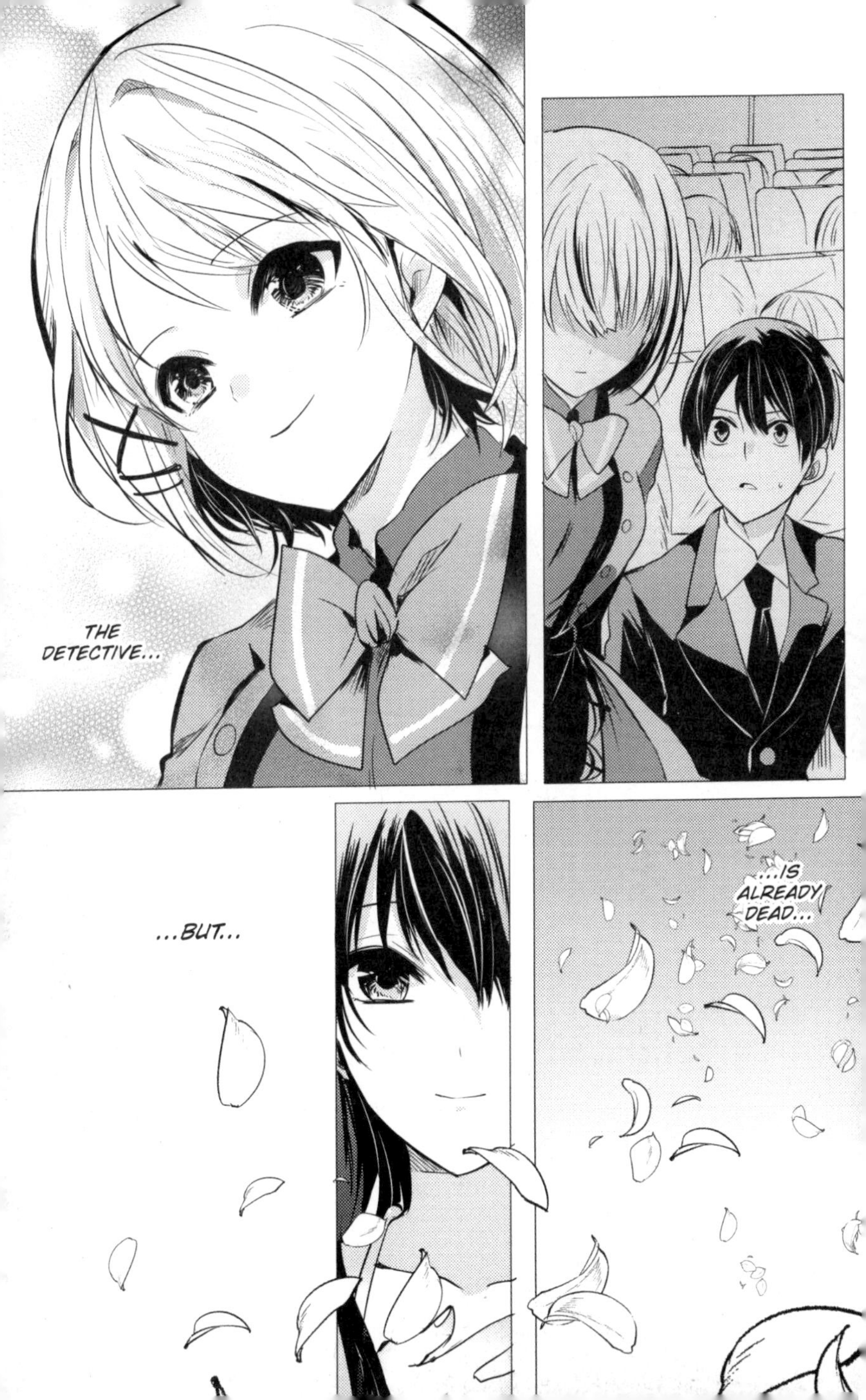
THE DETECTIVE...
...IS ALREADY DEAD...
...BUT...

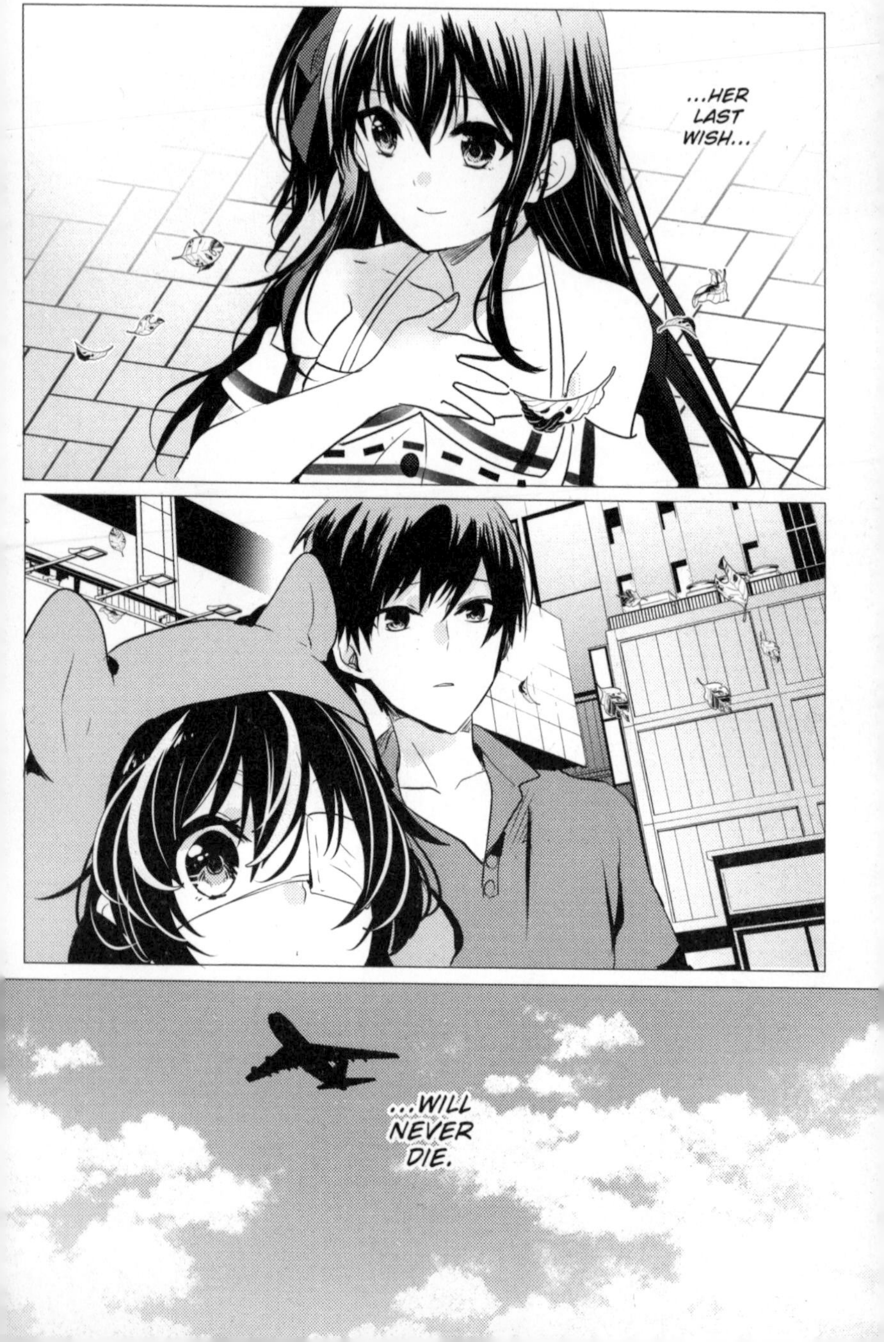
...HER LAST WISH...
...WILL NEVER DIE.

The Detective Is Already Dead

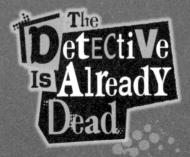

The Detective Is Already Dead

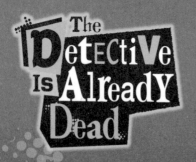

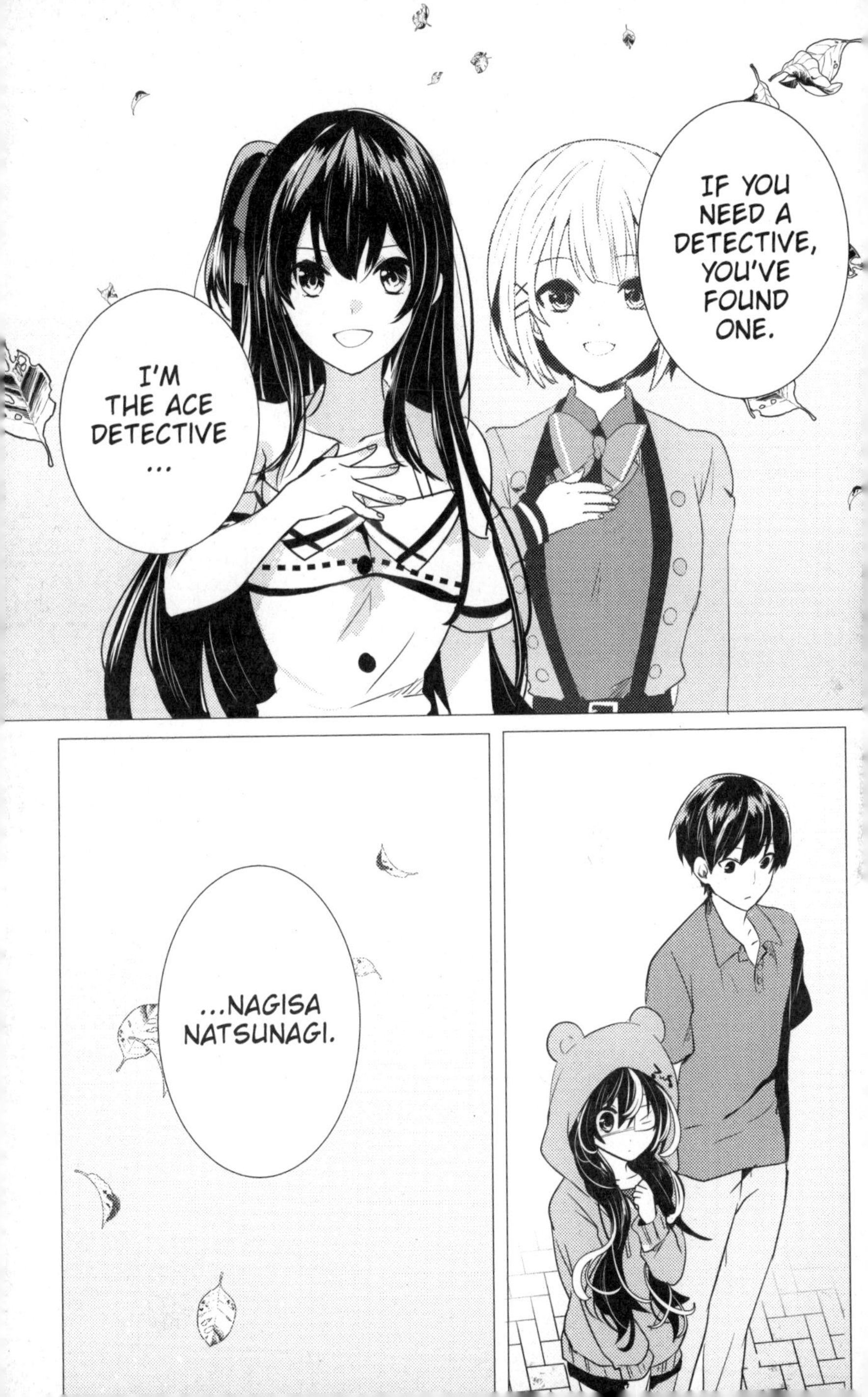
IF YOU NEED A DETECTIVE, YOU'VE FOUND ONE.
I'M THE ACE DETECTIVE ...
...NAGISA NATSUNAGI.

Episode. 10
A Simple Job: Protect a Three-Billion-Yen Family Treasure

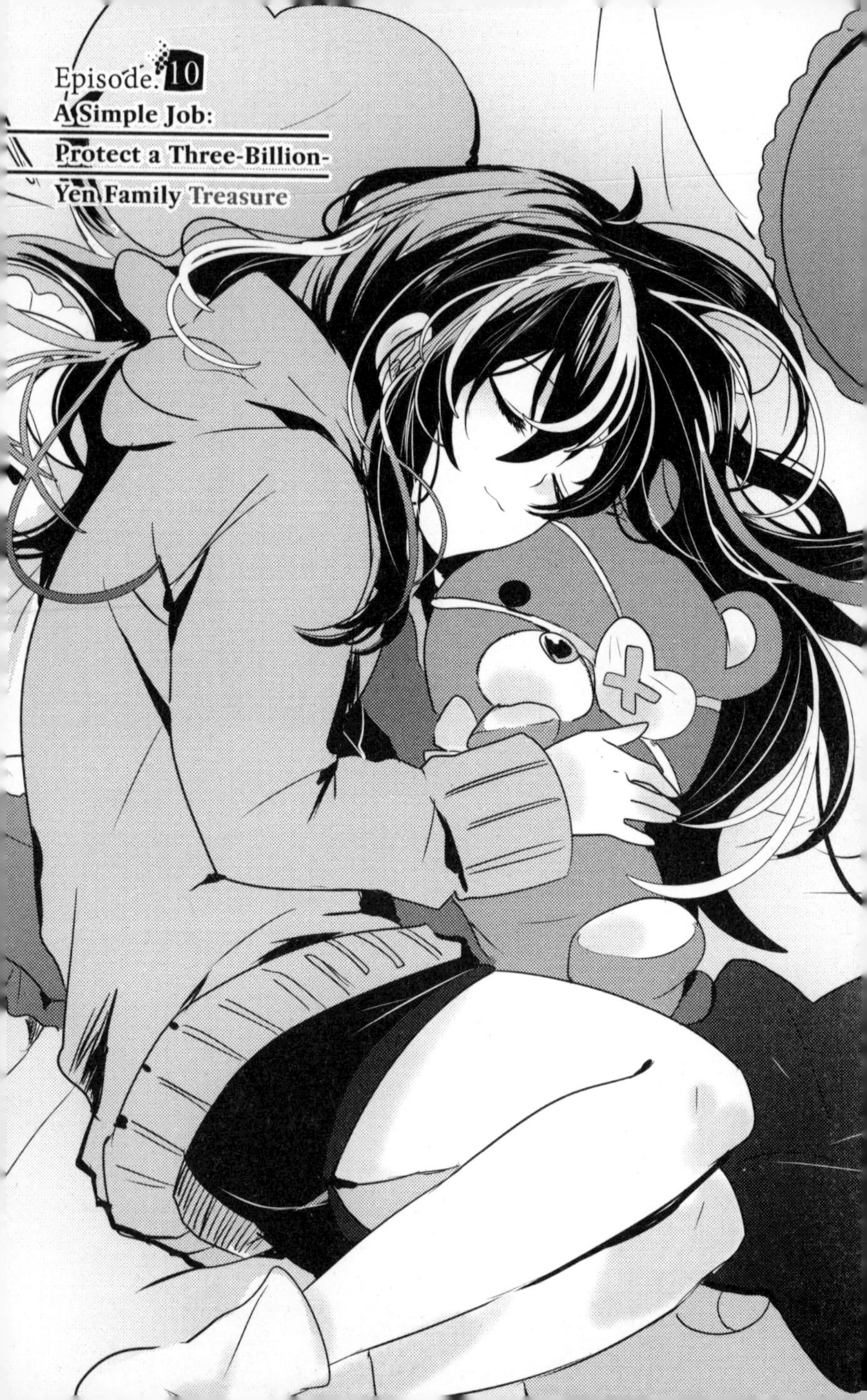

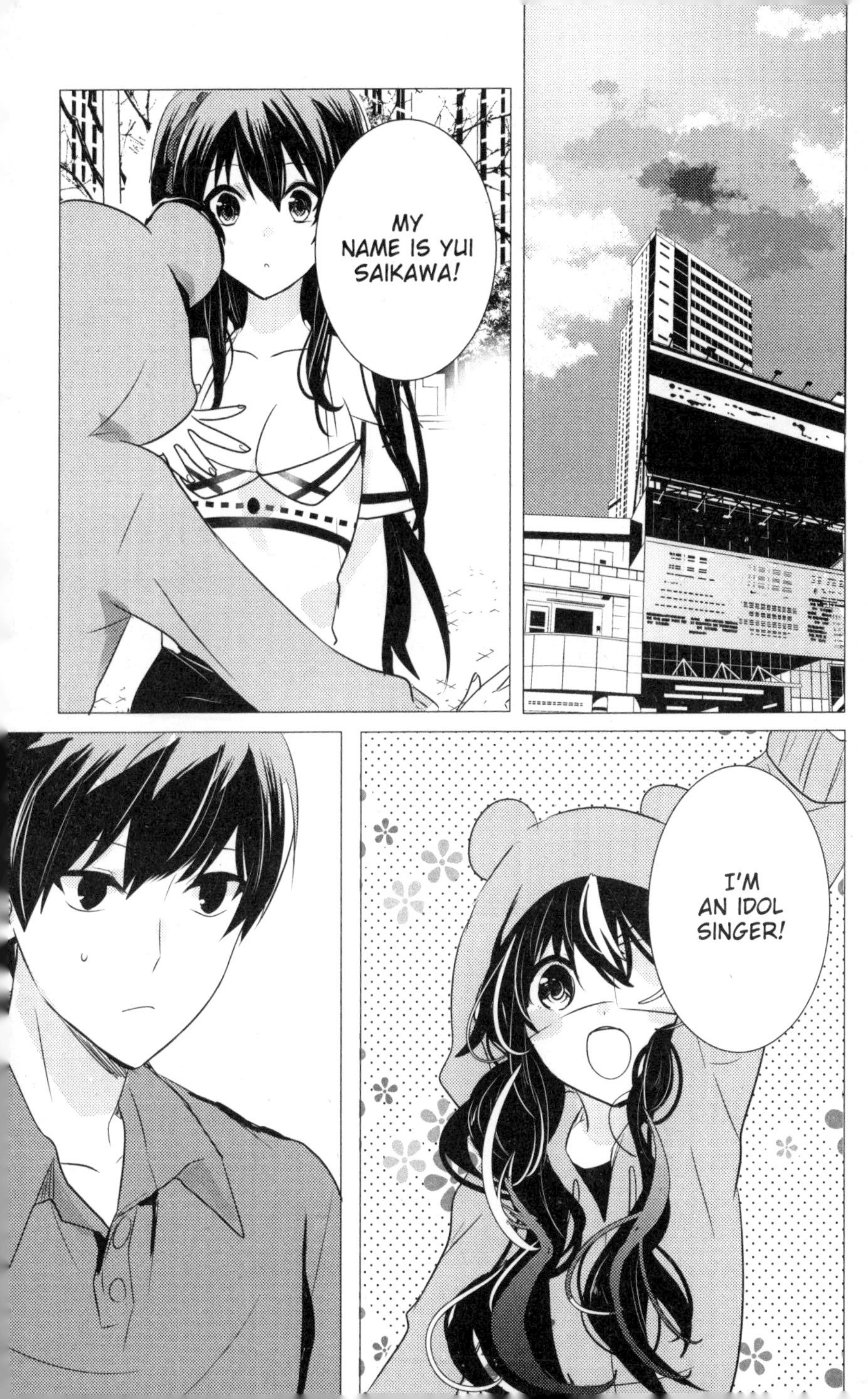
MY NAME IS YUI SAIKAWA!
I'M AN IDOL SINGER!

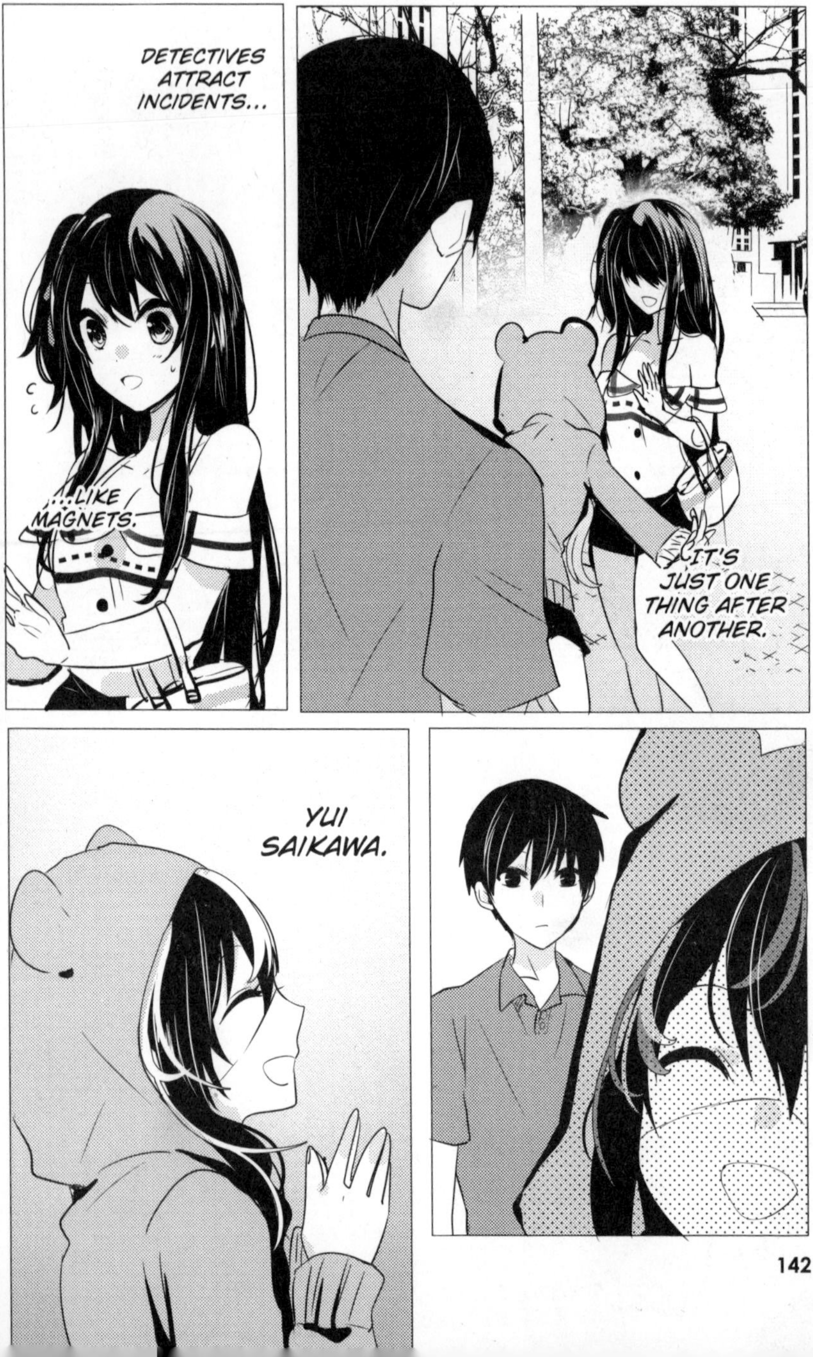
IT'S JUST ONE THING AFTER ANOTHER.
DETECTIVES ATTRACT INCIDENTS...
...LIKE MAGNETS.
YUI SAIKAWA.

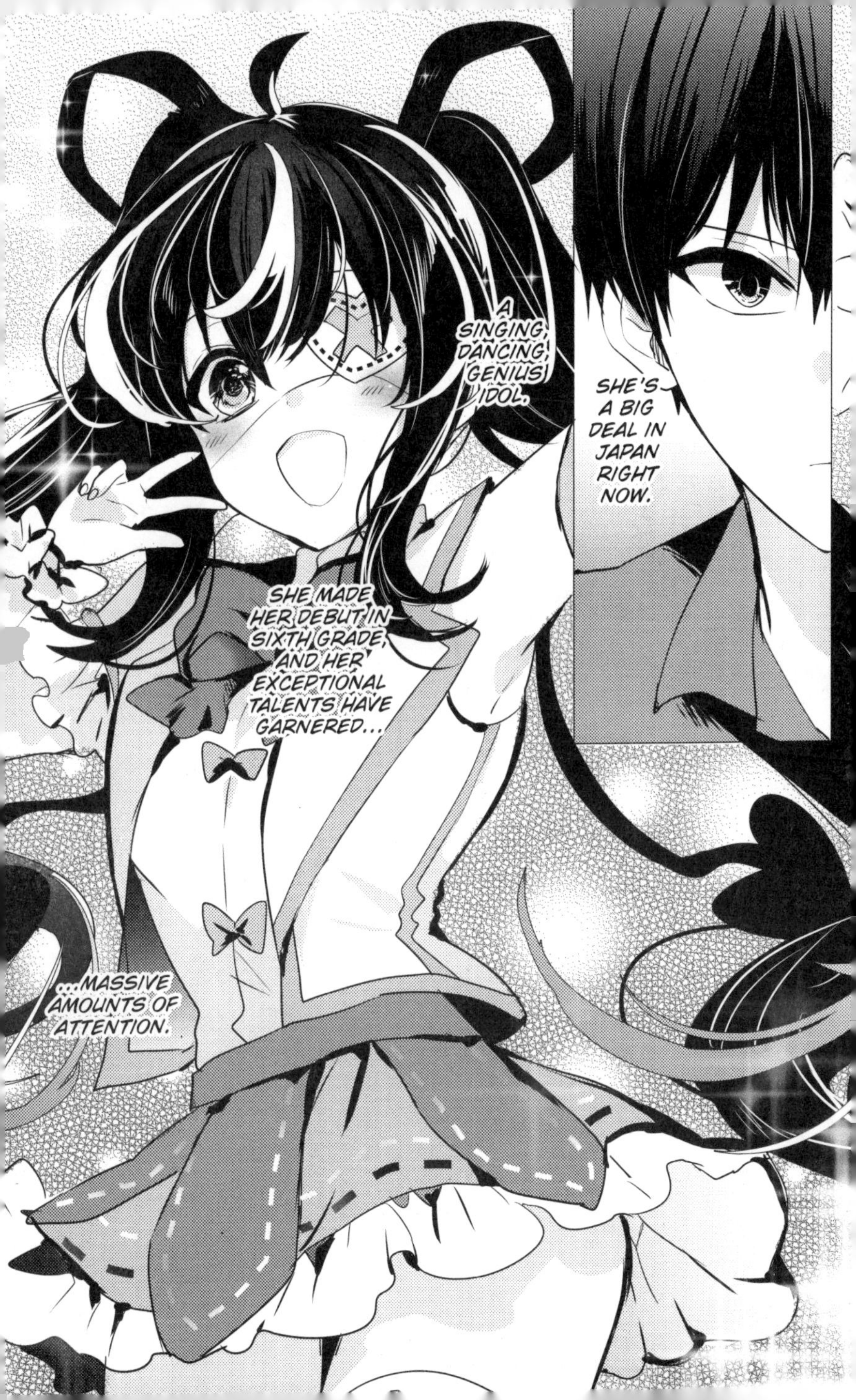
SHE'S A BIG DEAL IN JAPAN RIGHT NOW.
A SINGING, DANCING GENIUS IDOL.
SHE MADE HER DEBUT IN SIXTH GRADE, AND HER EXCEPTIONAL TALENTS HAVE GARNERED...
...MASSIVE AMOUNTS OF ATTENTION.

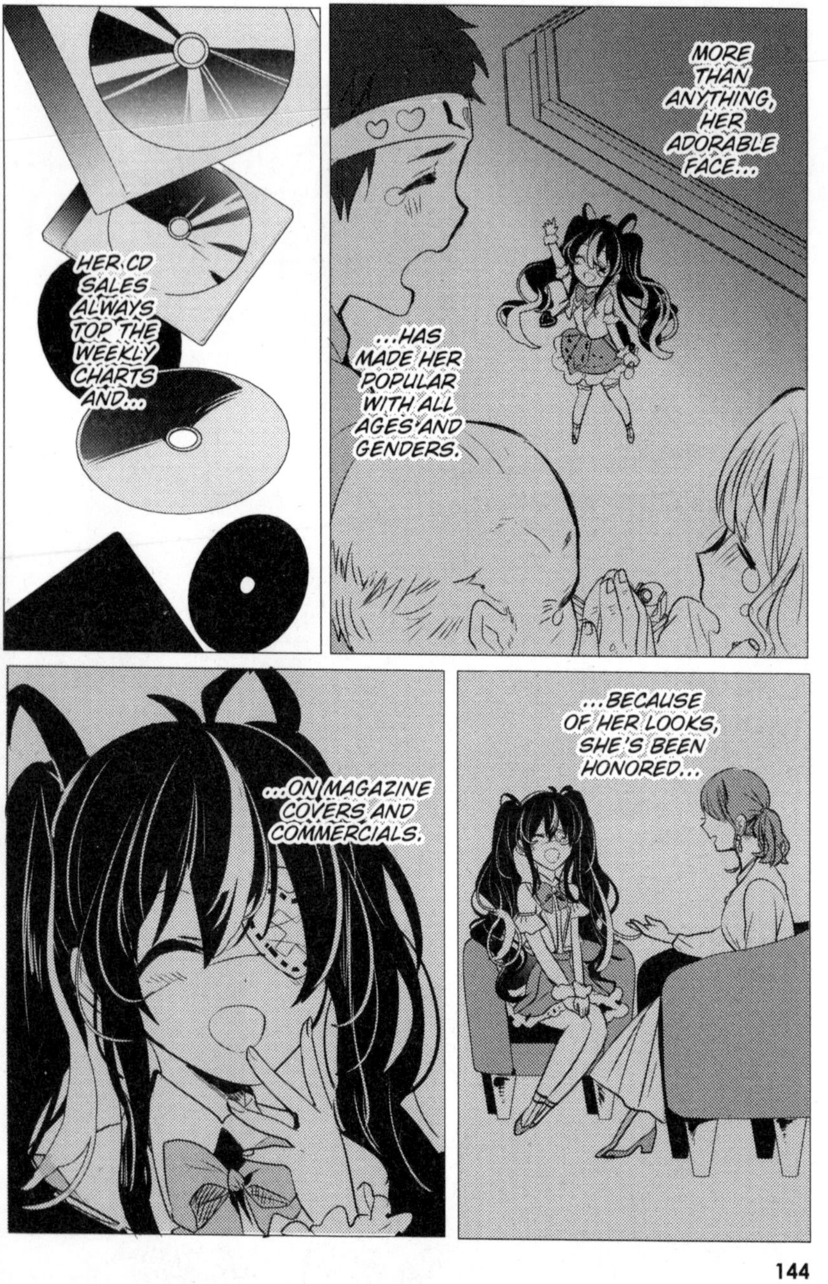
MORE THAN ANYTHING, HER ADORABLE FACE...
...HAS MADE HER POPULAR WITH ALL AGES AND GENDERS.
HER CD SALES ALWAYS TOP THE WEEKLY CHARTS AND...
...BECAUSE OF HER LOOKS, SHE'S BEEN HONORED...
...ON MAGAZINE COVERS AND COMMERCIALS.

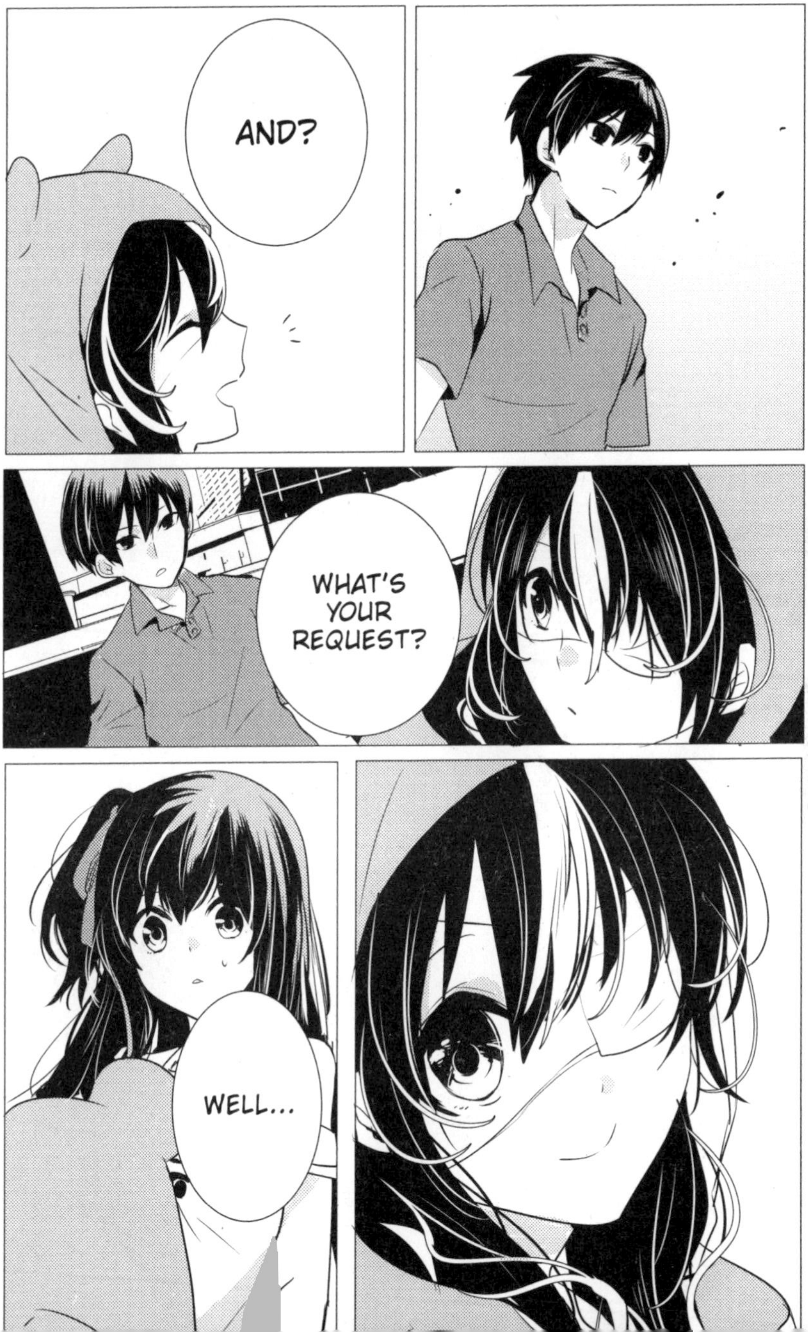
AND?
WHAT'S YOUR REQUEST?
WELL...

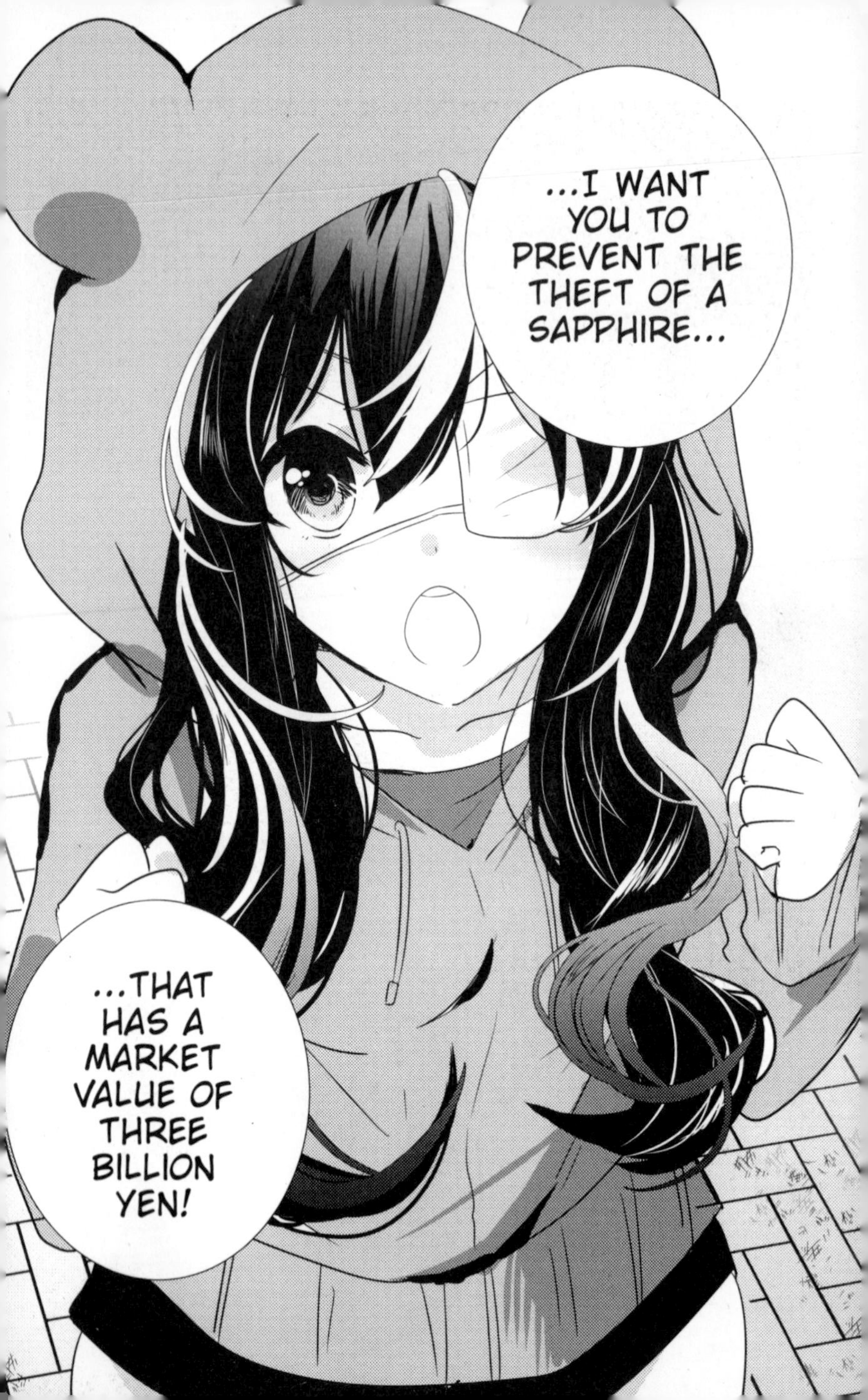
...I WANT YOU TO PREVENT THE THEFT OF A SAPPHIRE...
...THAT HAS A MARKET VALUE OF THREE BILLION YEN!

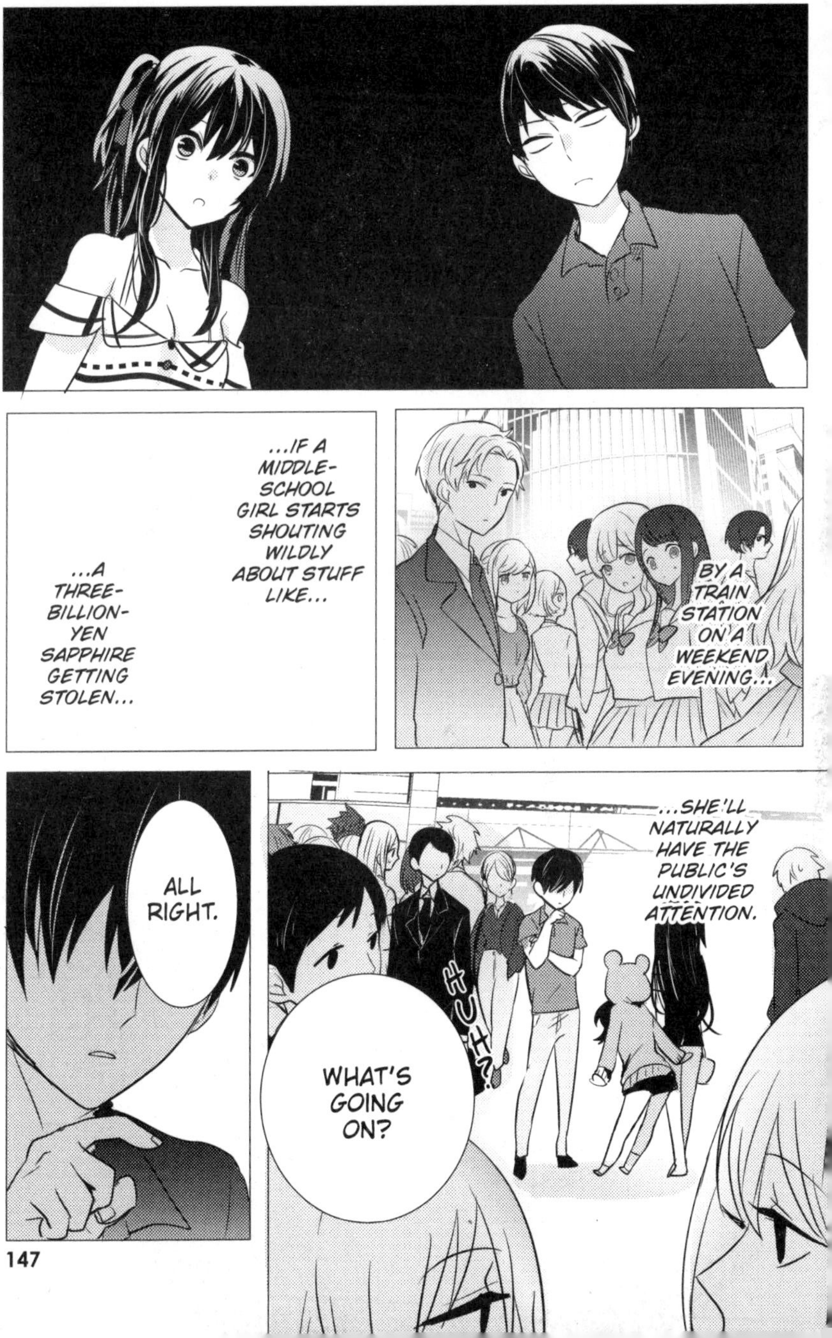
BY A TRAIN STATION ON A WEEKEND EVENING...
...IF A MIDDLE-SCHOOL GIRL STARTS SHOUTING WILDLY ABOUT STUFF LIKE...
...A THREE-BILLION-YEN SAPPHIRE GETTING STOLEN...
...SHE'LL NATURALLY HAVE THE PUBLIC'S UNDIVIDED ATTENTION.
HUH?
WHAT'S GOING ON?
ALL RIGHT.

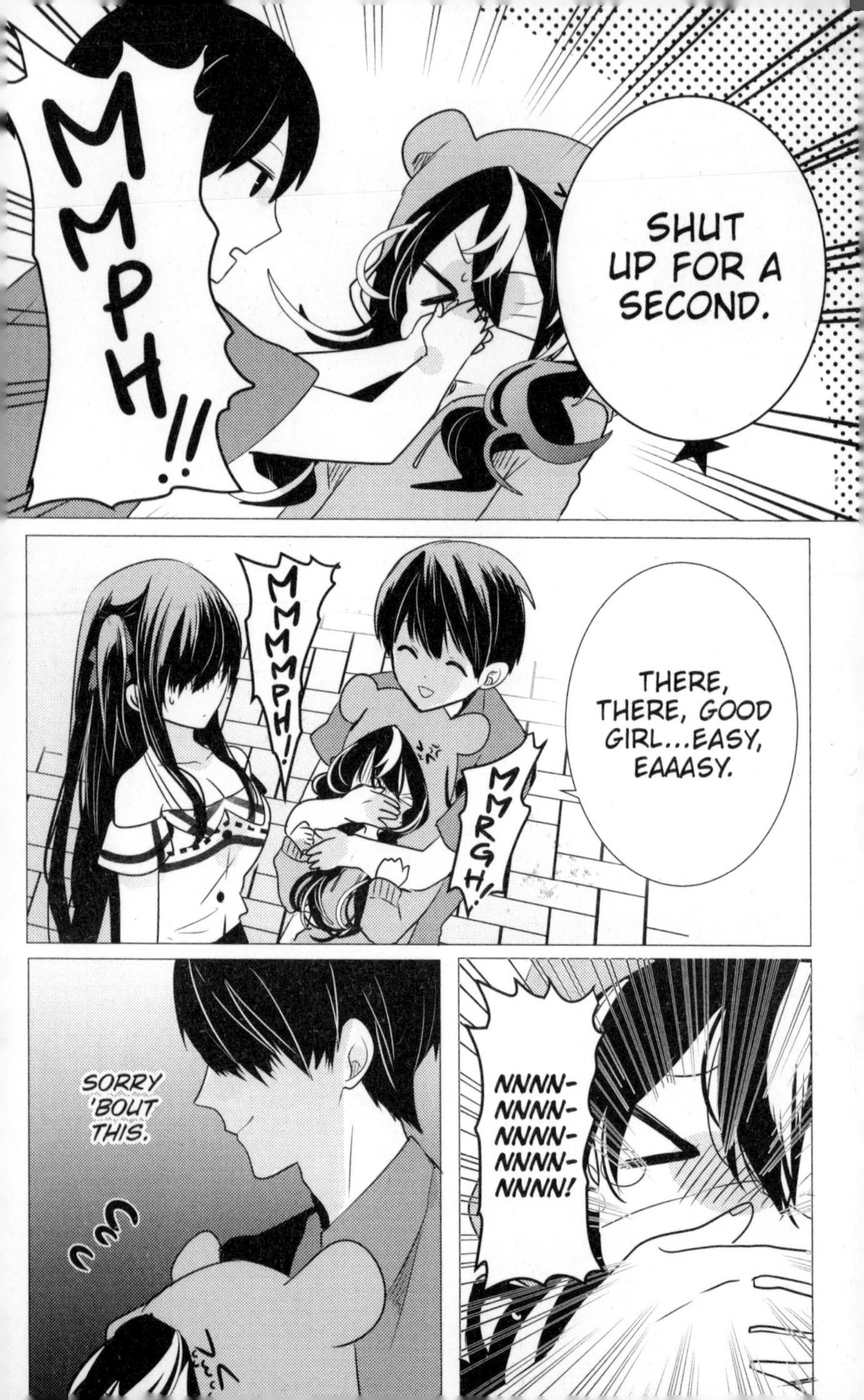
SHUT UP FOR A SECOND.
MMMPH!!
THERE, THERE, GOOD GIRL...EASY, EAAASY.
MMMMPH!
MMRGH!
NNNN-NNNN-NNNN-NNNN-NNNN!
SORRY 'BOUT THIS.

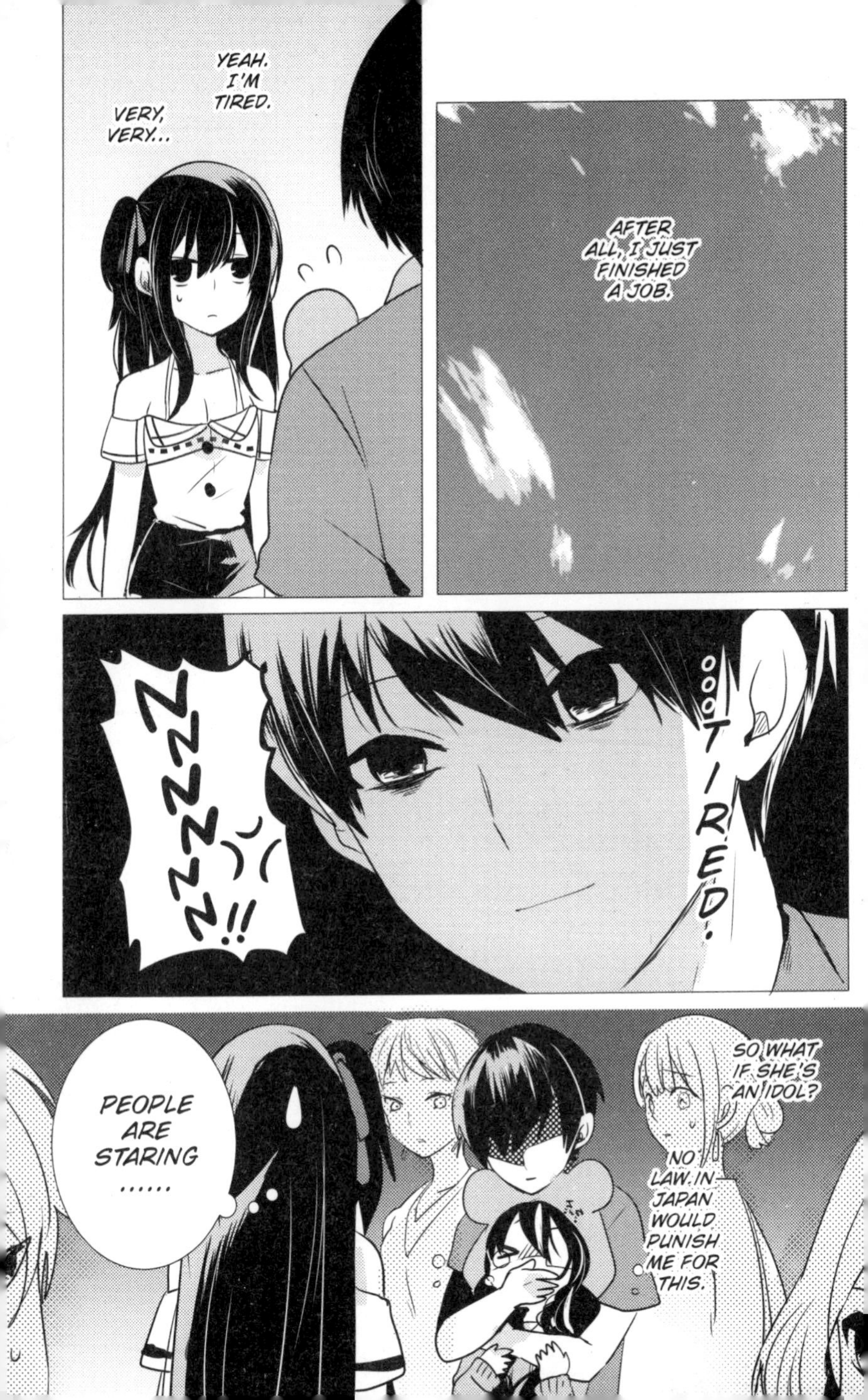
AFTER ALL, I JUST FINISHED A JOB.
YEAH. I'M TIRED.
VERY, VERY...
OOOTIRED.
NNNNNNN!!
SO WHAT IF SHE'S AN IDOL?
NO LAW IN JAPAN WOULD PUNISH ME FOR THIS.
PEOPLE ARE STARING......

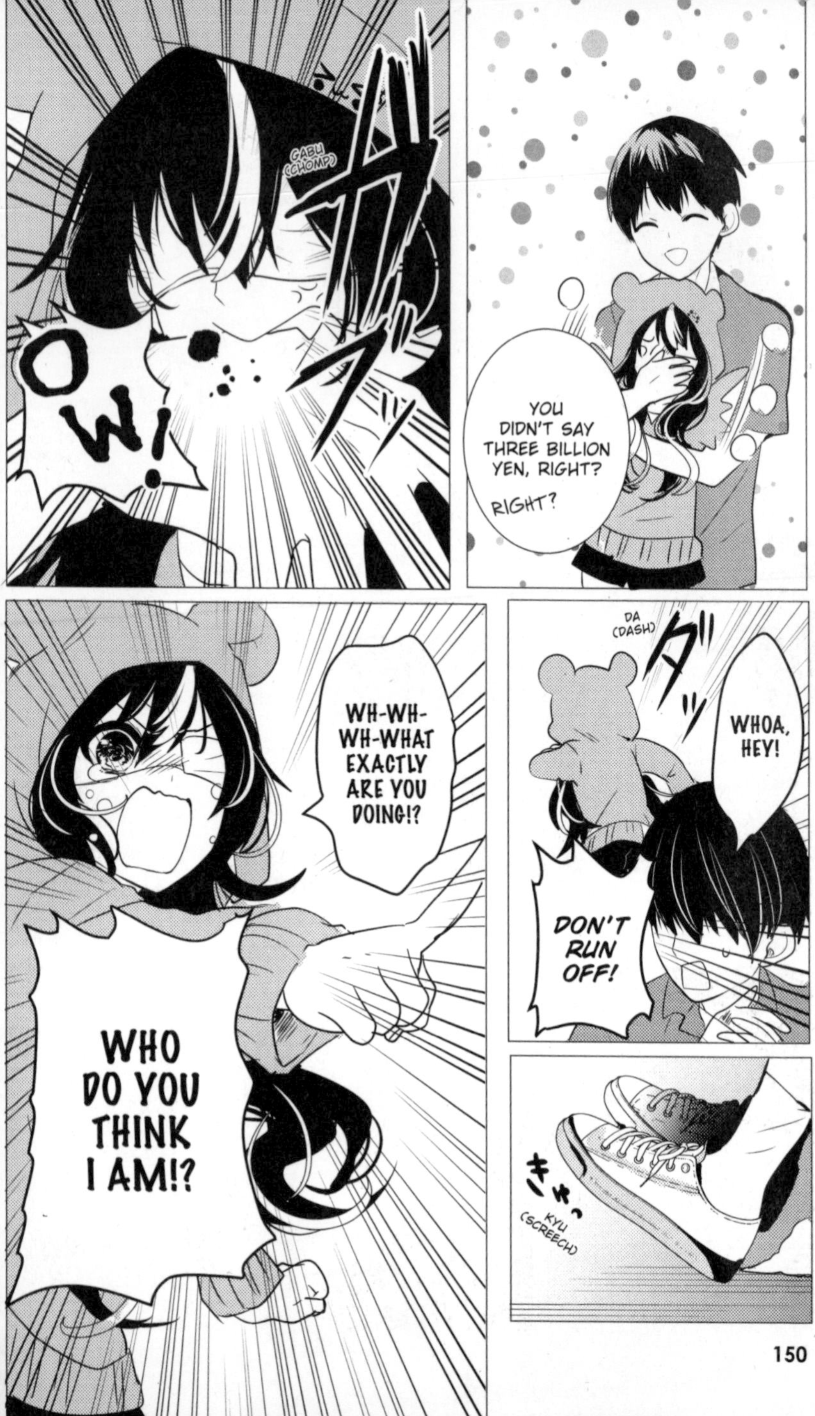
YOU DIDN'T SAY THREE BILLION YEN, RIGHT?
RIGHT?
GABU (CHOMP)
OW!
DA (DASH)
WHOA, HEY!
DON'T RUN OFF!
KYU (SCREECH)
WH-WH-WH-WHAT EXACTLY ARE YOU DOING!?
WHO DO YOU THINK I AM!?

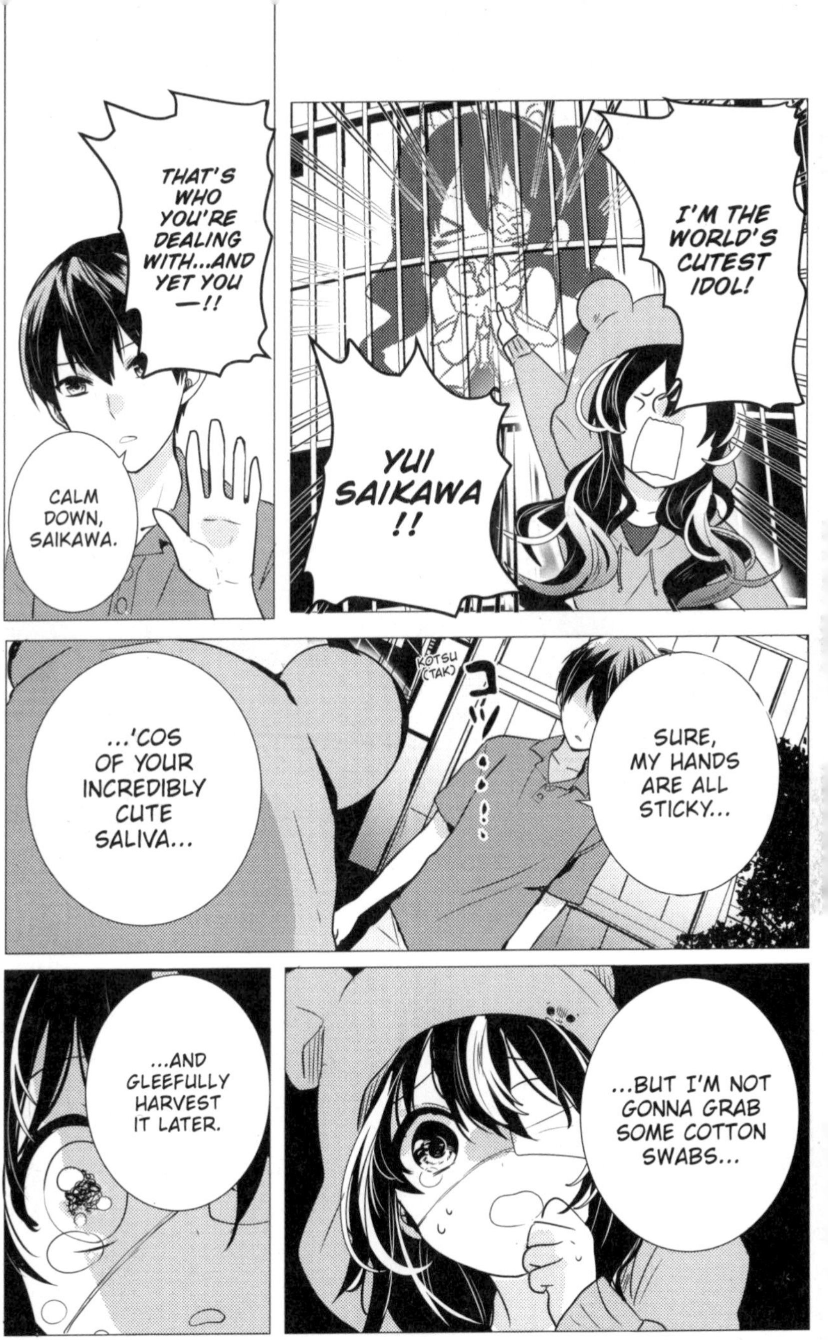
I'M THE WORLD'S CUTEST IDOL!
YUI SAIKAWA!!
THAT'S WHO YOU'RE DEALING WITH...AND YET YOU—!!
CALM DOWN, SAIKAWA.
SURE, MY HANDS ARE ALL STICKY...
KOTSU (TAK)
...'COS OF YOUR INCREDIBLY CUTE SALIVA...
...BUT I'M NOT GONNA GRAB SOME COTTON SWABS...
...AND GLEEFULLY HARVEST IT LATER.

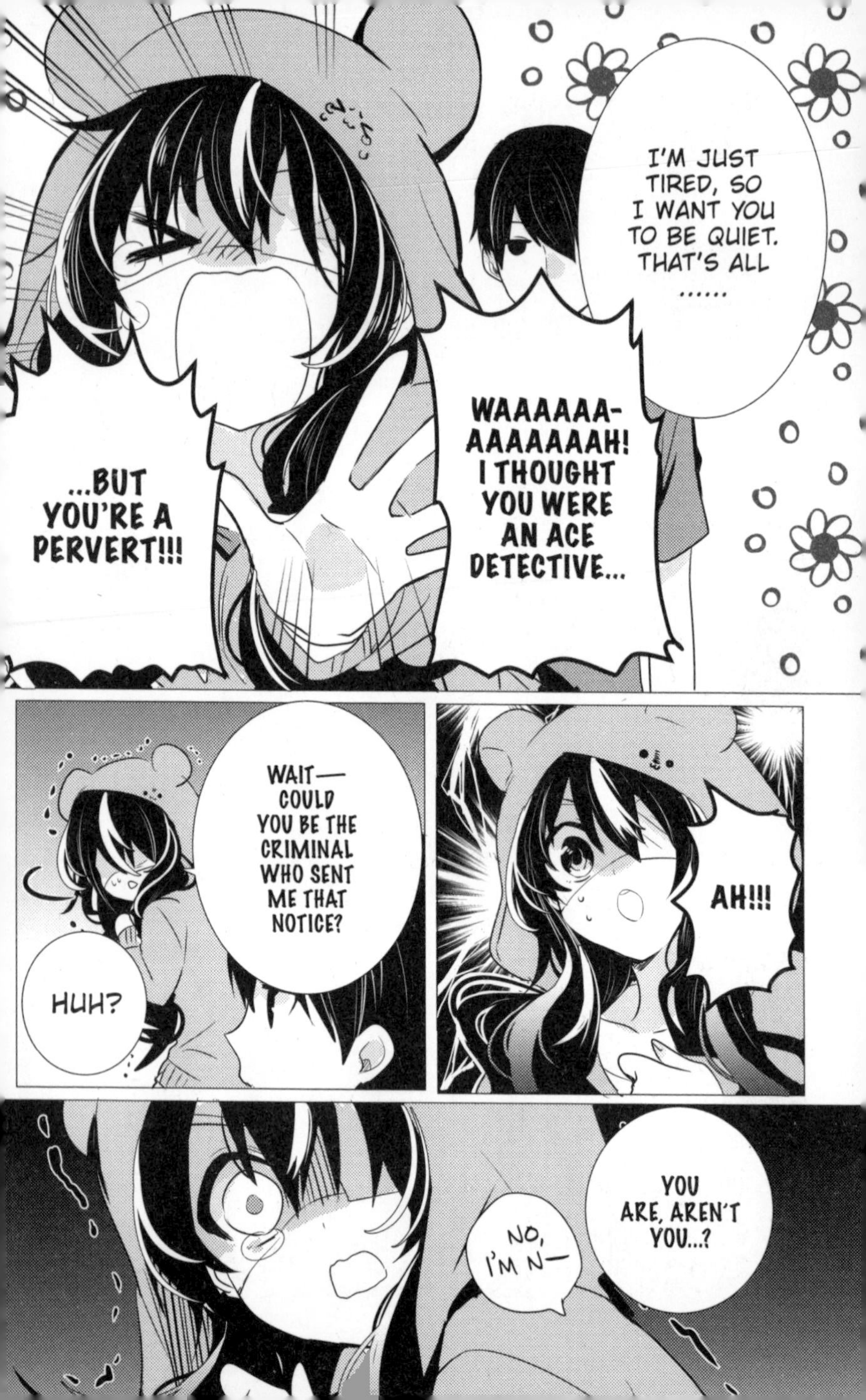
I'M JUST TIRED, SO I WANT YOU TO BE QUIET. THAT'S ALL ......
WAAAAAA-AAAAAAAH! I THOUGHT YOU WERE AN ACE DETECTIVE...
...BUT YOU'RE A PERVERT!!!
AH!!!
WAIT— COULD YOU BE THE CRIMINAL WHO SENT ME THAT NOTICE?
HUH?
YOU ARE, AREN'T YOU...?
NO, I'M N—

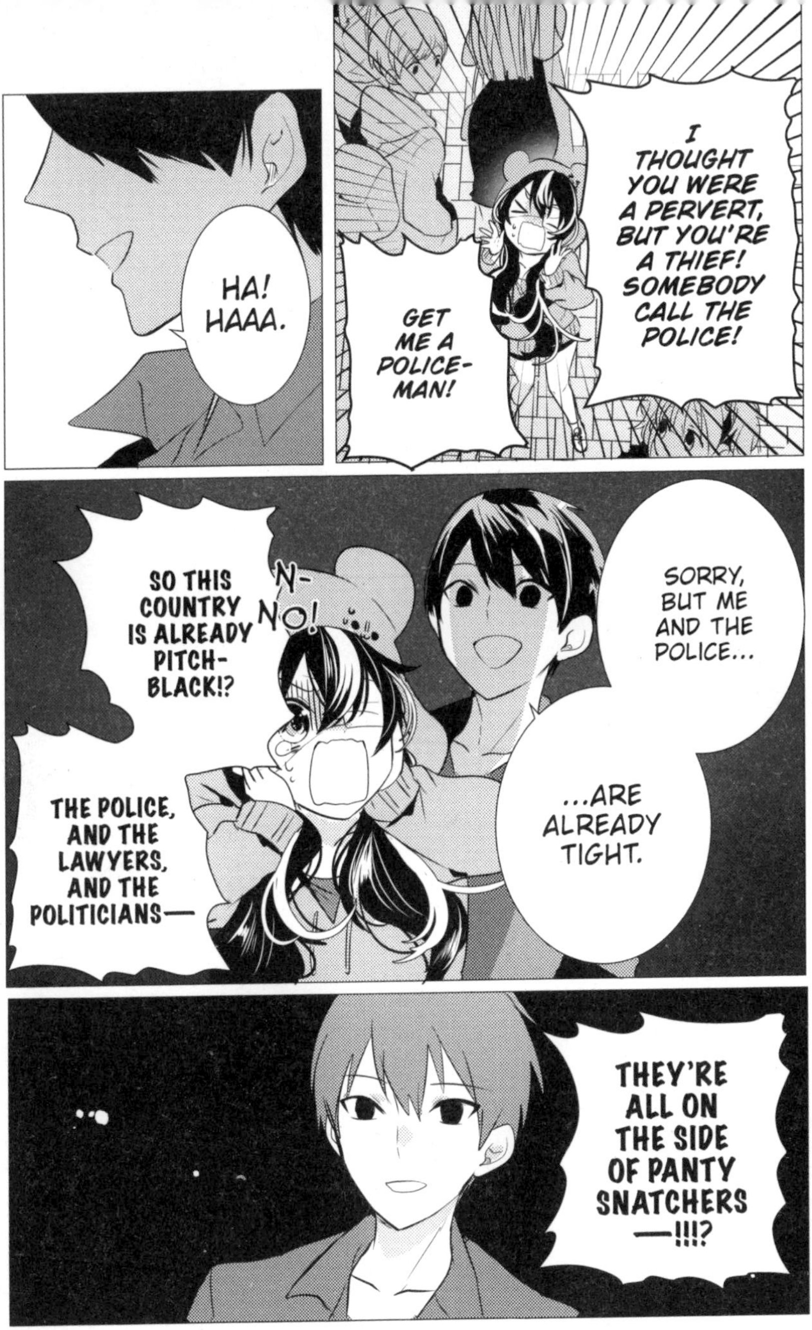
I THOUGHT YOU WERE A PERVERT, BUT YOU'RE A THIEF! SOMEBODY CALL THE POLICE!
GET ME A POLICE-MAN!
HA! HAAA.
SORRY, BUT ME AND THE POLICE...
...ARE ALREADY TIGHT.
N-NO!
SO THIS COUNTRY IS ALREADY PITCH-BLACK!?
THE POLICE, AND THE LAWYERS, AND THE POLITICIANS—
THEY'RE ALL ON THE SIDE OF PANTY SNATCHERS—!!!?

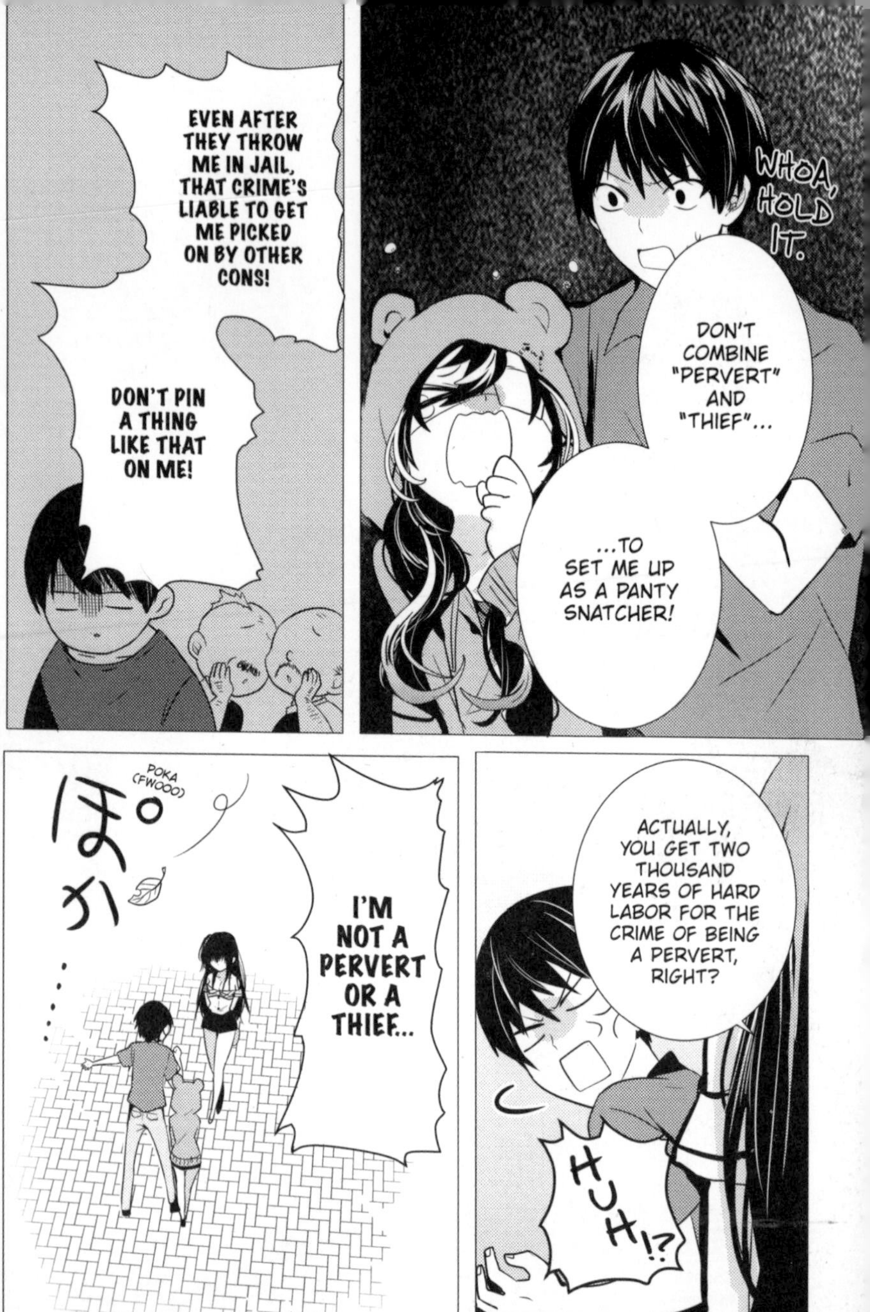
WHOA, HOLD IT.
DON'T COMBINE "PERVERT" AND "THIEF"...
...TO SET ME UP AS A PANTY SNATCHER!
EVEN AFTER THEY THROW ME IN JAIL, THAT CRIME'S LIABLE TO GET ME PICKED ON BY OTHER CONS!
DON'T PIN A THING LIKE THAT ON ME!
ACTUALLY, YOU GET TWO THOUSAND YEARS OF HARD LABOR FOR THE CRIME OF BEING A PERVERT, RIGHT?
HUH!?
I'M NOT A PERVERT OR A THIEF...
POKA (FWOOO)
ぽか
...

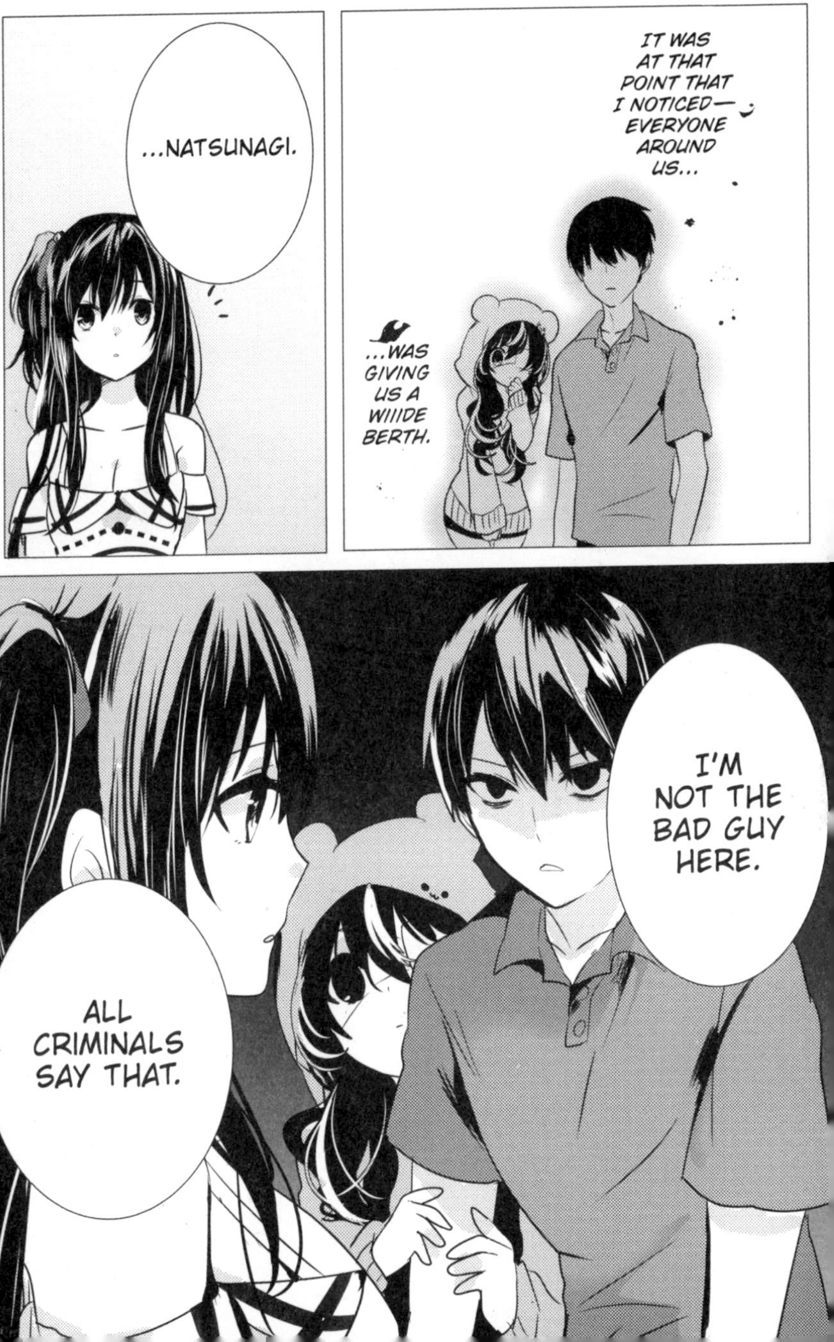
IT WAS AT THAT POINT THAT I NOTICED— EVERYONE AROUND US...
...WAS GIVING US A WIIIDE BERTH.
...NATSUNAGI.
I'M NOT THE BAD GUY HERE.
ALL CRIMINALS SAY THAT.

HEM, AHEM!

THE NEXT DAY

THAT'S FINE...

...BUT, UM...

I APOLOGIZE FOR LOSING MY COMPOSURE YESTERDAY!

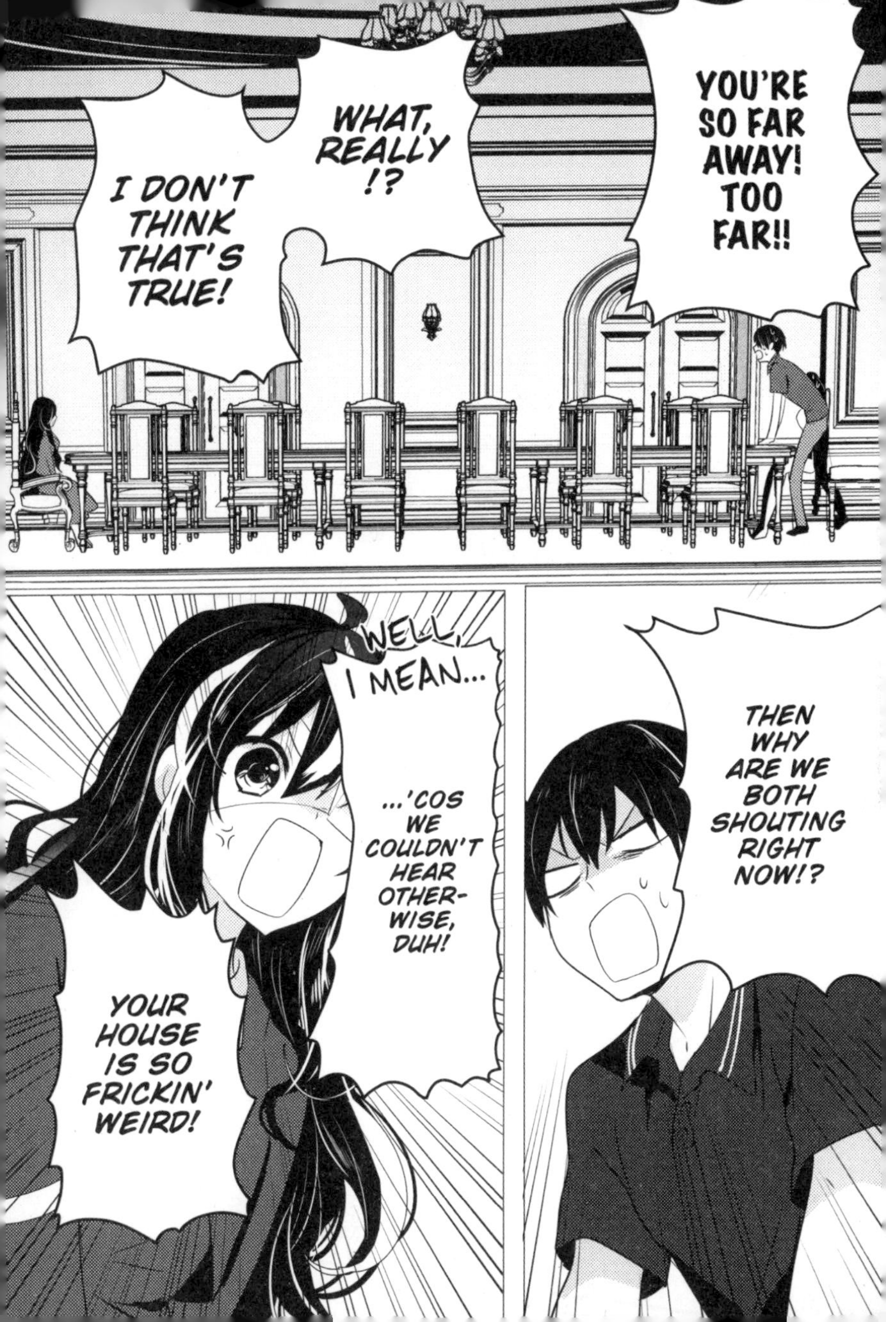
YOU'RE SO FAR AWAY! TOO FAR!!
WHAT, REALLY !?
I DON'T THINK THAT'S TRUE!
THEN WHY ARE WE BOTH SHOUTING RIGHT NOW!?
WELL, I MEAN...
...'COS WE COULDN'T HEAR OTHER-WISE, DUH!
YOUR HOUSE IS SO FRICKIN' WEIRD!

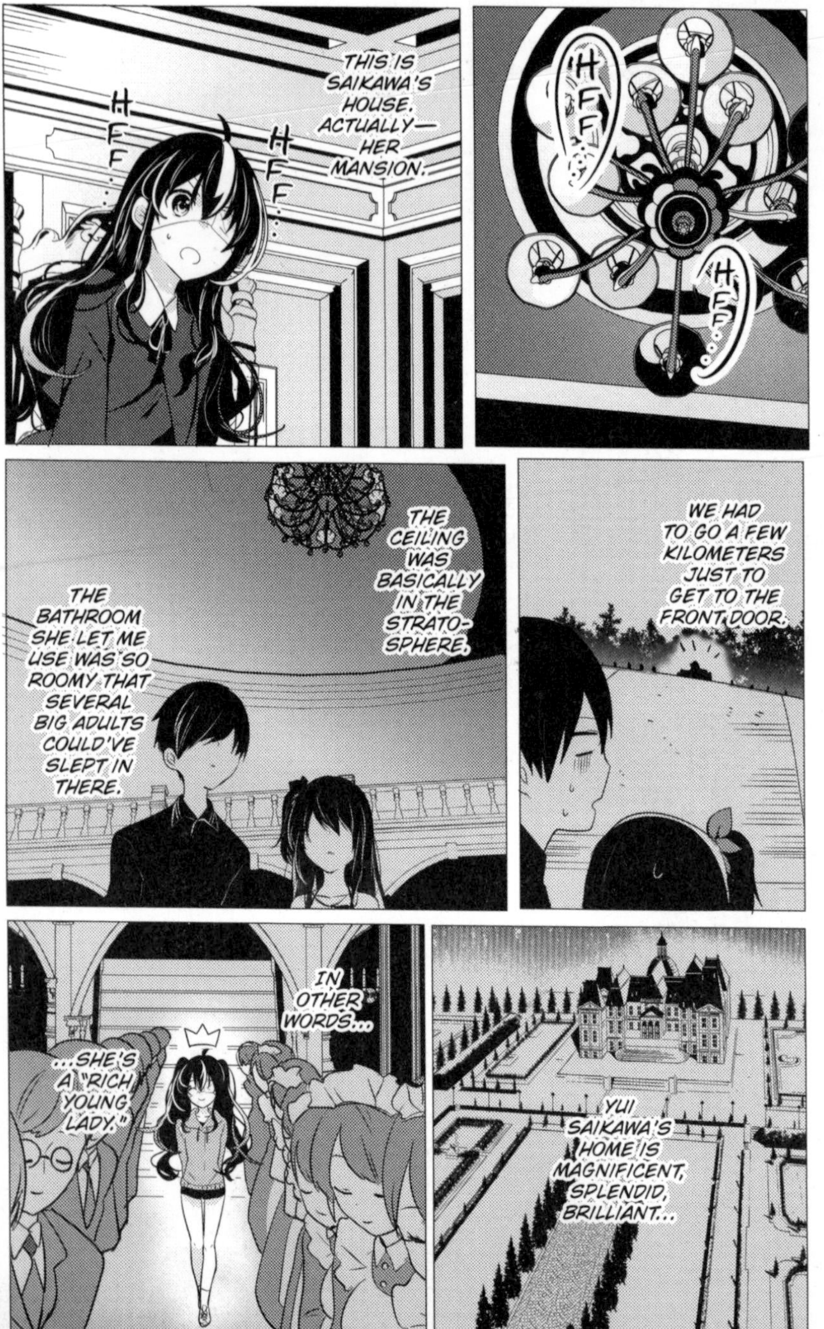
HFF...
HFF...
THIS IS SAIKAWA'S HOUSE. ACTUALLY—HER MANSION.
HFF...
HFF...
WE HAD TO GO A FEW KILOMETERS JUST TO GET TO THE FRONT DOOR.
THE CEILING WAS BASICALLY IN THE STRATOSPHERE.
THE BATHROOM SHE LET ME USE WAS SO ROOMY THAT SEVERAL BIG ADULTS COULD'VE SLEPT IN THERE.
YUI SAIKAWA'S HOME IS MAGNIFICENT, SPLENDID, BRILLIANT...
IN OTHER WORDS...
...SHE'S A "RICH YOUNG LADY."

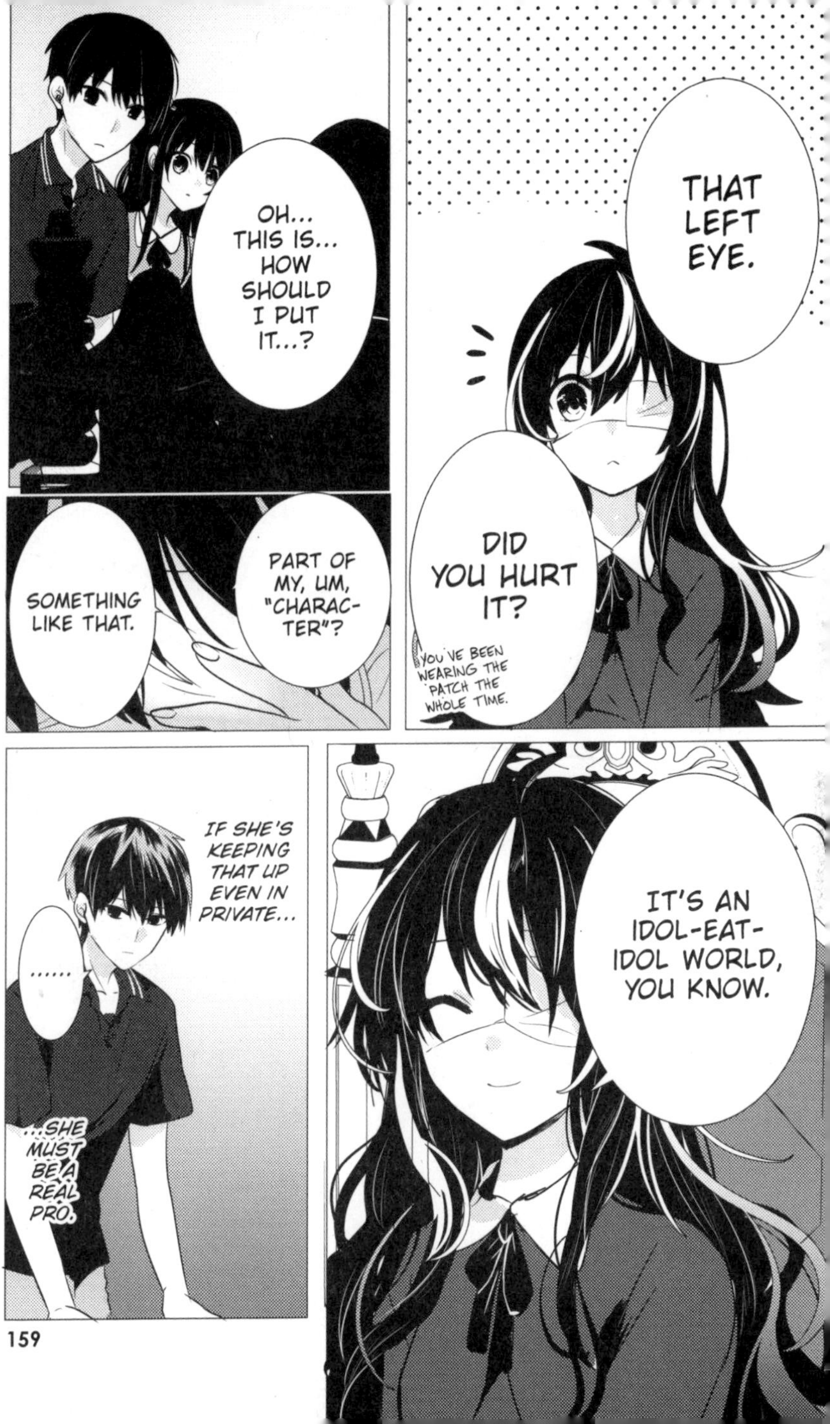
THAT LEFT EYE.
DID YOU HURT IT?
YOU'VE BEEN WEARING THE PATCH THE WHOLE TIME.
OH... THIS IS... HOW SHOULD I PUT IT...?
PART OF MY, UM, "CHARAC-TER"?
SOMETHING LIKE THAT.
IT'S AN IDOL-EAT-IDOL WORLD, YOU KNOW.
IF SHE'S KEEPING THAT UP EVEN IN PRIVATE...
......
...SHE MUST BE A REAL PRO.

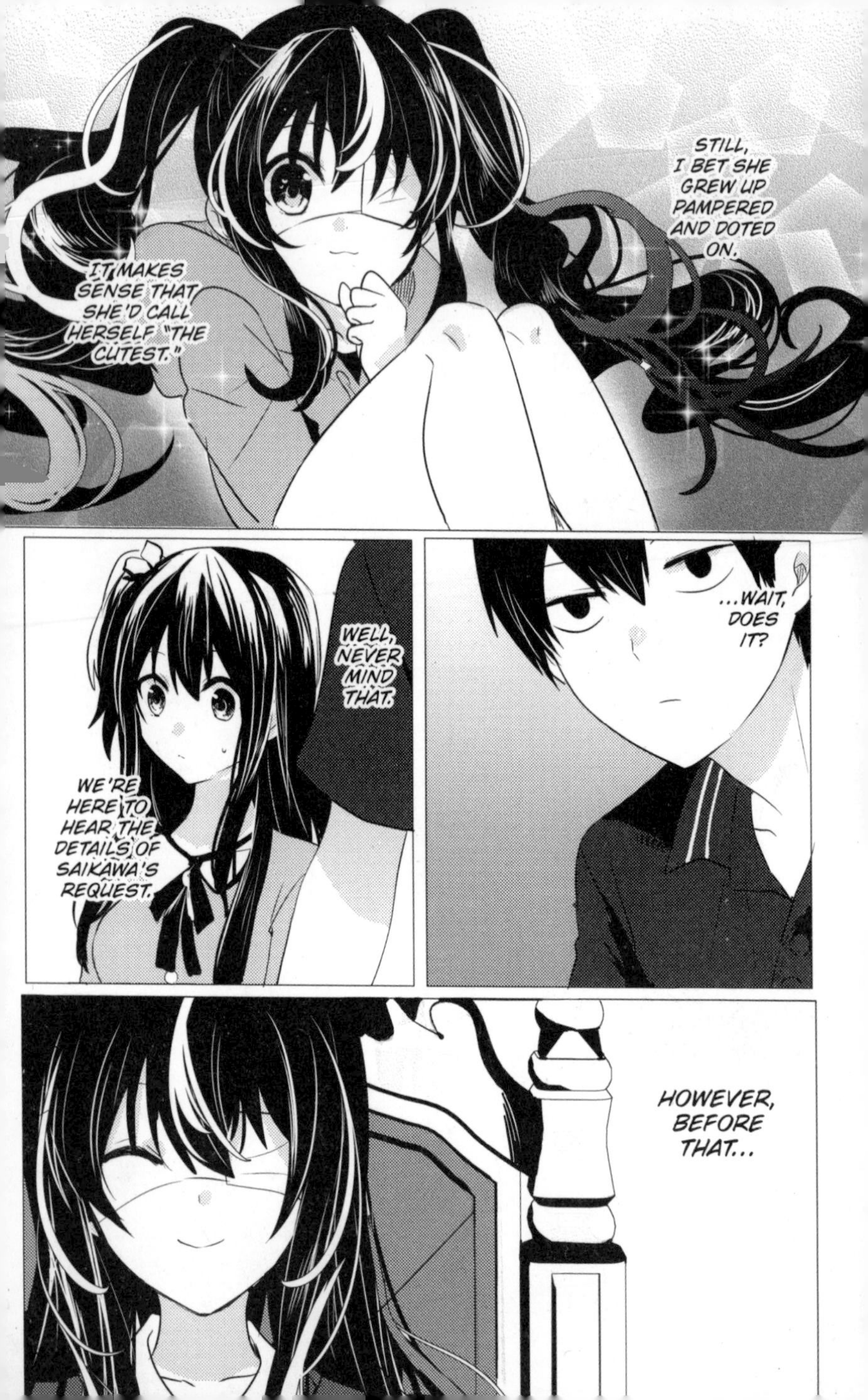
STILL, I BET SHE GREW UP PAMPERED AND DOTED ON.
IT MAKES SENSE THAT SHE'D CALL HERSELF "THE CUTEST."
...WAIT, DOES IT?
WELL, NEVER MIND THAT.
WE'RE HERE TO HEAR THE DETAILS OF SAIKAWA'S REQUEST.
HOWEVER, BEFORE THAT...

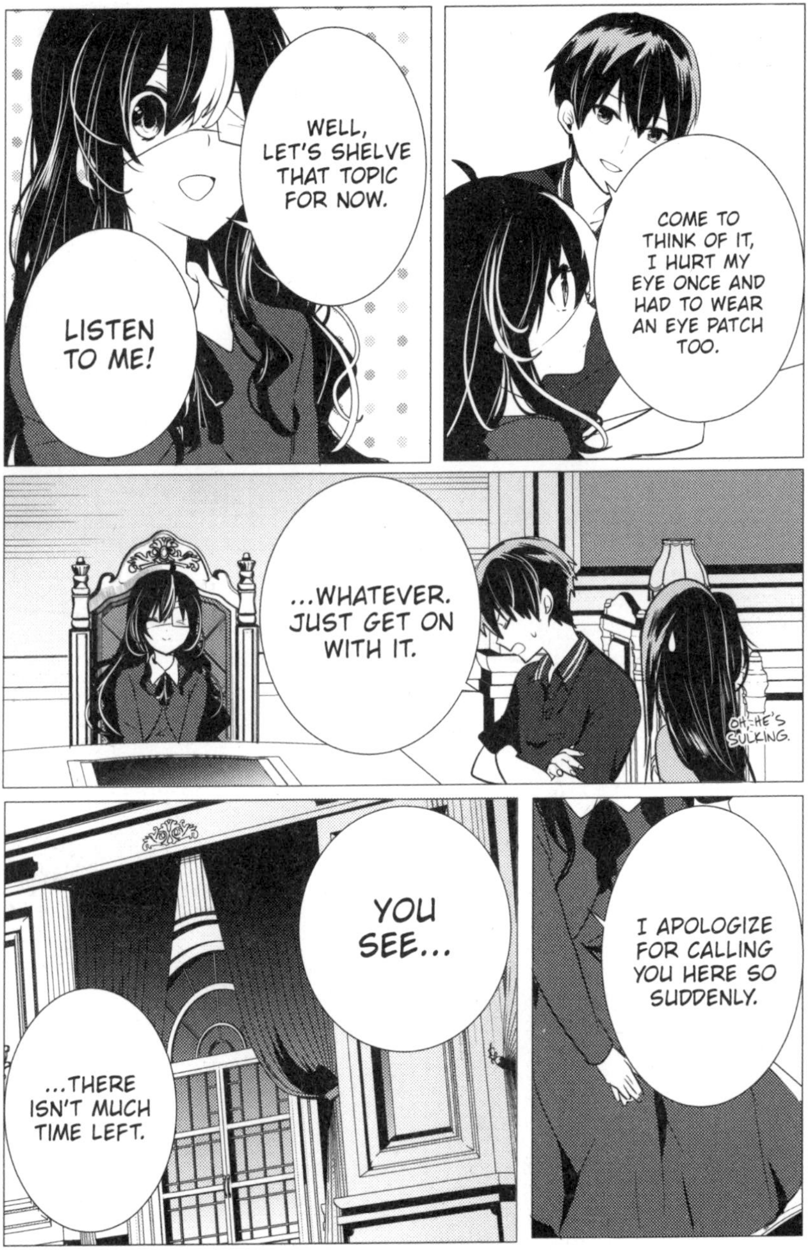
COME TO THINK OF IT, I HURT MY EYE ONCE AND HAD TO WEAR AN EYE PATCH TOO.
WELL, LET'S SHELVE THAT TOPIC FOR NOW.
LISTEN TO ME!
...WHATEVER. JUST GET ON WITH IT.
OH, HE'S SULKING.
I APOLOGIZE FOR CALLING YOU HERE SO SUDDENLY.
YOU SEE...
...THERE ISN'T MUCH TIME LEFT.

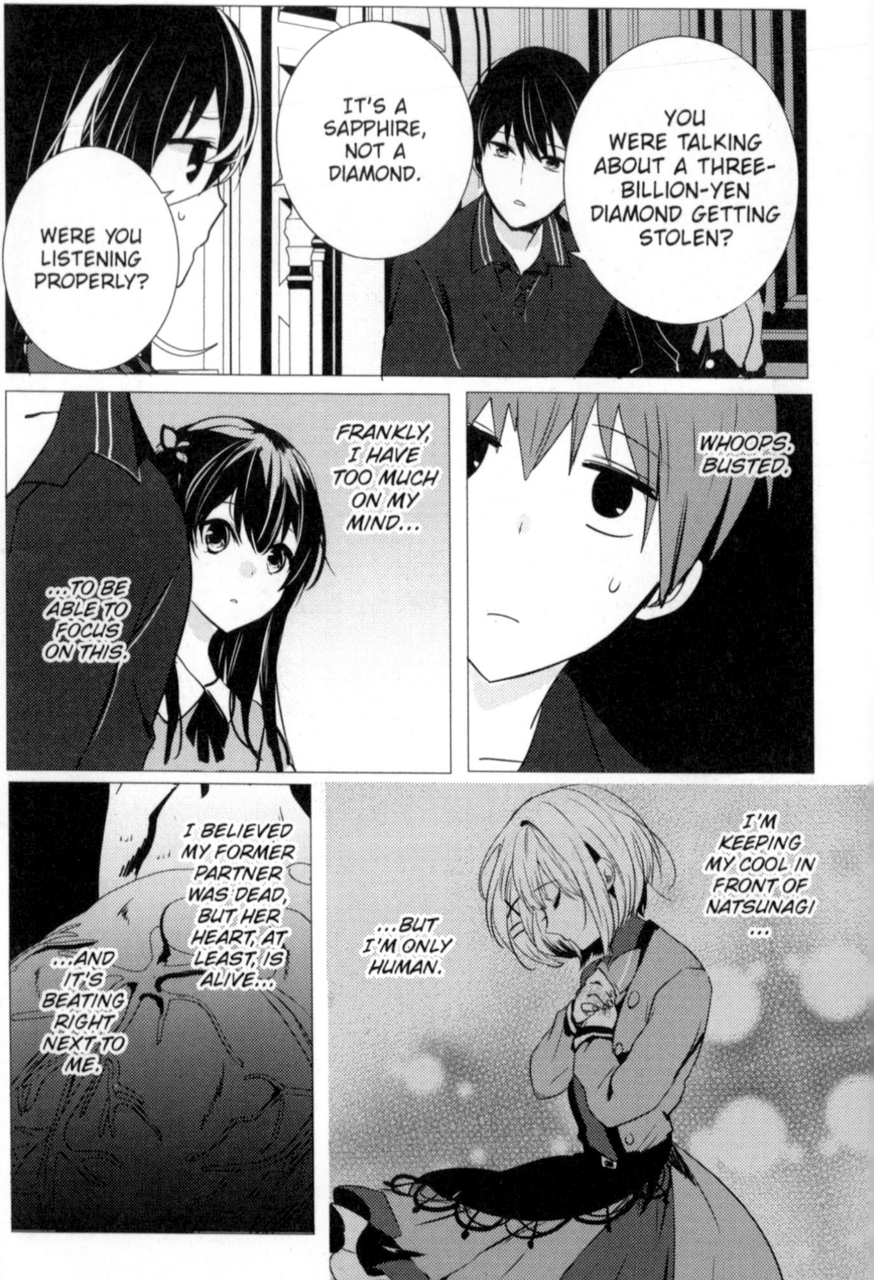
YOU WERE TALKING ABOUT A THREE-BILLION-YEN DIAMOND GETTING STOLEN?
IT'S A SAPPHIRE, NOT A DIAMOND.
WERE YOU LISTENING PROPERLY?
WHOOPS. BUSTED.
FRANKLY, I HAVE TOO MUCH ON MY MIND...
...TO BE ABLE TO FOCUS ON THIS.
I'M KEEPING MY COOL IN FRONT OF NATSUNAGI...
...BUT I'M ONLY HUMAN.
I BELIEVED MY FORMER PARTNER WAS DEAD, BUT HER HEART, AT LEAST, IS ALIVE...
...AND IT'S BEATING RIGHT NEXT TO ME.

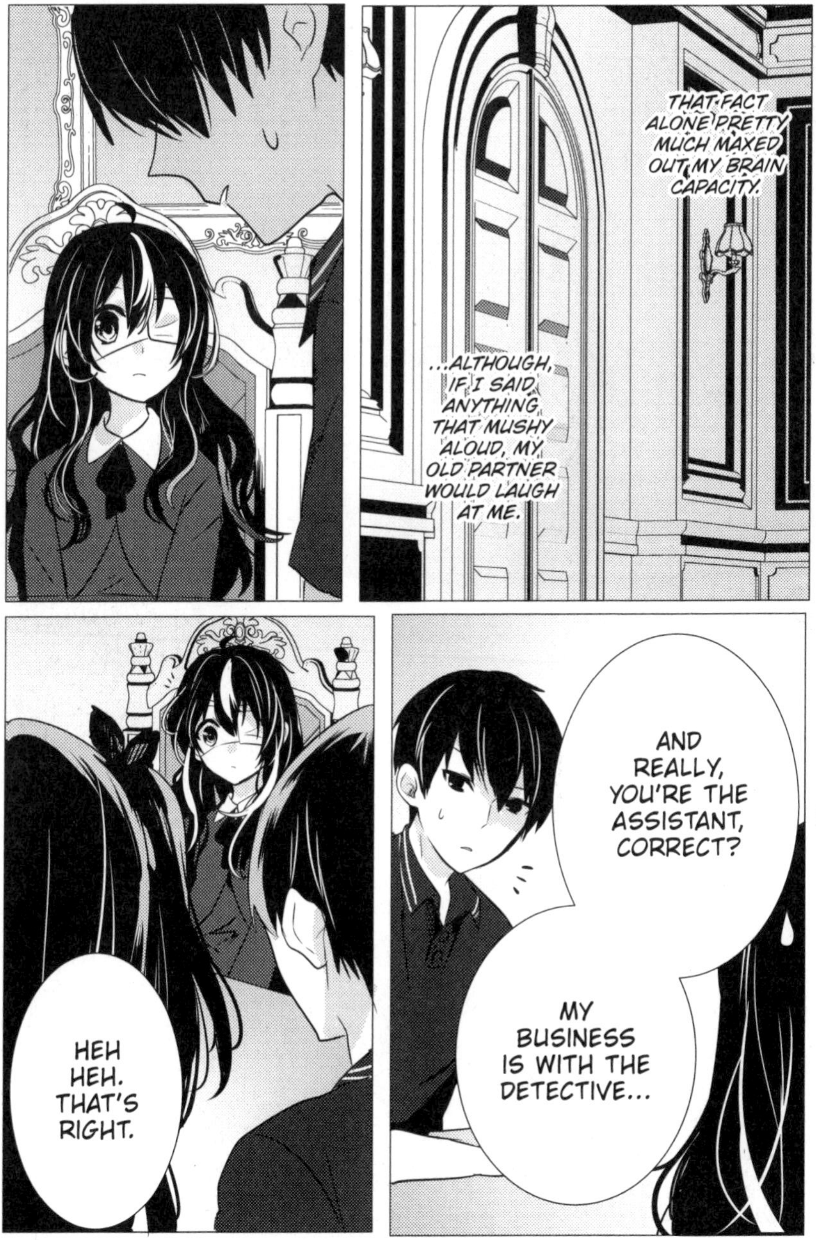
THAT FACT ALONE PRETTY MUCH MAXED OUT MY BRAIN CAPACITY.
...ALTHOUGH, IF I SAID ANYTHING THAT MUSHY ALOUD, MY OLD PARTNER WOULD LAUGH AT ME.
AND REALLY, YOU'RE THE ASSISTANT, CORRECT?
MY BUSINESS IS WITH THE DETECTIVE...
HEH HEH. THAT'S RIGHT.

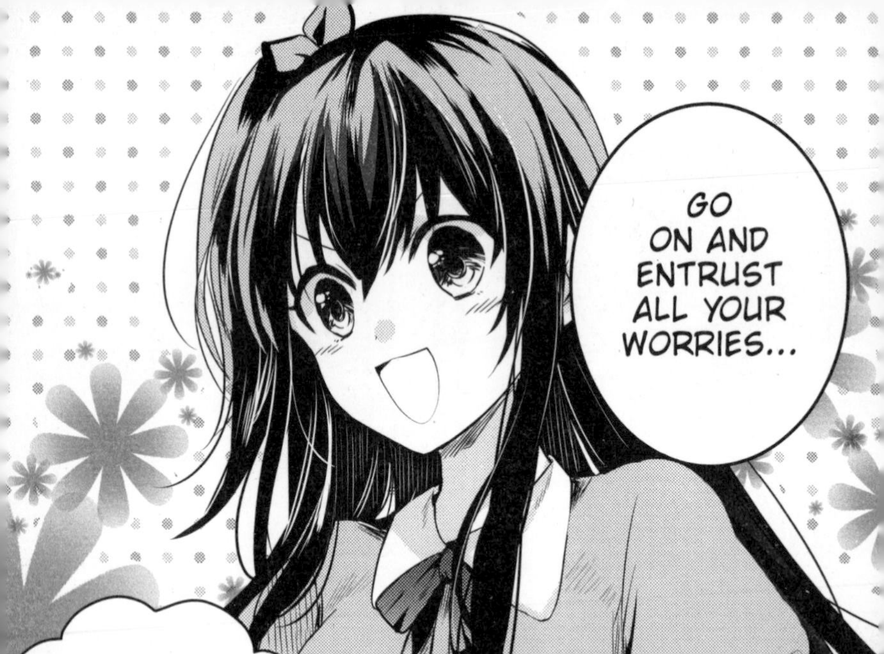
GO ON AND ENTRUST ALL YOUR WORRIES...
...TO THIS ACE DETECTIVE, NAGISA NATSUNAGI!

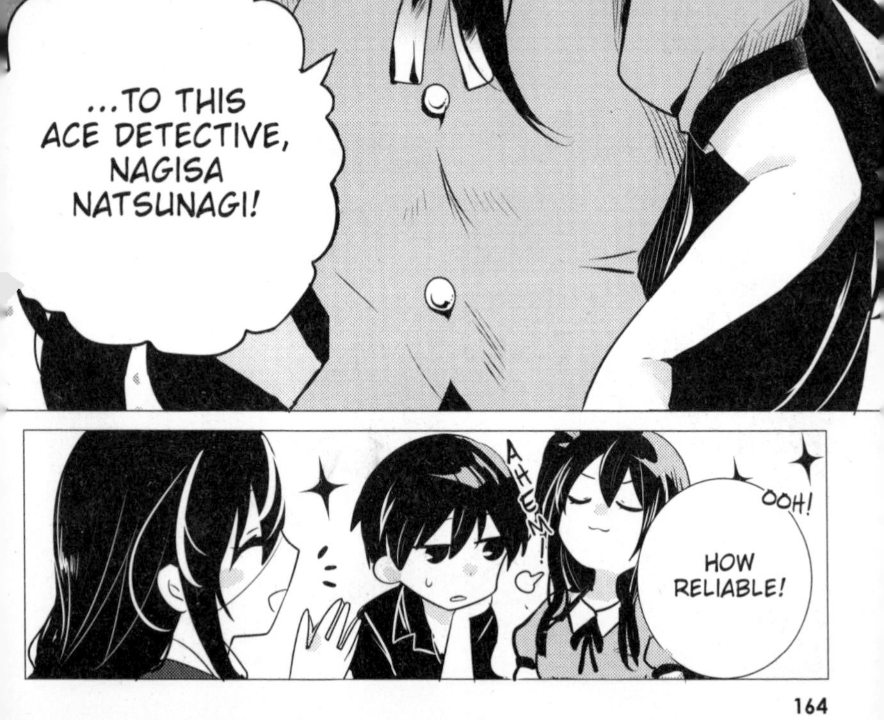
OOH!
HOW RELIABLE!
AHEM!

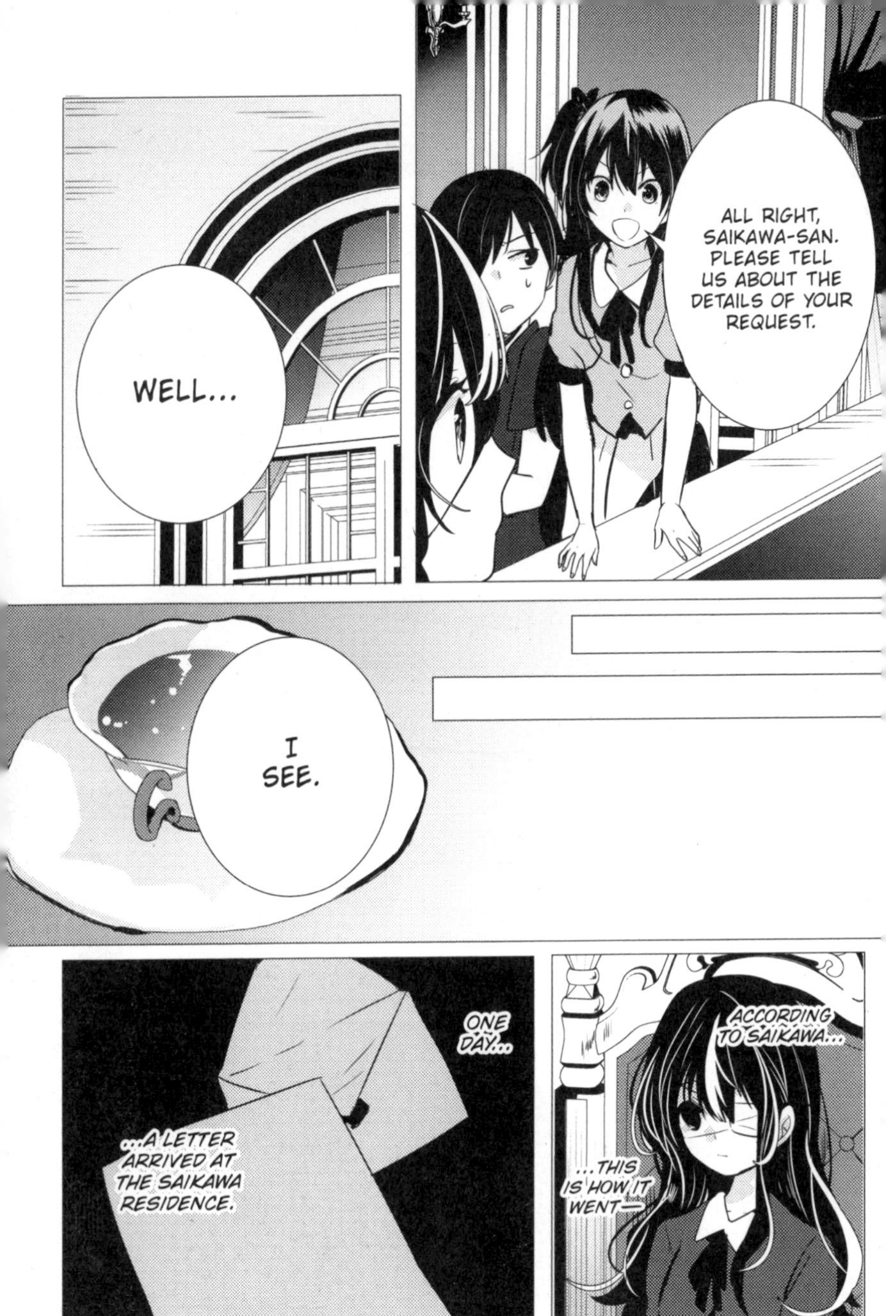
ALL RIGHT, SAIKAWA-SAN. PLEASE TELL US ABOUT THE DETAILS OF YOUR REQUEST.
WELL...
I SEE.
ACCORDING TO SAIKAWA...
...THIS IS HOW IT WENT—
ONE DAY...
...A LETTER ARRIVED AT THE SAIKAWA RESIDENCE.

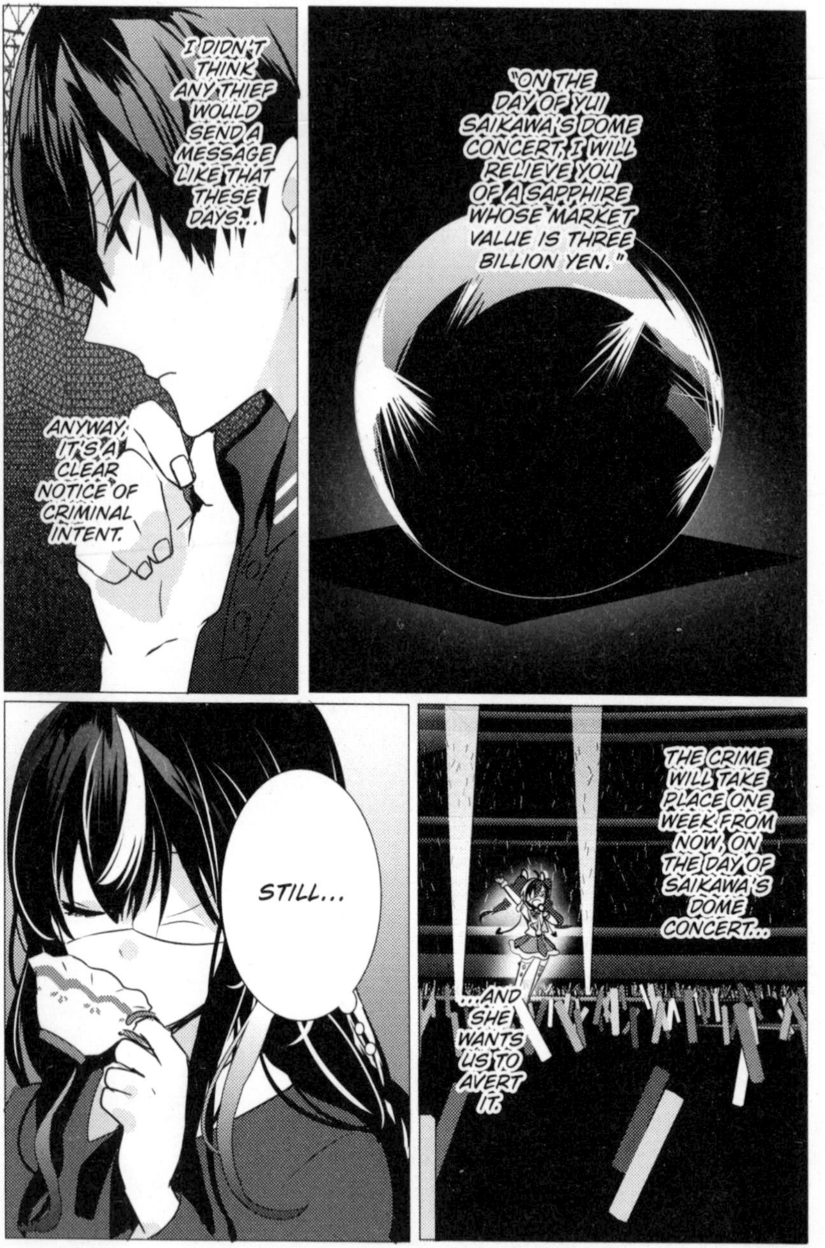
"ON THE DAY OF YUI SAIKAWA'S DOME CONCERT, I WILL RELIEVE YOU OF A SAPPHIRE WHOSE MARKET VALUE IS THREE BILLION YEN."
I DIDN'T THINK ANY THIEF WOULD SEND A MESSAGE LIKE THAT THESE DAYS...
ANYWAY, IT'S A CLEAR NOTICE OF CRIMINAL INTENT.
THE CRIME WILL TAKE PLACE ONE WEEK FROM NOW, ON THE DAY OF SAIKAWA'S DOME CONCERT...
...AND SHE WANTS US TO AVERT IT.
STILL...

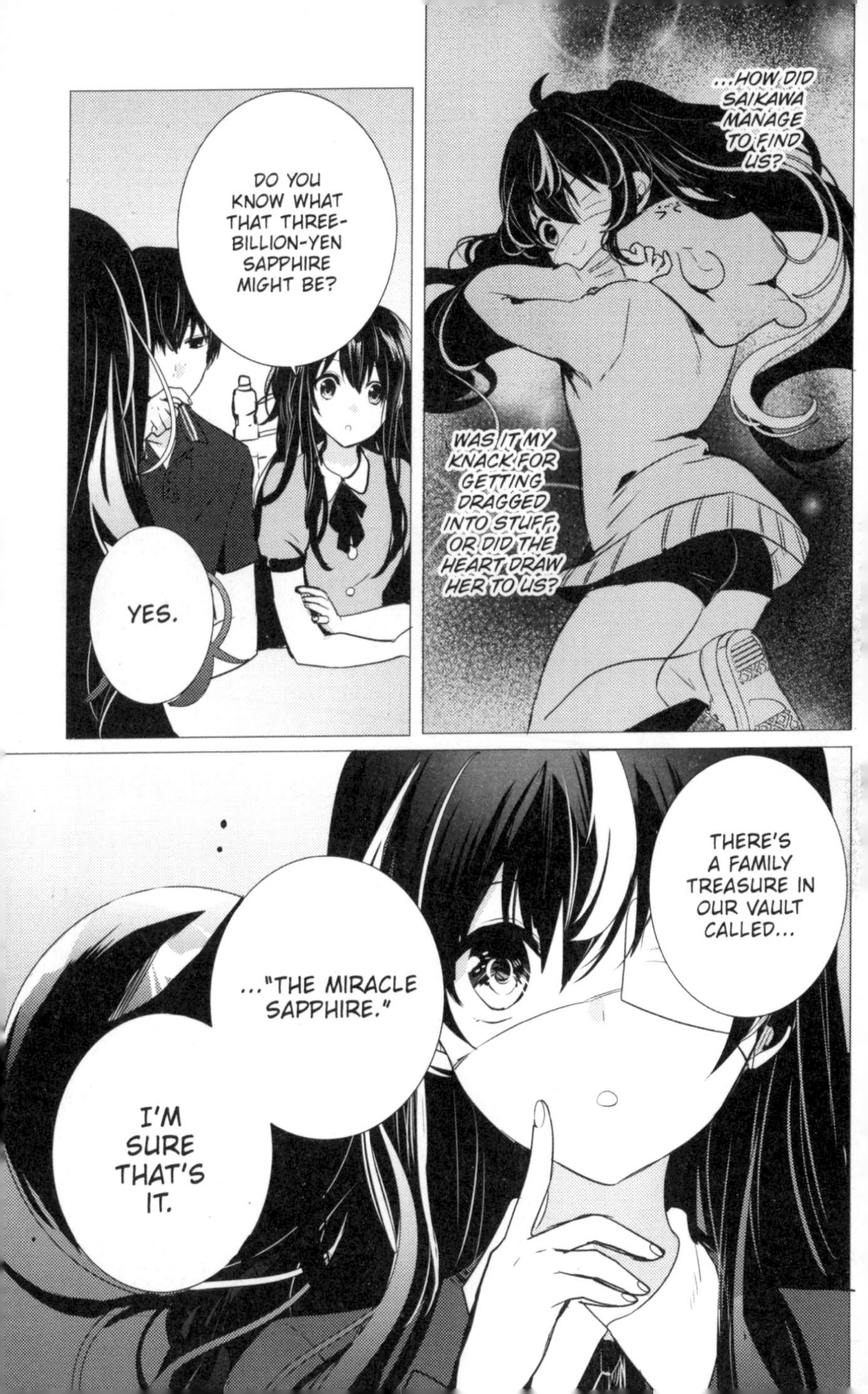
...HOW DID SAIKAWA MANAGE TO FIND US?
WAS IT MY KNACK FOR GETTING DRAGGED INTO STUFF, OR DID THE HEART DRAW HER TO US?
DO YOU KNOW WHAT THAT THREE-BILLION-YEN SAPPHIRE MIGHT BE?
YES.
THERE'S A FAMILY TREASURE IN OUR VAULT CALLED...
..."THE MIRACLE SAPPHIRE."
I'M SURE THAT'S IT.

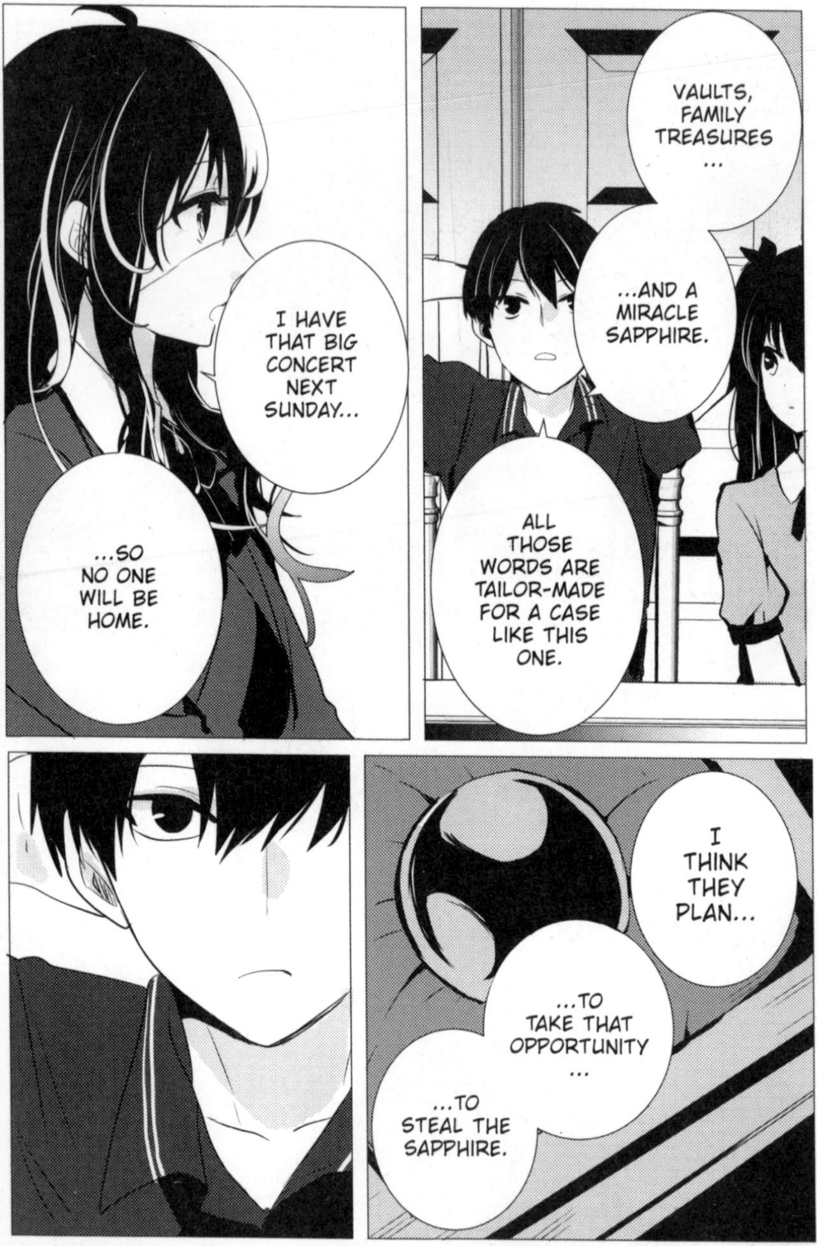
VAULTS, FAMILY TREASURES ...
...AND A MIRACLE SAPPHIRE.
ALL THOSE WORDS ARE TAILOR-MADE FOR A CASE LIKE THIS ONE.
I HAVE THAT BIG CONCERT NEXT SUNDAY...
...SO NO ONE WILL BE HOME.
I THINK THEY PLAN...
...TO TAKE THAT OPPORTUNITY ...
...TO STEAL THE SAPPHIRE.

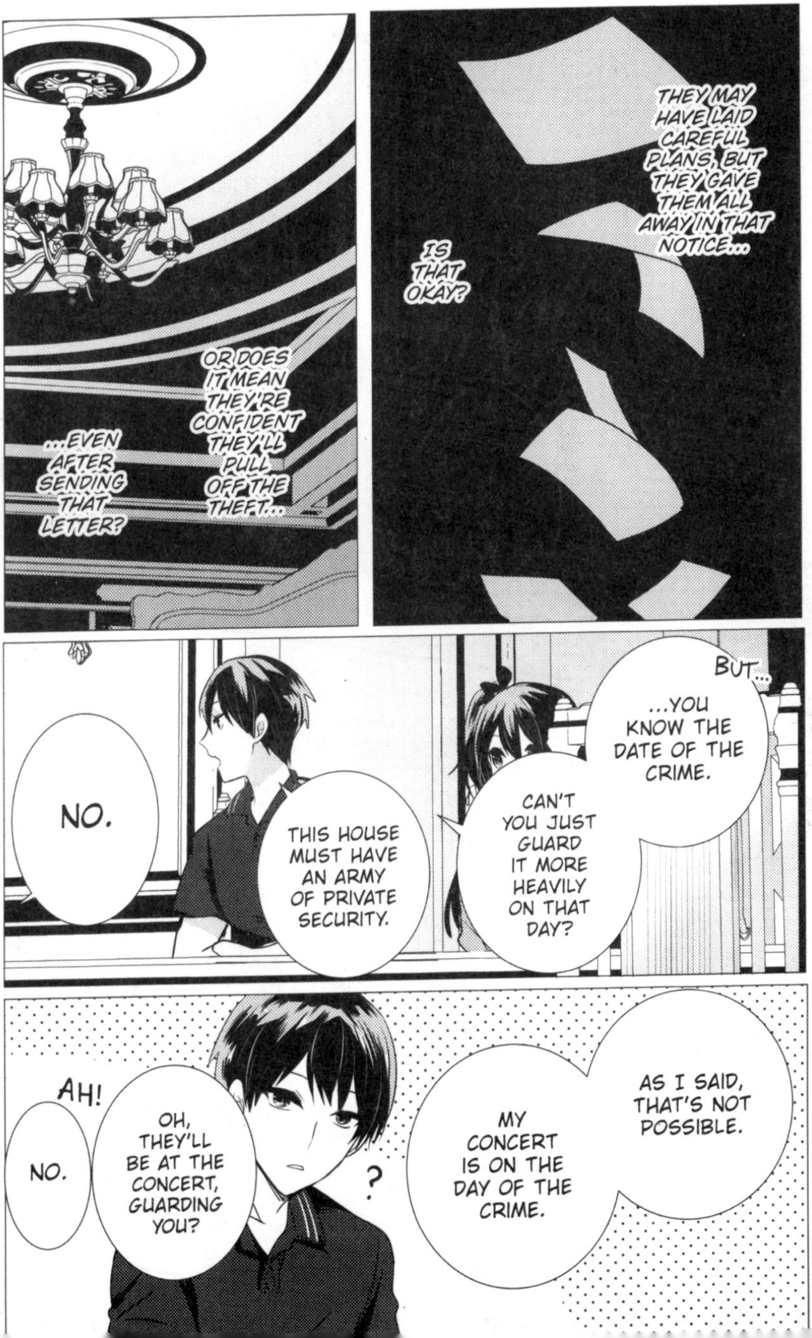
THEY MAY HAVE LAID CAREFUL PLANS, BUT THEY GAVE THEM ALL AWAY IN THAT NOTICE...
IS THAT OKAY?
OR DOES IT MEAN THEY'RE CONFIDENT THEY'LL PULL OFF THE THEFT...
...EVEN AFTER SENDING THAT LETTER?
BUT...
...YOU KNOW THE DATE OF THE CRIME.
CAN'T YOU JUST GUARD IT MORE HEAVILY ON THAT DAY?
THIS HOUSE MUST HAVE AN ARMY OF PRIVATE SECURITY.
NO.
AS I SAID, THAT'S NOT POSSIBLE.
MY CONCERT IS ON THE DAY OF THE CRIME.
?
OH, THEY'LL BE AT THE CONCERT, GUARDING YOU?
AH!
NO.

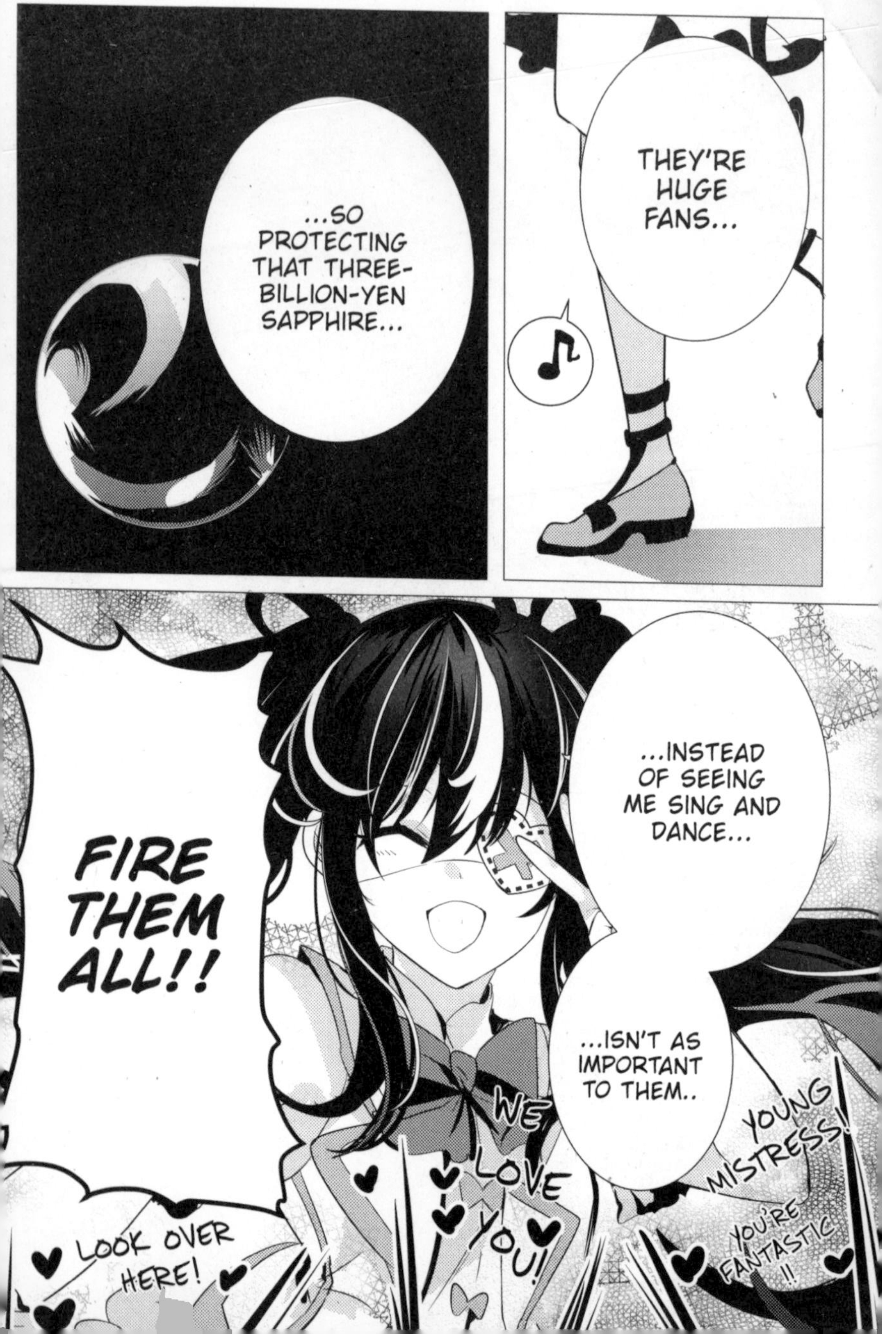
THEY'RE HUGE FANS...
♪
...SO PROTECTING THAT THREE-BILLION-YEN SAPPHIRE...
...INSTEAD OF SEEING ME SING AND DANCE...
...ISN'T AS IMPORTANT TO THEM..
YOUNG MISTRESS!
YOU'RE FANTASTIC!!
WE LOVE YOU!
FIRE THEM ALL!!
LOOK OVER HERE!

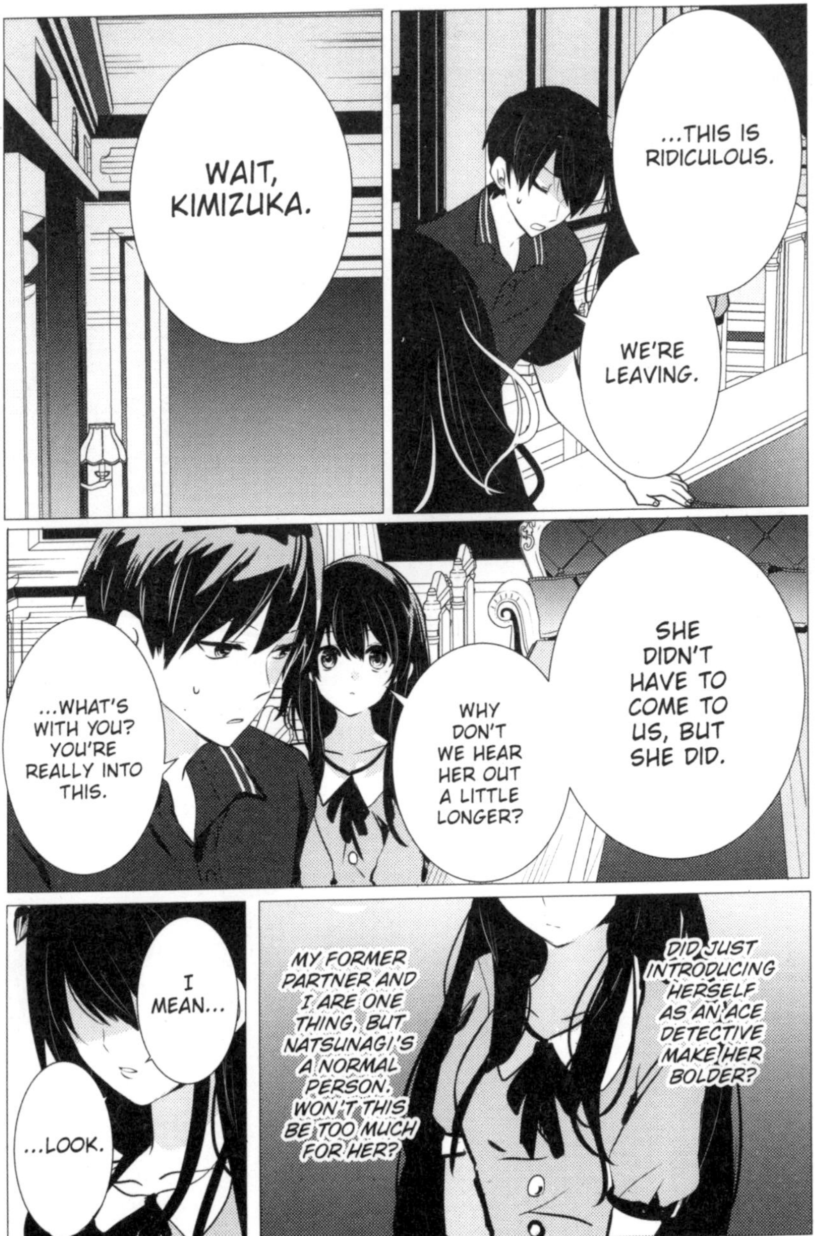
...THIS IS RIDICULOUS.
WE'RE LEAVING.
WAIT, KIMIZUKA.
SHE DIDN'T HAVE TO COME TO US, BUT SHE DID.
WHY DON'T WE HEAR HER OUT A LITTLE LONGER?
...WHAT'S WITH YOU? YOU'RE REALLY INTO THIS.
DID JUST INTRODUCING HERSELF AS AN ACE DETECTIVE MAKE HER BOLDER?
MY FORMER PARTNER AND I ARE ONE THING, BUT NATSUNAGI'S A NORMAL PERSON. WON'T THIS BE TOO MUCH FOR HER?
I MEAN...
...LOOK.

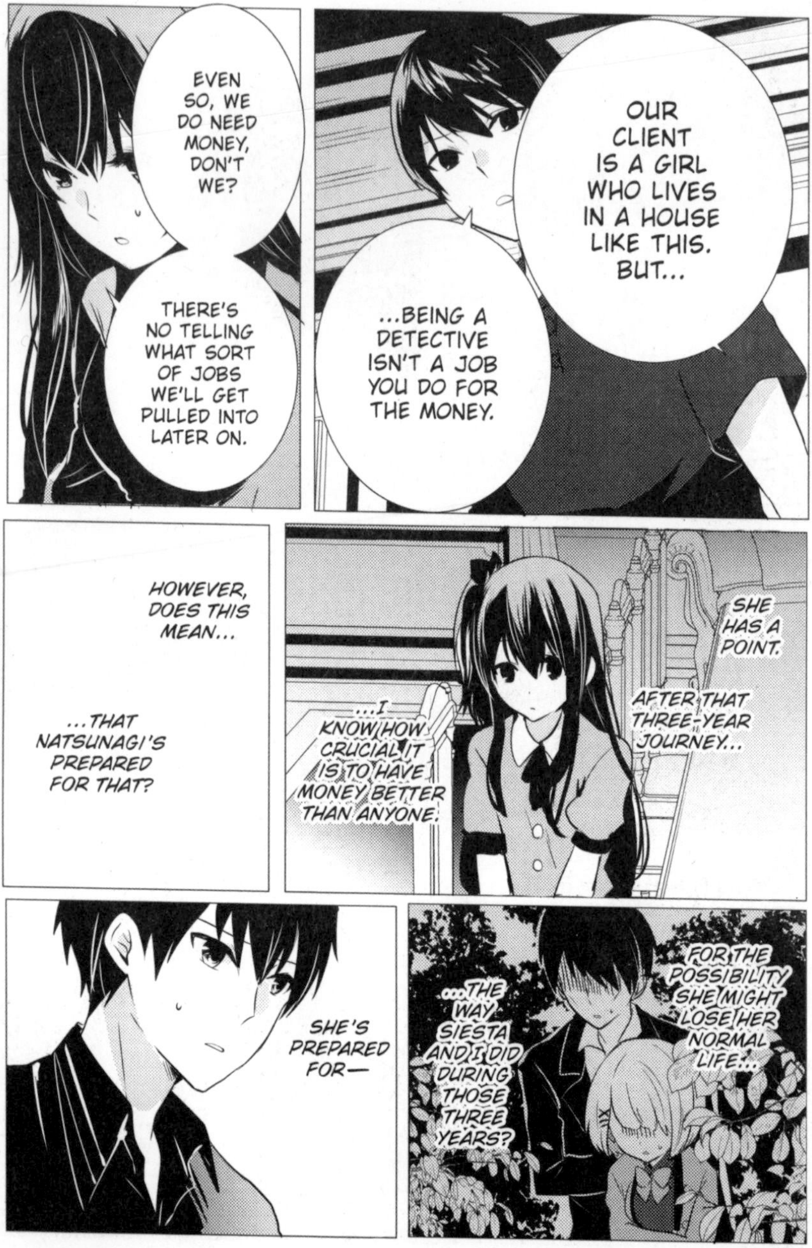
OUR CLIENT IS A GIRL WHO LIVES IN A HOUSE LIKE THIS. BUT...
...BEING A DETECTIVE ISN'T A JOB YOU DO FOR THE MONEY.
EVEN SO, WE DO NEED MONEY, DON'T WE?
THERE'S NO TELLING WHAT SORT OF JOBS WE'LL GET PULLED INTO LATER ON.
SHE HAS A POINT.
AFTER THAT THREE-YEAR JOURNEY...
...I KNOW HOW CRUCIAL IT IS TO HAVE MONEY BETTER THAN ANYONE.
HOWEVER, DOES THIS MEAN...
...THAT NATSUNAGI'S PREPARED FOR THAT?
FOR THE POSSIBILITY SHE MIGHT LOSE HER NORMAL LIFE...
...THE WAY SIESTA AND I DID DURING THOSE THREE YEARS?
SHE'S PREPARED FOR—

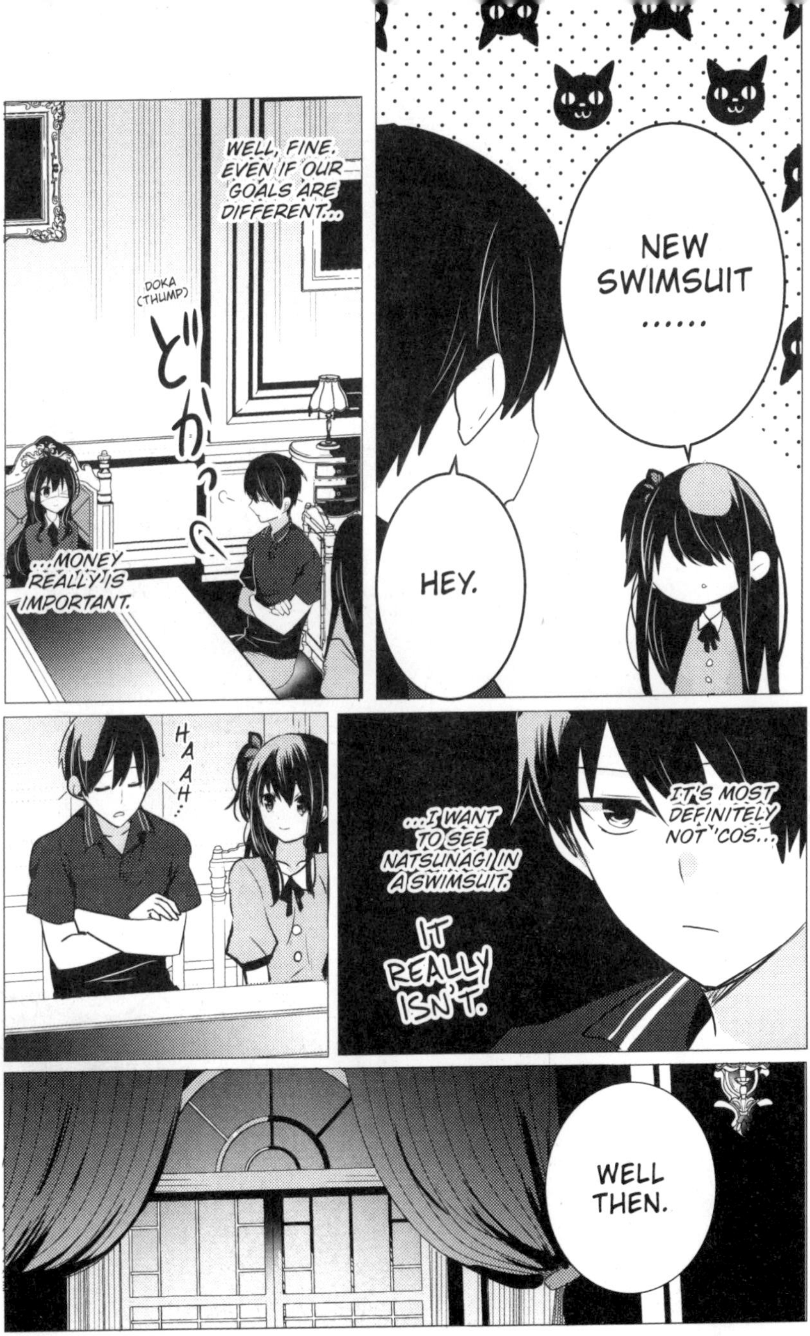
NEW SWIMSUIT ......
HEY.
WELL, FINE. EVEN IF OUR GOALS ARE DIFFERENT...
DOKA (THUMP)
どかっ
...MONEY REALLY IS IMPORTANT.
IT'S MOST DEFINITELY NOT 'COS...
...I WANT TO SEE NATSUNAGI IN A SWIMSUIT.
IT REALLY ISN'T.
HAAAH...
WELL THEN.

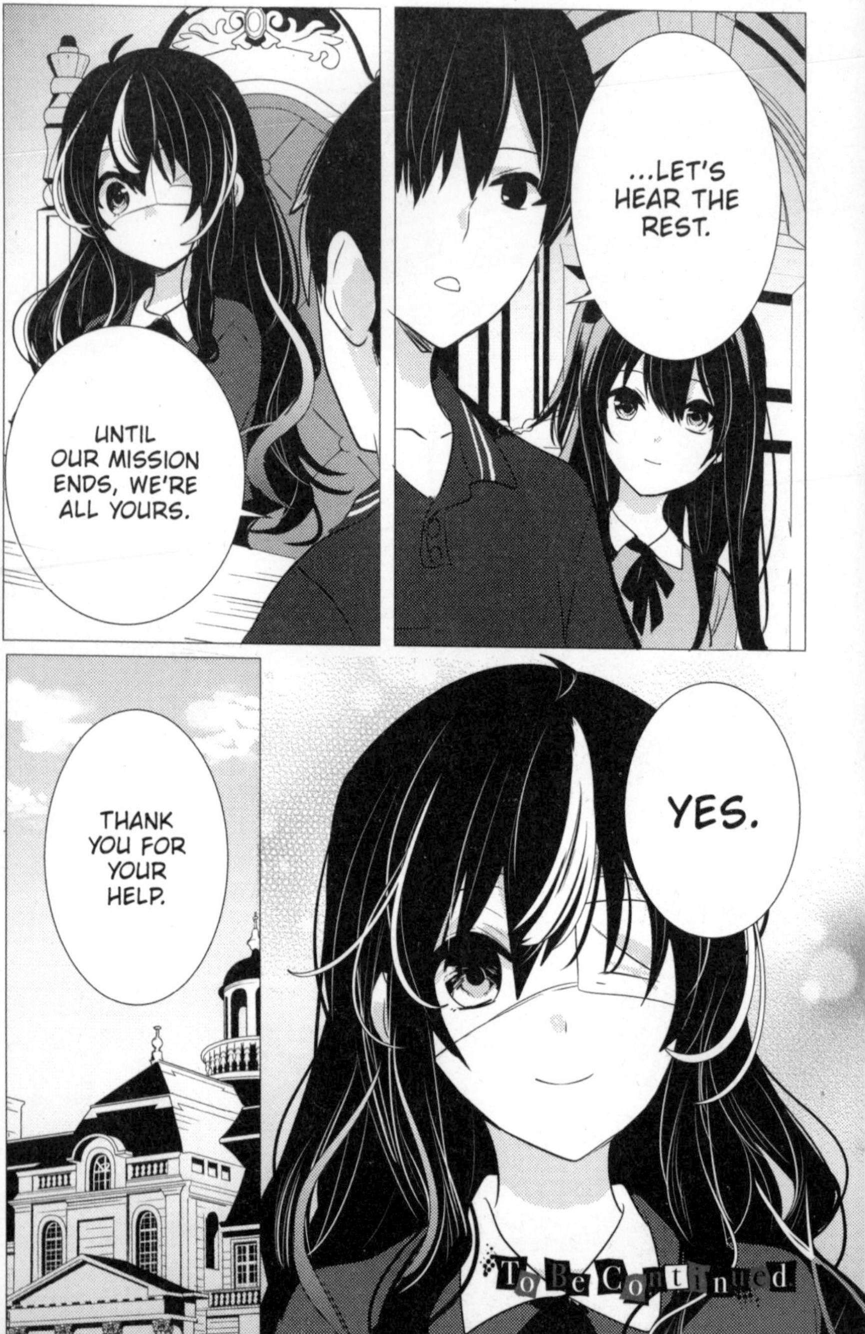
...LET'S HEAR THE REST.
UNTIL OUR MISSION ENDS, WE'RE ALL YOURS.
YES.
THANK YOU FOR YOUR HELP.
To Be Continued

The Detective Is Already Dead

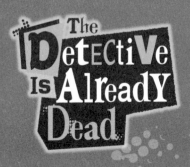

The Detective Is Already Dead

ORIGINAL AUTHOR COMMENTS:
NIGOZYU

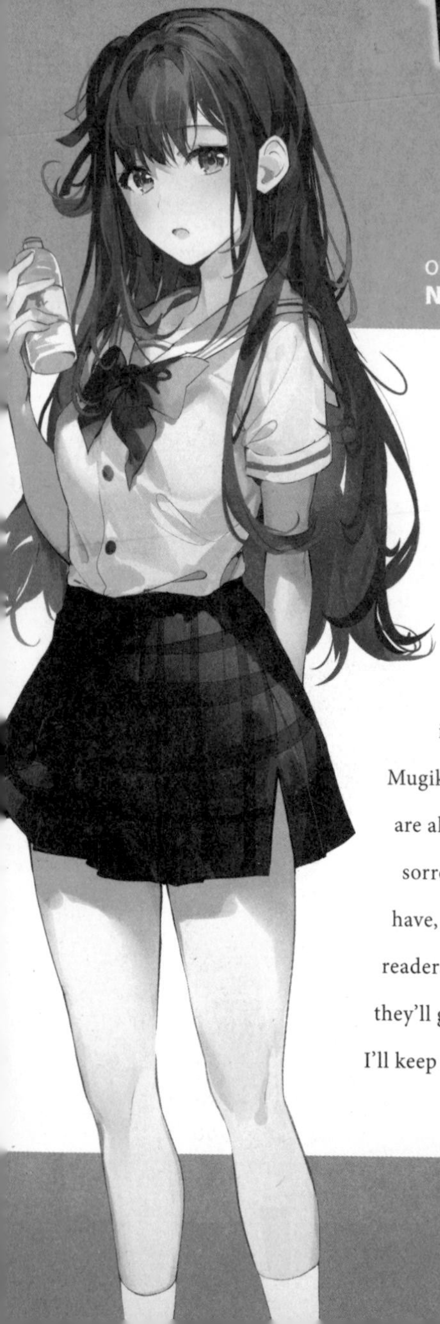

It's the second volume of the *Detective* manga! At this point, the story is shifting from the Natsunagi arc to the Saikawa arc. I think from this volume on, it'll be packed with enthusiasm, laughs, unbearable cuteness, and all sorts of other things—very *Detective*-esque indeed!

Mugiko-sensei's heroines (including Kimizuka) are all really expressive. They show joy, anger, sorrow and excitement with everything they have, running through the story at full tilt. If readers match the speed at which they live, I think they'll get to see scenery that's more entertaining. I'll keep running too!

ILLUSTRATION: **UMIBOUZU**

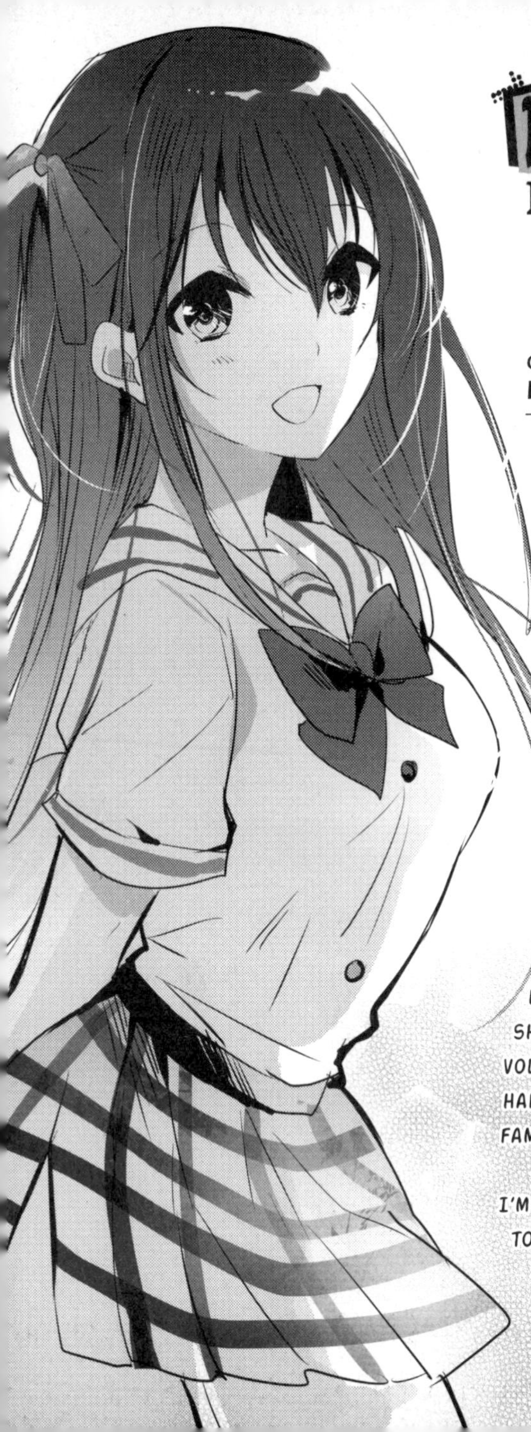

The Detective Is Already Dead

CREATOR AFTERWORD:
MUGIKO

THANK YOU FOR PICKING UP VOLUME 2 OF THE *THE DETECTIVE IS ALREADY DEAD* MANGA! I WANT TO DRAW THE *DETECTIVE* WORLD TO THE FULLEST, TO THE POINT WHERE IT KINDA HURTS EVERY DAY.

THIS VOLUME IS AN EXTRA-SPECIAL ONE THAT INCLUDES A SHORT STORY BY NIGOZYU-SENSEI! I'D ALWAYS DREAMED OF HAVING A SHORT STORY IN ONE OF MY VOLUMES, SO I COULDN'T BE HAPPIER. I'LL KEEP IT AS A FAMILY HEIRLOOM.

I'M REALLY LOOKING FORWARD TO THE ANIME TOO! I HOPE YOU'LL CONTINUE ENJOYING THE WORLD OF *DETECTIVE*.

Translation Notes

Common Honorifics

-san: The Japanese equivalent of Mr./Mrs./Miss. If a situation calls for politeness, this is the fail-safe honorific.

-kun: Used most often when referring to boys, this indicates affection or familiarity. Occasionally used by older men among their peers, but it may also be used by anyone referring to a person of lower standing.

-sensei: A respectful term for teachers, artists, or high-level professionals.

no honorific: Indicates familiarity or closeness; if used without permission or reason, addressing someone in this manner would constitute an insult.

Page 37

Kimi: Siesta's nickname for Kimihiko is a play on words. Not only does it work as a nickname for both his family name and his given name, but it also has the same reading as the Japanese word for "you."

Page 51

Cat in the box: Kimihiko is referring to Schrödinger's Cat, whose condition is unknown as long as it is concealed in the box. The well-known physics experiment is a popular motif in manga and anime.

Page 146

Three billion yen: In USD, the sapphire would be worth approximately $26 million.

Page 151

Cutest: Saikawa's title for herself is actually a pun on her name in Japanese. It comes from the word *sai*, or "most" and *kawa*, "cute." Put together "the most cute" or "cutest" is Saikawa.

Page 177

Ketchup spaghetti: A popular pasta dish native to Japan called *Napolitan*. It is usually made with spaghetti, ketchup or another tomato-based sauce, onions, mushrooms, green peppers, sausage, bacon, and occasionally hot sauce.

Turn to the back of the book for an original short story by **nigozyu**, the author of

The Detective Is Already Dead

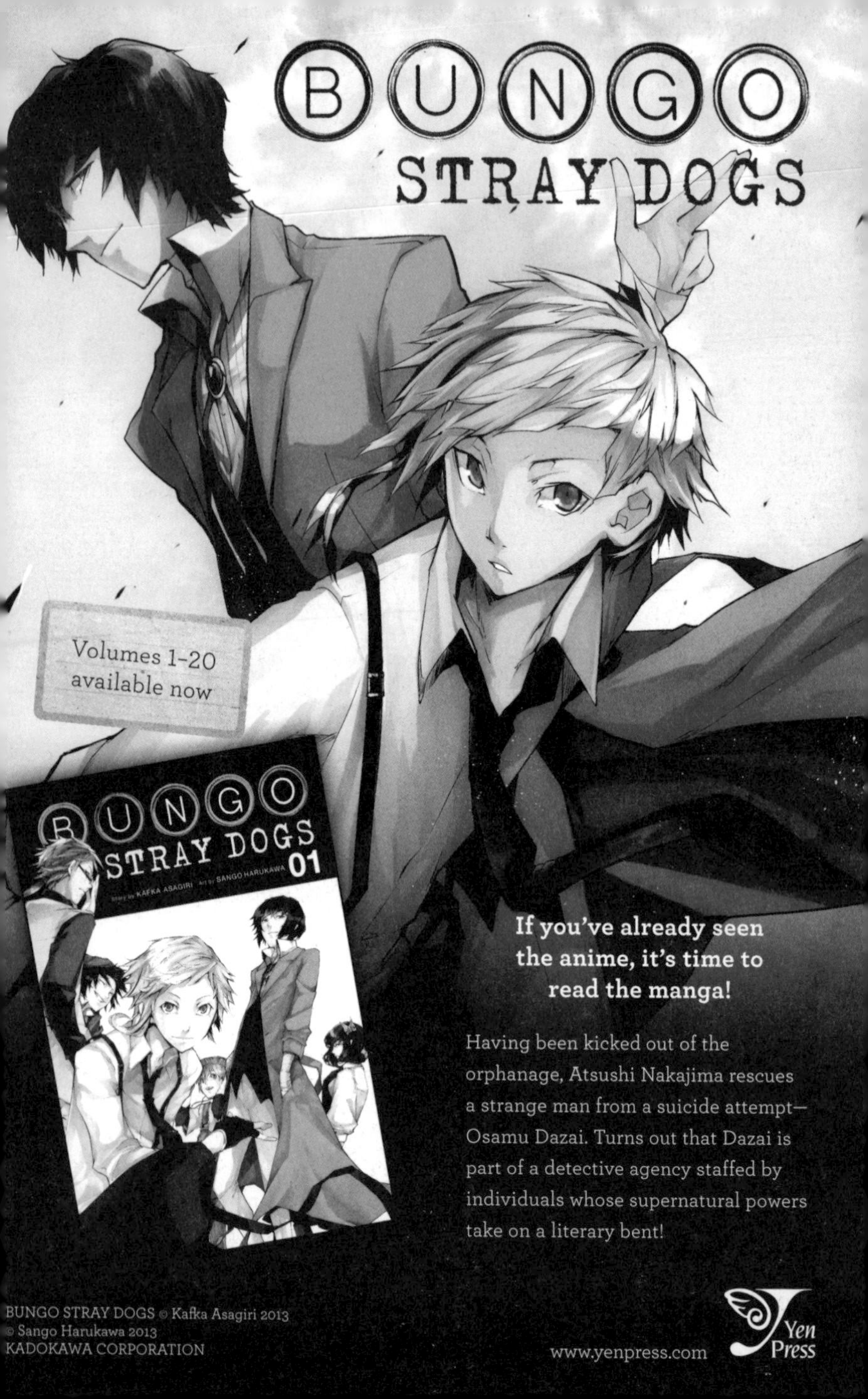
BUNGO
STRAY DOGS
Volumes 1–20 available now
BUNGO STRAY DOGS 01
KAFKA ASAGIRI
SANGO HARUKAWA
If you've already seen the anime, it's time to read the manga!
Having been kicked out of the orphanage, Atsushi Nakajima rescues a strange man from a suicide attempt—Osamu Dazai. Turns out that Dazai is part of a detective agency staffed by individuals whose supernatural powers take on a literary bent!
BUNGO STRAY DOGS © Kafka Asagiri 2013
© Sango Harukawa 2013
KADOKAWA CORPORATION
www.yenpress.com
Yen Press

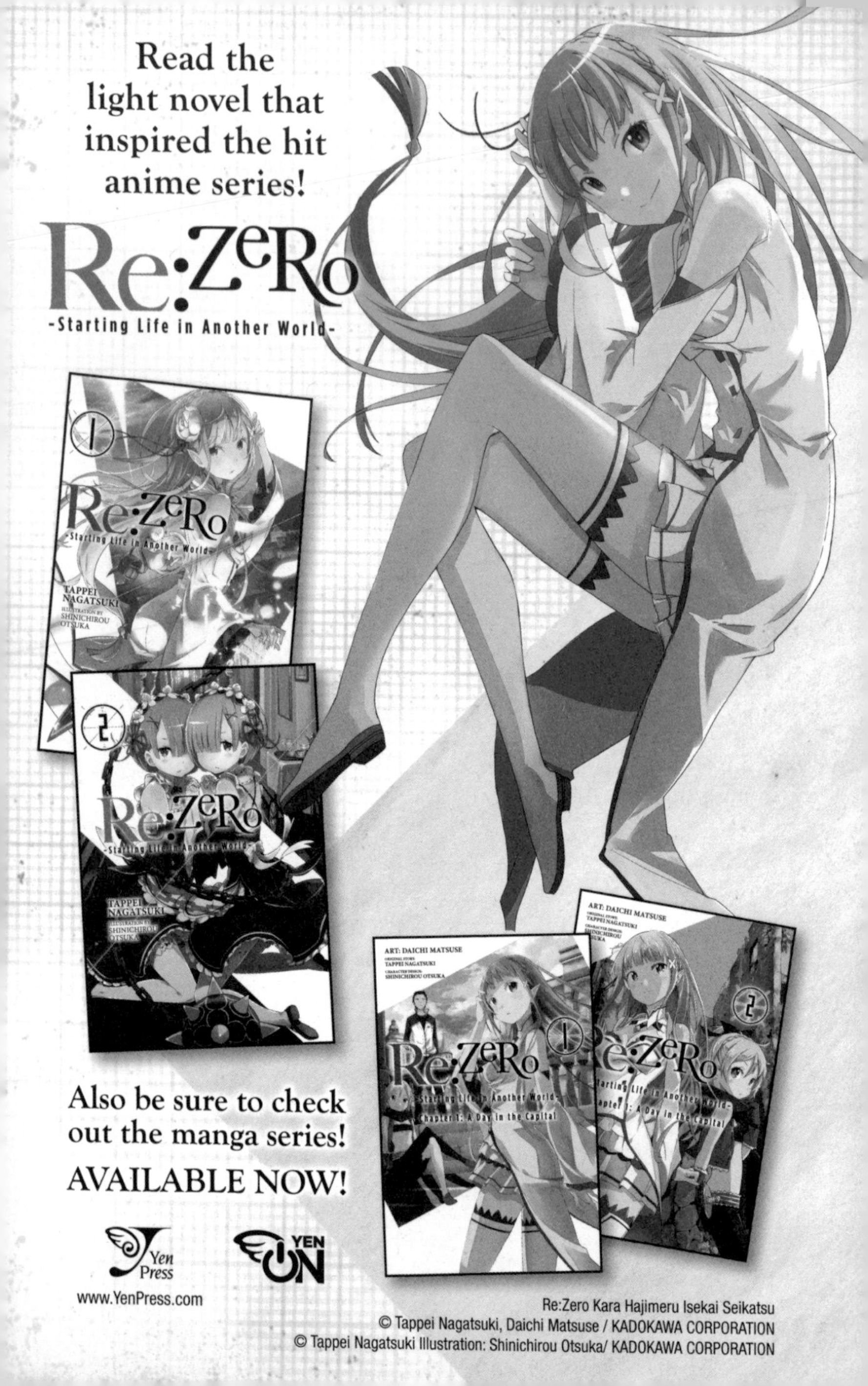
Read the light novel that inspired the hit anime series!
Re:ZeRo
-Starting Life in Another World-
TAPPEI NAGATSUKI
ILLUSTRATION BY SHINICHIROU OTSUKA
ART: DAICHI MATSUSE
Chapter 1: A Day in the Capital
Also be sure to check out the manga series!
AVAILABLE NOW!
Yen Press
YEN ON
www.YenPress.com
Re:Zero Kara Hajimeru Isekai Seikatsu
© Tappei Nagatsuki, Daichi Matsuse / KADOKAWA CORPORATION
© Tappei Nagatsuki Illustration: Shinichirou Otsuka/ KADOKAWA CORPORATION

In the world of Alcia, where rank is determined by **"counts,"** a young girl named Hina scours the land for the fabled Ace—the legendary hero of the Waste War. With only the last words of her missing mother to guide her search, she wanders from town to town until she meets Licht, a clownish masked vagrant with a count of −999. Girl-crazy and unpredictable, he's the exact opposite of a hero...or at least, that's how he appears...

PLUNDERER

VOLUMES 1-9 AVAILABLE NOW!

COMBATANTS WILL BE DISPATCHED!

AVAILABLE WHEREVER BOOKS ARE SOLD!

LIGHT NOVEL
VOLUMES 1-6

MANGA
VOLUMES 1-5

©Natsume Akatsuki, Kakao • Lanthanum 2017
KADOKAWA CORPORATION

©Masaaki Kiasa 2018 ©Natsume Akatsuki, Kakao • Lanthanum 2018
KADOKAWA CORPORATION

Always bring a gun to a sword fight!

With world domination nearly in their grasp, the Supreme Leaders of the Kisaragi Corporation—an underground criminal group turned evil megacorp—have decided to try their hands at interstellar conquest. A quick dice roll nominates their chief operative, Combat Agent Six, to be the one to explore an alien planet...and the first thing he does when he gets there is change the sacred incantation for a holy ritual to the most embarrassing thing he can think of. But evil deeds are business as usual for Kisaragi operatives, so if Six wants a promotion and a raise, he'll have to work much harder than that! For starters, he'll have to do something about the other group of villains on the planet, who are calling themselves the "Demon Lord's Army" or whatever. After all, this world doesn't need two evil organizations!

For more information
visit www.yenpress.com

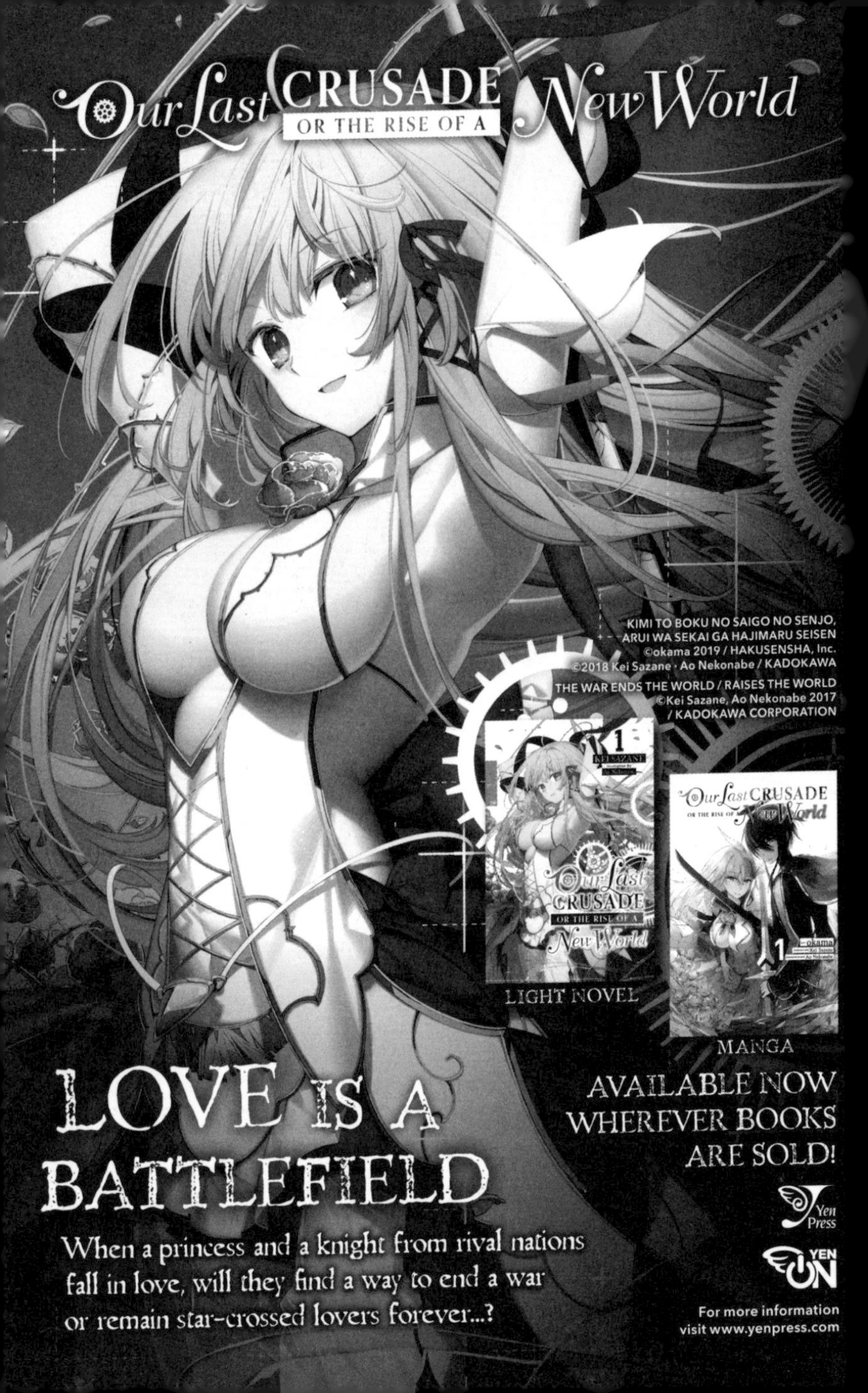
Our Last CRUSADE OR THE RISE OF A New World
KIMI TO BOKU NO SAIGO NO SENJO, ARUI WA SEKAI GA HAJIMARU SEISEN
©okama 2019 / HAKUSENSHA, Inc.
©2018 Kei Sazane · Ao Nekonabe / KADOKAWA
THE WAR ENDS THE WORLD / RAISES THE WORLD
©Kei Sazane, Ao Nekonabe 2017 / KADOKAWA CORPORATION
LIGHT NOVEL
MANGA
LOVE IS A BATTLEFIELD
When a princess and a knight from rival nations fall in love, will they find a way to end a war or remain star-crossed lovers forever...?
AVAILABLE NOW WHEREVER BOOKS ARE SOLD!
Yen Press
YEN ON
For more information visit www.yenpress.com

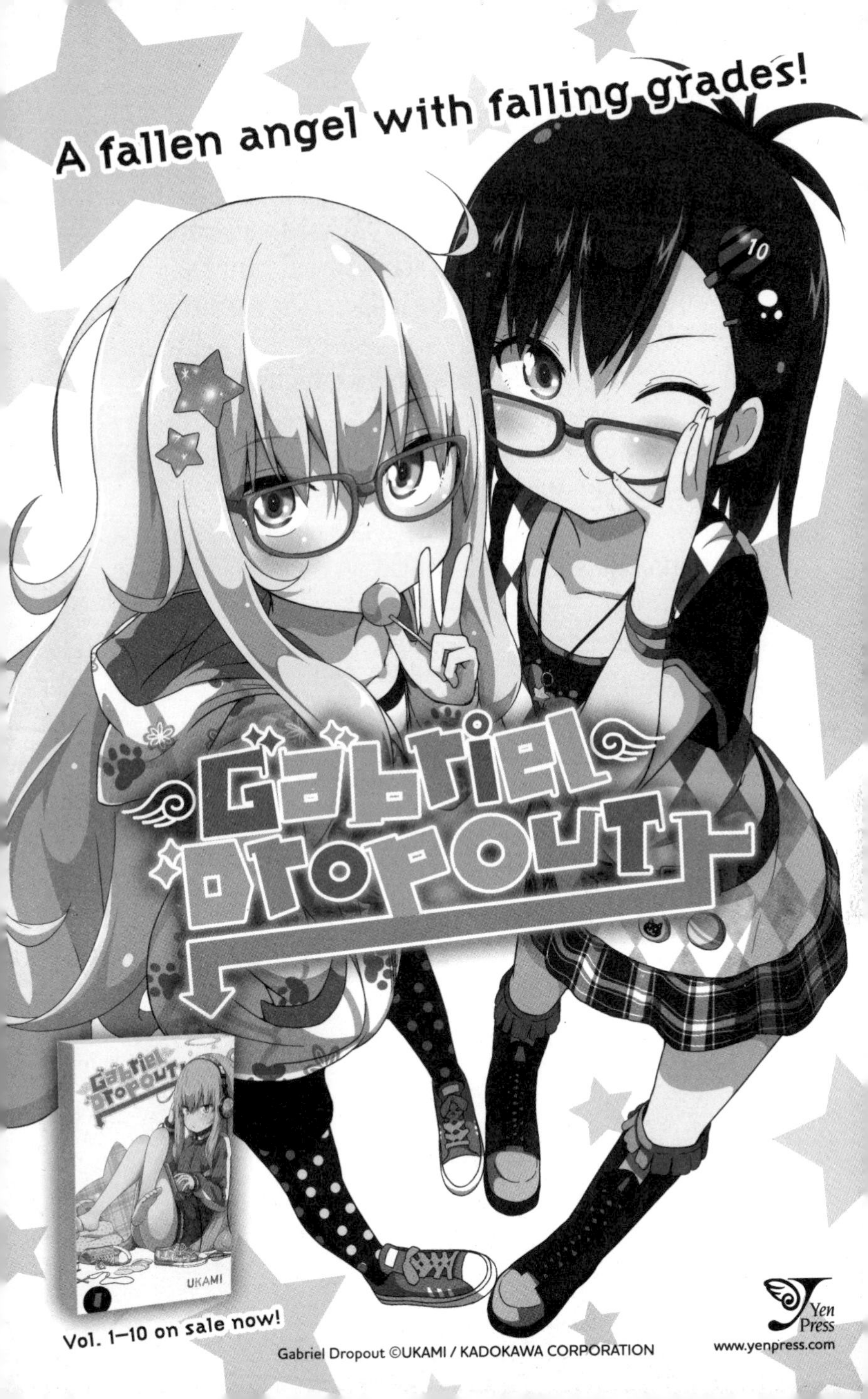
A fallen angel with falling grades!
Gabriel Dropout
Gabriel Dropout
UKAMI
Vol. 1–10 on sale now!
Gabriel Dropout ©UKAMI / KADOKAWA CORPORATION
Yen Press
www.yenpress.com

"...I don't think I'm the type who'd give my all for a guy like that." Natsunagi cocked her head dubiously. Then she said, "Yeah, I can cover it." She closed her wallet, then started skimming the menu again. Somewhere in there, she'd polished off her pasta.

"You're not done eating yet, high school girl?"

"I-it's fine, right? I'm the one who's paying anyway." Natsunagi lifted the menu, hiding the lower half of her face behind it.

Sheesh. Guess I'll have to keep her company a little while longer. I smiled wryly. "What are you getting?"

Natsunagi responded with a smile like the August sun.

"Apple pie!"

The End.

somewhere before. I might even remember who'd said it if I gave it a little thought, but I didn't want to think about the past too much.

"That's kind of you."

"It's the natural, human thing to do."

At least as far as I was concerned, the strength it took to declare that seemed like kindness.

"Wait, didn't you say you'd paid me in advance by letting me touch your chest?"

"...You know, that's suddenly embarrassing, so don't say it."

"You're breaking character way too much, way too early."

"Shut up!"

She slammed a solid low kick into my shin... I wish she'd stay in her fragile, sickly personality, since it seems like that's an option.

"...Haah. In that case, pay me by picking up the check here."

There was no guarantee I'd be able to fulfill her request, but we could call this a retainer fee.

"Well, if you're fine with that, then okay," Natsunagi responded lightly. Even as she said it, though, she peeked into her wallet. "...I wonder if I have enough."

"Make sure you don't let some weird leech of a boyfriend glom onto you later on down the road."

"Huh? Why?"

No real reason. The sight of her consulting her wallet just put that scene in my head.

"No, not that. You know, if you make me lunches, um, they'll probably start awkward rumors about us at school."

"...Huh?" She looked at me as if I were garbage. So unfair.

"I don't need a reward or anything this time." I took a sip of coffee, clearing my palate, and shifted the conversation back on topic.

"Um... But then you don't get anything out of taking my request."

"Right. That means the only reason I took this request is because I'm such a nice person."

"Wow, you're really irritating."

"Yeah, looks like we're hopelessly incompatible." But don't worry about it. Over the last three years, I got used to working for free.

Besides, for some reason, when I looked into Natsunagi's eyes and heard what she said, I just couldn't bring myself to turn her down.

"Hrmm. This just doesn't feel right." However, even as Natsunagi ate her pasta, she was wearing a pensive frown. Apparently she was still worried about the fact that I was working for free. Despite that gonzo first meeting, she seemed to have more common sense than I'd assumed she did.

"I mean, you're doing something for me. It's rude if I don't give you something in return. I feel bad just getting things," Natsunagi insisted petulantly.

I got the feeling I'd heard a similar line,

But when they learned about my talent for getting dragged into stuff, they all started drifting away. Just being around me was enough to get them involved in trouble they didn't need, so it was probably inevitable that they left.

Even so... There was one girl who knew about my talent and stayed with me anyway. Actually, she came to me specifically because of that talent and then stuck with me for three whole years. At this point, though, she's no longer—

"I'm sorry." Unexpectedly, Natsunagi apologized. But...

"Hey, don't gimme that poor, unfortunate soul look." Is it really so bad, not having friends?

"Ah-ha-ha! Oh, do you want me to make you a lunch every once in a while, then?"

If I resolved her request for her, she told me, that would be my reward.

Apparently the idea that I wasn't going to get paid in money was already an established fact. Well, that's fine—I wasn't expecting any in the first place.

"Are you a good cook?"

"I do live by myself, you know! So I'm... working on it."

Oh, you are, huh? You don't seem to know where to look right now.

"Either way, though. No lunches, please."

"Why not? ...Because any lunch I made couldn't possibly be good or something?" Natsunagi pouted.

small world after all.

"I mean, in my case, even though I finally got better, I don't have a family to celebrate with."

Natsunagi's lips quirked up in a forlorn smile. I had no intention on probing more deeply into her family's circumstances, especially given that my own parents rarely made an appearance at home due to the nature of their work.

"So you're like me," I murmured.

Natsunagi looked a little startled. Then she smiled at me. "Well, I've got friends at school. That's enough for me!"

"Yeah, we don't have that common..."

While we were talking, the ketchup spaghetti, pizza toast, and drinks we'd ordered after the fact arrived at our table.

"Thanks for the food," Natsunagi solemnly intoned after putting her hands together, before we both dug in together.

While enjoying the aroma of nicely toasted cheese, the first bite brought a few memories back along with it, too. "It's been a year since I had dinner with anybody."

"...Seriously?" Natsunagi paused in the act of winding spaghetti around her fork.

"Yeah. I only just realized it, and even I'm feeling weirded out."

"Why? What about your friends?"

"Shockingly, I've never made one."

Well, when I was a kid, I did have a few.......

"Don't mimic my voice and everything. Leave the past where it is."

Although, said past was really only a few minutes old.

"But splitting up right after we finish talking is boring. At least stay and have dinner with me."

Natsunagi called a waiter over and ordered ketchup spaghetti.

"What are you getting?" she asked, holding the menu out to me.

I gave it a quick once-over and ordered pizza toast.

"You like pizza?"

"I used to eat a lot of it."

Natsunagi glanced up and tilted her head slightly, looking puzzled.

It's an old story; just don't ask.

"Are you sure about this, though?" I queried. "You won't have room for dinner when you get home."

Natsunagi had already ordered, but I checked with her anyway.

"It's the other way around," she replied. "I'm eating here so I won't have to make anything at home."

"You live on your own, then?"

"You guessed that pretty quick. I'm guessing you do, too?"

I nodded. I'd thought solo living arrangements were pretty rare for high schoolers. Guess it's a

The Day of the Request—Backstage, Encore

※This story takes place just after Vol. 1, page 70.

"Let's see, what should I order...?"

It was after sunset. The girl in front of me was happily studying the café menu.

Her name was Nagisa Natsunagi.

She was in my grade at school—and the first client I'd had in a year, but...

"Geez. I thought we were done here."

I'd first met Natsunagi an hour ago, in a classroom after school. That's where she gave me a bizarre assignment: "I want you to find out who I'm looking for." As she filled me in on the details, I learned that her heart seems to hold some sort of clue.

After that, we'd agreed to meet again tomorrow, and I'd started to leave......but for some reason, Natsunagi stopped me. And so here we were.

"'You want to see X, right?' So painfully cool."

The Detective Is Already Dead

Short Story
The Day of the Request—Backstage, Encore

NIGOZYU

JUL 10/24

mugiko

Original Story **nigozyu**

Character Design **Umibouzu**

Translation **Taylor Engel**

Lettering **Chiho Christie**

TANTEI WA MO, SHINDEIRU. Vol. 2
©Mugiko 2021
©Nigozyu 2021
First published in Japan in 2021 by KADOKAWA CORPORATION, Tokyo.
English translation rights arranged with KADOKAWA CORPORATION, Tokyo, through Tuttle-Mori Agency, Inc., Tokyo.

Yen Press
150 West 30th Street, 19th Floor
New York, NY 10001

Visit us at yenpress.com ✽ facebook.com/yenpress ✽ twitter.com/yenpress
yenpress.tumblr.com ✽ instagram.com/yenpress

First Yen Press Edition: April 2022

Yen Press is an imprint of Yen Press, LLC.
The Yen Press name and logo are trademarks of Yen Press, LLC.

Library of Congress Control Number: 2021942345

ISBNs: 978-1-9753-4198-5 (paperback)
978-1-9753-4199-2 (ebook)

10 9 8 7 6 5 4 3 2 1

TPA

Printed in South Korea